For Ken, Elizabeth, Noah, and Gareth

The Great School Bus Controversy

Edited by
NICOLAUS MILLS

TEACHERS COLLEGE PRESS

Teachers College, Columbia University
New York and London

Copyright © 1973 by Teachers College, Columbia University
Library of Congress Catalog Card Number: 73-16469

Cataloging in Publishing Data:

Mills, Nicolaus, comp.
    The great school bus controversy.
    Includes bibliographical references.
    1. School integration—United States. 2. School
children—Transportation—United States. 3. Segregation in education—Law and legislation—United States.
I. Title.
LA210.M55   1973   370.19'342   73-16469

Manufactured in the United States of America

The Great School Bus Controversy

Also by Nicolaus Mills. . .

Comparisons: A Short Story Anthology

American and English Fiction in the Nineteenth Century

Acknowledgments

I want to express my gratitude to the ERIC/IRCD Center at Teachers College, Columbia University, for the support and freedom to work on this anthology. As with so much of my work at the Center, I am particularly indebted to the encouragement of Edmund Gordon, Erwin Flaxman, and Jean Barabas. I also owe special thanks to Bob and Elinor Linberg, whose sense of what education should be like for children and adults has influenced me in more ways they know. Lastly, I want to thank Craig Stark, who once again has tormented me into thinking that I was reluctant to do.

Introduction

NICOLAUS MILLS

A decade ago it would have seemed easy to answer the question, "Who supports busing for desegregation?" All one would have done is point to the black-liberal-labor coalition that made possible the 1964 Civil Rights Act. But in the 1970's that coalition no longer exists. Many of those who once belonged to it have indeed reversed their positions to the point where they are among the principal supporters of the view put forward within the Nixon administration by Presidential speech writer Patrick Buchanan: "The second era of Reconstruction is over; the ship of integration is going down; it is not our ship; it belongs to national liberalism—we cannot salvage it, and we ought not to be aboard."

In the 1972 elections, busing was in effect the "red-scare" issue, the code word for a series of widespread racial fears. The only candidates with unequivocal positions on busing were, like George Wallace, opposed to it. For left-of-center Democrats, busing was *at best* a tool for eliminating certain forms of segregation—generally those found in the South, the region they expected to lose anyway. A Harris Survey released in April 1972 shows the candidates were correct in judging where their self interest lay. According to the Harris figures, 73 percent of the public opposed busing for racial balance, 7 percent were unsure, and only 20 percent favored it.

Equally revealing, however, was another Harris finding, one that lends strong support to educator Kenneth Clark's charge that today "more pupils are being transported at public expense to racially *segregated* schools—including public schools, private schools, parochial schools, and recently organized Protestant church related 'academies'—than for purposes of school desegregation." The second Harris finding was that busing per se was not the issue in the school bus crisis. Of parents whose children are bused to school, the overwhelming majority, 89 percent, told the Harris pollsters they were not unhappy with busing, that they found their children's present arrangements "convenient."

What follows in this anthology is an attempt to put the great school bus controversy of the 1970's in perspective by providing a forum in which a series of widely differing views can be compared. Much of the writing collected here is accordingly concerned with hard data. How much busing is going on in the United States? What is its measurable effect on the education of black and white students? What are its costs? But no attempt has been made to suggest there is a statistical answer to the battle over busing. More than half the material in this anthology focuses on the implications of school busing. Who feels most threatened by it? What are its potential economic consequences? When does it become a new form of racism?

The first section, "Background and Legal History," is devoted to putting the busing controversy in a perspective that predates the 1970's. In my essay "Busing: Who's Being Taken for a Ride?" I focus on the history and scope of school busing in America. I trace the origins of busing back to the nineteenth century and the first pupil transportation laws, which were an outgrowth of the school consolidation movement, and then I shift to the present situation in which nearly 20 million children take the school bus every day. The question I am most concerned with answering, in view of the estimate by the Department of Health, Education, and Welfare that only three percent of the school busing in the country is for racial reasons, is: Who's being taken for a political ride? And in the last section of my essay, I examine a series of busing myths.

The perspective on busing that Christopher Jencks offers in his "Busing—The Supreme Court Goes North" turns on the problem of whether public schools are to be racially mixed or merely color blind. Jencks himself believes that a strong probusing effort entails more political risks than benefits. "It seems to me," he writes, "that direct efforts to assure better jobs for blacks would win more widespread support from both blacks and whites and would also yield more important benefits than busing." His article, which traces the legal history of busing from *Brown* to *Swann* to *Keyes* (the Supreme Court cases included at the end of this section) centers on the economic implications of busing and argues that it is these practical considerations that are finally most important.

Alexander Bickel, in his "Untangling the Busing Snarl," is also concerned with the practical consequences of the busing controversy but in a far different way than Jencks. Bickel worries over the possibility of a dangerous collision between the Congress and the President on one side and the Supreme Court on the other. Specifically, he fears Congress and the President will pass an antibusing law that the Supreme Court will declare unconstitutional, and the result will be a judicial crisis of disastrous proportions, no matter how it is settled. Bickel sees this situation stemming in large measure from the way the Supreme Court has verged on ordering integration rather than desegregation, but his remedy is not for the Court to pull back from the positions it has taken. Instead, he thinks the President and Congress should get school districts to change the reality to which the Court has been reacting. What this means to Bickel is "federal help for coherent, well-planned local efforts to improve primary and secondary education," and his article concludes with a discussion of the form such help might take.

The questions raised in section two of this anthology, "The Debate Over Evidence and Social Policy," are an extension of those raised earlier but with a crucial difference: they are directly concerned with establishing the criteria of a successful busing program and determining the relationship between government policy and social science. The exchange between David Armor and Thomas Pettigrew *et al.* with which this section opens provides the most explicit opportunity of all for exploring the kinds of standards, evidence, and interpretations used in evaluating busing.

Standards. At the heart of this issue is what comparative basis is to be used for judging busing programs. Professor Pettigrew charges Professor Armor with "establishing unrealistically high standards" for evaluating busing and desegregation, and Armor in turn replies, "I did not formulate these standards and expectations. They come from the programs themselves, buttressed by several noteworthy studies, particularly the Coleman report and the 1967 report of the U.S. Commission on Civil Rights." The nature of their disagreement can be seen very clearly in a case like New York City (Table 1 in Pettigrew's rebuttal, Table 4 in Armor's surrebuttal) in which whites in a desegregated school situation continue to outgain blacks but black reading scores improve faster than before. There are at least three different standards that can be used in such a situation: (1) A standard that suggests negative progress because whites in the integrated school continue to outgain blacks and increase the gap between them; (2) a standard that suggests minor progress because over a year integrated black students gained two more months than did segregated black students in the study; and (3) a standard that suggests important progress because in terms of national norms the black gain is much greater than the expected gain of black students, given no desegregation. The result in such a situation is that Armor, by focusing on the first two points, and Pettigrew and his colleagues, by focusing on the last, are able to arrive at vastly different conclusions. The specific facts of the case are not at all relevant to this disagreement. What is at issue is the model of progress each has in mind.

Evidence. The crux of the matter in this case is, What constitutes fair and complete findings? Professor Pettigrew charges Professor Armor with presenting an "incomplete list" of desegregation studies, one that is "selectively negative in its results." Armor answers that the studies he uses were consistent in their results and that the seven additional studies Pettigrew speaks of provide no reason for him to change his conclusions. The extent of Pettigrew's and Armor's disagreement over evidence is best illustrated not by a single situation but by a series of problems relating to evidence. For example, is a desegregation-busing study reliable when: Less money is spent on education after than before busing? Black students are consistently put in the lower tracks of the desegrated school? School officials contribute to feelings of racial tension rather than ease them? Armor argues, "I asked only the question: What *has* happened? My critics have confused the *has* with the *might* and the *should.*" It is a position that very clearly leads in a different direction from Pettigrew's insistence that the "critical conditions" under which busing and desegregation have taken place often make it impossible to judge such programs on their own terms.

Interpretation. The Armor-Pettigrew debate also shows that, even if one puts aside the question of evidence and standards, it is possible for two scholars to interpret matters so differently that they reach no final agreement. The example of black separatism in desegregated schools is a case in point. In this area Armor and Pettigrew quarrel over whether the result means worsened race relations. At issue is the difference between racial pride and antagonism, militancy and the desire for segregation, overt and covert expressions of racial tension, and once again a positive versus a negative argument for busing hangs in the balance.

These are not, to be sure, the only areas in which Professors Armor and Pettigrew disagree. But they are among the most important, and they reflect in heightened form the attempt that is made by all the writers in this section to find the solidest possible ground for their views on busing. Indeed, as the debate in this section goes on, it does not diminish in intensity, but expands to the point where questions of standards and evidence and interpretation become more and more intertwined.

By contrast, the writing in section three of this anthology is descriptive rather than analytic in emphasis. What it offers are a series of direct reports—many of them "new journalistic" in nature—on the impact of busing. Three accounts—Robert Coles's "Billy's Bus Driver," James A. Michener's "Pressing Decisions," and William Serrin's "They Don't Burn Buses Anymore in Pontiac"—reflect the range of experiences covered here especially well.

"Billy's Bus Driver" is a description of a man who five days a week drives a group of black children from Boston's inner city to a predominantly white school. For Coles, a child psychologist who also made the trip, Billy's driver and the world he creates on his bus are an important educational influence. "He has seen his own contribution. He is a strong, well-spoken, active man whom the children admire and talk to all the time, and find it a real pleasure to know," Coles writes. "I have often thought as I rode with him that he runs a kind of school on that bus of his. He points things out to the children. He asks them questions. They huddle close to his seat and listen to his stories, his jokes, his clever remarks full of irony and vigorous social satire." Coles never suggests that most bus drivers are like Billy's, but what he does destroy is the notion that a bus trip, even a long one, can't be a vital part of a child's school day.

Novelist James Michener's comments on busing are based on a very different experience: Pipersville, Pennsylvania, a small town with no blacks and no likelihood of blacks' being bused into its school district. The town, as Michener notes, has had busing for 60 years, and although some parents have complained about the early hours the buses start, everyone has supported the sending of Pipersville children to central schools miles away. But to Michener's surprise, when busing in the current racial context is discussed, opposition to it is intense, even from people he has known intimately. " 'Enough! We've reached a point where sensible comment is no longer possible'," a friend finally tells him after a long argument on busing. Michener's response is not, however, to dwell on his own shock or the pros and cons of busing, but to explore the anger that his questions cause and to suggest the need for finding alternatives to busing. It is at this point, unfortunately, that Michener himself comes up short. For, as he concedes, the alternatives he suggests—equal access to jobs and housing and the upgrading of all schools—show no likelihood of occurring.

William Serrin's "They Don't Burn Buses Anymore in Pontiac" takes up questions that Coles and Michener both consider, but in the context of a much more volatile situation: one in which buses were burned, children stoned, the Ku Klux Klan involved, and Irene McCabe's National Action Group (NAG) formed. What finally brought peace to Pontiac? As Serrin notes, it was not the two most powerful forces in this Michigan auto town, General Motors and the United Auto Workers. The company failed to provide the school system with the additional financial backing it could have used for busing, and the union failed to confront its membership on the question of segregation. Support for a workable busing program came, Serrin finds, from those most vulnerable to the antibusing forces, individual parents and students, and the Pontiac PTA. Serrin leaves no doubt that Pontiac has a long way to go before its busing troubles are finally over. Much remains uncertain—including the academic results of the Pontaic busing program. But as a student Serrin quotes observers, " 'There is a new kind of learning this year. We're learning from one another, and also what the entire Pontiac community is about.' "

The final section of this anthology, "Busing and Black Political Strategy," turns to the issue that may finally determine the outcome of the busing struggle. For, given the degree of white opposition to busing, black opposition or a strong division among blacks stands a good chance of being the factor that halts new busing.

In "The Nationalist vs. the Integrationist," Charles Hamilton puts the busing issue in perspective when he notes that, whereas in the 1950's there was virtually unanimous support by blacks for the Montgomery bus boycott, in 1972 only 52 percent of the blacks surveyed were committed to school busing. "This is no minor debate," Hamilton observes. "It relates to the broader issue of integration and what has happened to the civil rights movement in the last decade." Hamilton shows how the division within the black community over school busing parallels the struggle over issues as broad as neighborhood housing and racially-mixed adoption. The debate, as Hamilton points out, centers not only on what blacks find politically desirable, but on what they find politically feasible in view of current white attitudes. Hamilton offers no hard-and-fast predictions on the outcome of the school bus controversy, but he does give strong evidence for believing that it will be determined less by purely educational needs than by black political and economic strategy.

The concluding essays in this section represent the positions of two black groups, CORE and the NAACP Legal Defense and Educational Fund, once political allies, now in opposition on the school bus question. In CORE's "A Proposal for Community School Districts," two kinds of schools are seen as racist. The first are those segregated schools, typically in the South, in which a white school board has told blacks where they may or may not get an education. The second are those schools in both the North and the South desegregated on white terms with whites determining curriculum, teacher hiring, and financing. For CORE, racial isolation in the schools is not the crucial question. No one, their proposal contends, argues that all-white schools are inferior.

The crucial question is who controls the schools, and by so doing determines everything from their tone to what is studied. The CORE proposals included here maintain that the creation of school districts along "natural community lines" is the only solution for whites and blacks, and the closing section of the CORE essay is devoted to explaining how such a plan would work.

The arguments in the NAACP Legal Defense and Educational Fund's "It's Not the Distance, 'It's the Niggers'" trace the major problems in the school bus controversy to political exploitation of it, particularly by the Nixon administration. As the Legal Defense Fund notes, the proposals for a moratorium on busing, which "would curtail only one kind of busing—busing to desegregate schools—and not any other kind of pupil transportation, barely camouflage their racist motivation. They signal the reversal of the momentum for equal justice which during the 60's ended a century of Congressional silence on the legal rights of the nation's racial minorities." For the Legal Defense Fund the worst possible course of action would be a detente in which whites and blacks settled the school bus controversy by going their separate ways. The result, they hold, would mean not only a false solution of the school bus question, but a denial of what is at stake in it: "our sanity as a people, the independence and integrity of our courts, the fulfillment of our commitment to equal justice."

Contents

PART III
ON-THE-SCENE REPORTS

PART IV
BUSING AND BLACK POLITICAL STRATEGY

Contents

Background and Legal History

Busing: Who's Being Taken for a Ride?

NICOLAUS MILLS

Nicolaus Mills, scholar-in-residence at the ERIC/IRCD Center at Teachers College, Columbia University, specializes in the politics of education. He is also the author of *Comparisons: A Short Story Anthology* and *American and English Fiction in the Nineteenth Century.*

I would also like to restate my position as it relates to busing. I am against busing as that term is commonly used in school desegregation cases. I have consistently opposed the busing of our nation's school children to achieve a racial balance, and I am opposed to the busing of children simply for the sake of busing.

President Nixon, 1971

All things being equal, with no history of discrimination, it might well be desirable to assign pupils to schools nearest their homes. But all things are not equal in a system that has been deliberately constructed and maintained to enforce racial segregation.

Chief Justice Warren Burger, 1971

In its yearbook for 1953 the National Education Association describes school busing as follows: "The daily trip to and from school is an informal learning situation that reflects the feelings, the desires, the aspirations, the problems, the successes and the failures of pupils. While the morning ride carries the joys, the enthusiasm and sorrows of

Nicolaus Mills, "Busing: Who's Being Taken for a Ride?", *Commonweal*, March 24, 1972.

home, the afternoon ride from school back home brings together the reactions to the school activities of the day. . . . There is no better defined continuity of home and school life than may be observed on the bus as children leave home to ride to school and as these same children leave school in the afternoon to return home." Today this description reads like a Pollyanna fantasy. Yet one of the reasons it does is that we have allowed the present crisis over school busing to blind us to the way school busing is a traditional part of American life. We have—almost willfully it would seem—neglected to ask ourselves the most basic questions about school busing: What is its history? What is its extent? Who wants it and benefits most from it?

HISTORY OF BUSING

Like so many of our current educational problems, busing has a much deeper history than we generally acknowledge. Its origins not only predate the desegregation struggle, they predate the bus. In 1869, Massachusetts enacted the first law authorizing the spending of public funds to carry children to and from school. The vehicles employed in this task were, for the most part, horsedrawn wagons or carriages. A farmer in the neighborhood was usually contracted to provide the horses and buggies, and was paid in proportion to the number of students he hauled. (Interestingly enough, horsedrawn pupil transportation lasted well into the 1920's. In 1927–1928, 12 percent of the school transportation vehicles used in 32 states were still horse-powered rather than motor-powered.) Seven years after Massachusetts passed its pupil transportation act, Vermont followed suit, and then Maine and New Hampshire passed pupil transportation laws. By 1900, 18 states had some sort of pupil transportation law, and by 1919 pupil transportation at public expense was legal in all 48 states. What were the forces behind this development? In virtually all states they were two: compulsory attendance laws based on the belief that the welfare of the state required all children to receive some education; and the consolidation of school centers in rural areas, which formerly relied on inferior one-room school houses. In 31 states, school consolidation laws preceded school transportation laws, and in 14 states they were passed simultaneously. For rural children, this meant that the circumstances of their lives were not to be allowed to deprive them of the kind of education city children could assume by virtue of where they lived.

In the first two decades of this century, the demand for pupil transportation rose dramatically as rural population continued to decline and the school consolidation movement gathered greater acceptance.

TABLE 1. YEAR OF STATUTORY AUTHORIZATION FOR
SCHOOL CONSOLIDATION BY STATE, 1838–1913.

Date	State	Date	State
1838	Massachusetts	1901	California
1839	Connecticut	1901	Missouri
1843	Michigan	1901	Minnesota
1844	Vermont	1901	Pennsylvania
1847	Ohio	1902	Louisiana
1853	New York	1903	Virginia
1854	Maine	1903	Tennessee
1856	Wisconsin	1903	Oregon
1857	New Hampshire	1903	Oklahoma
1861	Delaware	1904	Maryland
1873	Iowa	1905	Illinois
1873	Indiana	1907	Arizona
1885	North Carolina	1907	New Mexico
1886	New Jersey	1908	Kentucky
1889	Florida	1908	West Virginia
1889	Nebraska	1909	Colorado
1890	Washington	1910	Alabama
1893	Texas	1910	Mississippi
1896	Utah	1911	Arkansas
1896	South Carolina	1911	Georgia
1897	Kansas	1913	Montana
1898	Rhode Island	1913	South Dakota
1899	North Dakota	1913	Wyoming
1900	Idaho	1913	Nevada

Source: J. F. Abel, *Consolidation of Schools and Transportation of Pupils,* Bulletin No. 41 (Washington, D.C.: U.S. Department of Interior, Bureau of Education, 1923), p. 22.

By the end of World War I, two other factors were also in operation. The first was the development of the automobile. The number of registered motor vehicles tripled between 1919 and 1929 and provided a new means of getting students to school. The second factor was the improvement of roads. During this period the number of surfaced roads almost doubled, with the result that transportation in bad weather become increasingly feasible.

In the last 25 years, these factors have continued to accelerate the demand for pupil transportation. Since the end of World War II, the number of school districts in the country has dropped from over 100,000 to 17,153. In addition, new forces have also spurred the rise in pupil transportation. In cities and suburbs, there has been growing recognition of the health benefits and educational savings that school busing affords, and the states themselves have come to assert financial leadership in the area of pupil transportation. This has meant

TABLE 2.   YEAR OF STATUTORY AUTHORIZATION FOR PUBLIC
PUPIL TRANSPORTATION BY STATE, 1869–1918.

Date	State	Date	State
1869	Massachusetts	1903	Virginia
1876	Vermont	1904	Maryland
1880	Maine	1905	Oklahoma
1885	New Hampshire	1905	Utah
1889	Florida	1907	Missouri
1893	Connecticut	1908	West Virginia
1894	Ohio	1909	Colorado
1895	New Jersey	1910	Mississippi
1896	New York	1911	Arkansas
1897	Iowa	1911	Georgia
1897	Nebraska	1911	Illinois
1897	Pennsylvania	1911	North Carolina
1897	Wisconsin	1912	Kentucky
1898	Rhode Island	1912	South Carolina
1899	Kansas	1912	Arizona
1899	North Dakota	1913	Idaho
1899	South Dakota	1913	Tennessee
1899	Indiana	1915	Nevada
1901	California	1915	Alabama
1901	Minnesota	1915	Texas
1901	Washington	1916	Louisiana
1903	Michigan	1917	New Mexico
1903	Montana	1919	Delaware
1903	Oregon	1919	Wyoming

Source: J. F. Abel, *Consolidation of Schools and Transportation of Pupils*, Bulletin No. 41 (Washington, D.C.: U.S. Department of Interior, Bureau of Education, 1923), p. 22.

not only more money for busing, but more uniform safety standards and economy measures. In most large school districts, the job of calculating bus routes has become a task for the computer rather than local officials with pen and pencil and a list of student addresses.

THE EXTENT OF BUSING

The extent of busing, no less than its history, goes against the assumptions generally made about it. As *New York Times* education writer Gene Maeroff noted, "Busing for desegregation is still only a small part of all school busing. For millions of American children who live too far from any school to walk, the institution known as the neighborhood school is not and never has been a reality." Recent surveys show that over 43 percent of the students in the country ride a school bus every day, and that 65 percent take either a school bus or use regular public transportation. The investment the nation makes in school busing breaks down as follows:

Number of children bused to school .... 19.6 million
Cost of busing (including replacement) .... $1.5 billion
Busing costs in states as percentages
of total education outlays .... 0.7% to 6.9%
Number of buses 256,000
Number of drivers 275,000
Miles traveled per year .... 2.2 billion

These statistics make school busing the greatest single transportation system in the country. They are indicative not only of its quantity but also its breadth. 80 percent of the school districts in the country maintain one or more vehicles for pupil transportation, with fleets in the largest school districts reaching 500 vehicles and the average fleet, 15.

On a national average these figures are consistent with the tendency in the last decade for the number of pupils bused to rise between .6 and 2.3 percent per year. They are, on the other hand, *less* than the percentage gains recorded over other ten-year periods. The gain from 1959–1960, when the proportion of pupils bused stood at 37.6 percent, to the present is, for example, approximately 6 percentage points. In 1949–1950, on the other hand, the proportion of pupils transported was 27.7 percent (a change of almost ten percentage points), and in 1939–1940 the proportion of pupils transported was 16.3 percent (a change in that decade of more than 11 percentage points). Table 3 below presents these and other figures in greater detail. It reaffirms, above all else, the degree to which busing was a normal and accepted part of public education long before it was thought of as a means of bringing about desegregation. (A 1972 HEW memorandum on the subject estimates a 3 percent increase in busing because of desegregation.)

THE USE AND BENEFITS OF BUSING

As the history and statistics of busing indicate, the greatest demand for it has come from rural states, where population is scattered and the consolidated school district is typical. Many states now transport almost 100 percent of those rural pupils who meet the distance standards set up as a requirement for transportation, and it is not uncommon to find rural schools where more than 95 percent of all pupils enrolled come to school in a bus. In states like Maine, West Virginia, Kentucky, and Missouri, more than 60 percent of all students

TABLE 3.   GROWTH OF SCHOOL TRANSPORTATION IN AMERICA.

Year	Number of Pupils Transported	Percent of Total Pupils in U.S. Transported
1919–1920	356,000	1.7
1921–1922	594,000	2.6
1923–1924	837,000	3.4
1925–1926	1,112,000	4.5
1927–1928	1,251,000	5.0
1929–1930	1,903,000	7.4
1931–1932	2,419,000	9.2
1933–1934	2,795,000	10.6
1935–1936	3,251,000	12.3
1937–1938	3,769,000	14.5
1939–1940	4,144,000	16.3
1941–1942	4,503,000	18.3
1943–1944	4,410,000	19.0
1945–1946	5,057,000	21.7
1947–1948	5,854,000	24.4
1949–1950	6,947,000	27.7
1951–1952	7,697,000	29.0
1953–1954	8,411,000	32.8
1955–1956	9,969,000	35.0
1957–1958	10,862,000	36.5
1959–1960	12,225,000	37.6
1961–1962	13,223,000	38.1
1963–1964	14,476,000	38.7
1965–1966	15,537,000	39.7
1967–1968	17,131,000	42.0
1969–1970	18,199,000	43.4

Note: Number of Pupils transported rounded to nearest thousand. Percentages from unrounded figures.

Sources: Stephen J. Knezevich and John Guy Fowlkes, *Business Management of Local School Systems* (New York: Harper and Row, 1960), p. 293. National Commission on Safety Education, National Education Association. U.S. Department of Health, Education, and Welfare.

are bused to school daily, and in Vermont, New Hampshire, North Carolina, Idaho, and Oregon, the percentages are not far behind. When one reads the educational literature put out by such states, it is also apparent that busing is an activity in which great pride is taken. To quote the State Board of Education on "Pupil Transportation in North Carolina," "As long as we accepted a narrow and limited education as satisfactory, the State discharged this responsibility primarily through the establishment of a small school within walking distance of most pupils. But demands on the school for a broadened program increased. . . . These and other factors have resulted in transportation of pupils to and from school becoming one of the most important of the auxiliary activities of the school." For those most sensitive to rural education problems, the need for greater busing has only increased of late. As Robert Isenberg of the American Association of School Administrators observed in testimony before the Select Committee on Educational Opportunity of the United States Senate, "Too many of the school systems in rural America still lack the capability of providing a quality education program. We need an improved delivery system."

The demand and need for more busing cannot, however, be confined to rural areas. Urban and suburban areas now use busing more heavily than before. Not only has busing become a safety factor in crowded urban areas or in suburbs where no sidewalks exist, it has also permitted these areas to develop special schools, designed to serve pupils with common interests. At present, some of the largest bus fleets in the country are those operating in and around urban areas.

The urban trend toward specialized schools shows that virtually all attempts at unique elementary and high school education now depend on some form of busing. Whether one has in mind an elite private school, like the Chapin School in New York, where most lower and middle school children ride the bus, or an educational complex that depends on the pooling of a wide variety of resources, the bus is critical. The parochial schools of this country, which have continually gone to court in order to have their students transported at public expense, provide perhaps the best-known example of the close ties between busing and special education. These schools have continually argued that their viability depends on pupil transportation, and have been instrumental in getting state school boards to transport nonpublic school students at public expenses. Four states—Delaware, New Jersey, New York, and Wisconsin—have constitutions that authorize such transportation, and a number of other states have statutory provisions for school boards to transport nonpublic school students at public expense.

Busing in urban areas is also used to deal with the population problem opposite to that in rural areas—overcrowing. In cities where shifts in population have made it impossible for neighborhood schools to cope with an influx of students, busing to less crowded areas has been adopted. St. Louis provides a classic example. There busing was used as an alternative to having double sessions, which would have set one group of children free in the morning and another in the afternoon.

For those transported, the benefits of the program were obvious, but they were not the only beneficiaries. As a report to the Superintendent of St. Louis Schools emphasized, "reduction of class size, through bus transportation and other expediencies . . . made it possible for *nontransported as well as transported* children residing in the districts of these seriously overcrowded schools to suffer minimal education loss."

Although demographic and geographic forces, coupled with the need for more sophisticated kinds of education, provide the major impetus for school busing, they still do not tell the whole story. 43 states have provision for the transportation of children with emotional or physical handicaps. The range of categories extends from those suffering retardation to the deaf and blind, and the most common provision is for the distance requirement to be waived with regard to the busing of such children. In any number of states these transportation programs are both expensive and thorough. In Illinois, for example, over 9,000 handicapped children are transported daily to and from their schools under arrangements *other* than regular school bus services. The state pays local districts as much as half the cost, up to the sum of $400 per year per child.

As a result, the school bus has come to be looked upon as anything but a necessary evil. More and more schools are using it not merely to get students to class but for curriculum trips and extracurricular activities. It is not uncommon to find educators referring to the bus as "an extending arm of the classroom," or to see an increasing number of studies that show bus trips themselves enlarging the student's horizon.

MYTHS AND REALITIES

With these observations in mind, it becomes possible to turn to the current crisis over busing and to begin sorting out the myths surrounding it. Five of these myths may, I think, be distinguished from the others:

1. *Busing goes against tradition and represents a break with past approaches to improving education.* The fact that the first pupil transportation bills were passed in the nineteenth century and that by the conclusion of World War I all the states had passed legislation on pupil transportation provides the clearest refutation of the idea that school busing is untraditional. What is equally important, however, is that school busing has historically been regarded as a way of equalizing educational opportunity. It has distinctly gone against the notion that children who live in areas where population factors make it hard to receive a quality education should be forced to "make do."

State boards of education have traditionally argued that consolidation and the need for improved education are at the root of busing. To quote from the literature of three states, Arkansas, Alabama, and Mississippi, normally associated with antibusing sentiment:

> Arkansas is now, and will long continue to be, predominantly a rural state. The rural children must be educated in standard schools, which, of course, is impossible with a one- and two-teacher school system. Large schools will have to be maintained where teachers who are specialists may be provided. . . . The transportation of children to school at public expense is now generally accepted by constituted educational authorities as a function of the state school system.

> Most of our area in Alabama is rural; therefore, it became necessary to provide students with transportation to centers where they could receive the best possible education.

> The public school districts of Mississippi, with few exceptions, own and operate their bus fleets. . . . The great majority of pupils being transported is due to school consolidation and the rural makeup of this state.

There is, it should be emphasized, nothing unusual in these statements. One could find similar sentiments in the literature of most any state with school busing.

2. *Busing is the exception and the neighborhood school is always the most desirable.* With the number of bused school children now 19.6 million and the proportion of bused children at 43.4 percent, it is no longer possible to regard busing as unusual. The same is also true for recent gains in busing. On a national scale, they are no greater than gains over the past decade, and less in terms of percentages than gains in other decades. In this regard it is also significant that in areas protesting most strongly about racial busing, there is often a long history of busing and a long history of disregard for neighborhood school patterns. The case of Charlotte-Mecklenburg provides a perfect example. As the Supreme Court noted in its 1971 ruling, the Charlotte school authorities did not purport to assign students on the basis of geographically drawn zones until 1965, and after that they still allowed almost unlimited transfer privileges. Moreover, the system as a whole, without regard to desegregation plans, planned to bus approximately 23,000 students in 1971 for an average daily round trip of 15 miles. More elementary school children than high school children were to be bused, and four- and five-year-olds were scheduled for the longest routes in the system. Charlotte-Mecklenburg is not, of course, unusual. All across the country the neighborhood school has become an educa-

tionally less viable institution for reasons generally having nothing to
do with desegregation.

3. *The decision to bus has, until recently, not been guided by
social beliefs or principles.* The history of pupil transportation offers
the most conclusive refutation of this idea. The growth of pupil transportation is inseparable from the belief that education is required for
the social welfare of the country and offers a chance for individual
social advancement. Ironically, the South provides the most dramatic
case of bus transportation being used to support a set of social values.
The dual school system of the South would not have been possible
without an elaborate pupil transporation system. As G. W. Foster, a
former consultant to the Office of Education and a professor of law, has
noted,

> In dual school systems it has been customary in many instances for
> separate buses to travel the same roads, one to pick up Negroes for the
> Negro school and the other to take whites to a different school. Again
> separate bus routes for Negro and white students have operated in
> some instances to place individual children of either or both races
> under the burden of going to a distant pick-up point when a pick-up
> point for the opposite race was much more convenient.

What busing to achieve desegregation has done is not introduce social
values to the concept of pupil transportation but introduce social
values that stir opposition.

4. *Riding on the school bus is bad for children.* There are a certainly occasions when long distance riding places a hardship on
students, and the courts have been especially sensitive to this problem.
Except when busing involves desegregation, this problem is rarely
raised, however. In the state literature on busing, it is apparent that
the bus ride to and from school is seen as a pleasant part of the school
day. The most frequent warnings in this area are against children being
carried away by their play and becoming a hazard to the bus driver.
Again, the attitude of the South toward busing is most revealing when
one considers its reputed bad effects. As the U. S. Civil Rights Commission noted, "in many cases, busing [in the South] was the exclusive
privilege of white children—black children often were required to
walk considerable distances. No complaints then were heard from
whites of any harmful effects." Indeed, rather than being bad for
children, busing has shown itself a safety as well as a health factor.

5. *Busing is invariably a financial burden on a community.* In a
number of instances, busing certainly has introduced expenses that a
community was avoiding when it had segregated schools. But it cannot be assumed that increased busing—racial or otherwise—is auto-

matically a drain on a community. The busing that eliminated the one-room schoolhouse was a financial saving for the community, and busing for desegregation purposes is often the same. In the case of a dual school system, busing eliminates not only overlapping bus routes but the kinds of inefficiencies the Civil Rights Commission found in Alabama when it discovered that black students in Selma, seeking to attend trade school, were bused 50 miles to Montgomery to a virtually all-black trade school rather than allowed to attend an all-white trade school nearby. In the North, the savings made possible by busing for desegregation purposes are often harder to locate, but they are present in a number of situations. For example, when the choice is between attempting to improve education through compensatory funding of schools or busing for integration, the latter is frequently the more economical choice. In testimony before the Senate's Select Committee on Equal Educational Opportunity, Dr. Wayne Carle, Superintendent of Schools in Dayton, Ohio, described how in his city busing for desegregation cost on a per pupil basis less than half of what compensatory funding did and was more effective in improving education. A second example of the economy of busing is to be found in New York City, where Dan Dodson, professor of education at New York University, has proposed a plan that would involve busing 215,000 students in order to achieve desegregation. In his plan, a large share of the cost would be made up for by the use of underutilized schools in areas outside Manhattan.

Much harder to come to terms with are the practical steps needed to resolve the school bus controversy. For the controversy is now so intimately tied to the political climate of the 1970's that history offers few specific solutions to it. All we can know for sure is that, if school busing is not understood in a far different context than it has been, what can we expect of the politics?

Busing—the Supreme Court Goes North

CHRISTOPHER JENCKS

Christopher Jencks is associate professor of education at Harvard University and a fellow of the Cambridge Policy Studies Institute. He is co-author, with David Riesman, of *The Academic Revolution* and with seven colleagues of *Inequality,* a study of the economic effects of schooling.

Sometime in the next few months the Supreme Court will decide the case of *Keyes v. School District No. 1.* School District No. 1 is in Denver, Colo., and the *Keyes* case deals with racial segregation in the Denver schools. The Court may decide the case on narrow grounds that have no clear implications for other Northern cities, but this seems unlikely. In all probability the *Keyes* decision will tell us whether the Court intends to launch a major attack on school segregation in the North.

Unlike some Northern school systems, Denver still has a white majority. About 15 percent of Denver's students are black and another 20 percent are Hispano (the local term for those with Latin-American roots). Most of the blacks live in central or northwestern Denver. The Hispanos are also concentrated in a few areas. Since Denver has traditionally assigned students to neighborhood schools, the blacks and Hispanos generally end up in different schools from the whites. Yet school segregation has not always been unavoidable in Denver, or even unintentional. A school board can draw neighborhood boundaries in

Christopher Jencks, "Busing—The Supreme Court Goes North," *The New York Times Magazine,* November 19, 1972. © 1972 by the New York Times Company. Reprinted by permission.

any way it finds politically convenient. The Denver School Board, like many others in America, has often used ethnic criteria to define neighborhoods. As the black population grew, the board deliberately redrew some neighborhood boundaries and built at least one new school in such a way as to keep blacks and whites in separate buildings. As a result, Denver's schools were even more segregated than they would have been under a color-blind neighborhood assignment system.

In 1969, the board briefly adopted a new policy, aimed at desegregating a number of schools in northeastern Denver. This plan involved busing some whites to schools in black neighborhoods and some blacks to white neighborhoods. Before this policy could be implemented, however, a school board election was held. Two board members who had supported desegregation were defeated, and the new board rescinded the plan. Advocates of desegregation therefore turned to the courts.

Both the Federal District Court and the conservative United States Court of Appeals for the 10th Circuit found that Denver's use of racial criteria to define neighborhood attendance zones violated the 14th Amendment's "equal protection" clause. It seems reasonably certain that the Supreme Court will uphold this judgment. The real question posed by this part of the *Keyes* case is not whether the Denver board acted illegally in the past, but rather what remedy it is now required to provide. The N.A.A.C.P. Legal Defense Fund, which represented the plaintiffs, has argued that the board engaged in *de jure* segregation of essentially the same kind as employed by Southern school boards. The Fund has therefore asked the Supreme Court to order the same kind of remedial efforts in Denver that it has ordered in Southern districts. If the Court agrees, Denver will have to redraw almost all its attendance zones, not just those it had previously gerrymandered. Furthermore, if Southern precedents are followed, it will not now suffice to redraw attendance zones on a color-blind basis. Instead, Denver will have to redraw its zones in such a way as to offset the effects of neighborhood segregation and produce racially mixed schools. This will mean busing some blacks to schools in white neighborhoods and some whites to schools in black neighborhoods.

A decision of this kind would have repercussions throughout the North. Virtually every Northern school board has done something at one time or another to keep blacks and whites in separate schools. If Northern school boards must now not only eliminate the direct consequences of their past discrimination but also neutralize the effects of residential segregation, almost every major city will eventually have to desegregate all its schools. In most big cities this will require two-way busing.

Desegregation would not occur overnight, because integrationists would have to assemble evidence that each Northern district had contributed in some deliberate way to segregating its schools. Such cases have, however, already been brought in a number of Northern cities, and Federal district judges have usually found them convincing. Last year in San Francisco, for example, Judge Stanley Weigel ordered complete desegregation of all San Francisco schools, on such grounds. Similarly, this year in Detroit, Judge Stephen Roth found a pattern of officially maintained segregation, and ordered desegregation of the entire metropolitan area. (This order has been stayed, pending a review by the Court of Appeals.) Ironically, many Southern segregationists are hoping that the Supreme Court will require a similar remedy in Denver. They believe that if the Supreme Court applies this principle to all Northern cities, they will be able to win Northern support for an antibusing constitutional amendment.

Mindful of this possibility, the Court could decide to reject N.A.A.C.P.'s contention that Denver is essentially similar to the South. The Court might hold that racial segregation was never official policy in Denver, that it was never anything like total and that it was therefore qualitatively different from segregation in the South. Thus the Court might simply require Denver to redraw attendance zones on a color-blind basis. Or, the Court might order the board to desegregate the specific schools where the plaintiffs have proved deliberate segregation but might allow other attendance zones to remain as they are.

Whether the Burger Court will start down a road leading to large-scale desegregation in the North depends on how much the Justices are influenced by public opinion, how much by social science and how much by the logic of past Supreme Court decisions. If the Court is guided primarily by public opinion, it will draw a clear distinction between Northern and Southern style *de jure* segregation and will only require school boards to eliminate segregation in those specific schools where the board originally caused the problem. If it is guided by social science, which is unlikely, the Court will have to render some sort of ambiguous verdict. If it is guided primarily by the logic of its own past decisions, it will treat cities like Denver just as it has treated their Sourthern counterparts and will order large-scale, two-way busing where this is necessary to achieve desegregation.

The politics of desegregation depends to a significant extent on the methods used to achieve it. The most popular and least effective method has been what Northerners call "open enrolment" and Southerners call "freedom of choice." Ideally, open enrolment ought to allow any child to attend any school in his district and provide him with free transportation. In practice, open enrolment programs usually give students who live near a school the right to attend it, and admit "outsiders" only if there are still vacancies. Some open enrolment programs also require parents to pay the transportation costs. In its ideal form, open enrolment could neutralize the effects of residential segregation by allowing black parents to send their children to schools in white neighborhoods. In practice, however, only 5 to 15 percent of black parents usually exercise this right, even when transporation is free and places are available. (This estimate is very rough. While many cities have tried open enrolment, few have collected statistics that showed how many of the eligible blacks used it to move to a desegregated school.)

Open enrolment seldom arouses as much white opposition as other approaches to desegregation, since it allows white children to attend their neighborhood schools, and these schools remain predominantly white. Indeed, whites sometimes use open enrolment more than blacks, since whites in racially mixed neighborhoods may be more anxious to transfer their children to predominantly white schools than blacks are. (Some open enrolment programs do not allow white transfers that increase the level of segregation.) Integrationists object to open enrolment because it does not eliminate all-black schools. Whites almost never move to schools in black areas, whereas blacks usually remain in them. For those whose primary concern is with the rights of individual black parents, this outcome may not seem particularly disturbing, since it is more or less voluntary. But for those who believe that black schools are educationally inferior, or that every school needs a substantial cadre of middle-class students, or that segregated schools breed racist alumni, a solution that leaves most schools segregated is unsatisfactory.

A second common approach to desegregation in the North has been to redraw neighborhood boundaries so as to achieve racial balance. In small cities, where most blacks live within walking distance of a white neighborhood, this often eliminates all-black schools or at least sharply reduces their number. In big cities, where many blacks live miles from the nearest white neighborhood, this approach is impossible. Regardless of city size, redrawing neighborhood boundaries is very unpopular with whites when it results in white children having to attend schools with large numbers of blacks or their having to walk through black areas to get to school. Indeed, white parents whose children get assigned to such schools often become strong supporters of citywide busing, because they want the whole city to share the burden of desegregation. In Seattle, for example, where blacks are still a small minority, some central-city whites see citywide busing as a device for maintaining a substantial white majority in every school. Redrawing neighborhood boundaries may also be unpopular with blacks as it may under open enrolment if they end up doing most of the walking or if they think it will cost them control over schools in black neighborhoods.

The third and least popular approach to desegregation is busing. Only a handful of American cities (for example, Berkeley and Riverside, Calif., and Evanston, Ill.) have voluntarily established two-way busing programs aimed at achieving racial balance in every school. Most two-way busing programs have been the result of court orders or strong state pressure. This is no accident. Most white parents are deeply fearful of sending their children to schools in black areas, whether by bus, by foot or by any other means. Many fear for their children's physical safety. White parents' anxieties on this score are not entirely groundless, any more than Southern black parents' fears were groundless when their children entered traditionally white schools. In addition, many white parents believe that predominantly black schools have low academic standards. Educational researchers have almost never found that white students' test scores actually fell as a result of being in desegregated schools. Nonetheless, both blacks and many whites have been proclaiming the inferiority of schools in black neighborhoods for a generation, so it is not surprising that many white parents believe the difference important.

Black attitudes toward mandatory busing seem to be mixed. Opinion polls show overwhelming black support for desegregated schooling, but experience with open enrolment suggests that only a small minority of blacks send their children to desegregated schools when this requires individual action and a long bus ride. Black parents' attitudes seem to depend, however, on how the choice is presented. In Hartford, for example, Project Concern picks random classrooms from black neighborhood schools and offers the parents a chance to send the children to schools in white suburbs. Almost all black parents accept this offer. The evidence suggests, then, that when busing is initiated by the school establishment and parents expect their children to be welcome in the new school, most black parents like the idea. But when busing requires individual initiative and may lead to an indifferent or hostile reception, as it may under open enrolment, relatively few black parents make the move.

The situation is further complicated by black suspicion. In the South, where whites have generally resisted each new step toward desegregation, black leaders tend to feel that desegregation is worth almost any price, including busing. In the North, where the white élite has often favored some degree of desegregation, blacks have been less certain that desegregation was worthwhile. They have suspected, probably rightly, that desegregation may in some cases cause blacks to lose control of their own schools. Yet where the threat of mandatory busing has solidified white resistance to desegregation, as it has in Detroit, black leaders have become more committed to it. In part this is because whites as well as blacks would be required to ride buses under Judge Roth's plan, and while this may be cold comfort to those black parents whose children end up on buses, it is important symbolically. Indeed, the whole issue is now symbolic, and many blacks who had no enthusiasm for busing a few years ago now feel that the black community cannot afford to "lose" the busing battle.

Whatever the state of black opinion, most local white politicians have concluded that they cannot publicly support mandatory busing, even when they privately favor it. In San Francisco, the Mayor has denounced mandatory busing and waged a successful campaign to displace a school board that supported busing on a limited basis. In Michigan, Judge Roth's efforts to desegregate the Detroit metropolitan area have evoked almost universal opposition from white politicians of otherwise diverse ideologies. In Congress, even some long-time supporters of civil rights legislation have gone on record against mandatory busing. Last summer, Congress tacked an amendment onto the higher-education bill, limiting the Federal Courts' powers to use busing to achieve racial balance. An even stronger bill was killed by a liberal Senate filibuster in the last days of the session, but it will be reintroduced next January.

Legal experts disagree over whether Congress has the power to set limits on what the courts may do to enforce the 14th Amendment. But while the Court could hold Congressional restrictions on busing unconstitutional, it is not likely to ignore the popular mood that motivates such legislation. For if Congress cannot achieve its objective by legislation, it may well try to do so by constitutional amendment. If passed, such an amendment would be a blow not only to school desegregation but also to the prestige and authority of the Court itself. Constitutional amendments are, of course, difficult to enact. During the nineteen-sixties both the school-prayer decision and the reapportionment decision led to proposals for amendments that would preserve the old arrangements. Neither effort succeeded, and within a few years both decisions were generally accepted. Opposition to busing may, however, prove less transient. Unless desegregation ushers in a new era of racial harmony faster than even its advocates expect, white parents whose children attend schools in black areas will continue to feel anxious every day as their children go off to school. This means that support for constitutional curbs on busing may persist long enough to be translated into action.

Even if the Court decides that the chances of a constitutional amendment are small and that it can safely ignore white opposition to busing, it will still have to decide whether large-scale desegregation in the North is desirable. In trying to adjudicate such questions, Federal district judges, including the district judge who heard the *Keyes* case, have placed considerable reliance on the opinions of social scientists. While the Supreme Court has been properly reluctant to enter this morass, some of the Justices may still be influenced by supposedly expert opinion about the effects of desegregation.

Social scientists have done a fair amount of research on school segregation and have reached contradictory conclusions. Most researchers have concentrated on the relationship between desegregation and black students' scores on standardized tests. The most famous single study of this subject is the "Coleman Report," which was based on a 1965 national survey of both segregated and desegregated schools. The survey found that the average Northern black sixth grader was about 18 months behind the average white sixth grader on tests of verbal ability, reading comprehension and arithmetic skill. Black sixth graders attending 50-per-cent to 75-per-cent white schools lagged only about 12 months. (Black first graders entering these schools had scores no higher than blacks entering other schools.) The situation in schools where whites constituted more than 75 percent of the enrolment was less encouraging. Blacks entering these schools had higher test scores than other blacks, but they appeared to lose ground between first and sixth grades. Most other surveys also suggest that blacks' test scores improve faster in predominantly white elementary schools than in predominantly black schools.[1] (The finding that blacks do worse when they are a small minority has not been replicated and may be wrong.) The Coleman data do not allow us to say much about the effects of segregation in junior high schools, but do imply that segregation has very little effect on changes in black students' test scores between ninth and twelfth grades.

Unfortunately, none of these surveys deals primarily with schools that had been desegregated by busing or by court order. When social scientists have studied busing programs, they have gotten mixed results. Busing almost never seems to hurt black students' test scores. In some cases it seems to help somewhat. In most cases, however, researchers report no statistically reliable difference between the test scores of blacks who were bused and whatever control group they chose to measure them against. Such findings should not be taken at face value, however. Most busing studies cover only one or two years.

---

[1] The best review of this research is probably the one published by Nancy St. John in *Review of Education Research,* February 1970.

If the cumulative effect of desegregated elementary schooling were to reduce the gap between blacks and whites by 20 to 30 percent, as the Coleman survey suggests, one year of desegregation might only reduce the gap by 3 to 5 percent. A difference of this kind could not be detected with certainty except by comparing very large groups. Busing studies almost all involve relatively small groups. Thus even if six years of busing could cut the test-score gap between blacks and whites by 20 to 30 percent, researchers might find that the effects of busing over one or two years were "statistically insignificant." The only way to overcome this difficulty would be to average all the different busing studies together. Since some studies report gains and virtually none report losses, it seems likely that the average effect is a gain.

Social scientists have also investigated the relationship between high school desegregation and black students' chances of attending college. Blacks are at much less of a disadvantage relative to whites in terms of staying in school and going to college than they are on standardized tests. Blacks today get a year less schooling than the average white. They get slightly *more* schooling than whites with comparable test scores. This is because blacks have higher educational aspirations than whites with comparable test scores. Desegregation does not seem to have consistent effects on either aspirations or college entrance rates. Blacks in segregated high schools have educational aspirations as high as similar blacks in desegregated high schools, and they are as likely to attend college as similar blacks from desegregated high schools. Blacks from desegregated high schools may attend colleges of higher academic and social status than blacks from segregated high schools, but the evidence for this is still very scanty.

We know far less about how desegregation affects black students' attitudes and values. Blacks get somewhat lower grades when they have to compete with whites than they get in segregated schools. As a result they seem to form a somewhat lower opinion of their own academic competence. At least in recent years, blacks who attended desegregated colleges have been more overtly hostile to whites than blacks who attended segregated colleges. This may not be true of blacks who have gone to desegregated elementary and secondary schools, however, and it may stop being true once traditionally white colleges adapt to having a sizable black minority.

The long-term effects of desegregated schooling on black adults have not been extensively studied. The one relevant study deals with blacks who were educated in the North before 1960. It found that blacks who attended desegregated Northern schools had parents of essentially the same social and economic status as blacks who attended segregated Northern schools. Yet when the two groups finished school, the desegregated blacks were slightly more likely to enter "nontraditional" occupations, that is, occupations that had relatively few blacks in them. Blacks from desegregated schools therefore earned $200 to $400 more per year than blacks who had attended segregated schools.

Social scientists have paid relatively little attention to the effects of desegregated schooling on white children. Some studies suggest that busing actually raises white children's test scores. In general, however, the most reasonable conclusion at present is that neither busing nor "natural" desegregation (that which results from residential desegregation) has much effect either way on whites' test scores

Social science does tell us one thing that makes most of the foregoing facts almost irrelevant in forming judgments about whether or not to desegregate the schools. Even when blacks have the same educational credentials and test scores as whites, they end up in much lower status occupations and earn substantially less money. Some whites blame this on black workers' attitudes and behavior on the job. Blacks mostly blame it on white racism. In some cases both expanations may be relevant, that is, white prejudice may lead blacks to act in ways their white employers regard as unacceptable. In other cases the problem is discrimination pure and simple. Sometimes this discrimination is overt, as when blacks are arbitrarily excluded from labor unions or from managerial jobs. Sometimes it is covert, as when blacks fail to hear about desirable jobs because they have no friends in the all-white organizations that have good jobs to offer. Unfortunately, we have no good evidence as to whether attending school with blacks makes whites less prejudiced as adults. Most people assume this is the case, but one could also argue the opposite view.

My own guess—and it is only that—is that school desegregation can have a profound effect if it is part of a larger effort to transform relations between blacks and whites, but that it has very little effect in and of itself. This suspicion derives largely from comparing the situations of Northern and Southern blacks. In 1959, Northern black families had incomes 71 percent of the Northern white average, while Southern black families had incomes 46 percent of the Southern white average. Less than a tenth of that difference between North and South could be traced to the fact that some Northern blacks had attended desegregated schools. Yet much of the difference between North and South may well have been traceable to the fact that the North had no official system of segregation, that Northern employers were less consciously racist and that discrimination, while widespread, was widely regarded as reprehensible. The fact that half of all Northern blacks had attended desegregated schools prior to 1960 was at least a symbol of this situation, and probably also one cause of it.

If this argument is correct, we should not evaluate busing primarily in terms of what happens to the children on the buses, any more than we should evaluate the effect of desegregating the University of Mississippi primarily by asking what happened to James Meredith. The most important effect of the *Brown* decision was not that it desegregated the schools of Topeka, Kan., or even that it eventually led to school desegregation throughout the South. The primary importance of *Brown* was that it served as both the symbol and the precedent for a sweeping attack on the entire Jim Crow system, not only in schools but in buses, restaurants, motels, toilets, voting and employment. It has not entirely eliminated the difference between black and white children's average reading scores, but it has certainly transformed the political and social mores of the South in a way that seemed almost inconceivable in 1954. One effect of this transformation has been to raise Southern black family income from 46 percent of the Southern white average in 1959 to 57 percent in 1969. None of this improvement was due to the direct effects of desegregated schools on black students' subsequent earning power, for virtually none of the Southern blacks who attended desegregated schools had entered the labor force in 1969. Furthermore, Northern experience suggests that even when these students do enter the labor force, they will not earn much more than those who attended segregated schools. Putting it the other way around, Northern experience also suggests that the benefits of desegregation would accrue to *all* blacks, including those who remained in segregated schools. The question about busing in the North, then, is whether it will make Northern whites less likely to discriminate against blacks, or whether it will intensify racism. On this question, social science is not helpful. The Court must, therefore, proceed on its own.

One of the difficulities of judicial policy making is that the judiciary has to pretend to be something else. The nine men who constitute the Supreme Court are inevitably guided by their notions about what America is, what it should become and what the Court's role should be in the transition. But they are also required to act as if their interpretations of the Constitution had always been implicit in it, rather than being read in when this seemed politically wise. This makes the Court worry more about consistency and tradition than other branches of government. Congress can make and unmake laws as it sees fit. The Court cannot announce that the Constitution means one thing in 1971 and another in 1972 without destroying the very legitimacy from which it derives authority. As a result, the Court will inevitably be concerned with trying to make its future decisions on Northern school segregation consistent with its past decisions on

Southern segregation, even though the membership on the Court has changed. The logic of these Southern decisions leads, in my judgment, to the conclusion that Northern and Southern segregation are different only in degree, not in kind. It would follow that Northern remedies should be essentially similar to Southern ones, and that Denver should use two-way busing to desegregate all its schools.

The crucial precedent in this regard is the *Swann* decision of 1971, which dealt with Charlotte, N.C. This decision came after the appointment of Justices Burger and Blackmun but before the appointment of Justices Powell and Rehnquist. The decision was unanimous. Charlotte was assigning pupils to the school nearest their homes (with some transfer privileges), and because Charlotte's neighborhoods were segregated, most of its schools were also segregated. The Court observed that the school board had been willing to bus when this helped maintain segregation. It inferred that the board had chosen a neighborhood system at least in part to maintain segregation. The Court, therefore, held that, given Charlotte's past history, the neighborhood assignment system was unconstitutional, and it ordered busing.

The analogy with Denver seems clear. Denver's attendance zones, like Charlotte's, are now mostly drawn on a color-blind basis, and those that are not easily could be. But Denver's commitment to neighborhood assignment is not color-blind, as its history of gerrymandering shows. The board's enthusiasm for neighborhood assignment seems to depend on the fact this keeps whites from having to attend schools in black or Hispano areas. If neighborhood schools did not have this effect, it seems safe to predict the current Denver board would find new virtues in busing. If such motives make neighborhood assignment unconstitutional in Charlotte, they have the same implications in Denver.

But while logical consistency may be of paramount importance to some judges and lawyers, it is not a satisfactory basis for making public policy. Whatever the Supreme Court decides in the *Keyes* case, civil-rights leaders still ought to be asking themselves whether two-way busing is worth the risks. If our goal is a "salt-and-pepper" society, in which every group of 10 includes at least one black face, school desegregation is essential by definition. But if our goal is to ensure that blacks get their share of social and economic privileges, further school desegregation may not be of high priority at the present time. Indeed, if school desegregation requires sending large numbers of white children to schools in black neighborhoods, it may arouse resentments that will make economic equality harder to achieve.

As I noted earlier, the main reason blacks have worse jobs than whites is not that they have low test scores or inadequate educational credentials. Economic equality between blacks and whites depends, instead, primarily on changing white employers' hiring and promotion practices. In the long run, sending blacks and whites to the same schools might reduce white hostility to blacks and black fears about whites. If so, more blacks might end up in good jobs. In the short run, however, efforts to achieve complete school desegregation may result in so much white resistance that its long-term effects never get tested. If the Supreme Court pushes ahead with two-way busing in the North, Congress may well pass a tough antibusing bill aimed at nullifying the Court's decisions. Worse yet, if the Court holds such legislation unconstitutional, Congress and 38 states may enact a constitutional amendment to stop busing, particularly with a President publicly committed against busing for racial balance. Such an amendment would be a political disaster of major proportions. Both blacks and whites would see it as a decisive defeat for the civil-rights movement and triumph for segregationism. Blacks would be demoralized, and white supremacists would be encouraged to attack on other fronts. The result might not only be to halt further progress toward racial equality but also to erode many of the gains made over the past decade. Many white employers would probably feel that they no longer had to worry about recruiting blacks. Some might even revert to overt discrimination in hiring and promotion.

All this may, of course, be unduly pessimistic. Liberal Senators may be able to filibuster for the foreseeable future. If they fail, the Court may strike down antibusing legislation. Opponents of a constitutional amendment may then be able to find 13 states where there are so few blacks that the white majority is not worried about busing. Nonetheless for a strategy whose benefit seems so uncertain, busing entails considerable political risk.

It seems to me that direct efforts to assure better jobs for blacks would win more widespread support from both blacks and whites and would also yield more important benefits than busing. It is true that getting blacks into white jobs takes more manpower and more persistence than bringing school desegregation suits. But demands for economic equality can unite blacks of almost all political hues, instead of setting the integrationists and the nationalists at one another's throats as busing does. Furthermore, while whites inevitably resist threats to the security and status of their jobs, their opposition has not been as bitter or as widespread as to busing. There are two reasons for this. First, adults are more willing to take risks themselves than to expose their children to risks. Second, once blacks get into a given job category and organization, white hostility is likely to diminish. This seems less likely with busing, which exposes white children to the hazards of black neighborhoods day after day and remains both an inconvenience and a threat for as long as it continues.

None of this means that school desegregation is undesirable. If the

Fourteenth Amendment means anything, it means we must guarantee black children the right to attend desegregated schools if they want to do so. We must guarantee this right even when it involves busing blacks to schools in white neighborhoods where whites do not want them. Busing whites to schools in black neighborhoods is another story. This is not a clear legal or moral issue. It should therefore be decided on practical grounds. Other things being equal, busing probably makes educational sense. But other things are rarely equal. If busing creates a political climate in which economic equality is more difficult to attain, it will not have been worthwhile. Conversely, if it can create a climate in which economic equality is easier to attain, it should be promoted even if its educational effects prove negligible.

Untangling the Busing Snarl

ALEXANDER M. BICKEL

Alexander M. Bickel is Chancellor Kent Professor of
Law and Legal History at Yale University and contrib-
uting editor to *The New Republic*. His books include
*The Unpublished Opinions of Mr. Justice Brandeis,
Politics and the Warren Court*, and *The Supreme Court
and the Idea of Progress*.

I

President Nixon, it is widely charged, is using the busing issue for
purely political purposes, irresponsibly heightening racial tension and
pandering to bigots. Busing children to school is a common practice
throughout the country, and the amount of additional busing required
by court decrees in racial cases is marginal. Busing, as the President
and other unscrupulous politicians talk about it, is not an issue, but
a code-word, a scare-word. So runs the charge.

But one man's code-word or scare-word is another man's symbol.
No doubt, a great deal of busing goes on to which no one objects, and
the busing to which the President draws attention is chiefly objected
to not for itself, but because of the ends to which it is put. It *is* a
handy symbol for those ends, however, and the President is not responsible for focusing attention on it; it is quite capable of drawing
sufficient attention by itself. The question of ends is no false issue. It is
serious, it has been a long time coming to a head and it will not go
away. Its context is a dilemma posed by the decision in *Brown v. Board
of Education,* now 18 years old, and its roots are in the ambivalence of
the reasoning on which the *Brown* decision rested.

Alexander M. Bickel, "Untangling the Busing Snarl," *The New Republic,* September 23 and 30, 1972. Reprinted by permission of *The New Republic,* © 1972,
Harrison-Blaine of New Jersey, Inc.

Brown decreed the end of legally enforced segregation. It is possible formally to abolish a system of legal segregation by simply wiping the laws that enforced it off the books. But if that had been all that *Brown* demanded, it would have amounted to a sham, since the law of segregation bespoke attitudes that were still widely held, and that would have continued to have effect. And so the *Brown* decision had to be administered in order that it might be made palpable. It had to be administered for the sake of maintaining the integrity and credibility of law. Dual school systems had to be visibly disestablished.

But when *was* a previously dual school system in fact disestablished; when could it be said to have become unitary? The courts groped for and were unable to find a principled answer to this question. Given the realities of American life and its pattern of racial as well as ethnic, and perhaps most particularly planned, residential and social separation, any answer short of enforced racial balance necessarily appeared arbitrary and incomplete; no more than a pragmatic, temporizing, political compromise.

By 1968, some rules of administration were reasonably well established and were achieving some visible results. But these rules still left all-black and all-white, or overwhelmingly white, schools in many places. Was that good enough? Could that situation now be described as *de facto,* and no longer *de jure* segregation, and could the courts sit back, satisfied that *Brown* had been complied with? And could they accept as *de facto,* and constitutionally unobjectionable, similar and sometimes even more massive racial concentration in schools in parts of the country that had never, or had not for better than half a century, enforced school segregation by law or by any other official action?

President Nixon's answer, in his statement on school desegregation of March 1970, was largely in the affirmative. We have tended, he said, to place "on the schools and the children too great a share of the burden of eliminating racial disparties throughout our society. A major part of this task falls to the schools. But they cannot do all or even most of it by themselves." This answer was unsatisfactory, however, to the traditional civil rights movement, white and black. No candid and public recognition of limits, of this or any other sort, was acceptable to those who had spent 15 years fighting for school desegregation in hundreds upon hundreds of Southern counties, because the struggle was symbolic as well as practical, and because they harbored an ever-present fear that any admission of limits would lead to backsliding.

As of 1970, applicable Supreme Court decisions left open considerable room for legislative action. But the President proposed none, and Northern liberals and moderates of both parties in Congress would hear of none. Proposals were made to give legislative guidance to the courts by presumptively, if not conclusively, defining the goals they should try to reach under *Brown* as either a neighborhood school system supplemented by state-supported transfers from black-majority into black-minority schools, or a system in which schools would have to conform to a black-white ratio within a certain range. Such proposals received no presidential endorsement and found no support among Northern liberals or moderates in the legislature.

Two and a half years later, much more drastic measures are in the offing. The President has sent up a bill forbidding any busing of pupils in the sixth grade and below that exceeds certain averages of present busing, and the House, with many Northern liberals not only joining in but actually taking the lead, passed a much more stringent bill, just about flatly mandating the neighborhood school, and allowing previously implemented desegregation plans to be reopened and rolled back to conform to the new mandates. All this in face of constitutional obstacles which did not exist in 1970, but which do exist today, as we shall see, because Supreme Court decisions have advanced considerably beyond the stage they had reached in 1970. The stringent House bill, or something like it, appears to have a fair chance of passage in the Senate, too. Such is the price of political timidity and of trying as long as possible to hide behind the judges' skirts.

It is to be added that the President's position is more respectable than that of Northern liberals who voted for the House bill, since the President's basic policy has been more or less consistent, and since 1970 he not only presided over but actively pushed to completion or to near-completion in the South a process of desegregation that could still be called that, rather than integration for racial balance.

During this same period, many lower federal courts, and in substantial measure ultimately the Supreme Court itself, rejected the policy expressed in the President's statement of March 1970, and blurred the distinction—uneasy and merely pragmatic, as it has always been—between desegregation on the one hand, and integration for racial balance on the other. One reason they did so is the original ambivalence in the Supreme Court's reasoning in the *Brown* case.

Of course, on its facts, *Brown* dealt only with *de jure*, legally enforced segregation; technically, this is all that was held unconstitutional. One branch of the holding in *Brown* is the simple, minimal proposition that the state may not, by legislation or administratively, in the schools or otherwise, classify the population along racial lines, except—and this point is problematic but the problem is not necessarily insoluble—for obviously remedial purposes. But another element in the *Brown* decision was the Supreme Court's concern not with race relations in general, but specifically with education. In this branch of its holding, the Court declared that separate schools are inherently unequal; they provide an inherently unequal education. This inequality is heightened, but merely heightened, when the separation has the sanction of law.

The implicit idea was that separate public schooling, whatever the cause of it or the means by which it was enforced, is unconstiutional because the function of the public school cannot be successfully performed unless children of all groups are taught in it together. If this is so, then the distinction between *de jure* and *de facto* segregation begins to vanish, and disestablishment of a legally enforced dual system cannot be said to have ocurred until the maximum amount of integration has taken place. The task then is not to draw a pragmatic line, but to achieve a principled end beyond desegregation, namely, integration.

In a group of cases decided in April 1971, of which *Swann v. Charlotte-Mecklenburg Board of Education* was the chief one, the Supreme Court edged quite near this end. The distinction between *de jure* segregation and *de facto* separation was not abandoned. Hence it is arguable that the rule of the *Swann* case is not necessarily to be applied where one or another discrete instance of *de jure* segregation is discovered in a school system that is otherwise not "deliberately operated to carry out a governmental policy to separate pupils in schools solely on the basis of race." Whether this is so or not we may find out when the Court decides the Denver, Colorado, case in which it granted *certiorari* earlier this year.

Again, it is an open question under *Swann* whether school district lines are subject to alteration by court decree. We may find out more about that as the Richmond, Virginia, and Detroit cases develop further. This June, in the *Emporia* and *Scotland Neck, N.C.* cases, in decisions very much tied to particular facts, the Court held that creation of new school districts out of old ones may be prevented by judicial decree, where creation of the new district would adversely affect the process of desegregation. In the *Emporia* case, the Court divided five to four, partly because the majority emphasized the *effect* of school board action virtually to the point of ignoring its *purpose;* the majority, in other words, suggested that if the action of a school board (presumably past or present) had the effect of causing racial separation, it did not matter, or mattered very little, what its purpose or motivation might have been. This position, if consistently maintained, would make short shrift of the *de jure–de facto* distinction.

Finally the Court in *Swann* by no means held that the Constitution requires racial balance, and as Chief Justice Burger has since pointed out, while it sanctioned busing, the Court certainly perceived possible limits on the use of busing, at least where it runs a risk to the health of children or where it significantly impinges on the educational process.

But the Court did in the *Swann* case declare a new objective to be achieved in the disestablishment of formerly dual school systems: school boards and district judges must "make every effort to achieve the greatest possible degree of actual desegregation." And by actual desegregation, it is perfectly plain in context, the Court meant dispersal of the school population through any given system. That is the objective. *Swann* lays its down as the law of the Constitution. The operative phrase, to repeat, is "greatest possible degree of actual desegregation."

The *Swann* ruling may yet end up being qualified by the Supreme Court itself, and its consequences in practice can be exaggerated. But for now, there it is. District judges have the responsibility of estimating the possible and practicing its art, "taking into account," as the Court remarked in a companion case from Mobile, "the practicalities of the situation" facing each of them. But there is no longer any question about what they must try to achieve.

So it is that we have arrived where we are. Where we are is not in the presence of hundreds of massive integration decrees in the South, let alone in the North, involving extensive shuffling of total school populations, by busing or otherwise. But we are in the presence of a fair number of such decrees; there are further ones impending North and South; and that is the direction which the Supreme Court has authoritatively indicated to lower federal judges. It will involve busing, more busing in many places than before, and busing to different ends than before.

Under the impact of *Swann*, moreover, it is doubtful that the *de jure–de facto* distinction can long survive. It is still part of the law, and *Swann* was strictly a *de jure* case in the Court's view. But even technically, the distinction is showing some cracks, as in the *Emporia* and *Scotland Neck* cases of last June. And it is fatally vulnerable in a larger sense. The enforcement of a requirement of racial dispersal of school population in one region of the country but not in other regions is morally and politically, and therefore ultimately legally, an untenable position on any permanent basis.

Now, the President and all those congressmen who voted for the House bill may be inflating a false issue when they talk about busing, but it is a false issue also that the Democratic platform addresses, if in deflationary rather than inflationary terms, when it declares that busing is one among other acceptable methods of desegregation and lets it go at that. That is an attempt to hide behind the judges' skirts again.

Desegregation is not the issue any longer. Something else is, whether or not it is called integration or racial balance. That something else is symbolized by the shorthand term, busing, and it must be faced.

II

President Nixon and the Republic platform are inflating busing as a political issue, and Senator McGovern and the Democratic platform seek to deflate it. The deflationary effort is not only less likely to succeed, it is also the less responsible form of political behavior. For if busing as such is a false issue, it has come to symbolize a real one: namely, what is the proper objective of federal policy toward racial concentration—or separation, or isolation—in the public schools, and beyond that, what are the proper priorities of federal policy in primary and secondary education?

The federal courts are well along toward a transition from enforcing what could still properly be called segregation to undertaking, in the South and in many places elsewhere, the integration of schools, so that they will be racially balanced. This is a policy that requires busing, and it is this policy that Mr. Nixon and the Republic platform oppose when they oppose busing. It is the issue raised by this policy that Senator McGovern and the Democratic platform evade when they seek to deflate the busing controversy by their characterization of busing as an acceptable method of desegregation. Of course it is, but we are past desegregating the schools in most places in the South and elsewhere. Should federal policy now be to integrate them?

An affirmative answer to this question necessarily means we have set priorities. Integrating the schools—which the federal government will have to do nationally or not at all—is likely, once it is undertaken, to be all we will be doing in primary and secondary education for the next decade or more. It is an absorbing task. If it is equally a moral imperative to abolish racial concentration in schools resulting from housing patterns, from demographic changes and other factors as it is to disestablish legally enforced segregation, then perhaps the question whether to proceed with racial dispersal answers itself. So it may also if integration is a necessary, or necessarily the best, means of improving the education of lower-class black children.

But there is a moral difference between what housing patterns do to schools, even where those patterns were encouraged by past government policies, and what a legally enforced system of rigid segregation does to schools. There is a moral difference at least sufficient to render relevant a further inquiry into the costs that a policy of integration must incur, into its prospects of success, and into its value as a means of improving the education of black children.

Not the most sanguine reading of the available data can lead to the conclusion that the attainment of racial balance in the schools is the only or always necessarily the most effective way to improve the education of black children. On the other hand, the demography of many areas is such that the rather delicate conditions of balance in which alone educational improvement can even be hoped for are unattainable. Nearly half the black population in the country is concentrated in 50 cities, and a third of the total in 15. This is not a Northern pattern. It is nationwide. The 50 cities include such places of great black concentration as Baltimore, Houston, New Orleans, Atlanta, St. Louis, Memphis, Dallas, Birmingham, Jacksonville, Kansas City, and Richmond. And of course Washington, D.C. In these places and places like them, only extensive busing across district lines can have any impact at all, and its costs are high. It entails not only the expenditure of funds, which are in short supply and could be put to other uses, but of political, moral and administrative resources, which are also not in unlimited supply, and for which other fruitful employment could also be found. And since we are not prepared to pay the additional costs of closing private schools or incorporating them into the public system, or of restricting the freedom of residential choice which the middle class enjoys, busing not infrequently fails to achieve its end, even after all its other costs have been borne.

What, then, is to be done? Congress passed a rider to the Higher Education Bill last summer ordering that lower-court decrees be stayed pending appeal, rather than being implemented immediately as has been the practice in cases where busing is used for the purpose of achieving racial balance. But this is a stopgap, and not very effective as such either, because busing decrees do not generally avow a purpose to achieve racial balance; they still speak the language of desegregation, even though they have often actually made the transition to integration. Other anti-busing measures—the President's, or the harsher one passed in the House, which is now up for consideration in the Senate—are also stopgaps, though in another sense. They are stopgaps because they are negative. They are not a school policy; they seek to ensure the absence of a school policy. Moreover, they encounter constitutional difficulties. In many applications, they are in conflict with decisions of the Supreme Court—the *Swann* case and companion cases of 1971, and the *Emporia* and *Scotland Neck* decisions of June 1972.

Now in one sense, that does not mean that the House bill is unconstitutional, or that the President acted unlawfully in proposing his bill. In the last analysis, nothing is unconstitutional until there is a judicial decree saying so on particular facts. Such a decree must be obeyed. Until then there are predictions and opinions, and Congress and the President are not only entitled to their own predictions and opinions, they are entitled to hold opinions contrary to those expressed by the Supreme Court, and to give statutory form to their own opinions in the hope that the Supreme Court will be persuaded to see the error of its ways and will reverse itself.

But if our system of government is to work well and retain the confidence of our people, and if the institutions of our government are not to destroy each other in chaotic conflict, Congress and the President ought to provoke a direct clash with the Supreme Court only as a very last, almost despairing resort. For only two outcomes of such a clash are possible. Either the Supreme Court digs in its heels and dashes popular expectations that Congress and the President have raised, thus discrediting Congress and the President, or itself, or more likely both. Or the Court surrenders, reverses itself, and leaves the indelible impression, at least for a generation, that it is not independent, that it does not follow the law and its own precedents, but rather the election returns. Neither result is beneficial.

The constitutional difficulty, moreover, is even greater. The President's bill and the House bill are supported as exercises of a power of Congress to control the Supreme Court by prescribing the remedies that the Court may administer. In other words, the argument is that without reversing itself, the Supreme Court could hold that Congress has the necessary power to lay down the law that the Court is bound to apply.

On analysis, I think this argument questions *Marbury v. Madison* itself, the very foundation of the power of judicial review. No one can guarantee that a majority of the Court would reject this claim to supreme legislative power. The Court has seldom been presented with this sort of challenge, in my judgment never with quite the challenge embodied in the House bill, and except as one reasons one's way to the proper conclusion from *Marbury v. Madison* itself, this has happily been a grey area of constitutional law. The question is not whether the congressional assertion of power to prescribe remedies would be held unconstitutional, but whether it should be, and what kind of pervasive change in the basic structure of our federal institutions, going well beyond the busing problem and affecting myriad other matters, we will have worked if the assertion of congressional power is accepted.

The President—so one had judged, for example, from his position on the 18-year-old vote issue, when he opposed trying to deal with it legislatively—is an institutional and constitutional conservative. So are many congressmen who voted for the House bill. But that bill, as well as the President's proposal, are recklessly radical in undertaking to alter the balance of power between the judiciary and the political institutions of the federal government.

Congress, it is said, though it cannot overrule the judicial definition of the substance of constitutional rights, has power to prescribe appropriate remedies for effectuating them, and to forbid the courts to employ other remedies. But in one of the companion cases to the *Swann* case of 1971, the Supreme Court had before it a North Carolina statute that provided as follows:

> No student shall be assigned or compelled to attend any school on account of race, creed, color or national origin, or for the purpose of creating a balance or ratio of race, religion, or national origins. Involuntary busing of students in contravention of this article is prohibited, and public funds shall not be used for any such busing.

The Court declared the statute unconstitutional because it operated "to hinder vindication of federal Constitutional guarantees."

Not only the prohibition of assignments of students on account of race, but even the prohibition against assignments for the purpose of creating racial balance, said the Court, "must inevitably conflict with the duty of school authorities to disestablish dual school systems." For even though racial balance was not mandated by the Constitution, some ratios were likely in many cases to be useful starting points in the shaping of a remedy. An absolute prohibition of ratios, even as a starting point, interfered unconstitutionally with the shaping of appropriate remedies. An absolute prohibition of busing of students assigned on the basis of race "will similarly hamper" the fashioning of effective remedies for constitutional violations. Bus transporation, said the Court, as it had noted in its main opinion in the *Swann* case, "has long been an integral part of all public educational systems, and it is unlikely that a truly effective remedy could be devised without continued reliance upon it."

Can Congress do what North Carolina could not? Section five of the Fourteenth Amendment gives Congress enforcement power. But there is clear historical evidence that section five was not meant to change the relationship between Congress and the judiciary. It merely confirmed, as do other amendments, general legislative power that Congress possesses anyway. That power enables Congress to dictate to the courts a choice among remedies, or to create new ones and substitute them for remedies the courts have been administering. But Congress ought not be held to have power to take away a remedy for a constitutional violation in circumstances in which the courts have decided that it is the only and the essential remedy, for which nothing can be substituted—and for which, for that matter, Congress provides no substitute. If Congress has this power, it has in fact, if not in form, the power to alter the substance of most constitutional rights, not merely the right to go to one or another school. If such a power is upheld, the school bus will have traveled to a far destination.

What Congress and the President can do, the only thing they can do without inviting a constitutional crisis, and what they must do is to try to change the reality on which the courts have been acting, rather than trying to alter the decisions the courts have been making. Congress and the President should address themselves not to the courts, but to the problems of primary and secondary education. These problems —affecting many private as well as public schools—include poor educational results as well as racial isolation. Busing and racial balance won't solve them in most places. And there is no panacea that will solve them everywhere. Hence no categorical national policy is possible. What is possible is federal help for coherent, well-planned local efforts to improve primary and secondary education.

Few such efforts are now being made, and federal programs are not designed to induce them. Federal programs are themselves incoherent, as they have to be, since no one is in possession of a panacea to be administered nationally. But they are at the same time over-administered from Washington—just enough to transmit their own incoherence from the national level, where it is inevitable, to the local level, where it is disastrous and avoidable. A thousand flowers—to borrow a saying—should bloom, but they should not bloom at random and untended in every school district. Conditions vary, but one condition is universal, and it is that if a school district uses a pot of federal money to buy three TV sets, two speech specialists and four other assorted devices one year, a little more or a little less of a different assortment the next year, and so forth, nothing at all will happen that makes a substantial difference.

Something might happen if the school district were required to look at itself in organized fashion, and consult its customers in committees that are sure to include representatives of all of them; and if it were then required to present a ten-year plan for self-improvement, taking into view the community's entire primary and secondary educational process, drawing on private as well as public resources, and seeking to enhance the process in both private and public schools. Such a plan would include measures to alleviate racial inbalance, it might include interracial educational projects involving children from private and public schools who are otherwise left in place, it might include school decentralization, it might include voucher projects opening a choice among schools that only the well-to-do enjoy now, and it would presumably include many things no one has yet tried. It would in any event embody a common local judgment—not a judge's and not a federal administrator's—of the direction of school policy over a foreseeable period of time.

Federal money would then be concentrated as a bloc grant and committed to the plan. A measure of supervisory federal controls would remain necessary, and the plan itself would need HEW approval before funds would flow into it. But the degree of federal control and administration would be greatly reduced from the present level.

There is a bill—HR 13552, introduced by Representatives Preyer (D., N.C.) and Udall (D., Ariz.)—that carries out the suggestion discussed above. Suppose it were enacted, would it have any chance of diverting the inexorable movement of the judicial bus? Well, the Supreme Court can see what others perceive. There is no reason to believe that a majority of the justices have a doctrinaire attachment to maximum integration. That is not why they order it. They order it for different reasons.

District judges before whom school suits are brought are made to confront what is usually a wasteland: a school district deteriorating in every way, sinking deeper and deeper into racial isolation, and doing nothing about it. So the judge orders integration and busing. That is all he can do, short of throwing up his hands, which after 18 years in the school business he no longer thinks he may do. The record of the wasteland and of the judge's response to it then moves up to the Supreme Court. There the doctrinal pull of *Brown v. Board of Education* again exerts its force, a principled line between any case and the one immediately preceding it is hard to find—if we said desegregation, why not more desegregation?—and what happens is what we have seen happen. But if Congress and the President, instead of fighting the courts, try to get school districts to fight the reality to which the courts have been reacting, and manage to present courts in the future with school districts embarked on concentrated long-range reforms, then, without needing to renege on prior decisions and without accepting any impairment of the general function of judicial review, courts will be able to say that they are now faced with new facts, with a new reality, which no longer calls for the old remedies. And the Supreme Court will agree. Or so—candor compels one to add—so one would expect.

Brown v. Board of Education—I

347 U.S. 483 (1954)
(May 17, 1954)

The *Brown* decision in 1954 decreed the end of legally enforced school segregation and asserted that dual school systems must be disestablished. All court rulings on busing stem from an interpretation of *Brown*.

MR. CHIEF JUSTICE WARREN delivered the opinion of the Court.

These cases come to us from the States of Kansas, South Carolina, Virginia, and Delaware. They are premised on different facts and different local conditions, but a common legal question justifies their consideration together in this consolidated opinion.

In each of these cases, minors of the Negro race, through their legal representatives, seek the aid of the courts in obtaining admission to the public schools of their community on a nonsegregated basis. In each instance they had been denied admission to schools attended by white children under laws requiring or permitting segregation according to race. This segregation was alleged to deprive the plantiffs of the equal protection of the laws under the fourteenth amendment. In each of the cases other than the Delaware case, a three-judge Federal district court denied relief to the plantiffs on the so-called separate but equal doctrine announced by this Court in *Plessy v. Ferguson*, 163 U.S. 537. Under that doctrine equality of treatment is accorded when the races are provided substantially equal facilities, even though these facilities be separate. In the Delaware case, the Supreme Court of Delaware adhered to that doctrine, but ordered that the plaintiffs be admitted to the white schools because of their superiority to the Negro schools.

The plaintiffs contend that segregated public schools are not "equal" and cannot be made "equal," and that hence they are deprived of the equal protection of the laws. Because of the obvious importance of the question presented, the Court took jurisdiction. Argument was heard in the 1952 term, and reargument was heard this term on certain questions propounded by the Court.

Reargument was largely devoted to the circumstances surrounding the adoption of the fourteenth amendment in 1868. It covered exhaustively consideration of the amendment in Congress, ratification by the States, then existing practices in racial segregation, and the views of proponents and opponents of the amendment. This discussion and our own investigation convince us that, although these sources cast some light, it is not enough to resolve the problem with which we are faced. At best, they are inconclusive. The most avid proponents of the post-war amendments undoubtedly intended them to remove all legal distinctions among "all persons born or naturalized in the United States." Their opponents, just as certainly, were antagonistic to both the letter and the spirit of the amendments and wished them to have the most limited effect. What others in Congress and the State legislatures had in mind cannot be determined with any degree of certainty.

An additional reason for the inconclusive nature of the amendment's history, with respect to segregated schools, is the status of public education at that time. In the South, the movement toward free common schools, supported by general taxation, had not yet taken hold. Education of white children was largely in the hands of private groups. Education of Negroes was almost nonexistent, and practically all of the race were illiterate. In fact, any education of Negroes was forbidden by law in some States. Today, in contrast, many Negroes have achieved outstanding success in the arts and sciences as well as in the business and professional world. It is true that public school education at the time of the amendment had advanced further in the North, but the effect of the amendment on northern States was generally ignored in the congressional debates. Even in the North, the conditions of public education did not approximate those existing today. The curriculum was usually rudimentary; ungraded schools were common in rural areas; the school term was but 3 months a year in many States; and compulsory school attendance was virtually unknown. As a consequence, it is not surprising that there should be so little in the history of the fourteenth amendment relating to its intended effect on public education.

In the first case in this Court construing the fourteenth amendment, decided shortly after its adoption, the Court interpreted it as proscribing all State-imposed discriminations against the Negro race.[1]

The doctrine of "separate but equal" did not make its appearance in this Court until 1896 in the case of *Plessy v. Ferguson, supra,* involving not education but transportation.[2] American courts have since labored with the doctrine for over half a century. In this Court, there have been six cases involving the "separate but equal" doctrine in the field of public education. In *Cumming v. County Board of Education,* 175 U.S. 528, and *Gong Lum v. Rice,* 275 U.S. 78, the validity of the doctrine itself was not challenged. In more recent cases, all on the graduate school level, inequality was found in that specific benefits enjoyed by white students were denied to Negro students of the same educational qualifications. *Missouri ex rel. Gaines v. Canada,* 305 U.S. 337; *Sipuel v. Oklahoma,* 332 U.S. 631; *Sweatt v. Painter,* 339 U.S. 629; *McLaurin v. Oklahoma State Regents,* 339 U.S. 637. In none of these cases was it necessary to reexamine the doctrine to grant relief to the Negro plaintiff. And in *Sweatt v. Painter, supra,* the Court expressly reserved decision on the question whether *Plessy v. Ferguson* should be held inapplicable to public education.

In the instant cases, that question is directly presented. Here, unlike *Sweatt v. Painter,* there are findings below that the Negro and white schools involved have been equalized, or are being equalized, with respect to buildings, curricula, qualifications and salaries of teachers, and other "tangible" factors. Our decision, therefore, cannot

---

[1] *Slaughter-House Cases,* 16 Wall. 36, 67–72 (1873); *Strauder v. West Virginia,* 100 U.S. 303, 307–308 (1880):

"It ordains that no State shall deprive any person of life, liberty, or property without due process of law, or deny to any person within its jurisdiction the equal protection of the laws. What is this but declaring that the law in the States shall be the same for the black as for the white; that all persons, whether colored or white, shall stand equal before the laws of the States, and, in regard to the colored race, for whose protection the amendment was primarily designed, that no discrimination shall be made against them by law because of their color? The words of the amendment, it is true, are prohibitory, but they contain a necessary implication of a positive immunity, or right, most valuable to the colored race,— the right to exemption from unfriendly legislation against them distinctively as colored,—exemption from legal discriminations, implying inferiority in civil society, lessening the security of their enjoyment of the rights which others enjoy, and discriminations which are steps towards reducing them to the condition of a subject race."

[2] The doctrine apparently originated in *Roberts v. City of Boston,* 59 Mass. 198, 206 (1850), upholding school segregation against attack as being violative of a state constitutional guarantee of equality. Segregation in Boston public schools was eliminated in 1855. But elsewhere in the North segregation in public education has persisted in some communities until recent years. It is apparent that such segregation has long been a nationwide problem, not merely one of sectional concern.

turn on merely a comparison of these tangible factors in the Negro and white schools involved in each of the cases. We must look instead to the effect of segregation itself on public education.

In approaching this problem, we cannot turn the clock back to 1868 when the amendment was adopted, or even to 1896 when *Plessy v. Ferguson* was written. We must consider public education in the light of its full development and its present place in American life throughout the Nation. Only in this way can it be determined if segregation in public schools deprives these plaintiffs of the equal protection of the laws.

Today, education is perhaps the most important function of State and local governments. Compulsory school attendance laws and the great expenditures for education both demonstrate our recognition of the importance of education to our democratice society. It is required in the performance of our most basic public responsibilities, even service in the armed forces. It is the very foundation of good citizenship. Today it is a principal instrument in awakening the child to cultural values, in preparing him for later professional training, and in helping him to adjust normally to his environment. In these days, it is doubtful that any child may reasonably be expected to succeed in life if he is denied the opportunity of an education. Such an opportunity, where the State has undertaken to provide it, is a right which must be made available to all on equal terms.

We come then to the question presented: Does segregation of children in public schools solely on the basis of race, even though the physical facilities and other "tangible" factors may be equal, deprive the children of the minority group of equal educational opportunities? We believe that it does.

In *Sweatt v. Painter, supra,* in finding that a segregated law school for Negroes could not provide them equal educational opportunities, this Court relied in large part on "those qualities which are incapable of objective measurement but which make for greatness in a law school." In *McLaurin v. Oklahoma State Regents, supra,* the Court, in requiring that a Negro admitted to a white graduate school be treated like all other students, again resorted to intangible consideration: ". . . his ability to study, to engage in discussions and exchange views with other students, and, in general, to learn his profession." Such considerations apply with added force to children in grade and high schools. To separate them from others of similar age and qualifications solely because of their race generates a feeling of inferiority as to their status in the community that may affect their hearts and minds in a way unlikely ever to be undone. The effect of this separation on their educational opportunities was well stated by a finding in the Kansas case by a court which nevertheless felt compelled to rule against the Negro plaintiffs:

> Segregation of white and colored children in public schools has a detrimental effect upon the colored children. The impact is greater when it has the sanction of the law; for the policy of separating the races is usually interpreted as denoting the inferiority of the Negro group. A sense of inferiority affects the motivation of a child to learn. Segregation with the sanction of law, therefore, has a tendency to [retard] the educational and mental development of Negro children and to deprive them of some of the benefits they would receive in a racial[ly] integrated school system.

Whatever may have been the extent of psychological knowledge at the time of *Plessy v. Ferguson*, this finding is amply supported by modern authority.[3] Any language in *Plessy v. Ferguson* contrary to this finding is rejected.

We conclude that in the field of public education the doctrine of "separate but equal" has no place. Separate educational facilities are inherently unequal. Therefore, we hold that the plaintiffs and others similarly situated for whom the actions have been brought are, by reason of the segregation complained of, deprived of the equal protection of the laws guaranteed by the fourteenth amendment. This disposition makes unnecessary any discussion whether such segregation also violates the due process clause of the fourteenth amendment.

Because these are class actions, because of the wide applicability of this decision, and because of the great variety of local conditions, the formulation of decrees in these cases presents problems of considerable complexity. On reargument, the consideration of appropriate relief was necessarily subordinated to the primary question—the constitutionality of segregation in public education. We have now announced that such segregation is a denial of the equal protection of the laws. In order that we may have the full assistance of the parties in formulating decrees, the cases will be restored to the docket, and the

---

[3] K. B. Clark. Effect of Prejudice and Discrimination on Personality Development (Midcentury White House Conference on Children and Youth, 1950); Witmer and Kotinsky, Personality in the Making (1952), c. VI; Deutscher and Chein, The Psychological Effects of Enforced Segregation: A Survey of Social Science Opinion, 26 J. Psychol. 259 (1948); Chein, What are the Psychological Effects of Segregation Under Conditions of Equal Facilities?, 3 Int. J. Opinion and Attitude Res. 229 (1949); Brameld, Educational Costs, in Discrimination and National Welfare (MacIver, ed., 1949), 44–48; Frazier, The Negro in the United States (1949), 674–681. And see generally Myrdal, An American Dilemma (1944).

parties are requested to present further argument on questions 4 and 5 previously propounded by the Court for the reargument this term.[4] The Attorney General of the United States is again invited to participate. The attorneys general of the States requiring or permitting segregation in public education will also be permitted to appear as *amici curiae* upon request to do so by September 15, 1954, and submission of briefs by October 1, 1954.

---

[4] "4. Assuming it is decided that segregation in public schools violates the Fourteenth Amendment

"(*a*) would decree necessarily follow providing that, within the limits set by normal geographic school districting, Negro children should forthwith be admitted to schools of their choice, or

"(*b*) may this Court, in the exercise of its equity powers, permit an effective gradual adjustment to be brought about from existing segregated systems to a system not based on color distinctions?

"5. On the assumption on which questions 4(*a*) and (*b*) are based, and assuming further that this Court will exercise its equity powers to the end described in question 4(*b*)

"(*a*) should this Court formulate detailed decrees in these cases;

"(*b*) if so, what specific issues should the decrees reach;

"(*c*) should this Court appoint a special master to hear evidence with a view to recommending specific terms for such decrees;

"(*d*) should this Court remand to the courts of the first instance with directions to frame decrees in these cases, and if so what general directions should the decrees of this Court include and what procedures should the courts of first instance follow in arriving at the specific terms of more detailed decrees?"

Brown v. Board of
Education—II

349 U.S. 294 (1955)
(May 31, 1955)

The second *Brown* case, in 1955, approached for the
first time the manner in which dual school systems
were to be ended. It did not advocate a single line of
attack so much as a practical flexibility.

MR. CHIEF JUSTICE WARREN delivered the opinion of the Court.

These cases were decided on May 17, 1954. The opinions of that
date, declaring the fundamental principle that racial discrimination
in public education is unconstitutional, are incorporated herein by
reference. All provisions of Federal, State, or local law requiring or
permitting such discrimination must yield to this principle. There
remains for consideration the manner in which relief is to be accorded.

Because these cases arose under different local conditions and their
disposition will involve a variety of local problems, we requested
further argument on the question of relief. In view of the nationwide
importance of the decision, we invited the Attorney General of the
United States and the attorneys general of all States requiring or
permitting racial discrimination in public education to present their
views on that question. The parties, the United States, and the States
of Florida, North Carolina, Arkansas, Oklahoma, Maryland, and Texas
filed briefs and participated in the oral argument.

These presentations were informative and helpful to the Court in
its consideration of the complexities arising from the transition to a
system of public education freed of racial discrimination. The presentations also demonstrated that substantial steps to eliminate racial discrimination in public schools have already been taken, not only in
some of the communities in which these cases arose, but in some of

the States appearing as *amici curiae,* and in other States as well. Substantial progress has been made in the District of Columbia and in the communities in Kansas and Delaware involved in this litigation. The defendants in the cases coming to us from South Carolina and Virginia are awaiting the decision of this Court concerning relief.

Full implementation of these constitutional principles may require solution of varied local school problems. School authorities have the primary responsibility for elucidating, assessing, and solving these problems; courts will have to consider whether the action of school authorities constitutes good faith implementation of the governing constitutional principles. Because of their proximity to local conditions and the possible need for further hearings, the courts which originally heard these cases can best perform this judicial appraisal. Accordingly, we believe it appropriate to remand the cases to those courts.

In fashioning and effectuating the decrees, the courts will be guided by equitable principles. Traditionally, equity has been characterized by a practical flexibility in shaping its remedies and by a facility for adjusting and reconciling public and private needs. These cases call for the exercise of these traditional attributes of equity power. At stake is the personal interest of the plaintiffs in admission to public schools as soon as practicable on a nondiscriminatory basis. To effectuate this interest may call for elimination of a variety of obstacles in making the transition to school systems operated in accordance with the constitutional principles set forth in our May 17, 1954, decision. Courts of equity may properly take into account the public interest in the elimination of such obstacles in a systematic and effective manner. But it should go without saying that the vitality of these constitutional principles cannot be allowed to yield simply because of disagreement with them.

While giving weight to these public and private considerations, the courts will require that the defendants make a prompt and reasonable start toward full compliance with our May 17, 1954, ruling. Once such a start has been made, the courts may find that additional time is necessary to carry out the ruling in an effective manner. The burden rests upon the defendants to establish that such time is necessary in the public interest and is consistent with good faith compliance at the earliest practicable date. To that end, the courts may consider problems related to administration, arising from the physical condition of the school plant, the school transportation system, personnel, revision of school districts and attendance areas into compact units to achieve a system of determining admission to the public schools on a nonracial basis, and revision of local laws and regulations which may be necessary in solving the foregoing problems. They will also consider the adequacy of any plans the defendants may propose to meet these problems and to effectuate a transition to a racially nondiscriminatory school system. During this period of transition, the courts will retain jurisdiction of these cases.

The judgments below, except that in the *Delaware* case, are accordingly reversed and the cases are remanded to the district courts to take such proceedings and enter such orders and decrees consistent with this opinion as are necessary and proper to admit to public schools on a racially nondiscriminatory basis with all deliberate speed the parties to these cases. The judgment in the *Delaware* case—ordering the immediate admission of the plaintiffs to schools previously attended only by white children—is affirmed on the basis of the principles stated in our May 17, 1954, opinion, but the case is remanded to the Supreme Court of Delaware for such further proceedings as that court may deem necessary in light of this opinion.

Swann v. Charlotte-Mecklenburg

402 U.S. 1, 15 (1971)
(April 20, 1971)

The *Swann* decision in 1971 represents the fullest statement to date by the Supreme Court on the use of busing to eliminate the effects of a dual school system.

MR. CHIEF JUSTICE BURGER delivered the opinion of the Court.

We granted certiorari in this case to review important issues as
to the duties of school authorities and the scope of powers of federal
courts under this Court's mandates to eliminate racially separate public
schools established and maintained by state action. *Brown v. Board of
Education*, 347 U.S. 483 (1954).

This case and those argued with it arose in states having a long
history of maintaining two sets of schools in a single school system deliberately operated to carry out a governmental policy to separate
pupils in schools solely on the basis of race. That was what *Brown v.
Board of Education* was all about. These cases present us with the
problem of defining in more precise terms than heretofore the scope
of the duty of school authorities and district courts in implementing
Brown I and the mandate to eliminate dual systems and establish
unitary systems at once. Meanwhile district courts and courts of appeals have struggled in hundreds of cases with a multitude and variety
of problems under this Court's general directive. Understandably, in
an area of evolving remedies, those courts had to improvise and experiment without detailed or specific guidelines. This Court, in *Brown
I*, appropriately dealt with the large constitutional principles; other
federal courts had to grapple with the flinty, intractable realities of
day-to-day implementation of those constitutional commands. Their
efforts, of necessity, embraced a process of "trial and error," and our
effort to formulate guidelines must take into account their experience.

I

The Charlotte-Mecklenburg school system, the 43d largest in the Nation, encompasses the city of Charlotte and surrounding Mecklenburg County, North Carolina. The area is large—550 square miles—spanning roughly 22 miles east-west and 36 miles north-south. During the 1968–1969 school year the system served more than 84,000 pupils in 107 schools. Approximately 71% of the pupils were found to be white and 29% Negro. As of June 1969 there were approximately 24,000 Negro students in the system, of whom 21,000 attended schools within the city of Charlotte. Two-thirds of those 21,000—approximately 14,000 Negro students—attended 21 schools which were either totally Negro or more than 99% Negro.

This situation came about under a desegregation plan approved by the District Court at the commencement of the present litigation in 1965, . . . based upon geographic zoning with a free transfer provision. The present proceedings were initiated in September 1968 by Petitioner Swann's motion for further relief based on *Green v. County School Board,* 391 U.S. 430 (1968), and its companion cases. All parties now agree that in 1969 the system fell short of achieving the unitary school system that those cases require.

The District Court held numerous hearings and received voluminous evidence. In addition to finding certain actions of the school board to be discriminatory, the court also found that residential patterns in the city and county resulted in part from federal, state, and local government action other than school board decisions. School board action based on these patterns, for example by locating schools in Negro residential areas and fixing the size of the schools to accommodate the needs of immediate neighborhoods, resulted in segregated education. These findings were subsequently accepted by the Court of Appeals.

In April 1969 the District Court ordered the school board to come forward with a plan for both faculty and student desegregation. Proposed plans were accepted by the court in June and August 1969 on an interim basis only, and the board was ordered to file a third plan by November 1969. In November the board moved for an extension of time until February 1970, but when that was denied the board submitted a partially completed plan. In December 1969 the District Court held that the board's submission was unacceptable and appointed an expert in education administration, Dr. John Finger, to prepare a desegregation plan. Thereafter in February 1970, the District Court was presented with two alternative pupil assignment plans—the finalized "board plan" and the "Finger plan."

The Board Plan. As finally submitted, the school board plan closed seven schools and reassigned their pupils. It restructured school attendance zones to achieve greater racial balance but maintained existing grade structures and rejected techniques such as pairing and clustering as part of a desegregation effort. The plan created a single athletic league, eliminated the previously racial basis of the school bus system, provided racially mixed faculties and administrative staffs, and modified its free transfer plan into an optional majority-to-minority transfer system.

The board plan proposed substantial assignment of Negroes to nine of the system's 10 high schools, producing 17% to 36% Negro population in each. The projected Negro attendance at the 10th school, Independence, was 2%. The proposed attendance zones for the high schools were typically shaped like wedges of a pie, extending outward from the center of the city to the suburban and rural areas of the county in order to afford residents of the center city area access to outlying schools.

As for junior high schools, the board plan rezoned the 21 school areas so that in 20 the Negro attendance would range from 0% to 38%. The other school, located in the heart of the Negro residential area, was left with an enrolment of 90% Negro.

The board plan with respect to elementary schools relied entirely upon gerrymandering of geographic zones. More than half of the Negro elementary pupils were left in nine schools that were 86% to 100% Negro; approximately half of the white elementary pupils were assigned to schools 86% to 100% white.

The Finger Plan. The plan submitted by the court-appointed expert, Dr. Finger, adopted the school board zoning plan for senior high schools with one modification: it required that an additional 300 Negro students be transported from the Negro residential area of the city to the nearly all-white Independence High School.

The Finger plan for the junior high schools employed much of the rezoning plan of the board, combined with the creation of nine "satellite" zones.[1] Under the satellite plan, inner-city Negro students were assigned by attendance zones to nine outlying predominately white junior high schools, thereby substantially desegregating every junior high school in the system.

The Finger plan departed from the board plan chiefly in its handling of the system's 76 elementary schools. Rather than relying solely upon geographic zoning, Dr. Finger proposed use of zoning,

---

[1] A "satellite zone" is an area which is not contiguous with the main attendance zone surrounding the school.

pairing, and grouping techniques, with the result that student bodies throughout the system would range from 9% to 38% Negro.

The District Court described the plan thus:

> Like the board plan, the Finger plan does as much by rezoning school attendance lines as can reasonably be accomplished. However, unlike the board plan, it does not stop there. It goes further and desegregates all the rest of the elementary schools by the technique of grouping two or three outlying schools with one black inner city school; by transporting black students from grades one through four to the outlying white schools; and by transporting white students from the fifth and sixth grades from the outlying white schools to the inner city black school.

Under the Finger plan, nine inner-city Negro schools were grouped in this manner with 24 suburban white schools.

On February 5, 1970, the District Court adopted the board plan, as modified by Dr. Finger, for the junior and senior high schools. The court rejected the board elementary school plan and adopted the Finger plan as presented. Implementation was partially stayed by the Court of Appeals for the Fourth Circuit on March 5, and this Court declined to disturb the Fourth Circuit's order.

On appeal the Court of Appeals affirmed the District Court's order as to faculty desegregation and the secondary school plans, but vacated the order respecting elementary schools. While agreeing that the District Court properly disapproved the board plan concerning these schools, the Court of Appeals feared that the pairing and grouping of elementary schools would place an unreasonable burden on the board and the system's pupils. The case was remanded to the District Court for reconsideration and submission of further plans. This Court granted certiorari, and directed reinstatement of the District Court's order pending further proceedings in that court.

On remand the District Court received two new plans for the elementary schools: a plan prepared by the United States Department of Health, Education, and Welfare (the HEW plan) based on contiguous grouping and zoning of schools, and a plan prepared by four members of the nine-member school board (the minority plan) achieving substantially the same results as the Finger plan but apparently with slightly less transportation. A majority of the school board declined to amend its proposal. After a lengthy evidentiary hearing the District Court concluded that its own plan (the Finger plan), the minority plan, and an earlier draft of the Finger plan were all reasonable and acceptable. It directed the board to adopt one of the three or in the alternative to come forward with a new, equally effective plan of its own; the court ordered that the Finger plan would remain in effect in the event the school board declined to adopt a new plan. On August 7, the board indicated it would "acquiesce" in the Finger plan, reiterating its view that the plan was unreasonable. The District Court, by order dated August 7, 1970, directed that the Finger plan remain in effect.

II

Nearly 17 years ago this Court held, in explicit terms, that state-imposed segregation by race in public schools denies equal protection of the laws. At no time has the Court deviated in the slightest degree from that holding or its constitutional underpinnings. None of the parties before us challenges the Court's decision of May 17, 1954, that

> in the field of public education the doctrine of "separate but equal" has no place. Separate educational facilities are inherently unequal. There-fore, we hold that the plaintiffs and others similarly situated . . . are, by reason of the segregation complained of, deprived of the equal protection of the laws guaranteed by the Fourteenth Amendment. . . .
>
> Because these are class actions, because of the wide applicability of this decision, and because of the great variety of local conditions, the formulation of decrees in these cases presents problems of con-siderable complexity. *Brown v. Board of Education.*

None of the parties before us questions the Court's 1955 holding in *Brown II*, that

> [s]chool authorities have the primary responsibility for elucidating, assessing, and solving these problems; courts will have to consider whether the action of school authorities constitutes good faith imple-mentation of the governing constitutional principles. Because of their proximity to local conditions and the possible need for further hearings, the courts which originally heard these cases can best perform this judicial appraisal. Accordingly, we believe it appropriate to remand the cases to those courts.
>
> In fashioning and effectuating the decrees, the courts will be guided by equitable principles. Traditionally, equity has been char-acterized by a practical flexibility in shaping its remedies and by a facility for adjusting and reconciling public and private needs. These cases call for the exercise of these traditional attributes of equity power. At stake is the personal interest of the plaintiffs in admission to public schools as soon as practicable on a nondiscriminatory basis. To effectuate this interest may call for elimination of a variety of obstacles in making the transition to school systems operated in ac-cordance with the constitutional principles set forth in our May 17,

1954, decision. Courts of equity may properly take into account the public interest in the elimination of such obstacles in a systematic and effective manner. But it should go without saying that the vitality of these constitutional principles cannot be allowed to yield simply because of disagreement with them.

Over the 15 years since *Brown II*, many difficulties were encountered in implementation of the basic constitutional requirement that the State not discriminate between public school children on the basis of their race. Nothing in our national experience prior to 1955 prepared anyone for dealing with changes and adjustments of the magnitude and complexity encountered since then. Deliberate resistance of some to the Court's mandates has impeded the good-faith efforts of others to bring school systems into compliance. The detail and nature of these dilatory tactics have been noted frequently by this Court and other courts.

By the time the Court considered *Green v. County School Board* in 1968, very little progress had been made in many areas where dual school systems had historically been maintained by operation of state laws. In *Green*, the Court was confronted with a record of a freedom-of-choice program that the District Court had found to operate in fact to preserve a dual system more than a decade after *Brown II*. While acknowledging that a freedom-of-choice concept could be a valid remedial measure in some circumstances, its failure to be effective in *Green* required that

> The burden on a school board today is to come forward with a plan that promises realistically to work . . . *now* . . . until it is clear that state-imposed segregation has been completely removed.

This was plain language, yet the 1969 Term of Court brought fresh evidence of the dilatory tactics of many school authorities. *Alexander v. Holmes County Board of Education* restated the basic obligation asserted in *Griffin v. School Board* (1964) and *Green, supra*, that the remedy must be implemented *forthwith*.

The problems encountered by the district courts and courts of appeals make plain that we should now try to amplify guidelines, however incomplete and imperfect, for the assistance of school authorities and courts. The failure of local authorities to meet their constitutional obligations aggravated the massive problem of converting from the state-enforced discrimination of racially separate school systems. This process has been rendered more difficult by changes since 1954 in the structure and patterns of communities, the growth of student population, movement of families, and other changes, some of which had marked impact on school planning, sometimes neutralizing or negating remedial action before it was fully implemented. Rural areas accustomed for half a century to the consolidated school systems implemented by bus transportation could make adjustments more readily than metropolitan areas with dense and shifting population, numerous schools, congested and complex traffic patterns.

III

The objective today remains to eliminate from the public schools all vestiges of state-imposed segregation. Segregation was the evil struck down by *Brown I* as contrary to the equal protection guarantees of the Constitution. That was the violation sought to be corrected by the remedial measures of *Brown II*. That was the basis for the holding in *Green* that school authorities are "clearly charged with the affirmative duty to take whatever steps might be necessary to convert to a unitary system in which racial discrimination would be eliminated root and branch."

If school authorities fail in their affirmative obligations under these holdings, judicial authority may be invoked. Once a right and a violation have been shown, the scope of a district court's equitable powers to remedy past wrongs is broad, for breadth and flexibility are inherent in equitable remedies.

> The essence of equity jurisdiction has been the power of the Chancellor to do equity and to mould each decree to the necessities of the particular case. Flexibility rather than rigidity has distinguished it. The qualities of mercy and practicality have made equity the instrument for nice adjustment and reconciliation between the public interest and private needs as well as between competing private claims. *Hecht Co. v. Bowles* (1944).

This allocation of responsibility once made, the Court attempted from time to time to provide some guidelines for the exercise of the district judge's discretion and for the reviewing function of the courts of appeals. However, a school desegregation case does not differ fundamentally from other cases involving the framing of equitable remedies to repair the denial of a constitutional right. The task is to correct, by a balancing of the individual and collective interests, the condition that offends the Constitution.

In seeking to define even in broad and general terms how far this remedial power extends it is important to remember that judicial powers may be exercised only on the basis of a constitutional violation. Remedial judicial authority does not put judges automatically in the shoes of school authorities whose powers are plenary. Judicial authority enters only when local authority defaults.

School authorities are traditionally charged with broad power to formulate and implement educational policy and might well conclude, for example, that in order to prepare students to live in a pluralistic society each school should have a prescribed ratio of Negro to white students reflecting the proportion for the district as a whole. To do this as an educational policy is within the broad discretionary powers of school authorities; absent a finding of a constitutional violation, however, that would not be within the authority of a federal court. As with any equity case, the nature of the violation determines the scope of the remedy. In default by the school authorities of their obligation to proffer acceptable remedies, a district court has broad power to fashion a remedy that will assure a unitary school system.

The school authorities argue that the equity powers of federal district courts have been limited by Title IV of the Civil Rights Act of 1964. The language and the history of Title IV show that it was not enacted to limit but to define the role of the Federal Government in the implementation of the *Brown I* decision. It authorizes the Commissioner of Education to provide technical assistance to local boards in the preparation of desegregation plans, to arrange "training institutes" for school personnel involved in desegregation efforts, and to make grants directly to schools to ease the transition to unitary systems. It also authorizes the Attorney General, in specified circumstances, to initiate federal desegregation suits. Section 2000c (b) defines "desegregation" as it is used in Title IV:

> "Desegregation" means the assignment of students to public schools and within such schools without regard to their race, color, religion, or national origin, but "desegregation" shall not mean the assignment of students to public schools in order to overcome racial imbalance.

Section 2000c–6, authorizing the Attorney General to institute federal suits, contains the following proviso:

> nothing herein shall empower any official or court of the United States to issue any order seeking to achieve a racial balance in any school by requiring the transportation of pupils or students from one school to another or one school district to another in order to achieve such racial balance, or otherwise enlarge the existing power of the court to insure compliance with constitutional standards.

On their face, the sections quoted purport only to insure that the provisions of Title IV of the Civil Rights Act of 1964 will not be read as granting new powers. The proviso in § 2000c–6 is in terms designed to foreclose any interpretation of the Act as expanding the *existing* powers of federal courts to enforce the Equal Protection Clause. There is no suggestion of an intention to restrict those powers or withdraw from courts their historic equitable remedial powers. The legislative history of Title IV indicates that Congress was concerned that the Act might be read as creating a right of action under the Fourteenth Amendment in the situation of so-called "de facto segregation," where racial imbalance exists in the schools but with no showing that this was brought about by discriminatory action of state authorities. In short, there is nothing in the Act which provides us material assistance in answering the question of remedy for state-imposed segregation in violation of *Brown I.* The basis of our decision must be the prohibition of the Fourteenth Amendment that no State shall "deny to any person within its jurisdiction the equal protection of the laws."

IV

We turn now to the problem of defining with more particularity the responsibilities of school authorities in desegregating a state-enforced dual school system in light of the Equal Protection Clause. Although the several related cases before us are primarily concerned with problems of student assignment, it may be helpful to begin with a brief discussion of other aspects of the process.

In *Green,* we pointed out that existing policy and practice with regard to faculty, staff, transportation, extra-curricular activities, and facilities were among the most important indicia of a segregated system. Independent of student assignment, where it is possible to identify a "white school" or a "Negro school" simply by reference to the racial composition of teachers and staff, the quality of school buildings and equipment, or the organization of sports activities, a *prima facie* case of violation of substantive constitutional rights under the Equal Protection Clause is shown.

When a system has been dual in these respects, the first remedial responsibility of school authorities is to eliminate invidious racial distinctions. With respect to such matters as transportation, supporting personnel, and extracurricular activities, no more than this may be necessary. Similar corrective action must be taken with regard to the maintenance of buildings and the distribution of equipment. In these areas, normal administrative practice should produce schools of like quality, facilities, and staffs. Something more must be said, however, as to faculty assignment and new school construction.

In the companion *Davis* case, the Mobile school board has argued that the Constitution requires that teachers be assigned on a "color blind" basis. It also argues that the Constitution prohibits district courts from using their equity power to order assignment of teachers to achieve a particular degree of faculty desegregation. We reject that contention.

In *United States v. Montgomery County Board of Education,* the District Court set as a goal a plan of faculty assignment in each school with a ratio of white to Negro faculty members substantially the same throughout the system. This order was predicated on the District Court finding that

> The evidence does not reflect any real administrative problems involved in immediately desegregating the substitute teachers, the student teachers, the night school faculties, and in the evolvement of a really legally adequate program for the substantial desegregation of the faculties of all schools in the system commencing with the school year 1968–69.

The District Court in *Montgomery* then proceeded to set an initial ratio for the whole system of at least two Negro teachers out of each 12 in any given school. The Court of Appeals modified the order by eliminating what it regarded as "fixed mathematical ratios" of faculty and substituted an initial requirement of "substantially or approximately" a five-to-one ratio. With respect to the future, the Court of Appeals held that the numerical ratio should be eliminated and that compliance should not be tested solely by the achievement of specified proportions.

We reversed the Court of Appeals and restored the District Court's order in its entirety, holding that the order of the District Judge

> was adopted in the spirit of this Court's opinion in *Green* . . . in that his plan "promises realistically to work, and promises realistically to work *now.*" The modifications ordered by the panel of the Court of Appeals, while of course not intended to do so, would, we think, take from the order some of its capacity to expedite, by means of specific commands, the day when a completely unified, unitary, nondiscriminatory school system becomes a reality instead of a hope. . . . We also believe that under all the circumstances of this case we follow the original plan outlined in *Brown II* . . . by accepting the more specific and expeditious order of [District] Judge Johnson . . . .

The principles of *Montgomery* have been properly followed by the District Court and the Court of Appeals in this case.

The construction of new schools and the closing of old ones is one of the most important functions of local school authorities and also one of the most complex. They must decide questions of location and capacity in light of population growth, finances, land values, site availability, through an almost endless list of factors to be considered. The result of this will be a decision which, when combined with one technique or another of student assignment, will determine the racial composition of the student body in each school in the system. Over the long run, the consequences of the choices will be far reaching. People gravitate toward school facilities, just as schools are located in response to the needs of people. The location of schools may thus influence the patterns of residential development of a metropolitan area and have important impact on composition of inner city neighborhoods.

In the past, choices in this respect have been used as a potent weapon for creating or maintaining a state-segregated school system. In addition to the classic pattern of building schools specifically intended for Negro or white students, school authorities have sometimes, since *Brown*, closed schools which appeared likely to become racially mixed through changes in neighborhood residential patterns. This was sometimes accompanied by building new schools in the areas of white suburban expansion farthest from Negro population centers in order to maintain the separation of the races with a minimum departure from the formal principles of "neighborhood zoning." Such a policy does more than simply influence the short-run composition of the student body of a new school. It may well promote segregated residential patterns which, when combined with "neighborhood zoning," further lock the school system into the mold of separation of the races. Upon a proper showing a district court may consider this in fashioning a remedy.

In ascertaining the existence of legally imposed school segregation, the existence of a pattern of school construction and abandonment is thus a factor of great weight. In devising remedies where legally imposed segregation has been established, it is the responsibility of local authorities and district courts to see to it that future school construction and abandonment is not used and does not serve to perpetuate or reestablish the dual system. When necessary, district courts should retain jurisdiction to assure that these responsibilities are carried out.

V

The central issue in this case is that of student assignment, and there are essentially four problem areas:

1. to what extent racial balance or racial quotas may be used as

an implement in a remedial order to correct a previously segregated system;

2. whether every all-Negro and all-white school must be eliminated as an indispensable part of a remedial process of desegregation;

3. what are the limits, if any, on the rearrangement of school districts and attendance zones, as a remedial measure; and

4. what are the limits, if any, on the use of transportation facilities to correct state-enforced racial school segregation.

1. Racial Balances or Racial Quotas

The constant theme and thrust of every holding from *Brown I* to date is that state-enforced separation of races in public schools is discrimination that violates the Equal Protection Clause. The remedy commanded was to dismantle dual school systems.

We are concerned in these cases with the elimination of the discrimination inherent in the dual school systems, not with myriad factors of human existence which can cause discrimination in a multitude of ways on racial, religious, or ethnic grounds. The target of the cases from *Brown I* to the present was the dual school system. The elimination of racial discrimination in public schools is a large task and one that should not be retarded by efforts to achieve broader purposes lying beyond the jurisdiction of school authorities. One vehicle can carry only a limited amount of baggage. It would not serve the important objective of *Brown I* to seek to use school desegregation cases for purposes beyond their scope, although desegregation of schools ultimately will have impact on other forms of discrimination. We do not reach in this case the question whether a showing that school segregation is a consequence of other types of state action, without any discriminatory action by the school authorities, is a constitutional violation requiring remedial action by a school desegregation decree. This case does not present that question and we therefore do not decide it.

Our objective in dealing with the issues presented by these cases is to see that school authorities exclude no pupil of a racial minority from any school, directly or indirectly, on account of race; it does not and cannot embrace all the problems of racial prejudice, even when those problems contribute to disproportionate racial concentrations in some schools.

In this case it is urged that the District Court has imposed a racial balance requirement of 71%–29% on individual schools. The fact that no such objective was actually achieved—and would appear to be impossible—tends to blunt that claim, yet in the opinion and order of the District Court of December 1, 1969, we find that court directing:

that efforts should be made to reach a 71–29 ratio in the various schools so that there will be no basis for contending that one school is racially different from the others . . . , that no school [should] be operated with an all-black or predominantly black student body, [and] that pupils of all grades [should] be assigned in such a way that as nearly as practicable the various schools at various grade levels have about the same proportion of black and white students.

The District Judge went on to acknowledge that variation "from that norm may be unavoidable." This contains intimations that the "norm" is a fixed mathematical racial balance reflecting the pupil constituency of the system. If we were to read the holding of the District Court to require, as a matter of substantive constitutional right, any particular degree of racial balance or mixing, that approach would be disapproved and we would be obliged to reverse. The constitutional command to desegregate schools does not mean that every school in every community must always reflect the racial composition of the school system as a whole.

As the voluminous record in this case shows, the predicate for the District Court's use of the 71%–29% ratio was twofold: first, its express finding, approved by the Court of Appeals and not challenged here, that a dual school system had been maintained by the school authorities at least until 1969; second, its finding, also approved by the Court of Appeals, that the school board had totally defaulted in its acknowledged duty to come forward with an acceptable plan of its own, notwithstanding the patient efforts of the District Judge who, on at least three occasions, urged the board to submit plans. As the statement of facts shows, these findings are abundantly supported by the record. It was because of this total failure of the school board that the District Court was obliged to turn to other qualified sources, and Dr. Finger was designated to assist the District Court to do what the board should have done.

We see therefore that the use made of mathematical ratios was no more than a starting point in the process of shaping a remedy, rather than an inflexible requirement. From that starting point the District Court proceeded to frame a decree that was within its discretionary powers, an equitable remedy for the particular circumstances.[2]

---

[2] In his August 3, 1970, memorandum holding that the District Court plan was "reasonable" under the standard laid down by the Fourth Circuit on appeal, the District Court explained the approach taken as follows: "This court has not ruled, and does not rule that 'racial balance' is required under the Constitution; nor that all black schools in all cities are unlawful; nor that all school boards must bus children or violate the Constitution; *nor that the particular order entered in this case would be correct in other circumstances not before this court.*"

As we said in *Green*, a school authority's remedial plan or a district court's remedial decree is to be judged by its effectiveness. Awareness of the racial composition of the whole school system is likely to be a useful starting point in shaping a remedy to correct past constitutional violations. In sum, the very limited use made of mathematical ratios was within the equitable remedial discretion of the District Court.

2. One-Race Schools

The record in this case reveals the familiar phenomenon that in metropolitan areas minority groups are often found concentrated in one part of the city. In some circumstances certain schools may remain all or largely of one race until new schools can be provided or neighborhood patterns change. Schools all or predominately of one race in a district of mixed population will require close scrutiny to determine that school assignments are not part of state-enforced segregation.

In light of the above, it should be clear that the existence of some small number of one-race, or virtually one-race, schools within a district is not in and of itself the mark of a system which still practices segregation by law. The district judge or school authorities should make every effort to achieve the greatest possible degree of actual desegregation and will thus necessarily be concernd with the elimination of one-race schools. No *per se* rule can adequately embrace all the difficulties of reconciling the competing interests involved; but in a system with a history of segregation the need for remedial criteria of sufficient specificity to assure a school authority's compliance with its constitutional duty warrants a presumption against schools that are substantially disproportionate in their racial composition. Where the school authority's proposed plan for conversion from a dual to a unitary system contemplates the continued existence of some schools that are all or predominately of one race, they have the burden of showing that such school assignments are genuinely nondiscriminatory. The court should scrutinize such schools, and the burden upon the school authorities will be to satisfy the court that their racial composition is not the result of present or past discriminatory action on their part.

An optional majority-to-minority transfer provision has long been recognized as a useful part of every desegregation plan. Provision for optional transfer of those in the majority racial group of a particular school to other schools where they will be in the minority is an indispensable remedy for those students willing to transfer to other schools in order to lessen the impact on them of the state-imposed stigma of segregation. In order to be effective, such a transfer arrangement must grant the transferring student free transportation and space must be made available in the school to which he desires to move.

3. Remedial Altering of Attendance Zones

The maps submitted in these cases graphically demonstrate that one of the principal tools employed by school planners and by courts to break up the dual school system has been a frank—and sometimes drastic—gerrymandering of school districts and attendance zones. An additional step was pairing, "clustering," or "grouping" of schools with attendance assignments made deliberately to accomplish the transfer of Negro students out of formerly segregated Negro schools and transfer of white students to formerly all-Negro schools. More often than not, these zones are neither compact [3] nor contiguous; indeed they may be on opposite ends of the city. As an interim corrective measure, this cannot be said to be beyond the broad remedial powers of a court.

Absent a constitutional violation there would be no basis for judicially ordering assignment of students on a racial basis. All things being equal, with no history of discrimination, it might well be desirable to assign pupils to schools nearest their homes. But all things are not equal in a system that has been deliberately constructed and maintained to enforce racial segregation. The remedy for such segregation may be administratively awkward, inconvenient and even bizarre in some situations and may impose burdens on some; but all awkwardness and inconvenience cannot be avoided in the interim period when remedial adjustments are being made to eliminate the dual school systems.

No fixed or even substantially fixed guidelines can be established as to how far a court can go, but it must be recognized that there are limits. The objective is to dismantle the dual school system. "Racially neutral" assignment plans proposed by school authorities to a district court may be inadequate; such plans may fail to counteract the continuing effects of past school segregation resulting from discriminatory location of school sites or distortion of school size in order to achieve or maintain an artificial racial separation. When school authorities present a district court with a "loaded game board," affirmative action in the form of remedial altering of attendance zones is proper to achieve truly non-discriminatory assignments. In short, an assignment plan is not acceptable simply because it appears to be neutral.

In this area, we must of necessity rely to a large extent, as this

---

[3] We said in *Green, supra,* at 439: "The obligation of the district courts, as it always has been, is to assess the effectiveness of a proposed plan in achieving desegregation. There is no universal answer to complex problems of desegregation; there is obviously no one plan that will do the job in every case. The matter must be assessed in light of the circumstances present and the options available in each instance."

Court has for more than 16 years, on the informed judgment of the district courts in the first instance and on courts of appeals.

We hold that the pairing and grouping of non-contiguous school zones is a permissible tool and such action is to be considered in light of the objectives sought. . . . Maps do not tell the whole story since non-contiguous school zones may be more accessible to each other in terms of the critical travel time, because of traffic patterns and good highways, than schools geographically closer together. Conditions in different localities will vary so widely that no rigid rules can be laid down to govern all situations.

4. Transportation of Students

The scope of permissible transportation of students as an implement of a remedial decree has never been defined by this Court and by the very nature of the problem it cannot be defined with precision. No rigid guidelines as to student transportation can be given for application to the infinite variety of problems presented in thousands of situations. Bus transportation has been an integral part of the public education system for years, and was perhaps the single most important factor in the transition from the one-room schoolhouse to the consolidated school. Eighteen million of the nation's public school children, approximately 39%, were transported to their schools by bus in 1969–1970 in all parts of the country.

The importance of bus transportation as a normal and accepted tool of educational policy is readily discernible in this and the companion case.[4] The Charlotte school authorities did not purport to assign students on the basis of geographically drawn zones until 1965 and then they allowed almost unlimited transfer privileges. The District Court's conclusion that assignment of children to the school nearest their home serving their grade would not produce an effective dismantling of the dual system is supported by the record.

Thus the remedial techniques used in the District Court's order were within that court's power to provide equitable relief; implementation of the decree is well within the capacity of the school authority.

The decree provided that the buses used to implement the plan

---

[4] During 1967–1968, for example, the Mobile board used 207 buses to transport 22,094 students daily for an average round trip of 31 miles. During 1966–1967, 7,116 students in the metropolitan area were bused daily. In Charlotte-Mecklenburg, the system as a whole, without regard to desegregation plans, planned to bus approximately 23,000 students this year, for an average daily round trip of 15 miles. More elementary school children than high school children were to be bused, and four- and five-year-olds travel the longest routes in the system.

would operate on direct routes. Students would be picked up at schools near their homes and transported to the schools they were to attend. The trips for elementary school pupils average about seven miles and the District Court found that they would take "not over 35 minutes at the most." [5] This system compares favorably with the transportation plan previously operated in Charlotte under which each day 23,600 students on all grade levels were transported an average of 15 miles one way for an average trip requiring over an hour. In these circumstances, we find no basis for holding that the local school authorities may not be required to employ bus transportation as one tool of school desegregation. Desegregation plans cannot be limited to the walk-in school.

An objection to transportation of students may have validity when the time or distance of travel is so great as to risk either the health of the children or significantly impinge on the educational process. . . . It hardly needs stating that the limits on time of travel will vary with many factors, but probably with none more than the age of the students. The reconcilation of competing values in a desegregation case is, of course, a difficult task with many sensitive facets but fundamentally no more so than remedial measures courts of equity have traditionally employed.

VI

The Court of Appeals, searching for a term to define the equitable remedial power of the district courts, used the term "reasonableness." In *Green, supra,* this Court used the term "feasible" and by implication, "workable," "effective," and "realistic" in the mandate to develop "a plan that promises realistically to work, and . . . to work *now.*" On the facts of this case, we are unable to conclude that the order of the District Court is not reasonable, feasible and workable. However, in seeking to define the scope of remedial power or the limits on remedial power of courts in an area as sensitive as we deal with here, words are poor instruments to convey the sense of basic fairness inherent in equity. Substance, not semantics, must govern, and we have sought to suggest the nature of limitations without frustrating the appropriate scope of equity.

---

[5] The District Court found that the school system would have to employ 138 more buses than it had previously operated. But 105 of those buses were already available and the others could easily be obtained. Additionally, it should be noted that North Carolina requires provision of transportation for all students who are assigned to schools more than one and one-half miles from their homes.

At some point, these school authorities and others like them should have achieved full compliance with this Court's decision in *Brown I*. The systems will then be "unitary" in the sense required by our decisions in *Green* and *Alexander*.

It does not follow that the communities served by such systems will remain demographically stable, for in a growing, mobile society, few will do so. Neither school authorities nor district courts are constitutionally required to make year-by-year adjustments of the racial composition of student bodies once the affirmative duty to desegregate has been accomplished and racial discrimination through official action is eliminated from the system. This does not mean that federal courts are without power to deal with future problems; but in the absence of a showing that either the school authorities or some other agency of the State has deliberately attempted to fix or alter demographic patterns to affect the racial composition of the schools, further intervention by a district court should not be necessary.

For the reasons herein set forth, the judgment of the Court of Appeals is affirmed as to those parts in which it affirmed the judgment of the District Court. The order of the District Court dated August 7, 1970, is also affirmed.

Keyes v. Denver School District No. 1

93 S. Ct. 2686 (1973)
(June 21, 1973)

Keyes v. Denver School District No. 1 represents the
most far-reaching decision the Supreme Court has
taken to date on segregation in the North. It has
enormous implications for the future of busing. In returning the case to District Court, the Supreme Court
ruled by a 7–1 margin that proof of state-imposed
segregation in a substantial part of a school district
will suffice to support a finding of a dual school system
unless school authorities can show the area in question
is a separate and unrelated part of the district. In the
Keyes case, Justice William Rehnquist dissented, and
Justice Byron White, a former Colorado resident, did
not participate. The majority opinion of the Court is
included here. As with the other cases in this collection,
an effort has been made to limit the length of the text
by deleting references of an essentially technical
nature and reducing the number of footnotes.

MR. JUSTICE BRENNAN delivered the opinion of the Court.

This school desegregation case concerns the Denver, Colorado,
school system. That system has never been operated under a constitutional or statutory provision that mandated or permitted racial
segregation in public education.[1] Rather, the gravamen of this action,

---

[1] To the contrary, Art. IX, § 8, of the Colorado Constitution expressly prohibits "any classification of pupils . . . on account of race or color." As early as
1927, the Colorado Supreme Court held that a Denver practice of excluding black
students from school programs at Manual High School and Morey Junior High
School violated state law.

brought in June 1969 in the District Court for the District of Colorado by parents of Denver school children, is that respondent School Board alone, by use of various techniques such as the manipulation of student attendance zones, school site selection and a neighborhood school policy, created or maintained racially or ethnically (or both racially and ethnically) segregated schools throughout the school district, entitling petitioners to a decree directing desegregation of the entire school district.

The boundaries of the school district are co-terminus with the boundaries of the City and County of Denver. There were in 1969 119 schools with 96,580 pupils in the school system. In early 1969, the respondent School Board adopted three resolutions . . . designed to desegregate the schools in the Park Hill area in the northeast portion of the city. Following an election which produced a Board majority opposed to the resolutions, the resolutions were rescinded and replaced with a voluntary student transfer program. Petitioners then filed this action, requesting an injunction against the rescission of the resolutions and an order directing that the respondent School Board desegregate and afford equal educational opportunity "for the School District as a whole." The District Court found that by the construction of a new, relatively small elementary school, Barrett, in the middle of the Negro community west of Park Hill, by the gerrymandering of student attendance zones, by the use of so-called "optional zones," and by the excessive use of mobile classroom units, among other things, the respondent School Board had engaged over almost a decade after 1960 in an unconstitutional policy of deliberate racial segregation with respect to the Park Hill schools. The court therefore ordered the Board to desegregate those schools through the implementation of the three rescinded resolutions.

Segregation in Denver schools is not limited, however, to the schools in the Park Hill area, and not satisfied with their success in obtaining relief for Park Hill, petitioners pressed their prayer that the District Court order desegregation of all segregated schools in the city of Denver, particularly the heavily segregated schools in the core city area. But that court concluded that its finding of a purposeful and systematic program of racial segregation affecting thousands of students in the Park Hill area did not, in itself, impose on the School Board an affirmative duty to eliminate segregation throughout the school district. Instead, the court fractionated the district and held that petitioners must make a fresh showing of *de jure* segregation in each area of the city for which they seek relief. Moreover, the District Court held that its finding of intentional segregation in Park Hill was not in any sense material to the question of segregative intent in other areas of the city. Under this restrictive approach, the District Court concluded that petitioners' evidence of intentionally discriminatory School Board action in areas of the district other than Park Hill was insufficient to "dictate the conclusion that this is *de jure* segregation which calls for an all-out effort to desegregate. It is more like *de facto* segregation, with respect to which the rule is that the court cannot order desegregation in order to provide a better balance."

Nevertheless, the District Court went on to hold that the proofs established that the segregated core city schools were educationally inferior to the predominantly "white" or "Anglo" schools in other parts of the district—that is "separate facilities . . . unequal in the quality of education provided." Thus, the court held that, under the doctrine of *Plessy v. Ferguson* (1896), respondent School Board constitutionally "must at a minimum . . . offer an equal educational opportunity," and, therefore, although all-out desegregation "could not be decreed, . . . the only feasible and constitutionally acceptable program—the only program which furnishes anything approaching substantial equality—is a system of desegregation and integration which provides compensatory education in an integrated environment." The District Court then formulated a varied remedial plan to that end which was incorporated in the Final Decree.

Respondent School Board appealed, and petitioners cross-appealed, to the Court of Appeals for the Tenth Circuit. That court sustained the District Court's finding that the Board engaged in an unconstitutional policy of deliberate racial segregation with respect to the Park Hill schools and affirmed the Final Decree in that respect. As to the core city schools, however, the Court of Appeals reversed the legal determination of the District Court that those schools were maintained in violation of the Fourteenth Amendment because of the unequal educational opportunity afforded, and therefore set aside so much of the Final Decree as required desegregation and educational improvement programs for those schools. In reaching that result, the Court of Appeals also disregarded respondent School Board's deliberate racial segregation policy respecting the Park Hill schools and accepted the District Court's finding that petitioners had not proved that respondent had a like policy addressed specifically to the core city schools.

We granted petitioners' petition for certiorari to review the Court of Appeals' judgment insofar as it reversed that part of the District Court's Final Decree as pertained to the core city schools. The judgment of the Court of Appeals in that respect is modified to vacate instead of reverse the Final Decree. The respondent School Board has cross-petitioned for certiorari to review the judgment of the Court of

Appeals insofar as it affirmed that part of the District Court's Final Decree as pertained to the Park Hill schools. The cross-petition is denied.

I

Before turning to the primary question we decide today, a word must be said about the District Court's method of defining a "segregated" school. Denver is a tri-ethnic, as distinguished from a bi-racial, community. The overall racial and ethnic composition of the Denver public schools is 66% Anglo, 14% Negro and 20% Hispano.[2] The District Court, in assessing the question of *de jure* segregation in the core city schools, preliminarily resolved that Negroes and Hispanos should not be placed in the same category to establish the segregated character of a school. Later, in determining the schools that were likely to produce an inferior educational opportunity, the court concluded that a school would be considered inferior only if it had "a concentration of either Negro or Hispano students in the general area of 70 to 75 percent." We intimate no opinion whether the District Court's 70% to 75% requirement was correct. The District Court used those figures to signify educationally inferior schools, and there is no suggestion in the record that those same figures were or would be used to define a "segregated" school in the *de jure* context. What is or is not a segregated school will necessarily depend on the facts of each particular case. In addition to the racial and ethnic composition of a school's student body, other factors such as the racial and ethnic composition of faculty and staff and the community and administration attitudes toward the school must be taken into consideration. The District Court has recognized these specific factors as elements of the definition of a "segregated" school, and we may therefore infer that the court will consider them again on remand.

We conclude, however, that the District Court erred in separating Negroes and Hispanos for purposes of defining a "segregated" school. We have held that Hispanos constitute an identifiable class for purposes of the Fourteenth Amendment. . . . Indeed the District Court recognized this in classifying predominantly Hispano schools as "segregated" schools in their own right. But there is also much evidence that in the Southwest Hispanos and Negroes have a great many things in

---

[2] The parties have used the terms "Anglo," "Negro," and "Hispano" throughout the record. We shall therefore use those terms.

"Hispano" is the term used by the Colorado Department of Education to refer to a person of Spanish, Mexican, or Cuban heritage.

common. The United States Commission on Civil Rights has recently published two Reports on Hispano education in the Southwest. Focusing on students in the States of Arizona, California, Colorado, New Mexico, and Texas, the Commission concluded that Hispanos suffer from the same educational inequities as Negroes and American Indians. In fact, the District Court itself recognized that "[o]ne of the things which the Hispano has in common with the Negro is economic and cultural deprivation and discrimination." This is agreement that, though of different origins, Negroes and Hispanos in Denver suffer identical discrimination in treatment when compared with the treatment afforded Anglo students. In that circumstance, we think petitioners are entitled to have schools with a combined predominance of Negroes and Hispanos included in the category of "segregated" schools.

II

In our view, the only other question that requires our decision at this time is that subsumed in Question 2 of the Questions Presented by petitioners, namely, whether the District Court and the Court of Appeals applied an incorrect legal standard in addressing Petitioners' contention that respondent School Board engaged in an unconstitutional policy of deliberate segregation in the core city schools. Our conclusion is that those courts did not apply the correct standard in addressing that contention.

Petitioners apparently concede for the purposes of this case that in the case of a school system like Denver's, where no statutory dual system has ever existed, plaintiffs must prove not only that segregated schooling exists but also that it was brought about or maintained by intentional state action. Petitioners proved that for almost a decade after 1960 respondent School Board had engaged in an unconstitutional policy of deliberate racial segregation in the Park Hill schools. Indeed, the District Court found that "[b]etween 1960 and 1969 the Board's policies with respect to those northeast Denver schools show an undeviating purpose to isolate Negro students" in segregated schools "while preserving the Anglo character of [other] schools." This finding did not relate to an insubstantial or trivial fragment of the school system. On the contrary, respondent School Board was found guilty of following a deliberate segregation policy at schools attended, in 1969, by 37.69% of Denver's total Negro school population, including one-fourth of the Negro elementary pupils, over two-thirds of the Negro junior high pupils, and over two-fifths of the Negro high school pupils. In addition, there was uncontroverted evidence that teachers and staff had for years been assigned on a minority teacher-to-minority school basis throughout the school system. Respondent argues, however, that a finding of state-imposed segregation as to a substantial portion of the school system can be viewed in isolation from the rest of the district, and that even if state-imposed segregation does exist in a substantial part of the Denver school system, it does not follow that the District Court could predicate on that fact a finding that the entire school system is a dual system. We do not agree. We have never suggested that plaintiffs in school desegregation cases must bear the burden of proving the elements of *de jure* segregation as to each and every school or each and every student within the school system. Rather, we have held that where plaintiffs prove that a current condition of segregated schooling exists within a school district where a dual system was compelled or authorized by statute at the time of our decision in *Brown v. Board of Education* (*Brown I*), the State automatically assumes an affirmative duty "to effectuate a transition to a racially nondiscriminatory school system," *Brown v. Board of Education* (*Brown II*), see also *Green v. County School Board*, that is, to eliminate from the public schools within their school system "all vestiges of state-imposed segregation." *Swann v. Charlotte-Mecklenburg Board of Education.*

This is not a case, however, where a statutory dual system has ever existed. Nevertheless, where plaintiffs prove that the school authorities have carried out a systematic program of segregation affecting a substantial portion of the students, schools, teachers and facilities within the school system, it is only common sense to conclude that there exists a predicate for a finding of the existence of a dual school system. Several considerations support this conclusion. First, it is obvious that a practice of concentrating Negroes in certain schools by structuring attendance zones or designating "feeder" schools on the basis of race has the reciprocal effect of keeping other nearby schools predominantly white. Similarly, the practice of building a school— such as the Barrett Elementary School in this case—to a certain size and in a certain location, "with conscious knowledge that it would be a segregated school," has a substantial reciprocal effect on the racial composition of other nearby schools. So also, the use of mobile classrooms, the drafting of student transfer policies, the transportation of students, and the assignment of faculty and staff, on racially identifiable bases, have the clear effect of earmarking schools according to their racial composition, and this, in turn, together with the elements of student assignment and school construction, may have a profound reciprocal effect on the racial composition of residential neighborhoods within a metropolitan area, thereby causing further racial concentration within the schools. We recognized this in *Swann* when we said:

> They [school authorities] must decide questions of location and capacity in light of population growth, finances, land values, site availability, through an almost endless list of factors to be considered. The result of this will be a decision which, when combined with one technique or another of student assignment, will determine the racial composition of the student body in each school in the system. Over the long run, the consequences of the choices will be far reaching. People gravitate toward school facilities, just as schools are located in response to the needs of people. The location of schools may thus influence the patterns of residential development of a metropolitan area and have important impact on composition of inner-city neighborhoods.
>
> In the past, choices in this respect have been used as a potent weapon for creating or maintaining a state-segregated school system. In addition to the classic pattern of building schools specifically intended for Negro or white students, school authorities have sometimes, since *Brown,* closed schools which appeared likely to become racially mixed through changes in neighborhood residential patterns. This was sometimes accompanied by building new schools in the areas of white suburban expansion farthest from Negro population centers in order to maintain the separation of the races with a minimum departure from the formal principles of "neighborhood zoning." Such a policy does more than simply influence the short-run composition of the student body of a new school. It may well promote segregated residential patterns which, when combined with "neighborhood zoning," further lock the school system into the mold of separation of races. Upon a proper showing a district court may consider this in fashioning a remedy.

In short, common sense dictates the conclusion that racially inspired school board actions have an impact beyond the particular schools that are the subjects of those actions. This is not to say, of course, that there can never be a case in which the geographical structure of or the natural boundaries within a school district may have the effect of dividing the district into separate, identifiable and unrelated units. Such a determination is essentially a question of fact to be resolved by the trial court in the first instance, but such cases must be rare. In the absence of such a determination, proof of state-imposed segregation in a substantial portion of the district will suffice to support a finding by the trial court of the existence of a dual system. Of course, where that finding is made, as in cases involving statutory dual systems, the school authorities have an affirmative duty "to effectuate a transition to a racially nondiscriminatory school system." (*Brown II.*)

On remand, therefore, the District Court should decide in the first instance whether respondent School Board's deliberate racial segregation policy with respect to the Park Hill schools constitutes the entire Denver school system a dual school system. We observe that on the record now before us there is indication that Denver is not a school district which might be divided into separate, identifiable and unrelated units. The District Court stated, in its summary of findings as to the Park Hill schools, that there was "a high degree of interrelationship among these schools, so that any action by the Board affecting the racial composition of one would almost certainly have an effect on the others." And there was cogent evidence that the ultimate effect of the Board's actions in Park Hill was not limited to that area: the three 1969 resolutions designed to desegregate the Park Hill schools changed the attendance patterns of at least 29 schools attended by almost one-third of the pupils in the Denver school system. This suggests that the official segregation in Park Hill affected the racial composition of schools throughout the district.

On the other hand, although the District Court did not state this or indeed any reason why the Park Hill finding was disregarded when attention was turned to the core city schools—beyond saying that the Park Hill and core city areas were in its view "different"— the areas, although adjacent to each other, are separated by Colorado Boulevard, a six-lane highway. From the record, it is difficult to assess the actual significance of Colorado Boulevard to the Denver school system. The Boulevard runs the length of the school district, but at least two elementary schools, Teller and Steck, have attendance zones which cross the Boulevard. Moreover, the District Court, although referring to the Boulevard as "a natural dividing line," did not feel constrained to limit its consideration of *de jure* segregation in the Park Hill area to those schools east of the Boulevard. The court found that by building Barrett Elementary School west of the Boulevard and by establishing Colorado Boulevard as the eastern boundary of the Barrett attendance zone, the Board was able to maintain for a number of years the Anglo character of the Park Hill schools. This suggests that Colorado Boulevard is not to be regarded as the type of barrier that of itself could confine the impact of the Board's actions to an identifiable area of the school district, perhaps because a major highway is generally not such an effective buffer between adjoining areas. But this is a factual question for resolution by the District Court on remand. In any event, inquiry whether the District Court and the Court

of Appeals applied the correct legal standards in addressing petitioners'
contention of deliberate segregation in the core city schools is not
at an end even if it be true that Park Hill may be seperated from the
rest of the Denver school district as a separate, identifiable and unrelated unit.

III

The District Court proceeded on the premise that the finding as to
the Park Hill schools was irrelevant to the consideration of the rest of
the district, and began its examination of the core city schools by
requiring that petitioners prove all of the essential elements of *de jure*
segregation—that is, stated simply, a current condition of segregation
resulting from intentional state action directed specifically to the core
city schools. The segregated character of the core city schools could
not be and is not denied. Petitioners' proof showed that at the time of
trial 22 of the schools in the core city area were less than 30% in
Anglo enrolment and 11 of the schools were less than 10% Anglo.
Petitioners also introduced substantial evidence demonstrating the
existence of a disproportionate racial and ethnic composition of faculty
and staff at these schools.

On the question of segregative intent, petitioners presented evidence tending to show that the Board, through its actions over a
period of years, intentionally created and maintained the segregated
character of the core city schools. Respondents countered this evidence
by arguing that the segregation in these schools is the result of a
racially neutral "neighborhood school policy" and that the acts of
which petitioners complain are explicable within the bounds of that
policy. Accepting the School Board's explanation, the District Court
and the Court of Appeals agreed that a finding of *de jure* segregation
as to the core city schools was not permissible since petitioners had
failed to prove "(1) a racially discriminatory purpose and (2) a
causal relationship between the acts complained of and the racial imbalance admittedly existing in those schools." This assessment of petitioners' proof was clearly incorrect.

Although petitioners had already proved the existence of intentional school segregation in the Park Hill schools, this crucial finding
was totally ignored when attention turned to the core city schools.
Plainly, a finding of intentional segregation as to a portion of a school
system is not devoid of probative value in assessing the school authorities' intent with respect to other parts of the same school system. On
the contrary, where, as here, the case involves one school board, a
finding of intentional segregation on its part in one portion of a school

system is highly relevant to the issue of the board's intent with respect to other segregated schools in the system. This is merely an application of the well-settled evidentiary principle that "the prior doing of other similar acts, whether clearly a part of a scheme or not, is useful as reducing the possibility that the act in question was done with innocent intent." . . .

Applying these principles in the special context of school desegregation cases, we hold that a finding of intentionally segregative school board actions in a meaningful portion of a school system, as in this case, creates a presumption that other segregated schooling within the system is not adventitious. It establishes, in other words, a prima facie case of unlawful segregative design on the part of school authorities, and shifts to those authorities the burden of proving that other segregated schools within the system are not also the result of intentionally segregative actions. This is true even if it is determined that different areas of the school district should be viewed independently of each other because, even in that situation, there is high probability that where school authorities have effectuated an intentionally segregative policy in a meaningful portion of the school system, similar impermissible considerations have motivated their actions in other areas of the system. We emphasize that the differentiating factor between *de jure* segregation and so-called *de facto* segregation to which we referred in *Swann* is *purpose* or *intent* to segregate. Where school authorities have been found to have practiced purposeful segregation in part of a school system, they may be expected to oppose system-wide desegregation, as did the respondents in this case, on the ground that their purposefully segregative actions were isolated and individual events, thus leaving plaintiffs with the burden of proving otherwise. But at that point where an intentionally segregative policy is practiced in a meaningful or significant segment of a school system, as in this case, the school authorities can not be heard to argue that plaintiffs have proved only "isolated and individual" unlawful segregative actions. In that circumstance, it is both fair and reasonable to require that the school authorities bear the burden of showing that their actions as to other segregated schools within the system were not also motivated by segregative intent.

This burden-shifting principle is not new or novel. There are no hard and fast standards governing the allocation of the burden of proof in every situation. The issue, rather, "is merely a question of policy and fairness based on experience in the different situations." In the context of racial segregation in public education, the courts, including this Court, have recognized a variety of situations in which "fairness" and "policy" require state authorities to bear the burden of explaining actions or conditions which appear to be racially motivated. Thus, in *Swann,* we observed that in a system with a "history of segregation," "where it is possible to identify a 'white school' or a 'Negro school' simply by reference to the racial composition of teachers and staff, the quality of school buildings and equipment, or the organization of sport activities, a *prima facie* case of violation of substantive constitutional rights under the Equal Protection Clause is shown." Again, in a school system with a history of segregation, the discharge of a disproportionately large number of Negro teachers incident to desegregation "thrust[s] upon the School Board the burden of justifying its conduct by clear and convincing evidence." . . . Indeed, to say that a system has a "history of segregation" is merely to say that a pattern of intentional segregation has been established in the past. Thus, be it a statutory dual system or an allegedly unitary system where a meaningful portion of the system is found to be intentionally segregated, the existence of subsequent or other segregated schooling within the same system justifies a rule imposing on the school authorities the burden of proving that this segregated schooling is not also the result of intentionally segregative acts.

In discharging that burden, it is not enough, of course, that the school authorities rely upon some allegedly logical, racially neutral explanation for their actions. Their burden is to adduce proof sufficient to support a finding that segregative intent was not among the factors that motivated their actions. The courts below attributed much significance to the fact that many of the Board's actions in the core city area antedated our decision in *Brown.* We reject any suggestion that remoteness in time has any relevance to the issue of intent. If the actions of school authorities were to any degree motivated by segregative intent and the segregation resulting from those actions continues to exist, the fact of remoteness in time certainly does not make those actions any less "intentional."

This is not to say, however, that the prima facie case may not be met by evidence supporting a finding that a lesser degree of segregated schooling in the core city area would not have resulted even if the Board had not acted as it did. In *Swann,* we suggested that at some point in time the relationship between past segregative acts and present segregation may become so attenuated as to be incapable of supporting a finding of *de jure* segregation warranting judicial intervention. . . . We made it clear, however, that a connection between past segregative acts and present segregation may be present even when not apparent and that close examination is required before concluding that the connection does not exist. Intentional school segregation in the past may have been a factor in creating a natural environment for the growth of further segregation. Thus, if respondent School Board cannot disprove segregative intent, it can rebut the prima facie case only by showing that its past segregative acts did not create or contribute to the current segregated condition of the core city schools.

The respondent School Board invoked at trial its "neighborhood school policy" as explaining racial and ethnic concentrations within the core city schools, arguing that since the core city area population had long been Negro and Hispano, the concentrations were necessarily the result of residential patterns and not of purposefully segregative policies. We have no occasion to consider in this case whether a "neighborhood school policy" of itself will justify racial or ethnic concentrations in the absence of a finding that school authorities have committed acts constituting *de jure* segregation. It is enough that we hold that the mere assertion of such a policy is not dispositive where, as in this case, the school authorities have been found to have practiced *de jure* segregation in a meaningful portion of the school system by techniques that indicate that the "neighborhood school" concept has not been maintained free of manipulation. Our observations in *Swann* are particularly instructive on this score:

> Absent a constitutional violation there would be no basis for judicially ordering assignment of students on a racial basis. All things being equal, with no history of discrimination, it might well be desirable to assign pupils to schools nearest their homes. But all things are not equal in a system that has been deliberately constructed and maintained to enforce racial segregation. . . . "Racially neutral" assignment plans proposed by school authorities to a district court may be inadequate; such plans may fail to counteract the continuing effects of past school segregation resulting from discriminatory location of school sites or distortion of school size in order to achieve or maintain an artificial racial separation. When school authorities present a district court with a "loaded game board," affirmative action in the form of remedial altering of attendance zones is proper to achieve truly nondiscriminatory assignments. In short, an assignment plan is not acceptable simply because it appears to be neutral.

Thus, respondent School Board having been found to have practiced deliberate racial segregation in schools attended by over one-third of the Negro school population, that crucial finding establishes a prima facie case of intentional segregation in the core city schools. In such case, respondent's neighborhood school policy is not to be determinative "simply because it appears to be neutral."

IV

In summary, the District Court on remand, *first,* will afford respondent School Board the opportunity to prove its contention that the Park Hill area is a separate, identifiable and unrelated section of the school district that should be treated as isolated from the rest of the district. If respondent School Board fails to prove that contention, the District Court, *second,* will determine whether respondent School Board's conduct over almost a decade after 1960 in carrying out a policy of deliberate racial segregation in the Park Hill schools constitutes the entire school system a dual school system. If the District Court determines that the Denver school system is a dual school system, respondent School Board has the affirmative duty to desegregate the entire system "root and branch" (*Green v. County School Board*). If the District Court determines, however, that the Denver school system is not a dual school system by reason of the Board's actions in Park Hill, the court, *third,* will afford respondent School Board the opportunity to rebut petitioners' prima facie case of intentional segregation in the core city schools raised by the finding of intentional segregation in the Park Hill schools. There, the Board's burden is to show that its policies and practices with respect to school site location, school size, school renovations and additions, student attendance zones, student assignment and transfer options, mobile classroom units, transportation of students, assignment of faculty and staff, etc., considered together and premised on the Board's so-called "neighborhood school" concept, either were not taken in effectuation of a policy to create or maintain segregation in the core city schools, or, if unsuccessful in that effort, were not factors in causing the existing condition of segregation in these schools. Considerations of "fairness" and "policy" demand no less in light of the Board's intentionally segregative actions. If respondent Board fails to rebut petitioners' prima facie case, the District Court must, as in the case of Park Hill, decree all-out desegregation of the core city schools.

The judgment of the Court of Appeals is modified to vacate instead of reverse the parts of the Final Decree that concern the core city schools, and the case is remanded to the District Court for further proceedings consistent with this opinion.

The Debate Over Evidence
and Social Policy

The Evidence on Busing

DAVID J. ARMOR

David J. Armor is a sociologist specializing in research
methods and social statistics. He played a leading role
in research on the Boston METCO study, one of the
earliest evaluations of the effects of busing on black
students.

The legal basis of the national policy of integration—and of the school
busing issue today—is the declaration of the Supreme Court in 1954
that

> to separate [black children] from others of similar age and qualifications
> solely because of their race generates a feeling of inferiority as to their
> status in the community that may affect their hearts and minds in a way
> unlikely ever to be undone.

Few decisions of the Court have provoked so much controversy for so
long, or have had so much impact on the way of life of so many persons, as the case of *Brown v. the Board of Education of Topeka*, where
this doctrine is stated. Policy makers have used it to restructure political, economic, and social institutions. Groups have rioted and states
have divided over actions, direct and indirect, that have flowed from
this ruling. And social scientists have proudly let it stand as a premier
axiom of their field—one of the few examples of a social theory that
found its way into formal law.

    Few persons, perhaps, know of the role played by the social
sciences in helping to sustain the forces behind desegregation. It would
be an exaggeration to say they are responsible for the busing dilemmas
facing so many communities today, yet without the legitimacy provided by the hundreds of sociological and psychological studies it

David J. Armor, "The Evidence on Busing," *The Public Interest*, No. 28 (Summer
1972), pp. 90–126. Copyright © National Affairs Inc., 1972.

would be hard to imagine how the changes we are witnessing could have happened so quickly. At every step—from the 1954 Supreme Court ruling, to the Civil Rights Act of 1964, to the federal busing orders of 1970—social science research findings have been inextricably interwoven with policy decisions.

And yet, the relation between social science and public policy contains a paradox in that the conditions for adequate research are often *not* met until a policy is in effect, while the policy itself often cannot be justified until supported by the findings of science. In consequence, the desire of scientists to affect society and the desire of policy makers to be supported by science often lead to a relation between the two that may be more political than scientific. Further, this can mean that the later evaluation research of a social action program may undo the very premises on which the action is based—as is the case somewhat in the Coleman Report on the effect of schools on achievement. There are obvious dangers for both social science and public policy in this paradox. There is the danger that important and significant programs —which may be desirable on moral grounds—may be halted when scientific support is lacking or reveals unexpected consequences; conversely, there is the danger that important research may be stopped when the desired results are not forthcoming. The current controversy over the busing of school children to promote integration affords a prime example of this situation.

The policy model behind the Supreme Court's 1954 reasoning— and behind the beliefs of the liberal public today—was based in part on social science research. But that research did not derive from the conditions of induced racial integration as it is being carried out today. These earlier research designs were "ex post facto"—i.e., comparisons were made between persons already integrated and individuals in segregated environments. Since the integration experience occurred *before* the studies, any inferences about the effects of *induced* integration, based on such evidence, have been speculative at best. With the development of a variety of school integration programs across the country there arose the opportunity to conduct realistic tests of the integration policy model that did not suffer this limitation. While it may have other shortcomings, this research suffers neither the artificial constraints of the laboratory nor the causal ambiguity of the cross-sectional survey. The intent of this essay is to explore some of this new research and to interpret the findings. What we will do, first, is to sketch the evolution of the social science model which became the basis of public policy, and then review a number of tests of this model as revealed in recent social science studies of induced school integration and busing.

THE INTEGRATION POLICY MODEL: STAGE I

The integration model which is behind current public policy is rooted in social science results dating back to before World War II. The connections between segregation and inequality were portrayed by John Dollard [1] and Gunnar Myrdal [2] in the first prestigious social science studies to show how prejudice, discrimination, segregation, and inequality operated to keep the black man in a subordinate status. Myrdal summarized this process in his famous "vicious circle" postulate: White prejudice, in the form of beliefs about the inferior status of the black race, leads to discrimination and segregation in work, housing, and social relationships; discrimination reinforces social and economic inequality; the resulting inferiority circles back to solidify the white prejudice that started it all. The vicious circle theory was the integration policy model in embryonic form.

Along with these broad sociological studies there also appeared a number of psychological experiments which were to play a crucial role in the policy decisions. The most notable were the doll studies of Kenneth and Mamie Clark.[3] They found that preschool black children were much less likely than white children to prefer dolls of their own race. Though this tendency tapered off among older children, the Clarks concluded that racial awareness and identification occurred at an early age and that the doll choices suggested harmful and lasting effects on black self-esteem and performance. Other studies confirmed these early findings.[4] These studies added a psychological dynamic to explain the operation of the vicious circle: Prejudice and segregation lead to feelings of inferiority and an inability to succeed among the blacks; these sustain inequality and further reinforce the initial white prejudice. In other words, segregation leads to serious psychological damage to the black child; that damage is sufficient to inhibit the kind of adult behavior which might enable the black man to break the circle.

How could the circle be broken? This question plagued a genera-

---

[1] John Dollard, *Caste and Class in a Southern Town* (New York: Doubleday, 1937).

[2] Gunnar Myrdal, *An American Dilemma* (New York: Harper and Bros., 1944).

[3] Kenneth B. Clark and M. P. Clark, "Racial Identification and Preference in Negro Children," in T. M. Newcomb and E. L. Hartley (Eds.), *Readings in Social Psychology* (New York: Holt, Rinehart and Winston, 1947).

[4] Harold Proshansky and Peggy Newton, "The Nature and Meaning of Negro Self-Identity," in M. Deutsch, *et al.* (Eds.), *Social Class, Race and Psychological Development* (New York: Holt, Rinehart and Winston, 1968); and Judith Porter, *Black Child, White Child* (Cambridge, Mass.: Harvard University Press, 1971).

tion of social scientists in quest of a solution to America's race problems. Of a number of studies appearing after the war, two which focused upon the effects of segregation and integration upon white racial attitudes had especial impact. The first was a section of Samuel Stouffer's massive research on the American soldier during World War II.[5] Stouffer found that white soldiers in combat companies with a black platoon were far more likely to accept the idea of fighting side by side with black soldiers than were white soldiers in non-integrated companies. The second was the study by Morton Deutsch and Mary Evans Collins of interracial housing.[6] Comparing residents of similar backgrounds in segregated and integrated public housing projects, they found that whites in integrated housing were more likely to be friendly with blacks, to endorse interracial living, and to have positive attitudes towards blacks in general than were whites living in the segregated projects. Though neither of these studies could ascertain the beliefs of these individuals *prior* to integration, neither author had reason to believe that the integrated whites differed from the segregated whites before the former's experience with blacks. They concluded, therefore, that the positive results were due to the effect of interracial *contact* and not to prior positive belief.

The culmination of this research was Gordon Allport's influential work, *The Nature of Prejudice*.[7] Using the work of Stouffer, Deutsch and Collins, and others, he formulated what has come to be known as the "contact theory":

> Contacts that bring knowledge and acquaintance are likely to engender sounder beliefs about minority groups. . . . Prejudice . . . may be reduced by equal status contact between majority and minority groups in the pursuit of common goals. The effect is greatly enhanced if this contact is sanctioned by institutional supports (i.e., by law, custom, or local atmosphere), and if it is of a sort that leads to the perception of common interests and common humanity between members of the two groups.

The clear key to breaking the vicious circle, then, was contact. By establishing integrated environments for black and white, white prejudice would be reduced, discrimination would decline, and damaging

---

[5] Samuel A. Stouffer, *et al.*, *The American Soldier*, Vol. II (Princeton: Princeton University Press, 1949).

[6] Morton Deutsch and Mary Evans Collins, *Interracial Housing: A Psychological Evaluation of a Social Experiment* (Minneapolis: University of Minnesota Press, 1951).

[7] Gordon W. Allport, *The Nature of Prejudice* (Cambridge, Mass.: Addison-Wesley, 1954).

effects upon the black child's feelings and behavior would be reduced.

While the Supreme Court based its 1954 decision upon the narrower relationship between legally sanctioned segregation and psychological harm, it is clear that the *modus operandi* by which the damage would stop is implied by the contact theory. With the 1954 decision, then, contact theory became an officially sanctioned policy model, and the Southern public school systems became prime targets for its implementation.

THE INTEGRATION POLICY MODEL: STAGE II

In the eyes of the Northerner, segregation had always been a Southern problem. The Supreme Court's action at first reinforced this belief, since state-sanctioned school segregation was rare outside the South. But events in the 1960's changed this for good. While the modern civil rights movement began in the South, its zenith was reached in the March on Washington in the late summer of 1963. Organized to dramatize the failure of court action to end segregation in the South, the March brought together 250,000 persons in the most impressive organized protest meeting in the history of the United States, and showed President Kennedy and the Congress the deep and massive support for anti-discrimination legislation.

The Congress answered this appeal by passing the Civil Rights Act of 1964, the strongest such act since the Reconstruction period. The Act included strong sanctions against discrimination in education, employment, housing, and voting (the last supplemented by the Voting Rights Act of 1965), and while its thrust was still aimed at the South, it also set standards that could be used against de facto segregation in the North (for example, the Title VI provisions directed the withholding of federal funds from localities which intentionally maintain segregated schools—and this has recently been applied to the city of Boston). Equally important, it set in motion a social science study that was to have an immense impact upon public policy in the North as well as the South. As part of the Act, the Congress commissioned the United States Office of Education to conduct a survey "concerning the lack of equal educational opportunities for individuals by reason of race, color, religion, or national origin in public educational institutions at all levels in the United States. . . ." Sociologist James Coleman was selected to head a team to design and conduct the survey.

The Coleman Report,[8] as it has come to be known, contained

---

[8] James Coleman, *et al.*, *Equality of Educational Opportunity* (Washington, D.C.: U.S. Government Printing Office, 1966).

striking evidence of the extent of school segregation not only in the South but in all parts of the country. While the South was more segregated than the North, fully 72 percent of black first graders in the urban North attended predominantly black schools. The report also confirmed one of the basic assumptions of the Stage I model: that black students performed poorly compared to white students. Using results from a variety of achievement tests, Coleman reported that throughout all regions and all grade levels, black students ranged from two to six years behind white students in reading, verbal, and mathematics performance. Equally, black students were shown to have lower aspirations, lower self-esteem about academic ability, and a more fatalistic attitude about their ability to change their situation.

The Coleman study, however, also reported some findings that surprisingly were not in accord with the early model. For one thing, black children were already nearly as far behind white children in academic performance in the *first* grade as they were in later grades. This raised some question about whether school policies alone could eliminate black/white inequalities. Adding to the significance of this finding were the facts that black and white schools could not be shown to differ markedly in facilities or services, and that whatever differences there were could not be used to explain the disparities in black and white student achievement. This led Coleman to conclude that

> schools bring little influence to bear on a child's achievement that is independent of his background and general social context; and this very lack of an independent effect means that the inequalities imposed on children by their home, neighborhood, and peer environment are carried along to become the inequalities [of their adult life].

While the findings about segregation and black/white differences have been widely publicized and largely accepted, this concluding aspect of Coleman's findings has been ignored by educational policy makers. Part of the reason may derive from the methodological controversies which surrounded these findings,[9] but the more likely and important reason is that the implications were devastating to the rationale of the educational establishment in its heavy investment in school rehabilitative programs for the culturally deprived; the connection between public policy and social science does have its limitations.

We must return to the policy makers one more time for an important input into the final policy model. In 1965, President Johnson

---

[9] See, for example, Samuel Bowles and Henry Levin, "The Determination of Scholastic Achievement: An Appraisal of Some Recent Evidence," *The Journal of Human Resources,* Vol. III, No. 1 (1968).

requested the United States Commission on Civil Rights to conduct an investigation into the effects of de facto segregation in the nation and to make recommendations about how it might be remedied. He expressed hope that the findings "may provide a basis for action not only by the federal government but also by the states and local school boards which bear the direct responsibility for assuring quality education." The Commission recommendations, in its 1967 volume entitled *Racial Isolation in the Public Schools,* constitute the most comprehensive policy statement to date on the subject of school integration; it is the policy which is, indeed, being followed by many states and local school boards throughout the country.

Using data from the Coleman study and several other original studies prepared for the Commission, the report concluded that

> Negro children suffer serious harm when their education takes place in public schools which are racially segregated, whatever the source of such segregation may be. Negro children who attend predominantly Negro schools do not achieve as well as other children, Negro and white. Their aspirations are more restricted than those of other children and they do not have as much confidence that they can influence their own futures. When they become adults, they are less likely to participate in the mainstream of American society, and more likely to fear, dislike, and avoid white Americans. The conclusions drawn by the U.S. Supreme Court about the impact upon children of segregation compelled by law—that it "affects their hearts and minds in ways unlikely ever to be undone"—applies to segregation not compelled by law.

To remedy this situation, the Commission recommended that the federal government establish a uniform standard for racial balance and provide financial assistance to states that develop programs to meet the standard. The Commission did not recommend a precise standard, but it did suggest that the standard be no higher than 50 percent black in any single school. Likewise, the Commission did not specifically recommend that busing be the method whereby integration is accomplished. But the realities of residential segregation in many cities throughout the nation offered little alternative to the use of busing if these integration standards were to be attained.

This, then, became the basis for the integration policy model as applied to public schools. While the implementation of racial balance programs has differed from one locality to the next, the underlying rationale of all these programs is similar to that first formulated by the Supreme Court and extended by the Civil Rights Commission. The full policy model may be summarized as follows: The starting point is white prejudice consisting of stereotyped beliefs about black people.

These beliefs lead to discriminatory behavior in employment, housing, schooling, and social relationships in general. Discrimination in turn leads to social and economic inequality on the one hand, and segregation on the other hand. Inequality and segregation are mutually reinforcing conditions, reflecting not only the judicial doctrine that separation is inherently unequal, but also the social reality that segregation of a deprived group can cut off channels and networks that might be used to gain equality. Segregation and inequality combine to cause psychological damage in children resulting in lower achievement, lower aspirations, and less self-esteem. As the child grows older, this damage leads, on the one hand, to further social and economic inequalities in the form of inadequate education and inferior jobs and, on the other hand, to black alienation, prejudice, and hostility towards whites. This in turn leads to increased white prejudice (the vicious circle) and a general polarization of race relations. Given these cause and effect relations, the elimination of segregation in schooling should act as a countervailing force for black students by increasing achievement, raising aspirations, enhancing self-esteem, reducing black/white prejudices and hostility, and enabling black students to find better educational and occupational opportunities. It then follows that social and economic inequalities would be lessened and the vicious circle would be bent if not broken.

It must be stressed that this model is construed from public policy. While many of the causal relationships assumed in the model are, indeed, based on many years of scientific research in psychology and sociology, it is doubtful that any two specialists in the field of race relations would agree on all of the components of the model. Be that as it may, it is more to the point to stress that we are not setting out to test the *full* model. *We are specifically interested in those aspects of the model that postulate positive effects of school integration for black students; namely, that school integration enhances black achievement, aspirations, self-esteem, race relations, and opportunities for higher education.* We do not have data on the effects of integration on adults, nor on the effects of other types of integration, such as neighborhood housing, employment, and other forms. More important, the school integration programs we review here have two important characteristics in common that may limit generalizability. First, they are examples of "induced" integration as opposed to "natural" integration. Induced integration is brought about by the decision of a state or local agency to initiate a school integration program (sometimes voluntary, sometimes mandatory), rather than by the "natural" process whereby a black family makes an individual decision to relocate in a predominantly white community. Second, all of these programs have had to use varying amounts of busing to accomplish integration. This makes it difficult to separate out the potential effects of busing, if any, from the integration experience *per se*. In other words, *we will be assessing the effects of induced school integration via busing,* and not necessarily the effects of integration brought about by the voluntary actions of individual families that move to integrated neighborhoods. This is a more limited focus, yet induced integration, usually necessitating some amount of busing, is precisely the policy model that has been followed (or is being considered) in many communities throughout the country.

THE DATA

Many of the cities which desegregated their schools to achieve a racial balance have conducted research programs to evaluate the outcomes of desegregation. It is from these studies that we can derive data to test the school and busing hypotheses stemming from the integration policy model. Since the evaluations were conducted independently, the variables studied and the research designs differ from one study to the next, and the quality of the research and the reports varies considerably. Accordingly, we have been selective in choosing studies to include in our analysis. Our choices have been guided by two considerations: (1) A study must employ a longitudinal time-span design, with the same tests administered at different times during the integration experience so that *actual* changes can be assessed; and (2) a study must have a control group for comparison with integrated black students. The ideal control group, of course, would consist of black students who are identical to the integrated students in every way except for the integration experience. Since such studies are rare, an "adequate" control group for our present purposes is either a group of non-bused black students who are reasonably comparable to the bused black students, or a group of white students in the same school as the bused black students. In the latter case, the effects of integration are revealed in the changes in the black/white differential for the measure in question.[10]

The data we will use can be classified into two parts. The first part consists of findings from a study of Boston's METCO program, for

---

[10] In spite of these precautions, we must still warn that it is difficult to make comparisons and generalizations when data are derived from different studies. Also, all of the studies we review were done in Northern cities, so that our findings may not be generalizable to the South. Nonetheless, the studies do reveal sufficiently clear and consistent findings in certain areas to enable at least a preliminary assessment of the effects of induced integration in de facto segregated cities of the North.

whose research design, execution, and analysis we are partly responsible.[11] The data are more complete and offer a more thoroughgoing
test of the policy model than many other studies we have seen. The
METCO program buses black students of all age levels from Boston
to predominantly white middle-class schools in the suburbs. Approximately 1500 black students and 28 suburban communities have participated since the program began in 1966; the study from which our
data will be taken covers the period from October 1968 to May 1970.
The study used a longitudinal design that called for achievement testing for all students and a questionnaire for the junior and senior high
students in three waves: the first at the beginning of the school year
in October 1968; a second in May 1969; and a third in May 1970. (For
a variety of reasons, the achievement testing was not done for the third
wave.) The questionnaire covered several areas, including academic
performance, aspirations and self-concept, relations with and attitudes
toward white students, and attitudes toward the program.

The METCO study also included a small control group consisting
of siblings of the bused students matched by sex and grade levels.[12]

---

[11] Herbert J. Walberg, "Student Achievement and Perception of Class Learning Environments" (Boston: METCO, 1969) (unpublished manuscript); and
David J. Armor and William J. Genova, "METCO Student Attitudes and Aspirations: A Three-Year Evaluation" (Boston: METCO, 1970) (unpublished manuscript). The data summarized in these reports were subjected to extensive reanalysis for the present study.

[12] The number of junior and senior high students participating in the METCO
study are as follows: wave one, 357 bused (80 per cent of the total population)
and 112 controls (54 per cent of the eligible population); wave two, 229 bused
(51 per cent) and 67 controls (32 per cent); wave three, 492 bused (87 per cent)
and 232 controls (65 per cent). Because of clerical errors in relating achievement
tests to questionnaires, the questionnaire data for waves one and two are based on
about 10 per cent fewer respondents in each group. Given the low turnout rates
for wave two and other factors (drop-outs, graduates, transfers from control to
bused status), our panel of secondary school students with achievement data for
both testing periods consists of 195 bused students and 41 control students; for the
questionnaire data the panel consists of 135 bused students with data from all
3 waves and 36 control students with data from wave one and wave three. (Only
16 students in the control group had questionnaire data from all three waves. Of
the initial sample of control students, over a third had either graduated or transferred into the busing program by the third wave.) In addition, achievement
data for elementary grades is available for panels of 147 bused students (66 per
cent of the wave one sample) and 41 controls (44 per cent). Given the relatively
small proportion of both bused and control students in the panels, there is the
chance that the panels are not representative of the full population of bused
students and their matched siblings. In the comparisons we make in the next
section, therefore, we shall also present data from the complete cross-sections for
all waves. The bused panel does not differ significantly from the full cross-section
of bused students, and the control panel differs in no way that would affect our
main conclusions. In other words, the cross-sectional data can be used as a check
on the panel data; the absence of any divergence between the two sets of find-

The fact that the siblings were from the same families as the bused students means that there is an automatic control for social class and other tangible and intangible family factors. Since the high application rate usually prevented the busing program from taking more than one applicant per family, we had reason to believe that the control students would not differ substantially from the bused students along the important dimensions of ability, aspirations, and so forth. This belief is confirmed by the findings presented in the next section.

In addition to the data for black students, there are also data from a single cross-sectional study done in the spring of 1969 to assess the impact of the program on white sophomores in eight of the suburban schools.[13] We will cite some of the findings from the Useem study whenever such comparisons seem relevant.

The second part of the data comes largely from reports on integration programs in four other Northern cities throughout the country.[14] In 1964, White Plains, New York, closed down one racially imbal-

---

ings indicates that the attrition of the panels does not invalidate the panel findings. (Analysis was carried out on the 240 bused students who were in both waves one and three, representing 74 per cent of the wave one sample, and there were no important differences between these results and the results from the smaller three-wave panel.)

[13] Betsy Useem, "White Suburban Secondary Students in Schools with Token Segregation," unpublished Ph.D. dissertation, Graduate School of Education, Harvard University, 1971; and Betsy Useem, "Correlates of Racial Attitudes Among White High School Students" (unpublished manuscript, 1972).

[14] Research reports for a number of widely-discussed busing programs were not included for various reasons. For example, the Berkeley, California, busing program has not been systematically studied; a report is available, however, which shows that black student achievement is as far behind (or *further* behind) white achievement after two years of integration as before integration (Arthur Dambacher, "Comparison of Achievement Test Scores made by Berkeley Elementary Students, Pre and Post Integration," unpublished report, Berkeley Unified School District, Berkeley, California, 1971). A study of the Rochester busing program also lacked a proper pre-test design ("Final Report: A Three-Year Longitudinal Study to Assess a Fifteen Point Plan to Reduce Racial Isolation," Rochester City School District, Rochester, New York, 1970). The study had pre-test and post-test achievement scores from *different tests*, and control groups with generally lower pre-test scores; and it used analysis of covariance to make adjustments for post-test scores. Such statistical adjustments do no necessarily eliminate initial differences between the bused and control groups. A third study—of the Evanston integration program—was received too late for inclusion (Jayjia Hsia, "Integration in Evanston, 1967–71," Educational Testing Services, Evanston, Illinois, 1971). This report did show, however, that after two to three years of integration, integrated black students were still as far—or farther—behind white students as before integration. This research also confirmed the reduction in black academic self-concept after integration and the tendency for black student grades to decline. We know of no other studies of induced school integration in the North which have the research design necessary for establishing cause and effect relationship—to wit, a longitudinal design with a control group.

anced inner-city elementary school and began busing the children
to predominantly white inner-city schools; the study we cite covers a
two-year period from 1964 to 1966.[15] In Ann Arbor, Michigan, there
was a similar pattern: A racially imbalanced elementary school was
closed in 1965 and the students were bused to predominantly white
schools; the study covers a one-year period with a three-year follow-
up.[16] A program in Riverside, California, followed a graduated program
of closing its racially imbalanced elementary schools and integrating
its predominantly white schools; the program began in 1965 and the
study covers a five-year period.[17] The fourth program, Project Concern,
is similar to METCO. Elementary school children from two inner cities
(Hartford and New Haven, Connecticut) are bused to suburban schools
in surrounding towns; this program began in 1966—the studies selected
cover two years for Hartford [18] and one year for New Haven.[19] In
addition to these five major studies, we will also refer at certain points
to studies of other integration programs that seem relevant. One such
study is an evaluation of A Better Chance (ABC), a program which
places high-ability black students in white preparatory schools in the
Northeast.[20] This evaluation research used techniques and instruments
similar to those used in the METCO study; therefore comparisons
with ABC may be more valid than comparisons with some of the other
studies.

To test the integration policy model we can group our findings
under five major headings—the effects of busing and integration on:
(1) academic achievement; (2) aspirations; (3) self-concept; (4)
race relations; and (5) educational opportunities. In addition, we will
examine a sixth area, program support. In each case, we shall compare
bused students with the control groups to assess those changes that
might be uniquely associated with the effects of induced integration.

---

15 White Plains Public Schools, "White Plains Racial Balance Plan Evaluation,"
White Plains, New York, 1967.

16 Patricia M. Carrigan, "School Desegregation via Compulsory Pupil Transfer: Early Effects on Elementary School Children," Final Report for Project No.
6-1320, Contract No. OEC-3-6-061320-0659, U.S. Office of Education (Washington, D.C.: U.S. Office of Education, 1969).

17 Mabel Purl and Judith Dawson, "The Achievement of Pupils in Desegregated Schools," unpublished manuscript, Riverside Unified School District,
California, 1971; and Harold Gerard and Norman Miller, "Factors Contributing to
Adjustment and Achievement in Racially Desegregated Schools," unpublished
manuscript, Department of Psychology, University of California at Los Angeles.

18 Thomas W. Mahan, Project Concern—1966–1968 (Hartford: Hartford
Public Schools, 1968).

19 Ronald R. Clinton, "A Study of the Improvement in Achievement of Basic
Skills of Children Bused from Urban to Suburban School Environments," unpublished master's thesis, Southern Connecticut State College, 1969.

20 George Perry, "A Preliminary Evaluation of the Effects of ABC on College
Attendance" (Boston: A Better Chance, 1972) (unpublished report).

THE FINDINGS: ACHIEVEMENT

None of the studies were able to demonstrate conclusively that integration has had an effect on academic achievement as measured by standardized tests. Given the results of the Coleman study and other evaluations of remedial programs (e.g., Head Start), many experts may not be surprised at this finding. To date there is no published report of *any* strictly educational reform which has been proven substantially to affect academic achievement; school integration programs are no exception.

The changes in reading achievement for elementary and secondary students in the METCO program are shown in Figures 1 and 2.[21] For

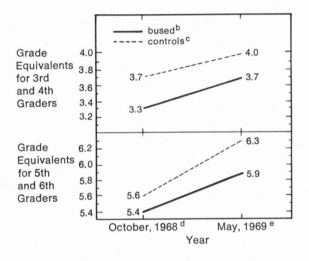

FIGURE 1. *Reading Achievement—Elementary.*[a]

[a] Metropolitan Achievement Tests; no statistically significant gains when bused compared to controls for either age group.
[b] N = 88 for Third-Fourth graders and 59 for Fifth-Sixth graders.
[c] N = 14 for Third-Fourth graders and 27 for Fifth-Sixth graders.
[d] Full cross-sections for grades:
    3-4: bused 3.4 (N = 131); control 3.7 (N = 38)—not significant (sd = .96).
    5-6: bused 5.5 (N = 90); control 5.4 (N = 55)—not significant (sd = 1.5).
[e] Full cross-sections for grades:
    3-4: bused 3.7 (N = 111); control 3.8 (N = 23)—not significant (sd = 1.1).
    5-6: bused 6.0 (N = 74); control 5.8 (N = 52)—not significant (sd = 1.7).

[21] About half of the elementary students and two thirds of the secondary students were new to the program in 1968. However, there were no differences in gain scores for the newly-bused compared to the previously-bused students.

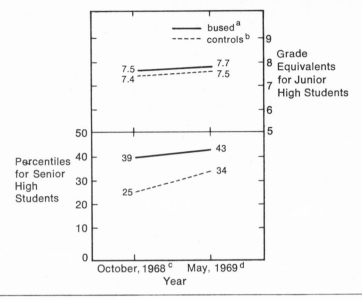

FIGURE 2.   *Reading Achievement—Junior and Senior High.*

a N = 123 for junior high and 72 for senior high (no statistically significant changes).
b N = 27 for junior high and 14 for senior high (no statistically significant changes).
c Full cross-section for junior high: bused 7.5 (N = 197); control 7.4 (N = 74)—n.s. (sd = 1.9).
   Full cross-section for senior high: bused 36 (N = 160); control 28 (N = 35)—n.s. (sd = 24).
d Full cross-section for junior high: bused 7.7 (N = 143); control 7.3 (N = 47)—n.s. (sd = 1.9).
   Full cross-section for senior high: bused 44 (N = 86); control 34 (N = 20)—n.s. (sd = 25).

the elementary students, the grade-equivalent gains for bused third and fourth graders after one year are somewhat greater than those for the control group (.4 to .3), but this is not a statistically significant difference. For grades 5 and 6 the situation is reversed; the control group outgained the bused group (.7 and .5), but again the difference is not significant. We can see that the control group is somewhat higher initially for both grade levels, but this difference, too, is not significant.[22]

In the case of high school students the bused group score somewhat higher than the control groups initially (but not significantly

22 Initial differences between the newly-bused and the previously-bused revealed no particular pattern; for third and fourth graders the previously-bused were higher by .15 points, but for fifth and sixth graders the newly-bused were higher by .5 points; in any event there were no statistically significant differences in gain scores.

so).[23] Nonetheless, the gain scores present no particular pattern. While the bused junior high students increased their grade-equivalent score from 7.5 to 7.7, the control group improved from 7.4 to 7.5; the bused gain is not significantly different from that for the control group. For senior high students the effect is reversed; the control students gain more than the bused students (9 percentile points compared to 4 points), but again the gains are not statistically significant for either group.

The results for reading achievement are substantially repeated in a test of arithmetic skills; the bused students showed no significant gains in arithmetic skills compared to the control group, and there were no particular patterns in evidence.

The White Plains, Ann Arbor, and Riverside studies also found no significant changes in achievement level for bused students in the elementary grades when comparisons were made with control groups. Although the White Plains report did show some achievement gains among the bused students, these were not significantly different, statistically, from gain scores of inner-city black students in 1960. Moreover, when comparisons were made with white students in the integrated schools, the black/white achievement gap did not diminish during the period of the study. The Ann Arbor study compared bused black student gains to white gains and to black student gains in a half-black school.[24] The bused students did not gain significantly more than the black control group, nor did their gains diminish the black/white gap in the integrated schools. On the contrary, a followup done three years later showed that the integrated black students were even further behind the white students than before the integration project began.[25] The Riverside study compared minority students (black and Mexican-American) who had been integrated for differing numbers of years with the city-wide mean (which consisted of about 85 percent white students). The minority/white gap had not diminished for fourth graders who had been integrated since kindergarten; the gap in 1970 was as great as it was in 1965 when the program began.[26] Similar

[23] The newly-bused students were somewhat higher than the previously-bused initially for both junior and senior high students (.3 and 2.5, respectively), but the differences were not significant.

[24] The control school was a "naturally" integrated school with an increasing proportion of black students; it was scheduled to be closed down the following year.

[25] The pattern of black achievement falling further behind white achievement at later grade levels has been extensively documented in Coleman, *Equality of Educational Opportunity,* and Michael Rosenfeld and Thomas L. Hilton, "Negro-White Differences in Adolescent Educational Growth," *American Educational Research Journal,* VIII (1971).

[26] Purl and Dawson, "Achievement of Pupils."

results occurred for minority pupils at other grade levels with differing numbers of years in the integration program.

Studies in the fifth program, Project Concern, showed mixed results. A study of the Hartford students compared bused black students who received special supportive assistance with non-bused inner-city black students.[27] (Although two separate one-year periods were covered, problems with missing data allow valid comparisons for only one full academic year, fall 1967 to spring 1968.) The bused students showed significant IQ gains only in grades two and three; the gains in kindergarten and grades one, four, and five were either insignificant or, in two cases, favored the control group. In a study of New Haven students, second and third grade students were randomly assigned to bused and non-bused conditions and were given reading, language, and arithmetic tests in October 1967 (when the busing began) and again in April 1968.[28] Of the six comparisons possible (three tests and two grades), only two showed significant differences favoring the bused students.[29]

While none of these studies are flawless, their consistency is striking. Moreover, their results are not so different from the results of the massive cross-sectional studies. An extensive reanalysis of the Coleman data showed that even without controlling for social class factors, "naturally" integrated (i.e., non-bused) black sixth-grade groups were still one and one-half standard deviations behind white groups in the same schools, compared to a national gap of two standard deviations.[30] This means that, assuming the Coleman data to be correct, the *best* that integration could do would be to move the average black group from the second percentile to the seventh percentile (on the *white* scale, where the average white group is at the fiftieth percentile). But the social class differences of integrated black students in the Coleman study could easily explain a good deal of even this small gain. Other investigators, after examining a number of studies, have come to similar conclusions.[31]

---

27 Mahan, *Project Concern.*

28 Clinton, "Improvement in Achievement."

29 Even these two significant results might not have occurred if the data had been analyzed differently. The author controlled for pre-busing scores using analysis of covariance rather than analyzing gain scores (see footnote 14). Since the author did not present pre-test means, we cannot know if the bused and control groups differed initially.

30 David J. Armor, "School and Family Effects on Black and White Achievement," in Frederic Mosteller and Daniel Moynihan (Eds.), *On Equality of Educational Opportunity* (New York: Randon House, 1972).

31 Nancy St. John, "Desegragation and Minority Group Preference," *Review of Educational Research,* XL (1970), 111–134.

While there are no important gains for the METCO group in standardized test scores, there were some important differences in school grades (see Figure 3). Even though the bused secondary school students have somewhat higher test scores than the control group, the bused group was about half a grade-point *behind* the control group in 1969, and the bused students dropped even further behind by 1970.[32] The average control student is able to maintain a grade average at above a B— level in the central city, while the average bused student in the suburbs is just above a C average. Although it is not shown in Figure 3, from the Useem study we can estimate the average white student *academic* grade average (i.e., excluding non-academic courses—an exclusion not made for the black students) at about 2.45, or between a B— and C+ average.

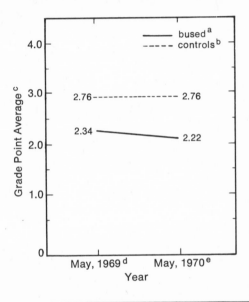

FIGURE 3. *Grade Point Average—Junior and Senior High.*

a N = 165; statistically significant change (.01 level).
b N = 23; no significant change.
c Self-reported; a grade of A is 4.0, B is 3.0, etc.
d Full cross-section: bused 2.33 (N = 210); control 2.73 (N = 59)—significant at .001 level.
e Full cross-section: bused 2.20 (N = 467); control 2.59 (N = 228)—significant at .001 level.

32 The grade-point system used here has an A as 4 points, B as 3 points, and so on.

Again, if we take into account the Coleman findings, we should not be too surprised. Since black students of the same age are, on average, behind white students in all parts of the country with respect to academic achievement, we should expect their grades to fall when they are taken from the competition in an all-black school to the competition in a predominantly white school. In addition, the bused students may not be adequately prepared for this competition, at least in terms of the higher standards that may be applied in the suburban schools.

ASPIRATION AND SELF-CONCEPT

In the METCO study we found that there were no increases in educational or occupational aspiration levels for bused students (see Figures 4 and 5); on the contrary, there was a significant decline for

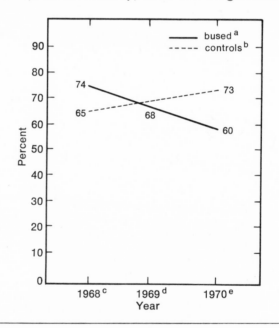

FIGURE 4.   *Per Cent Wanting a Bachelor's Degree.*

[a] N = 132; bused changes significantly different from control changes (0.2 level).
[b] N = 34.
[c] Full cross-section: bused 71% (N = 323); controls 68% (N = 87)—not significant.
[d] Full cross-section: bused 69% (N = 211); controls 68% (N = 60)—not significant.
[e] Full cross-section: bused 60% (N = 486); controls 56% (N = 228)—not significant.

the bused students, from 74 percent wanting a college degree in 1968 to 60 percent by May 1970. The control panel actually increased its college aspirations over the same period, but this is probably not a meaningful finding. (The cross-sectional data show a slight decline for the control group in 1970; this cautions us about our interpretation.)

At the very least, we can conclude that the bused students do not improve their aspirations for college. The same is true for occupational aspirations, and in this case both the bused students and the controls show a similar pattern. We should point out, however, that the initial aspiration levels are already very high; Coleman found that only 54 percent of white twelfth graders in the urban North aspired to college, and 53 percent expected a professional or technical occupation. Therefore, even the slight decline we have found still leaves the bused students with relatively high aspirations compared to a regional norm. Moreover, when achievement is taken into account, black students actually have higher aspirations than white students at

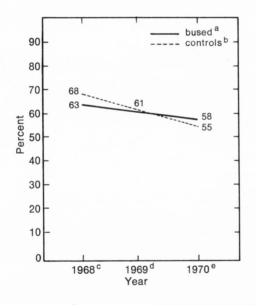

FIGURE 5. *Per Cent Expecting a Professional or Technical Occupation.*

[a] N = 130; bused changes not significantly different from control changes.
[b] N = 31.
[c] Full cross-section: bused 63% (N = 311); controls 55% (N = 91)—not significant.
[d] Full cross-section: bused 62% (N = 203); controls 52% (N = 58)—not significant.
[e] Full cross-section: bused 66% (N = 482); controls 66% (N = 228)—not significant.

similar levels of achievement.[33] In this respect, some educators have hypothesized that integration has a *positive* effect in lowering aspirations to more realistic levels; of course, others would argue that any lowering of aspirations is undesirable. However, we shall see in a later section that the METCO students were more likely to start college than the control group.

Since the other cities in our review included only elementary students, they do not provide data on regular educational or occupational aspirations.[34] But two of the studies did examine a concept closely related to aspirations—"motivation for achievement." The findings of the Ann Arbor and Riverside studies corroborate the pattern of high aspirations for black children in both the pre- and post-integration periods. In addition, the Ann Arbor researchers concluded that the overly high aspiration of black boys may have been lowered by the integration experience. The Riverside study, on the other hand, concluded that there were no significant changes in achievement motivation.

In the METCO study we also found some important differences with respect to academic self-concept (Figure 6). The students were asked to rate how bright they were in comparison to their classmates. While there were some changes in both the bused and control groups, the important differences are the gaps between the bused students and controls at each time period. The smallest difference is 15 percentage points in 1970 (11 points for the full cross-section), with the control students having the higher academic self-concept. Again, this finding makes sense if we recall that the academic performance of the bused students falls considerably when they move from the black community to the white suburbs. In rating their intellectual ability, the bused students may simply be reflecting the harder competition in suburban schools.

Both the Ann Arbor and Riverside studies made much more extensive inquiry into the realm of self-esteem of black children, although there were no directly comparable data for our academic self-concept measure. The Riverside study did report that, in a special test, minority children (black and Mexican-American) tended to choose white students more often than black students as "the [ones] with good

---

[33] David J. Armor, "The Racial Composition of Schools and College Aspriations of Black Students," Appendix C2 of *Racial Isolation in the Public Schools* (Washington, D.C.: U.S. Commission on Civil Rights, 1967); and Alan B. Wilson, "Educational Consequences of Segregation in a California Community," Appendix C3 of *Racial Isolation.*

[34] The Ann Arbor study did include a measure of occupational aspiration, but the variation was so great (not to speak of the coding problems presented by such choices as "superman" and "fairy princess") that interpretation was difficult.

grades." While we will not go into detail on the many other measures used in these studies, we can summarize their findings briefly as follows: (1) Minority children do tend to have lower self-esteem before integration, particularly in the later elementary grades; and (2) integration does not seem to affect the self-esteem measures in any clearly consistent or significant way.

RACE RELATIONS

One of the central sociological hypotheses in the integration policy model is that integration should reduce racial stereotypes, increase tolerance, and generally improve race relations. Needless to say, we were quite surprised when our data failed to verify this axiom. Our surprise was increased substantially when we discovered that, in fact, the converse appears to be true. The data suggest that, under the

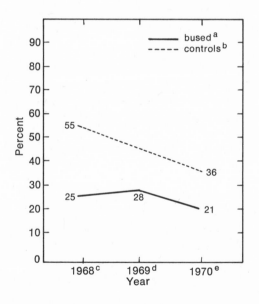

FIGURE 6. *Per Cent Feeling More Intelligent than Classmates.*

[a] N = 130; bused changes not significantly different from control changes.
[b] N = 33.
[c] Full cross-section: bused 25% (N = 320); controls 47% (N = 99)—significance under .01.
[d] Full cross-section: bused 31% (N = 211); controls 42% (N = 60)—not significant.
[e] Full cross-section: bused 23% (N = 483); controls 34% (N = 230)—significance under .01.

circumstances obtaining in these studies, integration heightens racial identity and consciousness, enhances ideologies that promote racial segregation, and reduces opportunities for actual contact between the races.

There are several indicators from the METCO study that point to these conclusions. The question which speaks most directly to the 50 percent racial balance standard suggested by the Civil Rights Commission asked: "if you could be in any school you wanted, how many students would be white?" Figure 7 reports the percentage which responded in favor of 50 percent or fewer white students. While both the control and the bused students started out fairly close together in 1968 (47 percent and 51 percent, respectively), two school years later the bused students were 15 percentage points *more* in favor of attending *non-white* schools than the controls (81 percent compared to 66 percent), although the differential change is not statistically

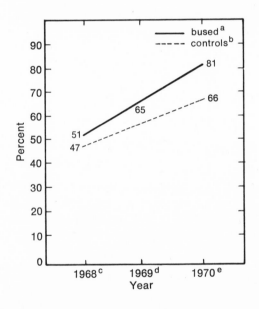

FIGURE 7. *Per Cent Wanting to be in a School with no More than 50 Per Cent White Students.*

[a] N = 133; bused change not significantly different from control change.
[b] N = 36.
[c] Full cross-section: bused 56% (N = 323); controls 56% (N = 97).
[d] Full cross-section: bused 67% (N = 209); controls 59% (N = 61)—not significant.
[e] Full cross-section: bused 71% (N = 485); controls 62% (N = 229)— significance under .001.

significant. The changes for the controls (both the panel and the full cross-sections) indicate that the black community as a whole may be changing its attitudes toward school integration, but the bused students appear to be changing at a more rapid rate. Ironically, just as white America has finally accepted the idea of school integration,[35] blacks who begin experiencing it may want to reject it.

That these changes reflect ideological shifts is supported by Figures 8 and 9. The bused students are much more likely to support the idea of black power than the control students, going from a difference of 11 points in 1969 to 36 points in 1970. We were also able to construct a Separatist Ideology Index from responses to a series of statements about black/white relations (e.g., 1. "Most black people should live and work in black areas, and most whites should live and

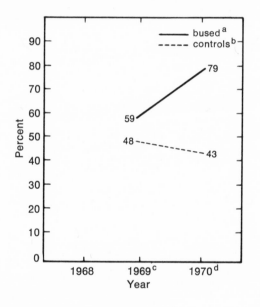

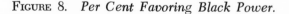

FIGURE 8. *Per Cent Favoring Black Power.*

[a] N = 167; bused change significantly different from control change (.05 level).
[b] N = 21.
[c] Full cross-section: bused 59% (N = 211); controls 52% (N = 59)—not significant.
[d] Full cross-section: bused 76% (N = 479); controls 55% (N = 220)—significance under .001.

[35] Andrew M. Greeley and Paul B. Sheatsley, "Attitudes Toward Racial Integration," *Scientific American,* Vol. 225, No. 6 (1971).

work in white areas." 2. "Black and white persons should not inter-marry."). The scores range from 0 (anti-separatist) to 4 (pro-separatist). From 1968 to 1970 the control group barely changes, increasing from 1.4 to 1.5. The bused group, however, changed from 1.4 to 1.8—a statistically significant change of about one half a standard deviation. This is the clearest indication in our data that integration heightens black racial consciousness and solidarity.

The changes do not appear to be in ideology alone. From 1969 to 1970 the bused students reported less friendliness from whites, more free time spent with members of their own race, more incidents of

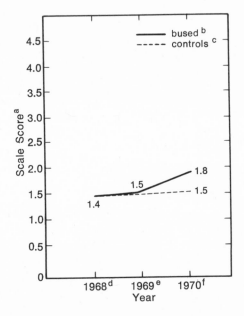

FIGURE 9.   *Separatist Ideology Index.*

a A score of 4 indicates strongest separatist feelings; reliability = .76; sd = .8.
b N = 135; bused change significantly greater than control change (under .01 level).
c N = 34.
d Full cross-section: bused 1.4 (N = 324); controls 1.4 (N = 97)—not significant.
e Full cross-section: bused 1.6 (N = 213); controls 1.5 (N = 60)—not significant.
f Full cross-section: bused 1.8 (N = 489); controls 1.5 (N = 230)—sig-nificance under .001.

prejudice, and less frequent dating with white students (Figure 10). In other words, the longer the contact with whites, the fewer the kinds of interracial experiences that might lead to a general improvement in racial tolerance.

To what extent might these changes be a result of negative experiences with white students in the schools? We do not doubt that there has been considerable hostility shown by certain groups of white students. Nonetheless, although the evidence is not complete, what we have indicates that the white students themselves were negatively affected by the contact. Support for the busing program was generally high among white sophomores in the eight high schools studied, especially among middle-class students in the college preparatory tracks.[36] For example, 46 percent of all students were "very favorable" to METCO (only 11 percent were "not favorable"); 73 percent felt METCO should be continued; and 52 percent agreed that there should be more METCO students (20 percent disagreed and 27 percent were not sure). But those students who had direct classroom

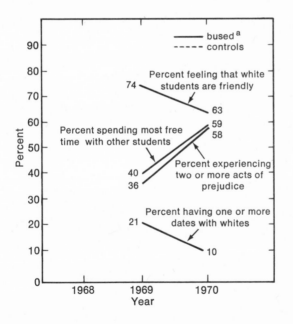

FIGURE 10.   *Bused Students' Relations with White Students.*

[a] N's range from 146 to 159; all changes significant at or under .02 level.

[36] Useem, "Correlates of Racial Attitudes."

contact with bused black students showed *less* support for the busing program than those without direct contact. In fact, the kind of students who were generally the most suportive—the middle-class, high-achieving students—showed the largest decline in support as a result of contact with bused black students. This finding is based on cross-sectional data and does not indicate a change over time, but it is suggestive of the possibility that a general polarization has occurred for both racial groups.

The data from the Ann Arbor and Riverside studies give some support to these findings, although again there were no directly comparable measures. Moreover, it is unlikely that the concept of ideology is relevant to elementary students. The Ann Arbor study included a sociometric test, whereby children could indicate how much they liked each classmate. Black students at all grade levels suffered a loss of peer status when they switched from a segregated to an integrated school, although the results were statistically significant only for second and third grade girls and fourth and fifth grade boys. That is, these black children were liked less by their new white peers than by their previously all-black peers. Also, the level of acceptance was considerably lower for black students than for white students. On the other hand, the black students tended to be more positive about their white peers after integration than they were about their black peers before integration, although the changes are not statistically significant.

The Riverside data more clearly support the conclusion that integration heightens racial identity and solidarity. Data from a test in which children rate pictures of faces portraying various ethnic and racial groups showed that fewer cross-racial choices were made after integration than before integration. For example, one rating task required that the children choose the face that they would "most like for a friend." Both black and white children tended to choose their own race to a greater extent after one year of integration than before integration.[37] The Riverside study also concluded that these effects were stronger with increasing age; that is, the cross-racial choices declined more in the later grades than in the earlier grades.

To avoid any misinterpretation of these findings, we should caution that the measures discussed here do no necessarily indicate increased *overt* racial hostility or conflict. This may occur to some extent in many busing programs, but our impression based on the METCO program is that overt racial incidents initiated by black or white students are infrequent. The polarization that we are describing, and

---

[37] Gerard and Miller, "Factors Contributing to Adjustment."

that our instruments assess, is characterized by ideological solidarity and behavioral withdrawal. Our inferences pertain to a lack of racial togetherness rather than to explicit racial confrontations or violence. While it is conceivable that a connection may exist between these ideological shifts and open racial conflicts, such a connection is not established by the studies reviewed.

There are two other qualifications we must place on the interpretation of these data. First, as of 1970 the *majority* of the bused METCO students still supported general integration ideology. Only 40 percent of the METCO students would ideally prefer schools with a majority of black students (compared to 28 percent of the controls); 60 percent of METCO students believe that "once you really get to know a white person, they can be as good a friend as anyone else" (compared to 78 percent of the controls); and 58 percent of METCO students do not agree that "most black people should live and work in black areas, and most whites should live and work in white areas" (compared to 71 percent of the control students).

The main point we are making is that the integration policy model predicts that integration should cause these sentiments to *increase,* while the evidence shows they actually *decrease,* leaving the bused students *more opposed* to integration than the non-bused students. Only further research can determine whether this trend will continue until the majority of bused students shifts to a general anti-integration ideology.

Second, group averages tend to obscure important differences between individual students. While we do not deny the existence of racial tension and conflict for some students, other students and families (both black and white) have had every meaningful relationships with one another, relationships made possible only through the busing program. It is very difficult, indeed, to weigh objectively the balance of benefit and harm for the group as a whole. The main point to be made is that a change in a group average does not necessarily reflect a change in every individual group member.

LONG-TERM EDUCATIONAL EFFECTS

In view of the fact that most of the short-term measures do not conclusively demonstrate positive effects of busing in the area of achievement, aspirations, self-concept, and race relations, it becomes even more important to consider possible longer-term changes that may relate to eventual socio-economic parity between blacks and whites. Since no busing program has been in operation for more than seven years or so, this area, obviously, has not been studied extensively. There are, however, some preliminary findings on long-term educational effects. Specifically, two studies have investigated the effects of integration on college attendance, and some tentative conclusions have emerged.

Seniors from the 1970 graduating class in the METCO program, as well as the seniors in the 1970 control group, formed samples for a follow-up telephone interview in the spring of 1972. Approximately two thirds of both groups were contacted, resulting in college data for 32 bused students and 16 control group students. The results of the follow-up are striking and they are summarized in Figure 11. The bused students were very much more likely to start college than the control group (84 percent compared to 56 percent), but by the end of the second year the bused students resembled the control group (59 percent compared to 56 percent). In other words, the METCO program seems to have had a dramatic effect upon the impetus for college, and many more of the bused students actually started some form of higher education. But the bused drop-out rate was also sub-

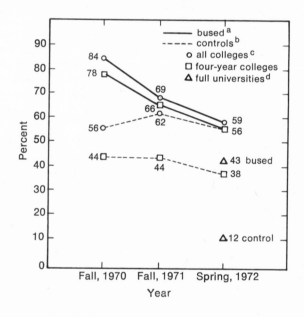

FIGURE 11.   *Per Cent Attending College Full-time.*

a N = 32 for all time periods.
b N = 16 for all time periods.
c Includes 2-year junior college; bused change significantly greater than control change (.05 level).
d Universities with a gradute program.

stantially higher, so that towards the end of the sophomore year the bused students were not much more likely to be enrolled full-time in college than the control group.

In spite of this higher drop-out rate, the bused students were still enrolled in what are generally considered higher-quality institutions. That, is, 56 percent of the bused students were in regular four-year colleges, compared to 38 percent for the control group. An even greater difference was found for those enrolled in full universities (which include a graduate school). The figures are 47 percent and 12 percent for bused and control students, respectively.

Similar findings emerged from a special college follow-up study of the ABC programs.[38] A group of ABC students were matched with a control group of high-ability black students not in the ABC program. Since ABC is a highly selective program, the matching was carried out so that the ABC and control groups had very similar family backgrounds, socio-economic status, and achievement levels. Approximately 40 matched pairs were followed until their first year of college (academic year 1971–72). All of the ABC students entered college, whereas only half of the control group did so. While it is too early to assess differential drop-out rates, it is very clear from the data that even if half of the ABC students drop out of college, the quality of colleges attended by the ABC students is considerably higher than those attended by the control group. Of the matched pairs attending college, two thirds of the ABC students attended higher-quality institutions.

Neither of these studies is large enough, of course, to draw any definite conclusions. But there does seem to be some strong evidence that middle-class suburban or prep schools have an important "channeling" effect not found in black schools. The effect is probably due to better counseling and better contacts with college recruiting officers. Whatever the reason, black students attending such schools may have doors opened for them that are closed to students attending predominantly black schools. Given the lack of positive effects in other areas, these findings may have great significance for future busing programs, and further research is urgently needed.

PROGRAM SUPPORT

Although it is not explicitly part of the integration policy model we are testing, it seems appropriate to consider the extent of the support for the busing program among the students and communities involved. As might be expected from the changes already described, there was

---

[38] Perry, "Preliminary Evaluation."

a general decline in the enthusiasm for the METCO program over time, with the bused students showing greater changes than the controls: 80 percent of the bused group said they were "very favorable" to the program in 1968, compared to 50 percent by 1970. Yet we cannot infer from this alone that there is a decline in support for the program. The drop-out rate in the METCO program is almost non-existent in spite of some of the changes we have reported. The families involved in the program appear to feel that their children will get a better education in the suburbs in spite of the inconvenience and the problems. Our data indicated that the most important reason cited by the bused students for being in the busing program was to receive "a better education." Moreover, this did not change as much as many of our other indicators from 1969 to 1970; 88 percent said this was a "very important" reason in 1969, and 81 percent indicated the same in 1970. Very few reported that "getting out of the city" or "more contact with whites" were important reasons for being in the program.

In other words, the justification of the program in the black community has little to do with the contact-prejudice components of the policy model; instead, busing is seen in the context of enlarging educational opportunities for the black students.

We do not have much systematic data from the white receiving schools other than those cited earlier (i.e., a sample of white sophomore students was generally supportive of the program in 1969). It is our impression, however, that most of the 28 communities that receive METCO students are enthusiastic about the program, and only a few communities have turned down the opportunity to participate. The other programs reviewed receive moderate to strong support from the community and participants. In Project Concern the drop-out rate was only 10 percent, half of which was due to the program directors' initiative in withdrawing students. After two years of urban-to-suburban busing, nine additional suburban towns chose to participate and over 1,000 additional elementary school children were bused to suburban schools. In White Plains both black and white parents expressed more positive than negative attitudes about integration, although black parents were more favorable to the program than white parents after two years of desegregation. In Ann Arbor the black parents felt more positive toward the program after one year of desegregated schooling, but the children were slightly less positive than they were prior to the integration experience. In both groups, however, support was high; only 20 percent of each group expressed negative attitudes toward the program.

We must conclude that the busing programs we have reviewed seem to have considerable support from both the black and white communities. In most cases, black parents were highly supportive of the various busing programs. Like the students in our own study, black parents stressed quality education as the most important benefit of such programs, whereas white parents in receiving schools tended to stress the experience of coming into contact with other races. We must point out, however, that *none* of the programs reviewed involved *mandatory* busing of white students into black communities; cities facing this situation might present a very different picture of white support. Moreover, it is unlikely that many in the black community have seen the data on achievement reported here; much black support may be based upon premises regarding academic gain which our findings call into question. Whether or not black support will be affected by such findings remains to be seen.

SOCIAL CLASS AND OTHER BACKGROUND FACTORS

Most of the data we have presented so far summarize the effects of busing on all students considered as a single group. A question might be raised about whether these effects (or lack of same) are consistent for all students regardless of their background. In particular, it might be hypothesized that social class differences between black and white students can explain the changes (or lack of changes) we have reported. We shall briefly indicate the major trends for students of differing social class and other characteristics, such as sex and age level.

It is difficult to separate race and social class, since black families as a group tend to be lower than white families on most socioeconomic measures. To the extent that the distinction can be made, however, no uniquely social class factors have been reported that would contradict the findings presented so far. The Riverside study selected a group of white students whose social class scores were less than or equal to the minority students; achievement test scores of the black students were still significantly lower than the low-SES white students (although the original difference was diminished somewhat).[39] For the METCO data, special analyses were made of the race relations changes among bused students who were children of blue-collar as compared to white-collar workers; no significant differences emerged. What small changes there were usually revealed that the black students from white-collar families changed more (in a negative direction) than those from blue-collar families.

There is also the possibility that, contrary to the assumptions behind many school integration programs, some of the predominantly

---

[39] Gerard and Miller, "Factors Contributing to Adjustment."

white schools to which black students are sent are in fact worse than the inner-city black schools. In the METCO study there were no data to examine this issue in detail, but it is our impression that perhaps only one or two suburbs would approximate the inner-city socio-economic level. In any event, while there were some differences from one town to another in the absolute levels of the various measures, there were no important variations in the *changes* over time that appeared to be related to any socio-economic differences in the communities.

With the exception of achievement test scores, there was some sex and age differential on various measures both before and after integration; but there were no important differences in the relative *changes* in these groups due to integration. That is, in METCO we found that girls generally had a more difficult time adjusting to the program (reflected in lower program support, stronger separatist ideology, and less contact with white students). There seemed to be some important differences in cross-sex, cross-race relationships, which were better between black boys and white girls than between white boys and black girls. This situation seems to have left some black girls with resentful feelings over white girls "stealing their men." But the amount of interracial contact was small for both groups, and, more important, the *changes* in our race relations measures for bused students were about the same for both boys and girls. A similar finding emerged for age levels. Younger students were somewhat more supportive of the program and were more positive of the various race relations measures than older students, but the degree and direction of *change* were similar for all ages. This was true for the METCO secondary school data as well as the Riverside elementary school data.

In sum, while there were some over-all differences according to the sex and age levels of students in busing programs, the effects of busing on *changes* (if any) in achievement and attitudes tended to be uniform for all groups.

It seems clear from the studies of integration programs we have reviewed that four of the five major premises of the integration policy model are not supported by the data, at least over the one- to five-year periods covered by various reports. While this does not deny the possibility of longer-term effects or effects on student characteristics other than those measured, it does mean that the model is open to serious question.

The integration policy model predicted that achievement should improve as black students are moved from segregated schools to integrated schools. This prediction was based in part upon the classical works of Kenneth Clark and others which argue that, because of segregation, black students have lower regard for themselves. It was also based in part upon reanalyses of the Coleman data which showed that black students achieve less than white students, but that black students in integrated schools achieve more than black students in segregated schools. But four of the five studies we reviewed (as well as the Berkeley and Evanston data discussed in footnote 14) showed no significant gains in achievement scores; the other study had mixed results. Our own analyses of the Coleman data were consistent with these findings.[40]

Although there were no gains in general standardized achievement scores that we might attribute to integration, neither were there any losses for black or white students. Unfortunately, we cannot say the same about academic grades of black students. The grades of the METCO secondary students in suburban schools dropped considerably. We did not measure the bused students' grades before they entered the program, but the fact that their test scores are somewhat *higher* than the control group's offers substantial evidence that this difference does represent a change. Along with this change we observed a difference in academic self-concept that seems to indicate that the bused students are aware that they are experiencing more difficult competition in the suburbs. While we might expect this result if we believe the Coleman finding of black/white achievement differences, it does not mean there is no problem. It is possible that there are psychological consequences of this increased competition that may be harmful to black children. Being moved from an environment where they are above average to one in which they are average or below may be frustrating and discouraging. It might be one of the reasons why the bused black students have become less supportive of the program and more supportive of black separatism.

We tested this latter possibility by examining the relationship between support for the Black Panthers and academic grades in our 1970 sample from METCO (see Figure 12). Consistent with our findings, the bused students are more favorable to the Panthers than the control group. But among the bused students we find that the METCO group which has college aspirations but which has a C average or below stands out clearly as more pro-Panther than the other groups. In other words, the increased militancy and anti-integration sentiments among the bused students may arise partly from the fact that their aspirations remain at a very high level even though their performance declines to the point where they may question their ability to compete with whites at the college level. The fact that this

---

[40] See Armor, "School and Family Effects."

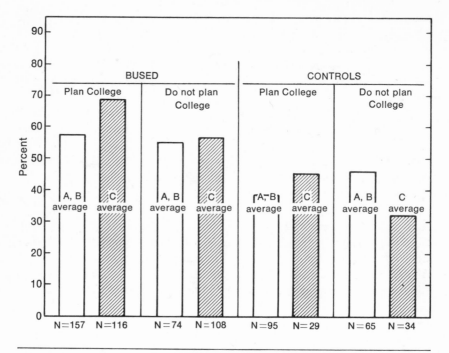

FIGURE 12. *Percentage of Bused and Control Students Who Sympathize with the Black Panthers, by College Plans and Academic Performance.*

group is proportionally a large one (about 25 percent of the total bused group compared to 13 percent for the analogous control group) may be an indication of a potentially serious problem.

The integration policy model predicted that integration should raise black aspirations. Again, our studies reveal no evidence for such an effect. Unlike poor achievement, however, low aspirations do not appear to be much of a problem. The black students in our busing program seem to have aspirations as high as or higher than white students. If anything, given their academic records in high school, these aspirations may be unrealistic for some students. The emphasis on equality of educational opportunity may be pushing into college many black students whose interests and abilities do not warrant it. The fact that only half of the 1970 METCO seniors are still enrolled in four-year colleges (after over 80 percent had started) may attest to this possibility.

The integration policy model predicted that race relations should improve as the result of interracial contact provided by integration programs. In this regard the effect of integration programs seems the opposite of that predicted. It appears that integration increases racial identity and solidarity over the short run and, at least in the case of black students, leads to increasing desires for separatism. These effects are observed for a variety of indicators: attitudes about integration and black power; attitudes towards whites; and contact with whites. The trends are clearest for older students (particularly the METCO high school students), but similar indications are present in the elementary school studies as well. This pattern holds true for whites also, insofar as their support for the integration program decreases and their own-race preferences increase as contact increases.

It is this set of findings that surprised us most. Although many recent studies have questioned the meaning of black/white differences in achievement and aspirations, to our knowledge there have been no research findings which challenged the contact theory. The idea that familiarity lessens contempt has been a major feature of liberal thought in the western world, and its applicability to racial prejudice has been supported for at least two decades of social science research. It may be true that, under certain conditions, greater contact will lead to a reduction of prejudicial feelings among racial or ethnic groups. But the induced integration of black and white students as it is being carried out in schools today does not fulfill the conditions.

In all fairness to the Allport contact theory, it must be said that he placed many qualifications upon it. One major qualification was that the contact must be made under equal-status conditions. Many behavioral scientists might assume that an integration program presumes equality of status, at least in the formal sense that all races are treated equally and have equal access to educational resources. But there is another way to look at status. Integrating black and white students does very little, in the short term, to eliminate the *socio-economic* and *academic* status differentials between black and white students that exist before integration. Therefore, we have to question whether integration programs for black and white children fulfill the equal-status conditions as long as socio-economic and academic inequalities are not eliminated. Allport warned that contact under the wrong conditions can reinforce stereotyped beliefs rather than reduce them; this may be occurring in our current integration programs. In other words, the social class differences between blacks and whites—the differences that integration programs are supposed to eliminate eventually—may heighten the sense of black identity and solidarity, leading to an increasing opposition to integration.

What Allport did not say, but what his emphasis on equal-status conditions may imply, is that contact between two groups with strong initial prejudices may increase prejudice to the extent that stereotypes are reflected by actual group differences. For black students, initial stereotypes about white students as snobbish, intellectual, and "straight" may be partially confirmed by actual experience; the same may be true for white stereotypes of black students as non-intellectual, hostile, and having different values. We might make the same observations about some of the other ethnic and religious conflicts we see in the world today, particularly the Protestant-Catholic conflict in Northern Ireland and the Israeli-Arab battles in the Middle East. It is certainly true in these cases that the amount of contact has not lessened the hostilities; it seems to have heightened them to dangerous levels in the first place.

Why has the integration policy model failed to be supported by the evidence on four out of five counts? How can a set of almost axiomatic relationships, supported by years of social science research, be so far off the mark? Part of the reason may be that the policy model has failed to taken into account some of the conditions that must be placed upon contact theory; but we believe that there may be other reasons as well having to do with (1) inadequate research designs, (2) induced versus "natural" factors, and (3) changing conditions in the black cultural climate.

Most of the methodological procedures which have been used to develop various components of the integration policy model are not adequate. The single most important limitation is that they have been cross-sectional designs. That is, the studies have measured aspects of achievement or race relations at a single point in time, with causal inferences being drawn from comparisons of integrated groups with segregated groups. Such inferences are risky at best, since the cross-sectional design cannot control for self-selection factors. For example, the Coleman study showed that integrated black students had slightly higher achievement than segregated students, but it is more than likely that families of higher-achieving students move to integrated neighborhoods in the first place (for reasons of social class or other issues involving opportunity). Thus the cause-and-effect relationship may be the opposite to that suggested by the U.S. Civil Rights Commission report. In the Deutsch and Collins housing study, which found that integrated whites were more tolerant of blacks than segregated whites, it is possible that self-selection factors were operating which led the more tolerant white persons to choose the integrated housing project in the first place. It is fair to say that none of the studies before the ones we have reviewed had an opportunity to study the effects of large-scale induced integration over a reasonable period of time. Yet this is the only way the effects of integration can be storted out from differences which may originally exist between any two groups of persons.

The second reason for our findings in the race relations realm may have to do with the relatively contrived nature of current school integration programs. In all of the programs reviewed, the integration has been induced by the actions of state or local agencies; it has not occurred in a more natural way through individual voluntary actions. The use of busing, the relatively instantaneous transition from an all-black to an all-white environment, the fact of being part of a readily identifiable group in a new and strange setting, may all combine to enhance racial solidarity and increase separatist tendencies for black students. (We might find a very different picture for black families that move into predominantly white neighborhoods and allow their children some time to adjust to the new environment.) On the other hand, this set of mechanisms would not explain why white student attitudes in the receiving schools also tended to become less favorable to black students, as shown in the Ann Arbor, Riverside, and METCO studies. Moreover, these mehcanisms—if they are, in fact, operating—do not invalidate our evaluation of those current policies that focus precisely on induced school integration.

The final major reason why the integration policy model may fail is that the racial climate has changed drastically in the years since the Allport work and the Supreme Court decision. The most noteworthy change, of course, has been in the attitudes of black people. Although the majority of blacks may still endorse the concept of integration, many younger black leaders deemphasize integration as a major goal. Black identity, black control, and black equality are seen as the real issues, and integration is regarded as important only insofar as it advances these primary goals. Some black leaders, albeit the more militant ones, feel that integration might actually defeat attainment of these goals by dispersing the more talented blacks throughout the white community and thereby diluting their power potential. Integration is also seen as having white paternalistic overtones and as the means whereby the white man allays his guilty conscience while ignoring reform on the really important issues. Given these sentiments, school integration programs are seen by blacks not as a fulfillment of the goal of joining white society, but only as a means of obtaining better educational opportunities, which would ultimately lead to a more competitive position in the occupational and economic market.

Integrated schools *per se* are not the real issue; if schools in the black community provided education of the same quality as those in white communities, blacks would not be so interested in busing programs. In fact, when we asked students in the METCO program this question, almost 75 percent said they would prefer to attend their own community school if it were as good as the suburban schools. Of course, it is by no means clear that the suburban schools actually offer better education. Any improvement in facilities or teacher quality (the ultimate importance of which is called into question by the Coleman report) may be counteracted, as our data show, by stiffer competition and a more hostile and unfriendly student atmostphere. Black leaders who view school integration only as a means to better opportunity must take these other factors into account.

In the context of these new black attitudes, the Allport model may not be applicable, and contact with white students provided by induced school integration may enhance ideological tedencies towards separatism. The reality of contact seems to sensitize black students to the heightened racial identity and separatism that has been growing in the black community since the late 1960's. The explanation may be, in part, that the large socio-economic differences between black and white students are fully recognized only when contact enables them to witness these differences. The difficulty of bridging this gap, coupled with the knowledge that they are viewed by whites as having lower status, leads black students to reject white standards and relationships. They turn inward, as it were, stressing the uniqueness and value of their own race, shutting off contact with whites, and embracing a point of view which endorses separatism as a means toward preserving and elevating their own position. Those black students not in contact with whites may exhibit some of these tendencies due to the over-all contact with white society, but the lack of direct contact postpones the problem or avoids it altogether. This type of "contact-conflict" model may be used to explain the conflicts which occur between two different cultural groups which come into direct contact (e.g., Catholics and Protestants in Northern Ireland; Israelis and Arabs in the Middle East). Whether or not it is applicable on a larger scale, it would fit the data better and would provide a more realistic model for the school integration case.

It would be a mistake, of course, to view the increased racial solidarity of black students as a completely negative finding. The differences between black and white cultures make a certain amount of culture conflict inevitable and even necessary if an integrated society is to be realized. In fact, it would be reasonable *not* to expect conflict—which always accompanies the contact of two cultures—only if we did not believe that a distinct black culture exists in America. Although this belief was held at one time by a large number of social scientists, it is not so popular today. There is now growing recognition that a black culture does exist, at least in the eyes of many blacks, and that this culture stresses values, goals, and behavioral patterns that differ considerably from those of the predominant white culture.[41]

Up to this point, we have said little about the one positive finding of our research, the "channeling" effect whereby black students who attend white middle-class schools tend to get into higher quality colleges (even though they may not finish college at a higher rate than segregated black students). This finding should be heartening to those who have believed that integration does provide educational opportunities not found in inner-city black schools, although the finding must be considered a tentative one since it has been shown in only two fairly small studies. Also, the positive effects are limited to the college-bound, so that there still may be a question about the benefits of integration for the non-college-bound black students. And it may be that the "channeling" effect works only when the number is relatively small. Nonetheless, this kind of longer-term effect—and perhaps others as yet undiscovered—may turn out to provide a basis for certain types of integration plans.

POLICY IMPLICATIONS

It is obvious that the findings of integration research programs have serious implications for policy. Given the momentum which has built up over the last few years for the school integration movement, however, it is likely that in some quarters the data we have presented will be attacked on moral or methodological grounds and then summarily ignored. In other quarters the data may be met with rejoicing over the discovery of a club which can be used to beat back the pro-integration forces. But we hope these extreme reactions will be avoided and that a more balanced interpretation of our findings will prevail.

The most serious question is raised for mandatory busing (or induced integration) programs. If the justification for mandatory busing is based upon an integration policy model like the one we have tested here, then that justification has to be called into question. The data do not support the model on most counts. There may be justifications for school integration other than those in the integration policy model, but then the burden must fall upon those who support a given school integration program to demonstrate that it has the intended effects (with no unintended, negative side-effects). It also must be demonstrated that any such program is at least supported by the black community.

---

[41] James Jones, *Prejudice and Racism* (Reading, Mass.: Addison-Wesley, 1972); and L. Paul Metzger, "American Sociology and Black Assimilation: Conflicting Perspectives," *American Sociological Review*, LXXVI (1971), 627–647.

We want to stress this last point. Decisions must be based upon feelings of the black community as well as the white community. Many liberal educators have been so intent on selling integration to reluctant white communities that they risk the danger of ignoring the opinion of the black community. While many black leaders favor school integration, there are also many black persons who would much prefer an upgrading of schools in their own community. The recent (March 1972) National Black Political Convention in Gary, Indiana, condemned mandatory busing and school integration, arguing that such plans are racist and preserve a black minority structure. These views may not represent the entire black community, but they are indicative of the complexity and heterogeneity of black political opinion.[42] Whether or not a white community wants integration (and there are obviously many that do not), we must take into account the feelings of the group on whose behalf integration is advocated.

Although the data may fail to support mandatory busing as it is currently justified, these findings should not be used to halt voluntary busing programs. For one thing, we have stressed that the studies of integration so far have been over fairly short periods (one to five years), and there are possibilities of longer-term effects which are not visible until adulthood (not to speak of effects on characteristics not measured by the present research). More important, however, we have tentatively demonstrated one very significant longer-term benefit of integration for college-bound blacks. The "channeling" effect, if substantiated by further research, could form a substantial basis for voluntary programs whose focus is upon the college-bound black student. Even for this subgroup, of course, we have documented the trend towards separatist ideology. But the gain in educational opportunity may well outweigh this consequence in the eyes of the black community, as indeed it does now for programs like METCO. In fact, some persons will view these ideological changes, as well as any conflict that may accompany them, as an inevitable consequence of contact between two different cultures. If blacks and whites are ever to live in an integrated culture, they must begin learning and accepting their differences; and this cannot happen without contact. If contact engenders a certain amount of racial friction, many persons will feel the gains from school integration—both long-term and symbolic—more than make up for it.

To these questions of the symbolic and long-run benefits of induced school integration, the existing studies provide no answer. What

---

[42] A recent Gallup Poll reported that 46 per cent of a national non-white sample are opposed to busing for racial balance; 43 per cent were in favor, and 11 per cent were undecided (August 1971).

they do show is that, over the period of two or three years, busing does *not* lead to significant measurable gains in student achievement or interracial harmony (although it does lead to the channeling of black students to better colleges). The available evidence thus indicates that busing is *not* an effective policy instrument for raising the achievement of black students or for increasing interracial harmony. On the other hand, the existing studies do not rule out the possibility that in the longer run, or in other respects, busing may indeed prove to have substantial positive consequences.

The available evidence on busing, then, seems to lead to two clear policy conclusions. One is that massive mandatory busing for purposes of improving student achievement and interracial harmony is not effective and should not be adopted at this time. The other is that *voluntary* integration programs such as METCO, ABC, or Project Concern should be continued and positively encouraged by substantial federal and state grants. Such voluntary programs should be encouraged so that those parents and communities who believe in the symbolic and potential (but so far unconfirmed) long-run benefits of induced integration will have ample opportunity to send their children to integrated schools. Equally important, these voluntary programs will permit social scientists and others to improve and broaden our understanding of the longer-run and other consequences of induced school integration. With a more complete knowledge than we now possess of this complicated matter, we shall hopefully be in a better position to design effective public education policies that are known in advance to work to the benefit of all Americans, both black and white.

Even in voluntary school integration programs, however, our data indicate that certain steps should be taken which might help alleviate the problems of achievement and race relations. Wholesale integration without regard to achievement levels of white and black students can lead to potentially frustrating experiences. Some selectivity might be desirable so that both groups reflect a similar achievement capacity. Although a certain amount of racial problems may be inevitable, full education of both groups about the possibilities and causes of differences might ameliorate the kind of polarization that would endanger the program.

One must also consider the possibility that other types of integration programs may be more successful. We have said since the outset that our data do not necessarily apply to neighborhood integration brought about by the individual choice of black families. It is possible that such programs would be more successful over the long run, at least in terms of race relations. Being a member of the community might tend to ameliorate black feelings of separateness that are fostered in the relatively contrived busing situation. Whether or not this kind of program could also change standardized achievement levels remains to be seen. Since the differences between black and white achievement are so large and consistent across so many different settings and studies, we must entertain the possibility that no plan of school integration will lessen this gap. Research will have to be continued in this area before the full causal mechanisms are understood and a firm basis is established on which social action can accordingly be planned.

Although we have been critical of some aspects of the connection between social science and public policy in the integration movement, we do not want to imply that their connection should be lessened. On the contrary, the real goals of social science and public policy are not in opposition; the danger is rather that the connection may not be close enough to enable us to make sound decisions. Society can only benefit by those ties which combine the advantage of scientific knowledge with a clear awareness of its limitations.

Busing: a Review of "The Evidence"

THOMAS F. PETTIGREW,
ELIZABETH L. USEEM,
CLARENCE NORMAND, AND
MARSHALL S. SMITH

Thomas F. Pettigrew is professor of social psychology at Harvard University. He is a specialist in race relations and has served as a consultant to the United States Commission on Civil Rights. His books include *Epitaph for Jim Crow, A Profile of the Negro American,* and *Racially Separate or Together?.* He is also one of the principal authors of the 1967 Civil Rights Commission report, *Racial Isolation in the Public Schools.* Elizabeth L. Useem is an assistant professor of sociology at Boston State College. Clarence Normand is a graduate student in sociology at Harvard University. Marshall Smith is an associate professor in the Graduate School of Education, Harvard University, and is one of the co-authors, with Christopher Jencks, of *Inequality.*

David Armor's "The Evidence on Busing" [1] presented a distorted and incomplete review of this politically charged topic. We respect Armor's

[1] David J. Armor, "The Evidence on Busing," *The Public Interest,* No. 28 (Summer 1972), pp. 90–126.

Thomas F. Pettigrew, Elizabeth L. Useem, Clarence Normand, and Marshall S. Smith, "Busing: A Review of 'The Evidence'," *The Public Interest,* No. 30 (Winter 1973), pp. 88–118. Copyright © National Affairs Inc., 1973.

right to publish his views against "mandatory busing." But we challenge his claim that these views are supported by scientific evidence.
A full discussion of our reading of the relevant research would be too
lengthy and technical for the non-specialist. We must limit ourselves
here to outlining and discussing briefly our principal disagreements
with Armor, which center on four major points.

First, his article begins by establishing unrealistically high standards by which to judge the success of school desegregation. "Busing," he claims, works only if it leads—in *one* school year—to increased
achievement, aspirations, self-esteem, interracial tolerance, and life opportunities for black children. And "busing" must meet these standards in *all* types of interracial schools; no distinction is made between
merely desegregated and *genuinely integrated* schools.

This "integration policy model," as it is labeled, is *not* what social
scientists who specialize in race relations have been writing about
over the past generation. Indeed, Armor's criteria must surely be
among the most rigid ever employed for the evaluation of a change
program in the history of public education in the United States.

Second, the article presents selected findings from selected studies
as "*the* evidence on busing." The bias here is twofold. On the one hand,
the few studies mentioned constitute an incomplete list and are selectively negative in results. Unmentioned are at least seven investigations
—from busing programs throughout the nation—that meet the methodological criteria for inclusion and report *positive* achievement results
for black students. These seven studies are widely known.

On the other hand, only cursory descriptions are provided of the
few investigations that are reviewed. Mitigating circumstances surrounding black responses to desegregation are not discussed. For
example, we are not told that educatonal services for the transported
black pupils were actually *reduced* with the onset of desegregation in
three of the cited cities. In addition, negative findings consistent with
the paper's anti-busing thesis are emphasized, while positive findings
from these same cities are either obscured or simply ignored. Newer
studies from three of the cited cities showing more positive results are
not discussed.

Positive findings are also obscured by the utilization of an unduly
severe standard. The achievement gains of black students in desegregated schools are often compared with white gains, rather than
with the achievement of black students in black schools. But such a
standard ignores the possibility that *both* racial groups can make
more meaningful educational advances in interracial schools. Indeed,
this possibility actually occurs in three of the cities mentioned by
Armor. Yet he does not inform us of this apparent dual success of

desegregation; instead, "busing" is simply rated a failure because the black children did not far outgain the improving white children.

Third, the paper's anti-busing conclusions rest primarily on the findings from one short-term study conducted by Armor himself. This investigation focused on a voluntary busing program in metropolitan Boston called METCO. Yet this study is probably the weakest reported in the paper. Our reexamination of its data finds that it has extremely serious methodological problems.

Two major problems concern deficiencies of the control group. To test the effects of "busing" and school desegregation, a control group should obviously consist exclusively of children who neither are "bused" nor attend desegregated schools. But our check of this critical point reveals that this is not the case. Among the 82 control students used to test the achievement effects of MECTO at all 10 grade levels, we obtained records on 55. Only 21 of these 55 actually attended segregated schools in the tested year of 1968–69. Many of the 34 (62 percent) desegregated children by necessity utilized buses and other forms of transportation to get to school.

Incredible as it sounds, then, Armor compared a group of children who were bused to desegregated schools with another group of children which included many who *also* were bused to desegregated schools. Not surprisingly, then, he found few differences between them. But this complete lack of adequate controls renders his METCO research of no scientific interest in the study of "busing" and school desegregation. Since this METCO investigation furnished the chief "evidence" against "busing," Armor's conclusions are severely challenged by this point alone.

Serious, too, is an enormous non-response rate in the second test administration, a problem alluded to by Armor only in a footnote. For the elementary students, only 51 percent of the eligible METCO students and 28 percent of the eligible "control" students took part in both of the achievement test sessions. The achievement results for junior and senior high students are also rendered virtually meaningless by the participation of only 44 percent of the eligible METCO students and 20 percent of the eligible "control" students. Compare these percentages to the survey standard of 70 to 80 percent, and one can appreciate the magnitude of the possible selection bias introduced into the METCO results by the widespread lack of student participation. Efforts to compensate for these high non-response rates through the use of cross-sectional samples that also suffer from extensive non-response are insufficient.

There are other problems in the METCO study. Some children were included who initially performed as well as the test scoring allowed and therefore could not possibly demonstrate "improvement"; in fact, these pupils comprise one sixth of all the junior high pupils tested for achievement gains in reading. Moreover, the conditions for the third administration of the attitude tests were different for the METCO students and the "controls": The former took the tests at school and the latter took them at home with their parents as proctors. Even apart from the severe control group problems, then, the faulty research design makes any conclusion about differences in racial attitudes between the two groups hazardous.

The inadequate discussion of the METCO study in Armor's article makes it virtually impossible for even the discerning reader to evaluate it properly. We uncovered its many errors only from unpublished earlier materials and from reanalyzing the data ourselves. The METCO discussion is inadequate in other ways. Differential statistical standards are employed, with less rigorous standards applied to findings congruent with the article's anti-busing thesis; attitude differences among METCO schools are not shown; and misleading claims of consistency with other research findings are made.

From this assortment of "evidence" Armor concludes authoritatively that "busing" fails on four out of five counts. It does not lead, he argues, to improved achievement, grades, aspirations, and racial attitudes for black children; yet, despite these failures, he admits that desegregated schools do seem somehow to lead more often to college enrolment for black students.

The picture is considerably more positive, as well as more complex, than Armor paints it. For example, when specified school conditions are attained, research has repeatedly indicated that desegregated schools improve the academic performance of black pupils. Other research has demonstrated that rigidly high and unrealistic aspirations actually deter learning; thus, a slight lowering of such aspirations by school desegregation can lead to better achievement and cannot be regarded as a failure of "busing." Moreover, "militancy" and "black consciousness and solidarity" are not negative characteristics, as Armor's article asserts, and their alleged development in desegregated schools could well be regarded as a further success, not a failure, of "busing." Finally, the evidence that desegregated education sharply expands the life opportunities of black children is more extensive than he has indicated.

Consequently, Armor's sweeping policy conclusion against "mandatory busing" is neither substantiated nor warranted. Not only does it rely upon impaired and incomplete "evidence," but in a real sense his paper is not about "busing" at all, much less "mandatory busing." Three of the cities discussed—among them Boston, the subject of

Armor's own research—had *voluntary*, not "mandatory busing." "Busing" was never cited as an independent variable, and many of the desegregation studies discussed involved some children who were not bused to reach their interracial schools. Indeed, in Armor's own investigation of METCO, some of the METCO children were not bused while many of the controls were.

Fourth, objections must be raised to the basic assumptions about racial change that undergird the entire article. Public school desegregation is regarded as largely a technical matter, a matter for social scientists more than for the courts. Emphasis is placed solely on the adaptive abilities of black children rather than on their constitutional rights. Moreover, the whole national context of individual and institutional racism is conveniently ignored, and interracial contact under any conditions is assumed to be "integration."

Now we wish to pursue these basic points in more detail.

I

Unrealistic Standards for Judging the Effects of "Busing"

The article advances an "integration policy model" which it claims grew out of social science and guided "the integration movement." The model allegedly maintained that *all* school desegregation would result in improved black achievement, aspirations, self-esteem, racial attitudes, and educational and occupational opportunities.[2] This interpretation of "the integration policy model" is at sharp variance with what specialists in this field have been writing over the past generation.[3] The fundamental premise of social scientists over these years was that racial segregation as it is typically imposed in the United States leads directly to a multitude of negative effects not only for black America but for the nation at large. (The evidence for this premise

---

[2] *Ibid.*, p. 96.

[3] This is true from the early statements on the desegregation process by Clark (Kenneth Clark, "Desegregation: An Appraisal of the Evidence," *Journal of Social Issues*, Vol. 9 [Fall 1953], 2–76), Williams and Ryan (Robin Williams and Margaret Ryan, *Schools in Transition: Community Experiences in Desegregation* [Chapel Hill: University of North Carolina Press, 1954]), Johnson (Guy Johnson, "A Sociologist Looks at Racial Desegregation in the South," *Social Forces*, Vol. 32 [1954], 1–10), and others (summarized in A. L. Coleman, "Social Scientists' Predictions About Desegregation," *Social Forces*, Vol. 38 [1960], 258–262) to more recent statements by Katz (Irwin Katz, "Review of Evidence Relating to Effects of Desegregation on the Intellectual Performance of Negroes," *American Psychologist*, Vol. 19 [1964], 381–399) and Pettigrew (Thomas F. Pettigrew, "The Negro in Education: Problems and Proposals," in I. Katz and P. Gurin, Eds., *Race and the Social Sciences* [New York: Basic Books, 1969]; and Thomas F. Pettigrew, *Racially Separate or Together?* [New York: McGraw-Hill, 1971]).

is extensive, and Armor does not contest the premise.) But social scientists have not made the error of contending that because enforced racial segregation has negative effects, *all* racial desegregation will have positive effects. It requires little imagination to think of hostile conditions of school desegregation that would limit its benefits for both races.

At the heart of this misconception is a persistent misreading of Gordon Allport's [4] theory of intergroup contact. Armor cites a quotation from Allport delineating the crucial conditions that he held to be essential before positive effects could be expected from intergroup contact: equal status, common goals, institutional supports, and a non-competitive atmosphere that is likely to lead to "'the perception of common interests and common humanity." Yet Armor summarizes this quotation by stating: "The clear key to breaking the vicious circle, then, was contact." This is *not* what Allport wrote; the key, Allport argued, is contact *under particular conditions.*

Later in his article Armor adds a brief discussion of one of these conditions—equal status between the two groups. Allport and other contact theorists have maintained that this condition is met by equal status, dignity, and access to resources *within* the contact situation itself.[5] Armor reinterprets this condition so that it is met only if the two groups bring equal societal status *to* the situation, a rigorous test indeed in a society where racial discrimination has long been endemic. We know of no relevant contact research that supports this reinterpretation of the theory, and vague references to conflict in Northern Ireland and the Middle East hardly suffice as evidence. But armed with his own reinterpretation, Armor writes: "Therefore, we have to question whether integration programs for black and white children can ever fulfill the equal status condition as long as socio-economic and academic inequalities are not eliminated." [6] Here the misreading of Allport's contact theory is fashioned into not only an explanation of presumed "negative" results from interracial schools but a not-so-subtle rationale for at best gradualism and at worst a return to racially segregated education throughout the nation.

The basic weakness, then, in this description of an "integration policy model" is that it assumes positive results for *all* interracial schools rather than for just those meeting the conditions for optimal contact. This erroneous assumption is best illustrated by reference to the chief policy document relied upon by Armor: *Racial Isolation in*

---

[4] Gordon W. Allport, *The Nature of Prejudice* (Cambridge, Mass.: Addison-Wesley, 1954).

[5] For example, Pettigrew, *Racially Separate or Together?*

[6] Armor, "Evidence," p. 111.

the Public Schools, issued by the U.S. Commission on Civil Rights.[7] The quotation Armor cites from this report emphasizes the harmful effects of racially isolated schooling, and it does not specify all of the five hypotheses which he somehow deduces from it. That the Commission clearly understood that interracial schools in and of themselves are not necessarily effective schools is demonstrated by the following passage which was not quoted:

> Whether school desegregation is effective depends on a number of factors. These include the leadership given by State and local officials; the application of the plan to all schools in the community; the measures taken to minimize the possibility of racial friction in the newly desegregated schools; the maintenance or improvement of educational standards; the desegregation of classes within the schools as well as the schools themselves, and the availability of supportive services for individual students who lag in achievement.

The Commission Report discusses these factors in detail for over eight pages, factors neither mentioned nor measured by Armor. "The integration policy model," then, sets up unrealistic standards for judging the effects of "busing" by ignoring the conditions specified by the two principal sources cited. Its five criteria for success constitute a "straw man," far exceeding the standards applied for the evaluation of other educational programs.

The Critical Distinction Between Desegregation and Integration is Ignored

The racial desegregation of schools is not a static but a complex, dynamic process. To evaluate it fairly, the critical conditions under which it takes place must be assessed. For this purpose, it is important to distinguish between desegregation and integration. Desegregation is achieved by simply ending segregation and bringing blacks and whites together; it implies nothing about the quality of the interracial interaction. Integration involves Allport's four conditions for positive intergroup contact, cross-racial acceptance, and equal dignity and access to resources for both racial groups.

The neglect of this distinction besets not only Armor's theoretical contentions but his empirical ones as well. No effort is made to look inside of the schools at the *process* of desegregation. The cursory descriptions of the "busing" investigations tell virtually nothing about the conditions of interracial contact that prevailed. (Indeed, a few

---

[7] United States Commission on Civil Rights, *Racial Isolation in the Schools* (Washington, D.C.: U.S. Government Printing Office, 1967).

of the initial reports of these studies failed to describe contact conditions.) For example, we should have been informed by Armor that transporated black children in some Riverside schools arrive and leave earlier than the untransported white children and that they have separate reading classes—hardly practices likely to generate interracial contact and lead to integration.[8] And we might have been told that minority students in Riverside who were most likely to be in interracial classrooms (high-ability students) performed far better after desegregation than before.[9]

In fact, in his Detroit deposition for school segregation, Armor admitted that he had no measures or knowledge in his own study of the METCO schools of such crucial factors as teacher expectations and preparation, the racial composition of the faculties, ability tracking practices, and curriculum changes. A review of "the evidence on busing" is misleading at best without consideration of these indicators of the desegregation versus integration distinction.

II

A Biased and Incomplete Selection of Studies

Armor's article makes no attempt to review all of the available evidence on "busing," as its title implies. Instead, the reader is told about only a small number of studies, selected with an apparent bias toward those reporting few positive effects. One hint of this selection is found in Armor's footnote 1, where we learn that he arbitrarily excludes the entire southern United States from his purview, though this severe restriction is not indicated either in his title or his conclusions against "mandatory busing." This unexplained exclusion seems unwarranted, for the bulk of court-ordered "mandatory busing" has occurred in the South.

Armor omits at least *seven* key desegregation investigations—only one of which is from the South—that reach conclusions in conflict with those of his paper. All seven of these desegregation programs involved "busing," and all seven of the studies meet the paper's two stated criteria for inclusion—longitudinal data and an adequate control group. Table 1 summarizes these neglected research reports. Though five of them spanned only one school year, all seven reach

---

[8] Harry Singer, "Effects of Integration on Achievement of Anglos, Blacks, and Mexican-Americans," unpublished paper, Department of Education, University of California, Riverside, 1972.

[9] Muriel C. Purl, "The Achievement of Pupils in Desegregated Schools," unpublished paper, Riverside Unified School District, Riverside, California, 1971.

positive conclusions concerning the effects of school desegregation upon the academic performance of black children. Moreover, none of them found that the process lowered white academic performance. No matter how Armor might wish to view these studies in retrospect, there was no reason for their omission in a paper that claimed to present "*the* evidence on busing."

Space limitations prevent a discussion here of these neglected investigations, but five points should be made about them. First, a number of them share methodological problems with the studies that Armor did choose to discuss. Indeed, reviewers of this research literature have uniformly found it methodologically weak.[10] Second, these seven by no means exhaust the relevant research literature that meets the paper's dual criteria for inclusion. There are studies on desegregation without busing that reveal positive achievement effects.[11] There are a few others that were also left out that found no significant achievement gains associated with desegregation.[12] From the perspective of the desegregation versus integration distinction, this mixed picture is precisely what one would expect. Third, these seven studies are not obscure reports; all but the more recent Goldsboro and Sacramento studies are cited in one or more of the standard reviews available on the topic.[13]

Fourth, the positive achievement effects revealed by these studies

---

[10] Robert A. Matthai, "The Academic Performance of Negro Students: An Analysis of the Research Findings from Several Busing Programs," unpublished paper, Graduate School of Education, Harvard University, 1968; Robert P. O'Reilly (Ed.), *Racial and Social Class Isolation in the Schools* (New York: Praeger, 1970); Nancy St. John, "Desegregation and Minority Group Performance," *Review of Educational Research,* Vol. 40 (1970), 111–134; and Meyer Weinberg, *Desegregation Research: An Appraisal* (Bloomington, Indiana: Phi Delta Kappa, 1968).

[11] Louis V. Anderson, "The Effects of Desegregation on the Achievement and Personality Patterns of Negro Children," unpublished doctoral dissertation, George Peabody College, 1966; James H. Fortenberry, "The Achievement of Negro Pupils in Mixed and Non-Mixed Schools," unpublished doctoral dissertation, University of Oklahoma, 1959; and Robert B. Frary and Thomas M. Goolsby, Jr., "Achievement of Integrated and Segregated Negro and White First Graders in a Southern City," *Integrated Education,* Vol. 8, No. 4 (1970), 48–52.

[12] For example, David J. Fox, "Free Choice Open Enrollment—Elementary Schools" (New York: Center for Urban Education, 1966) (unpublished paper); David J. Fox, "Evaluation of the New York City Title I Educational Projects 1966–1967; Expansion of the Free Choice Open Enrollment Program" (New York: Center for Urban Education, 1967) (unpublished paper); and David J. Fox, *et al.,* "Services to Children in Open Enrollment Receiving Schools: Evaluation of ESEA Title I projects in New York City, 1967–1968 (New York: Center for Urban Education, 1968) (unpublished paper).

[13] Matthai, "Academic Performance"; O'Reilly, *Racial and Social Class Isolation;* St. John, "Desegregation and Minority Group Performance"; and Weinberg, *Desegregation Research.*

TABLE 1. SEVEN NEGLECTED DESEGREGATION INVESTIGATIONS.

| | | | DESIGN | | | ACHIEVEMENT RESULTS | |
| STUDY | | | | | | | |
Place	Author(s)	Grade Level	Type of Comparison	Control Variables	Time of Desegregation	For Black Children	For White Children (If Tested)
SOUTHERN DESEGREGATION							
Goldsboro, N.C.	King & Mayer [a] McCullough [b]	7-11 cohort	White students and trend during segregation	Convergence curves for regression to mean effects and pre-desegregation trends	2 years	Statistically significant gains in reading closing part of black/white differential; gains in math scores do not close racial gap; gains greatest for initially high achievers	Both reading and math gains; gains greatest for high achievers
SUBURBAN BUSING PROGRAMS							
Newark-Verona, N.J.	Zdep & Joyce [c]	1-2	Comparable non-transfers	—	1 year	Statistically significantly greater total achievement gains for desegrated in both grades	No negative effects (only difference favors the desegregated)
Rochester-West Irondequoit, N.Y.	Rock *et al.* [d]	K-2	Comparable non-transfers	Teachers' ratings of ability	3 years	Statistically significantly greater verbal, reading, and math achievement gains on 13 of 27 comparisons for desegregated; no significant differences on remaining 14 comparisons	No negative effects (only differences favor the desegregated)
NORTHERN CENTRAL CITY DESEGREGATION							
Buffalo, N.Y.	Banks & DiPasquale [e]	5-7	Comparable non-transfers	—	1 year	2½ months greater achievement gain for the desegregated	No negative effects

132

Location	Study	Grades	Control	Controlled variables	Duration	Results	No negative effects
New York, N.Y.	Slone [f]	4	Comparable non-transfers	—	1 year	Statistically significantly greater math achievement gains, and somewhat greater reading gains ($p < .10$), for desegregated	No negative effects
Philadelphia, Pa.	Laird & Weeks [g]	4-6	Comparable non-transfers	I.Q., grade and sex	1 year	Statistically significantly greater reading, and somewhat greater math, achievement gains for desegregated in fourth and fifth grades	—
Sacramento, Cal.	Morrison & Stivers [h]	2-6	Comparable non-transfers	—	1 year	Statistically significantly greater gains on three of ten comparisons (5 classes on 2 tests) and greater gains on 6 more, for desegregated	—

[a] Similar results for a cohort of second through fifth grade students have also been obtained in Goldsboro. After two years of desegregated education the *standardized* verbal and mathematical computation achievement scores of both the black and white students had risen. The verbal gains, though not the mathematical computation gains, closed the racial differential slightly. Robert R. Mayer, University of North Carolina at Chapel Hill, personal communication. Charles E. King and Robert R. Mayer, "A Pilot Study of the Social and Educational Impact of School Desegregation," unpublished report, North Carolina Central University and University of North Carolina at Chapel Hill, 1971.

[b] James S. McCullough, "Academic Achievement Under School Desegregation in a Southern City," unpublished paper, Department of City and Regional Planning, University of North Carolina at Chapel Hill, January 1972.

[c] Stanley M. Zdep and Diane Joyce, "The Newark-Verona Plan for Sharing Educational Opportunity," (unpublished report PR-69-13) (Princeton: Educational Testing Service, 1969).

[d] William C. Rock, Joanne E. Long, Herman R. Goldberg, and L. William Heinrich, "A Report on a Cooperative Program Between a Suburban School District and a City School District," unpublished paper, Rochester School District, Rochester, New York, 1968.

[e] Ronald Banks and Mary E. DiPasquale, "A Study of the Educational Effectiveness of Integration," unpublished report, Buffalo Public Schools, Buffalo, New York, 1969.

[f] Irene W. Slone, "The Effects of One School Pairing on Pupil Achievement, Anxieties, and Attitudes," unpublished doctoral dissertation, New York University, 1968.

[g] Mary Alice Laird and Grace Weeks, "The Effect of Busing on Achievement in Reading and Arithmetic in Three Philadelphia Schools," unpublished paper, Division of Research, The School District of Philadelphia, 1966.

[h] Edward B. Morrison and James A. Stivers, "A Summary of the Assessments of the District's Integration Programs, 1964-1971," *Research Report No. 9 of Series 1971-72*, Sacramento City Unified School District, Sacramento, California, 1971.

are often not just statistically significant (Armor's criterion) but, more important, are educationally significant as well. The study from Buffalo by Banks and DiPasquale,[14] for example, found a 2.5 month achievement advantage for the desegregated children. Over a 12-year school career, were such an advantage to be replicated each year, this would constitute 2.5 extra years of achievement—a critical addition that could mean the difference between functional illiteracy and marketable skills. Finally, these seven studies do not measure the "pure" effects of desegregation any more than those cited by Armor. Probably there are no instances of school desegregation that are not confounded with curriculum changes, school quality, and other educational alterations. But our point is made: The few studies mentioned in Armor's article constitute an incomplete list and are selectively negative in results.

Biased and Incomplete Descriptions are Provided of the Few Studies Discussed

The cursory reviews of the few studies that Armor did select for attention allow only biased and incomplete descriptions. Since his article never probes the process going on inside the schools, it repeatedly omits mitigating circumstances surrounding black responses to desegregation. For example, no mention is made of the fact that educational services for the transported black students in Ann Arbor, Riverside, and Berkeley were actually *reduced* with the onset of desegregation.[15] Nor is there any indication that Riverside initially placed many of its bused minority children in the same classrooms, and often with low-achieving white children.[16] No "integration model," not even the new one devised by Armor, is fairly tested under such conditions.

Moreover, the positive findings that favor desegregation in these studies are often obscured or simply ignored by Armor. In the case of Hartford, for instance, only Wechsler I.Q. data are cited, while extensive results from the Primary Mental Abilities Test and measures of school achievement go undiscussed. When all three types of tests are considered together, a clear pattern of larger gains for the trans-

---

[14] Banks and DiPasquale, "Study of the Educational Effectiveness of Integration."

[15] Patricia M. Carrigan, "School Desegregation Via Compulsory Pupil Transfer: Early Effects on Elementary School Children," Final Report for Project No. 6–1320, U.S. Office of Education; Robert D. Frelow, "A Comparative Study of Resource Allocation: Compensatory Education and School Desegregation," unpublished doctoral dissertation, University of California, Berkeley, 1971; and Purl, "Achievement of Pupils."

[16] I. S. Henrick, "The Development of a School Integration Plan in Riverside, California: A History and Perspective," unpublished paper of the University of California, Riverside, and the Riverside Unified School District.

ported children emerges for all four grades from kindergarten through the third grade.[17] Likewise, black pupils in Ann Arbor attained a substantially higher mean I.Q. after one year of desegregation, but this fact is lost from sight by the use of a white comparison. A range of interesting results from Riverside is also omitted. Purl [18] found that: (a) Bused students who were more dispersed in the classes of their receiving schools outperformed those who—through ability grouping or other means—were clustered in near-segregation style. (b) While the mean achievement of minority pupils with low initial ability scores declined relative to grade level, the achievement of minority pupils with high initial ability scores rose in the desegregated schools. (c) Minority children transported to schools characterized by higher achievement of the receiving white students gain significantly more than comparable minority children transported to schools characterized by low achievement, an effect not linked to the social class levels of the receiving students. (d) The one group of bused minority students who began their schooling in interracial schools achieved better than those who had first experienced segregated education.

The incomplete descriptions also fail to reveal major methodological weaknesses in these cited studies. The Berkeley [19] investigation, as a case in point, utilized different tests for comparison over time, precisely the same defect for which an investigation in Rochester [20] showing a number of positive results is rejected without discussion. The White Plains [21] investigation employs inadequate control groups drawn from earlier time periods, a faulty procedure that confounds the effects of events over time with those of desegregation.[22] Indeed, the negative conclusions of a follow-up study in Ann Arbor are given without

---

[17] Thomas W. Mahan, *Project Concern—1966–1968* (Hartford: Hartford Public Schools, 1968).

[18] Purl, "Achievement of Pupils."

[19] Berkeley Unified School District, "Comparison of Achievement Test Scores Made by Berkeley Elementary Students Pre and Post Integration Eras, 1967–70," unpublished report, Berkeley, California, 1971.

[20] Rochester City School District, "Final Report: A Three-Year Longitudinal Study to Assess a Fifteen Point Plan to Reduce Racial Tension," Rochester, New York, 1970.

[21] White Plains Public Schools, "A Three-Year Evaluation of the White Plains Racial Balance Plan," unpublished report, White Plains, New York, 1967.

[22] Matthai, "Academic Performance," describes the White Plains research ("Three-Year Evaluation") as follows: "The small numbers of Negro students tested (33 desegregated students, 36 from previous years); the lack of explicitness about comparability of the groups under study and the rationale of sample selection; the occasionally contradictory figures and tables; the lack of significance tests; the selection of only one grade level for study (plus a truncated comparison of another grade level); and the almost impenetrable prose of the research report make this study utterly equivocal."

recording the fact that it failed to meet either of the criteria purportedly used for inclusion, for it had no control group whatsoever nor did it gather longitudinal data on the same test.[23]

Finally, several newer reports on these same cities that present results favorable to desegregation are not utilized. Mahan and Mahan,[24] for example, provide more refined analyses on the Hartford achievement data. Pooling the first, third, and fifth grades,[25] they show that the desegregated children in Project Concern do significantly better after two years than their comparable segregated controls on the Wechsler I.Q. and on both the verbal and quantitative scores of the Primary Mental Abilities Test.

Though he cited a Master's thesis on New Haven desegregation, Armor failed to cite a better-known doctoral dissertation on the same city.[26] Samuels[27] studied 138 black students who had all attended inner-city kindergartens in 1969 and then were assigned *randomly* to one of three conditions: bused into suburban schools, received intensive compensatory education in New Haven schools, or attended regular New Haven schools. After two years, Samuels found that the bused children possessed significantly higher reading scores than the two control groups as well as higher word knowledge scores that approach statistical significance ($p < .07$). Their self-image scores were slightly higher, but not significantly different. Comparisons on word analysis and mathematics yielded no significant differences.

In Berkeley, Frelow[28] studied the third and fourth grade achievement of poor children, most of them black, over a six-year period that

---

[23] F. D. Aberdeen, "Adjustment to Desegregation: A Description of Some Differences among Negro Elementary Pupils," unpublished doctoral dissertation, University of Michigan, 1969; and Carrigan, "School Desegregation Via Compulsory Pupil Transfer."

[24] Thomas Mahan and Alice Mahan, unpublished report, 1971.

[25] Grades two and four were excluded because of problems of sample dropout. Earlier work showed somewhat greater gains for the desegregated youngsters in the second grade and for the segregated youngsters in the fourth grade (Mahan, *Project Concern*), so the omission of these two grades should not bias the results of this new analysis (Thomas Mahan, personal communication).

[26] More recently, a study has been released by the Center for Urban Education concerning 25 black first, second, and third graders bused under Project Concern from Bridgeport to Westport, Connecticut. Though the sample size renders its findings tentative, it found marked academic improvement for the "bused" children during one-and-a-half years when compared with similar unbused children remaining in the segregated sending school in Bridgeport. The study also found no ill effects among the desegregated white children (Barabara Heller, Carla Drije, Barry Kaufman, and Morton Inger, *Project Concern: Westport, Connecticut* [New York: Center for Urban Education, 1972]).

[27] Joseph M. Samuels, "A Comparison of Projects Representative of Compensatory, Busing and Non-Compensatory Programs for Inner-City Students," unpublished doctoral dissertation, University of Connecticut, 1971.

[28] Frelow, "Comparative Study of Resource Allocation."

witnessed rapid changes in the city's schools. Though this design, like that used in White Plains, lacks contemporaneous controls, he found that achievement scores rose significantly after the introduction of compensatory programs and went slightly higher still after desegregation despite a reduction in services. Frelow concludes that "when gains are measured against level of instructional services, desegregation produces the most prominent achievement results."

The Use of White Control Groups
is Inadequate and Often Misleading

The contention that black children will learn more in integrated than in segregated schools is not tested when black data are compared with those of white control groups. Moreover, the use of a desegregated white control group ignores the possibility that *both* whites and blacks could benefit significantly from integration without "the racial gap" in achievement closing at all. As a matter of fact, precisely this possibility occurs in Riverside, Berkeley, and Ann Arbor—though this is not mentioned by Armor and is allowed to mask black gains in desegregated schools.

For Riverside, Armor reports that even for the fourth-grade group that had been desegregated since kindergarten "the minority/white gap had not diminished. . . ." But actually the white test scores being used for a comparison had improved after desegregation relative to national norms.[29] Thus, the fact that the minority students held the "gap" constant represents improvement; this is indicated, too, by these minority students' relative gains in grade equivalents.

For Berkeley, Armor reports in a footnote that "black achievement is as far behind (or *futher* behind) white achievement after two years of integration as before integration." But *both* white and black grade equivalents in grades one, two, and three went up across age cohorts after two years of desegregation; yet since they rose in virtually equal amounts, the "black/white gap" was not narrowed.[30] The measure here is grade equivalents, not percentiles. Thus, keeping "the racial gap" from expanding is an accomplishment in itself for desegregation, since the typical result of segregated schools is an ever-widening "racial gap" in grade equivalents.[31]

---

29 Purl, "Achievement of Pupils."

30 Berkeley Unified School District, "Comparison of Achievement Test Scores"; and Berkeley Unified School District, "Preliminary Report of Group Achievement Test Results for 1970–71," unpublished report, Berkeley, California, 1971.

31 James Coleman, *et al.*, *Equality of Educational Opportunity* (Washington, D.C.: U.S. Government Printing Office, 1966); and Frederick Mosteller and D. P. Moynihan, Eds., *On Equality of Educational Opportunity* (New York: Random House, 1972).

The most extreme case of this misleading use of white controls, however, occurs for Ann Arbor.[32] Here the bused black students were "a multi-problem group" with a greater incidence of "general health problems" and behavioral "problems requiring special professional help." Yet they gained an average of 3.86 I.Q. points during their first year of desegregation. They were compared with generally high-status white children, many of whom came from academic families, who gained an average of 4.28 I.Q. points. "Busing" failed, in Armor's terms, because "the racial gap" did not close. But can a program which utilizes fewer services with a multi-problem group of youngsters, and yet is associated with a nearly four-point average increase in I.Q. during one school year, be unquestionably ruled a failure? We think not, even if these "bused" pupils did not gain more than high-achieving white youngsters from a university community.

This point represents a crucial difference between our perspective and Armor's. We believe it to be unrealistic to expect any type of educational innovation to close most of the racial differential in achievement while gross racial disparties, especially economic ones, remain in American society. Furthermore, we know of no social scientists who ever claimed school desegregation alone could close most of the differential. We are pleased to note the many instances where effective desegregation has apparently benefited the achievement of both black and white children, and where over a period of years it appears to close approximately a fourth of the differential.

But to insist that "mandatory busing" must close most of the achievement differential by itself in a short time or be abolished is, to understate the case, an extreme position. Indeed, Armor himself has wavered on this point. In *The Public Interest* he wrote: "The ideal control group, of course, would consist of black students who are identical to the integrated students in every way except for the integrated experience,"[33] though white students in the same school constituted an "adequate" control. Later, however, while testifying in support of anti-busing legislation before the Senate Subcommittee on Education, he used white pupils as the critical comparison. This stern criterion leads to some strange conclusions. A desegregation program that dramatically raises the achievement levels of both racial groups is judged a failure when it does not close most of the racial disparity, but another desegregation program that entirely closes the gap by raising the blacks' scores and *lowering* the whites' scores would have to be deemed a success!

---

[32] Carrigan, "School Desegregation Via Compulsory Pupil Transfer."
[33] Armor, "The Evidence on Busing," p. 97.

III

Serious Weaknesses in the METCO Research

Armor's article relies most heavily upon his own research on Boston's suburban program known as METCO. Far greater space—including a dozen graphs—is devoted to the METCO research than to all of the other research combined; and the METCO work is the only investigation that is relied upon for support of all five of the conclusions concerning the effects of "busing." Yet a careful reanalysis of these METCO data reveals a host of serious weaknesses that center on five concerns: (a) the unrepresentativeness of the METCO program, and problems regarding (b) the control group, (c) the sample, (d) test administration, and (e) the analysis.

a. *Unrepresentativeness of METCO program.* Not only is "busing" not "mandatory" in METCO, but the program is highly atypical of desegregation efforts with "busing" around the nation. METCO is a voluntary program, and it has disproportionately attracted middle-class black students. This class bias may help explain why METCO children in the first year of the program attained a higher average I.Q. than the white national average [34] and why in Figures 1 and 2 of Armor's article all 10 grade levels show relatively high achievement scores. Moreover, METCO children comprise only a minute fraction of their student bodies, with less than four percent in any one school in 1969. Black faculty are rare in virtually all of the METCO schools. Indeed, some METCO schools have had all-white staffs, and until recently even all of the bus drivers were white. Thus, given METCO's "tokenism" in students and staff, as well as its social class bias, direct generalizations from this program to "busing" throughout the United States appear dubious at best.

b. *Control group problems.* The most serious weakness of the METCO research involves the students who were employed as "controls." The study's design obviously requires that none of these control students were either desegregated or "bused." But a careful review of the available records reveals that this essential condition is not met. [35] Among the 41 "control" youngsters at the elementary level, we obtained records on 17. Only seven of these 17 pupils were actually

---

[34] David K. Archibald, "Report on Change in Academic Achievement for a Sample of Elementary School Children: Progress Report on METCO," unpublished paper, Brookline, Massachusetts.

[35] We wish to thank Robert Hayden of METCO, the Boston School System, and the families of the children contacted for their helpful cooperation in securing these data.

attending segregated schools during 1968–69, while 10 (59 percent) were attending desegregated schools. Similarly, among the 38 (out of a total of 41) "controls" at the junior and senior high levels whose records we obtained, only 14 were in segregated schools during the tested year, while 24 (63 percent) were attending desegregated schools.

All told, then, of the 55 students whose records were secured, 34 (62 percent) actually went to desegregated schools and many of them used buses and other means of transporation.[36] Even if we assume that all 27 students whose records were unavailable went to segregated schools (an unlikely possibility), these data still mean that at least 41 percent (34/82) of the "control" students were in fact experiencing a racially desegregated education. Indeed, these desegregated "controls" were generally in schools with a greater inter-racial mixture than those attended by the METCO children.

This failure of the METCO study to have an adequate control group cannot be overemphasized. It means that *all* of the METCO comparisons between the METCO and "control" children in Armor's article are not valid indications of any differences attributable to "busing" or school desegregation. For such comparisons may also reflect the different effects of suburban versus inner-city desegrega-tion and token versus substantial desegregation. In short, we believe this weakness alone eliminates the METCO study from being relevant to "the evidence on busing," and makes our further criticisms of the study almost superfluous.

Other problems involve the use of siblings of METCO students as "controls." "This design feature by no means guarantees the equating of the groups," wrote Herbert Walberg [37] in the initial write-up of this investigation, "since there may be bias in the family's choice of the child to be bused. . . ." Indeed, there is potential bias in the selection by families, but the direction is not clear. The academically superior child might be chosen more often by his parents; or, as METCO officials suspect, the child having difficulties in Boston's schools might be chosen more often. Moreover, the use of siblings for

---

[36] We are here following the standard practice of defining a segregated school as one with a predominantly black student body. Had we employed a majority-white definition for a desegregated school, the "control" percentage attending desegregated would be 53 per cent (29/55) instead of 62 per cent (34/55). Small numbers of Chinese-American and Spanish-speaking students in a few of the schools explain the minor difference.

[37] Herbert J. Walberg, "An Evaluation of an Urban-Suburban School Busing Program: Student Achievement and Perception of Class Learning Environments" (unpublished paper) (Boston: METCO, 1969).

TABLE 2. METCO SAMPLE SIZES BY GRADE LEVEL
AND TYPE OF SCHOOL.

| Grade Level | METCO[a] | "Control" | Type of School Attended By "Controls" | | |
			Segregated	Desegre-gated	Unavailable
3rd & 4th	88	14	2	3	9
5th & 6th	59	27	5	7	15
Elementary School Totals	147	41	7	10	24
7th	47	11	6	5	0
8th	31	10	4	5	1
9th	47	6	1	4	1
Junior High School Totals	125	27	11	14	2
10th	53	4	0	3	1
11th	18	8	3	5	0
12th	1	2	0	2	0
Senior High School Totals	72	14	3	10	1

[a] These data are taken from our reconstructed data tapes. Armor lists 123 junior high METCO students in his Figure 2, but he inadevertently dropped two cases.

controls tends to confound sex, grade level, and age with family climate and social class.

c. *Sample problems.* The METCO research suffers, too, from both small numbers and a severe loss of eligible subjects. Limited sample size makes finding statistically significant differences in achievement between the experimental and "control" groups less likely; or, put differently, small sample sizes aid in supporting the anti-desegregation thesis of the article. The extent of this problem is shown in Table 2, which provides the sample sizes by grade level. The question arises as to how large the METCO group differences in achievement would have had to be before the sample sizes employed could have detected a statistically significant difference even at the .05 level of confidence? By our calculation, the answer at the junior high level, for example, is that the METCO students would have had to gain at least 0.4 of a grade *more* in average achievement on the test norms than the "control" group.[38] This is an unrealistic expectation over a duration of only

[38] Our projected sample sizes conservatively assume a standard deviation of the junior high gain scores of one grade level.

seven months, especially for comparisons among children who are close to grade level. An educationally meaningful average gain difference over such a short period would have been 0.2 of a grade more for the METCO students. But this would have required sample sizes of roughly 200 in each group to have reached statistical significance for a two-tailed test. Instead, only 125 METCO and 27 "control" junior high students were tested. The same point can be made about the other grade levels. We conclude, therefore, that the criterion of statistical significance was inappropriate for evaluating the METCO program when the sample sizes were so small.

The loss of subjects occurred in two stages. Among the elementary students, in the first test administration in October 1968, there was a 23 percent loss of eligible METCO students and a 35 percent loss of eligible "control" students.[39] In the second test administration in May 1969, 34 percent of the METCO and 56 percent of the "control" students who had taken the tests seven months earlier did not retake them. Combined, then, the achievement results on these students included only 51 percent of the eligible METCO and 28 percent of the eligible "control" participants. The situation was even worse for the junior and senior high students, whose achievement results were based on only 44 percent of the eligible METCO and only 20 percent of the eligible "control" participants. Furthermore, only eight percent of the "controls" took part in all three test administrations.

Contrast these percentages with Useem's [40] response rate of 87 percent in her study of white students in METCO schools. Compare them, too, with the accepted survey research standard of at least a 70 to 80 percent response rate, and one can appreciate the high level of potential bias introduced by this loss of subjects from Armor's study. An attempt to compensate for these impaired data by utilizing cross-sectional results is not an adequate remedy for many reasons, some of which are provided by Armor himself when he condemns cross-sectional investigations. Besides, there was a considerable loss of eligible subjects, and thus potential bias, in the cross-sectional data as well.

d. *Test administration problems.* "The control group," Armor

---

[39] Unfortunately for the discerning reader, Armor failed to mention these losses of elementary subjects in the one footnote he devotes to the subject. We obtained them from Walberg, "Evaluation of an Urban-Suburban Busing Program."

[40] Elizabeth Useem, "White Suburban Secondary Students in Schools with Token Desegregation," unpublished doctoral dissertation, Graduate School of Education, Harvard University, 1971; and Elizabeth Useem, "Correlates of Racial Attitudes Among White High School Students," unpublished paper presented at the American Educational Research Association meeting, 1972.

argued in his Detroit deposition for school segregation, "has to be measured in the same way that the treated group is." He further maintained that "we must measure them before the treatment, and put one through the treatment and one not, to assess the effect of a program." We agree, but his METCO research failed on both counts.

The third testing in May 1970, which involved attitudes but not achievement, took place under markedly contrasting conditions for the experimental and control groups. While the METCO children answered the questions in school, the control children answered them at home through a mailed questionnaire that explicitly requested the parents to serve as proctors. This procedure risks two related sources of bias. A wealth of research has demonstrated how different situations can lead to sharply different responses; and the home administration of the controls' testing opens the possibility for family members to influence the answers directly.

Armor expresses amazement that the METCO children revealed as a group more militant and ideological responses than the "control" children, but the differential testing administrations provide a possible explanation. Repeated surveys indicate that young black peers at school are far more likely to be militant and ideological than older parents at home;[41] and research in social psychology has shown that such different situational influences can have a sharp effect on group-linked attitudes.[42]

On the second point, measuring the groups *before* the treatment, the METCO research also fails. The METCO pupils were measured initially in October 1968, *after* all of them had begun for a month or more their year in the METCO school. Moreover, 45 percent of the METCO children were not beginning "the treatment" of suburban education, for they had already been in the program for either one or two years.

Finally, studies utilizing achievement tests require well-motivated students who are trying to do their best. We learn from those in attendance at both the first and second test administrations, however, that motivation was apparently not high. And no wonder. The students, METCO and control, had no special incentive for taking the lengthy

---

[41] A. Campbell and H. Schuman, "Racial Attitudes in Fifteen American Cities," in The National Advisory Commission on Civil Disorders, *Supplemental Studies* (Washington, D.C.: U.S. Government Printing Office, 1968); and Peter Goldman, *Report from Black America* (New York: Simon and Schuster, 1970).

[42] W. W. Charters, Jr., and T. M. Newcomb, "Some Attitudinal Effects of Experimentally Increased Salience of a Membership Group," in G. E. Swanson, T. M. Newcomb, and E. L. Hartley, Eds., *Readings in Social Psychology*, rev. ed. (New York: Holt, 1952).

tests on a holiday in a Boston technical school described by Walberg [43] as "an old, run-down, ill-cared-for building." This low level of motivation probably accounts for the small turnout for the second test.

e. *Analysis problems.* Even if there were no serious control group and sample problems, numerous data errors place Armor's analysis of the METCO results in serious question. One child was included who apparently did not take the verbal test initially at all; his post-test scores were then treated as a total gain from a base of zero. A sixth (25 of 151) of the junior high students initially scored virtually as high as the achievement test scoring allowed. Thus, this "ceiling effect" made it impossible for their post-test scores to advance, and their performance was treated as showing "no gain." Such problems, together with clerical errors, help explain why such talented children are shown to make such slight achievement gains in Armor's Figures 1 and 2. But given the irreparable control group and sampling problems, no purpose is served by a reanalysis of these data that corrects for these errors of analysis and data handling.

Inadequate Discussion of the METCO Research

The reader is not told enough in Armor's article to evaluate the METCO research fully. Most of our critical comments are based on information gleaned from a reanalysis of the raw data, the examination of unpublished papers on the research,[44] and a review of Armor's court testimony concerning the research. The discussion of the METCO work is also inadequate in other ways: (a) Differential statistical standards are employed; (b) attitude differences between METCO schools are not shown; and (c) misleading claims of consistency with other research findings are advanced.

a. *Differential statistical standards.* Rigid standards of statistical significance are uniformly applied to findings that favor school desegregation. Findings of positive effects in other studies that approach statistical significance are summarily dismissed as "not significant." But these standards are relaxed considerably when findings interpreted as negative to school desegregation are discussed. For instance, Figure 3 is provided to show how the grades of METCO's junior and senior high school pupils declined slightly, and this finding is emphasized in the conclusions.[45] Yet there is no significant difference between the

---

[43] Walberg, "Evaluation of an Urban-Suburban Busing Program."

[44] Archibald, "Report on Change in Academic Achievement"; Walberg, "Evaluaction of an Urban-Suburban Busing Program"; and David J. Armor and William J. Genova, "METCO Student Attitudes and Aspirations: A Three-Year Evaluation" (unpublished paper) (Boston: METCO, 1970).

[45] Armor, "Evidence on Busing," p. 109.

METCO and the control groups on changes in grades. Similarly, a slightly greater increase among METCO students in wanting a school with no more than half-white student bodies is emphasized.[46] Though ". . . the differential change is not statistically significant," Figure 7 is devoted to it. And later in the conclusions, this finding is utilized without qualification as part of the evidence that "bused" black students have become more supportive of "black separatism."

b. *Attitude differences between METCO schools are not shown.* Armor's article assumes that the METCO program consisted of the same "treatment" for all of the children participating in it. Consequently, attitude differences across METCO schools were not shown; nor, as noted earlier, were any variables utilized to take into account what type of educational programs were actually occurring inside the various METCO schools.

Actually, of course, there are as many different METCO programs under way as there are separate METCO schools. But consider the contrasting policy implications of providing only the total results as opposed to school-by-school results. Suppose a particular school program aimed at improving racial attitudes were attempted in eight schools, and that the overall effect was minimal. The policy implication would be to regard the program a disappointment and to consider abandoning it. Suppose further that a meaningful effect had in fact been registered in all but two schools, but that attitudes in these two were so unfavorable that they virtually obscured the favorable attitudes of the other six in the total data. Now the policy implication *from the same data* would be to regard the program as encouraging and to find out how to change the deviant two to make them more like the successful six schools. In short, the variability across schools is a critical consideration in judging a program.

Our Figure 1, from Useem,[47] shows that a situation similar to this existed for the METCO program in 1969. Note that schools F and A evince by far the most anti-METCO sentiment among both white and black pupils. Note, too, that black attitudes toward METCO are consistently more favorable than those of whites, though there is a positive relationship across schools in the attitudes of the two groups. With such wide differences between METCO schools, how can a simple judgment of success or failure be passed upon the entire program?

c. *Misleading claims of consistency with other research findings are advanced.* Two studies are cited as providing supporting evidence

---

[46] *Ibid.*, pp. 102–103.
[47] Useem, "White Suburban Secondary Students."

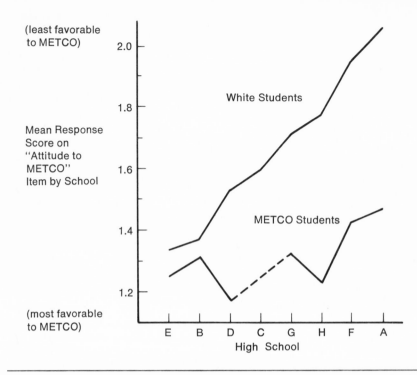

FIGURE 1. *Attitudes of METCO and White Students Toward the METCO Program by High School* [a]

[a] Data from METCO students in School C were not available. The Figure is taken from Useem, "White Suburban Secondary Students."

for the METCO results; but their descriptions are so incomplete as to be highly misleading. Useem's [48] METCO investigation is given as evidence for how interrical contact in METCO schools leads to worse race relations. Her complete findings, however, point to a different conclusion, and we shall return to these findings shortly. The other citation refers to Armor's earlier reanalysis of the Coleman report data:

> An extensive reanalysis of the Coleman data showed that even without controlling for social class factors, "naturally" integrated (i.e., non-bused) black sixth-grade groups were still one and one-half standard deviations behind white groups in the same schools, compared to a national gap of two standard deviations. This means that, assuming the Coleman data to be correct, the *best* that integration could do

---

[48] *Ibid.*, and Useem, "Correlates of Racial Attitudes."

would be to move the average black group from the second percentile to the seventh percentile (on the *white* scale, where the average white group is at the fiftieth percentile).[49]

Such a statement is extremely misleading, and it requires clarification. It appears to assert that there is some upper limit on the possible achievement gains through "busing" of blacks relative to whites. No such assertion is possible. Moreover, the evidence for this claim is based on data from *groups* of children who are in general not bused and for whom there are only Coleman's cross-sectional data. The statement, then, implies a causal relation from cross-sectional data, a practice correctly condemned earlier by Armor. The statement further implies that there is some intrinsic, if unspecified, connection between the gains possible from "busing" and the inferred gains estimated from cross-sectional data.

More misleading still is the use of *group* percentiles. Technically, it may be correct that the average black *group* mean in desegregated sixth grades is only at the seventh percentile when compared with the means of white *groups*. But the obvious misinterpretation that can easily arise is that the average individual black *student* in a desegregated school is only at the seventh percentile compared with the individual white student norms. Such an interpretation is patently *wrong*. Though Armor can argue that his statement is technically accurate, we feel that he has an obligation to inform the lay reader fully so that such a misinterpretation could not occur.

The misleading statement utilizes standard deviations based on group means rather than on individual scores. Group standard deviations are invariably smaller than standard deviations based on the individuals within the groups. Instead of the average black *group* in desegregated sixth grades being at the *seventh* percentile of white *group* norms, then, we estimate that the average black *individual* in desegregated sixth grades ranks between the *25th* and *30th* percentiles of white *individual* norms.[50] Indeed, Figure 2 of Armor's article shows

---

[49] Armor, "Evidence on Busing," p. 100.

[50] Using the Coleman report data, the standard deviation for groups of white students in desegregated schools in the Metropolitan North is only about 40 per cent as large as the standard deviation of the white individual scores; or, on Coleman's verbal test, roughly four points where the standard deviation of the individual whites is 10 points (Coleman, *et al., Equality of Educational Opportunity*). Since Armor finds that the mean for white groups in desegregated schools is roughly one-and-a-half group mean standard deviations larger than that for black groups in desegregated schools, we estimate that the average black child is roughly six points (1.5 x 4 points) behind the average white child. Translating this into individual percentiles and assuming that the average white in desegregated schools is at the 50th percentile, we arrive at our estimate that the average black pupil in desgregated schools is between the 25th and 30th percentiles.

that the black senior high students in METCO research average between the 25th and 43rd percentiles in individual reading achievement.

The Achievement Effects of "Busing" Are More Complex and Positive Than Reported

Armor concludes that "busing" fails on four of the five standards he alone sets for it. One of these alleged failures concerns the academic achievement of black students. From the selected findings of selected studies, Armor concludes that desegregation research throughout the nation has typically found no statistically significant enhancement of black achievement. Further, he claims that the METCO results support this conclusion. But we have noted how this conclusion was reached through the omission of at least seven busing investigations with positive black achievement results and through serious weaknesses in the METCO research.

This is not the place for a complete review of the relevant research literature. But our evaluation of the available evidence points to a more encouraging, if more tentative and complex set of conclusions. First, the academic achievement of both white and black children is not lowered by the types of racial desegregation so far studied. Second, the achievement of white and especially of black children in desegregated schools is generally higher when some of the following critical conditions are met: equal racial access to the school's resources; *classroom*—not just school—desegregation; [51] the initiation of desegregation in the early grades; interracial staffs; [52] substantial rather than token student desegregation; [53] the maintenance of or increase in school services and remedial training; and the avoidance of strict ability grouping.

Grading Changes Before and After Desegregation Are Meaningless If Differential Grading Practices Are Not Considered

"Busing" also fails, according to Armor, because the grade average of the METCO students in junior and senior high schools declined. The

---

[51] James McPartland, "The Segregated Student in the Desegregated Schools: Sources of Influence on Negro Secondary Students," *Report No. 21*, Department of Social Relations, The Johns Hopkins University, 1968.

[52] Bailey (S. K. Bailey, *Disruption in Urban Public Secondary Schools* [Washington, D.C.: National Association of Secondary School Principals, 1970]) has also shown that high school "disruptions" and racial tensions are far less likely to occur when the black staff percentage is equal to or greater than the black student percentage.

[53] Christopher Jencks and Marsha Brown, "The Effects of Desegregation on Student Achievement: Some New Evidence from the Equality of Educational Opportunity Survey," unpublished paper, Harvard Unievrsity, 1972.

average METCO grade decline is slight (−0.12 on a four-point scale), although he described it as "considerable." [54] Nor is the difference in grade changes between the METCO and control groups statistically significant. Moreover, the greater drop in METCO grades than in control grades may be an artifact of the enormous non-response rate discussed earlier, for the full cross-sectional data show the controls' grades falling as much as those of the METCO children (−0.14 to −0.13).

Black grades also fell after desegregation in Evanston, we are informed in Armor's footnote 14. But we are not informed that the same study shows that white grades also fell and that there were no significant differences "in the frequencies of earned grades within each group." [55] By contrast, when black pupils left a segregated junior high school in Sacramento in 1964, they soon received higher grades in the desegregated schools and maintained this improvement throughout their junior high years.[56] However, none of these results are convincing, since differential grading practices are not controlled.

Shifts in Aspirations and "Academic Self-Image" During Desegregation Are Positive in Meaning

Armor further contends that "busing" fails because it lowers both the aspirations and academic self-concept of black children. Several qualifications are briefly discussed initially,[57] but when the conclusions are drawn, this METCO "finding" has become unqualifiedly one of the four failures of "busing." [58]

Actually, the METCO data on the subject are by no means clear. Two of Armor's three relevant Figures (5 and 6), those concerned with occupational aspirations and with "feeling more intelligent than classmates," show no significant change differences between the METCO and "control" groups. And the non-response bias may account for the one significant change difference—in regard to the desire to obtain a bachelor's degree (Figure 4)—since the full cross-sectional samples reveal a similar decline for both groups (−11 percent to −12 percent).

Two careful desegregation investigations from Pittsburgh and Evanston, however, *have* found lower black aspirations combined with *better* academic performance. Black ninth graders in Pittsburgh had significantly higher arithmetic achievement and lower educational

---

[54] Armor, "Evidence on Busing," p. 109.

[55] Jayjia Hsia, *Integration in Evanston, 1967–1971* (Evanston: Educational Testing Service, 1971).

[56] Morrison and Stivers, "Summary of Assessments."

[57] Armor, "Evidence on Busing," pp. 101–102.

[58] *Ibid.*, p. 109.

aspirations in desegregated schools.[59] Similarly, *both black and white pupils* in Evanston's third, fourth, and fifth grades who had previously been in predominantly black schools reported somewhat lower academic self-concept scores after two years in predominantly white schools.[60] And we have noted that Evanston's black and white children made achievement gains during desegregation, though they were not statistically significant.[61] Since this effect occurred for *both* racial groups, these investigators inferred that this "social comparison effect" reflected adaptation to new norms and more realistic conceptions of academic performance.

The key to understanding the apparent paradox of reduced aspirations combined with increased achievement is the well-known psychological principle that achievement motivation and aspiration level are by no means identical. Researchers have repeatedly found that moderate motivational levels are best for learning and achievement.[62] Some of this motivational research directly concerns black children. Katz,[63] for example, has demonstrated experimentally how unduly high aspirations can doom black students to serious learning difficulties. In his view, desegregation benefits learning among black children by lowering their aspirations to more effective and realistic levels. Veroff and Peele [64] supported Katz's position in a study of desegregation in a small Michigan city. They found that achievement motivation, as measured by the choice of moderately difficult tasks, significantly increased for black boys after one year in a desegregated elementary school; black girls, however, did not evince the change.

If METCO had drastically curtailed black ambitions to low levels, this would have been a negative result. But METCO reduced these ambitions only slightly, for they remained as high or higher than the ambitions of white students in METCO schools.[65] In short, when

---

[59] Nancy St. John and Marshall S. Smith, "School Racial Composition, Achievement, and Aspiration," unpublished paper, Graduate School of Education, Harvard University, 1969.

[60] Stephen J. Weber, Thomas D. Cook, and Donald T. Campbell, "The Effect of School Integration on the Academic Self-Concept of Public School Students," unpublished paper presented at the Midwestern Psychological Association meeting, Detroit, 1971; and Hsia, *Integration in Evanston.*

[61] Hisa, *Integration in Evanston.*

[62] J. W. Atkinson, *An Introduction to Motivation* (Princeton: Van Nostrand, 1964).

[63] Irwin Katz, "The Socialization of Academic Motivation in Minority Group Children," in D. Levine, Ed., *Nebraska Symposium on Motivation, 1967* (Lincoln: University of Nebraska Press, 1967).

[64] Joseph Veroff and S. Peele, "Initial Effects of Desegregation on the Achievement Motivation of Negro Elementary School Children," *Journal of Social Issues,* Vol. 25, No. 3 (1969), 71–91.

[65] Useem, "White Suburban Secondary Students," studied white tenth graders' aspirations and attitudes in eight out of the nine secondary schools par-

desegregation lowers rigidly high aspirations of black students to moderate, effective levels, it should be considered a positive, not a negative effect.

Shifts in Racial Attitudes During Desegregation Are Exaggerated and Interpreted Too Narrowly

"Busing" fails again, in Armor's view, because he regards his METCO data as indicating that desegregation leads to negative effects for race relations. Once again, these METCO data are tenuous at best. Though much is made of it, the increase among METCO children in their desire to attend schools with at least half-black student bodies proves not to be significantly different from a similar increase among the "control" students (Figure 7). No control data are shown for black students' relations with white students (Figure 10), even though data without control comparisons are otherwise condemned by Armor and a large segment of the "control" group also attended interracial schools and had contact with white students. And as already noted, the differential administration of the third attitude questionnaire in 1970 is a critical factor which probably explains at least part of the difference between the two groups.

But if these supporting data are suspect, Armor's interpretations of them are even more suspect. "Militancy" and heightened "black consciousness and solidarity" are viewed as indicating "bad" race relations, though Armor adds, "It would be a mistake, of course, to view the increased racial solidarity of black students as a *completely* negative finding." [66] Similarly, support for "black power" and a preference for a school with a student body that is evenly divided between the races are believed necessarily to involve "black separatism." Even sympathy for the Black Panthers is regarded as indicative of "anti-integration sentiments"; this despite the fact that the Panthers do not support racial segregation and removed Stokely Carmichael as a member because of his insistence on racial separatism.

These interpretations involve a logical contradition in Armor's argument. He begins his article with the famous "hearts and minds" quotation of the 1954 Supreme Court ruling against *de jure* racial segregation of the public schools; and he employs it as evidence of the powerful influence of social science upon "the integration policy

---

ticipating in the METCO program during 1968–69. She found white aspirations just equal to or below those reported for blacks in the same schools. Thus, 74 per cent of the white students wanted to be above the middle of the class academically compared to about 80 per cent of the black students; and 26 per cent of the whites aspired to a professional or graduate school compared to 35 per cent of the blacks.

[66] Armor, "Evidence on Busing," p. 113 (italics added).

model." Yet the Supreme Court was maintaining that segregation led to black self-hate. Now when he interprets his data as showing that METCO "busing" leads to racial pride, militancy, and a desire to be among blacks as well as whites, Armor concludes that "the integration policy model" is proven wrong and that "busing" causes bad race relations.

The article admits that the METCO children are still supportive of the program, but emphasizes the trend toward "militancy." No consideration is given to the effects of the differential administration of the third-wave questionnaires; nor is any given to the possible effects of the study's having begun just after the 1968 assassination of Dr. Martin Luther King, Jr., a tragic event with wide repercussions for black/white interaction. Finally, the attitude results, like the achievement results, must be reinterpreted in the light of our discovery that much of the "control" group attends substantially desegregated schools. It could be, then, that the extreme tokenism of the METCO programs influenced these attitude results. They cannot be related to "busing" and desegregation, given the composition of the "control" group.

Nonetheless, Armor views these findings as a challenge to contact theory. To buttress this contention, he selectively cites a lone finding out of context from Useem's [67] 1969 study of white racial attitudes in METCO schools.

> Nonetheless, although the evidence is not complete, what we have indicates that the white students themselves were negatively affected by the contact. . . . [t]hose students who had direct classroom contact with bused black students showed *less* support for the busing program than those without direct contact. In fact, the kind of students who were generally the most supportive—the middle-class, high-achieving students—showed the largest decline in support as a result of contact with bused black students. This finding is based on cross-sectional data and does not indicate a change over time, but it is suggestive of the possibility that a general polarization has occurred for both racial groups.[68]

When drawing conclusions, however, he forgets his own caution against drawing causal inferences and flatly states that "white student attitudes in the receiving schools also tended *to become* less favorable to black students. . . ." [69]

---

[67] Useem, "White Suburban Secondary Students"; and Useem, "Correlates of Racial Attitudes."

[68] Armor, "Evidence on Busing," pp. 103–104.

[69] *Ibid.*, p. 112 (italics added).

The simple correlation between increased classroom contact and more negative feelings toward METCO among white students is statistically significant; but Armor fails to report that the relationship is no longer significant once such variables as sex, socio-economic status, and academic standing are taken into account. Moreover, this effect is limited to upper-status students of high ability who remain favorable to the program but who have their initially unrealistic expectations of blacks modified.

There is also a failure to report other relevant findings from Useem's work. For example, she found a statistically significant positive relationship between favorable white attitudes toward METCO and earlier equal status interracial contact in elementary school, summer camp, etc.; and this strong relationship remained significant after full controls were applied. Useem also found a relationship ($p < .08$) between support for METCO and interracial contact in extracurricular activities. Moreover, she found that having a METCO friend is strongly linked to support of METCO, and is best predicted by equal status contact with blacks as a child and with METCO students in class and school activities.[70]

The Evidence that School Desegregation "Channels" Blacks Into Greater Future Opportunities is Stronger than Presented

The one "success" of "busing," Armor admits, is that METCO appears to "channel" its students into colleges at higher rates than control students presumably from the same families. But this finding is couched with many qualifications that are conspicuously absent from his negative conclusions. Furthermore, his article actually understates METCO's success in this regard and fails to cite recent research that indicates that it may well be an important effect of interracial education in general.

Armor's article shows in its Figure 11 that 78 percent of the METCO graduating class of 1970 entered four-year colleges, compared to only 44 percent of the controls. By the fall of 1971, the percentages were 66 percent and 44 percent; and by the spring of 1971, 56 percent and 38 percent. (For universities, the spring 1971 figures were even more impressive, with 43 percent of the METCO graduates

---

[70] In his Detroit segregation testimony, Armor stated that he omitted these positive findings of contact because they were voluntary and therefore could have been caused by self-selection. But classrooms at the high school level often involve selection too. Besides, 72 percent of Useem's white students who had contact with METCO students in school activities had it in athletics. Armor's argument requires us to believe that tolerant white students would go out for football primarily to have contact with the few black players on the team.

and only 12 percent of the controls enrolled.) Similarly, positive results are cited from another special program.[71] But the article also
implies that the METCO drop-out rate from college is excessively
high, suggesting that the program pushes into college students who
do not belong there. This point is answered as soon as one compares
the METCO figures with other data on college attendance. For 1969
and 1970, the percentages of the *total* graduating classes of the METCO
high schools going on to four-year colleges were 61 percent and 62
percent—all well below the 1969 and 1970 METCO figures of 77 percent and 78 percent.[72] Moreover, the 84 percent college *retention* rate
of the 1970 METCO graduates who entered the second year of the
four-year colleges is *not* abnormally low. In fact, it is slightly above the
78 percent national retention rate for white students in four-year
colleges.[73]

Nor was the 1970 METCO graduating class unusual. Robert
Hayden, the director of METCO, kindly supplied us with data on the
32 METCO graduates of 1969. Twenty-eight (88 percent) entered
college in the fall of 1969, while four began full-time employment.
Three years later, attempts were made to contact the entire group,
and 22 of the 28 college-attenders were reached. One was in the
Army, and five had left college. Sixteen (73 percent), however, were
still enrolled in college.

Yet Armor belittles such concrete results. He emphasizes that such
findings are tentative, based on small samples, and may indicate that
the future benefits of biracial schooling are limited to the college-
bound. The importance of all three of these cautions is reduced,
however, by a major research effort that goes unmentioned. Robert
Crain,[74] using a 1966 survey of 1,624 adult blacks in the urban North,
focused upon the occupational and income outcomes of desegregated
education for high school graduates.[75] Crain concludes:

---

[71] George Perry, "A Preliminary Evaluation of the Effect of ABC on College
Attendance" (unpublished paper) (Boston: A Better Chance, 1972).

[72] Useem, "White Suburban Secondary Students." Data from one METCO
high school was unobtainable for 1970, but the similarity of the percentages for
the two years suggests that this does not introduce a serious bias.

[73] A. W. Astin, "College Dropouts: A National Profile," *American Council on
Education Research Reports*, Vol. 7, No. 1 (February 1972).

[74] Robert L. Crain, "School Integration and Occupational Achievement of
Negroes," *American Journal of Sociology*, Vol. 75 (1970), 593–606.

[75] From these same data, Crain (Robert L. Crain, "School Integration and
the Academic Achievement of Negroes," *Sociology of Education*, Vol. 44 [Winter
1971], 1–26) also finds "that those who attended integrated schools are more
likely to have graduated from high school, are more likely to have attended college, and score higher on a verbal test than those who attended northern segregated
schools. It seems likely that the higher achievement of Negroes in integrated

American Negroes who attend integrated public schools have better jobs and higher incomes throughout at least the next three decades of their life. The differences in income cannot be accounted for by the higher educational attainment of alumni of integrated schools, or by the higher differences in social background. The most significant effect of integrated schools is probably not "educational." It is probably more important that Negroes who attend integrated schools will have more contact with whites as adults, and tend to have more trust in whites than do Negroes from segregated schools. This in turn partially overcomes a crucial barrier to equal opportunity—the fact that information about employment opportunities is spread through types of informal social contacts to which few Negroes have access.

The Firm Policy Conclusion Against "Mandatory Busing" Is Not Substantiated by the Evidence Presented

For the many reasons discussed above, the evidence does not justify Armor's unqualified conclusion: "The available evidence on busing, then, seems to lead to two clear policy conclusions. One is that mandatory busing for purposes of improving student achievement and interracial harmony is not effective and should not be adopted at this time." [76] Interestingly, this conclusion was added to the final version after considerable publicity concerning Armor's paper had been generated by its repeated leaks to the mass media. An earlier draft had concluded only that "the data may fail to support mandatory busing as it is currently justified. . . ."

Armor also concludes that "voluntary busing" should continue for those who still believe in it and for the sake of social science research. Yet he never demonstrated, nor do we detect it when reviewing the evidence, that "mandatory" and "voluntary" desegregation lead to different effects. "Mandatory busing" is condemned out of hand even though his article rests most heavily on a voluntary program's effects, and rests entirely, except for Berkeley, upon token programs with small numbers and percentages of black children, while most "mandatory" programs involve larger numbers and percentages of black children in Southern cities excluded from consideration.

In a real sense, Armor's article does not concern itself with "busing" at all, save for its title and its conclusions. It does not provide us with direct evidence on the "busing" of school children for racial

---

schools can be attributed partly to differences in the character of their classmates, irrespective of race. In addition, however, there is evidence that attending integrated schools has an important impact in establishing social and psychological preconditions for achievement."

[76] Armor, "Evidence on Busing," p. 116.

desegregation, for it never treats "busing" as an independent variable. Rather, his article is an attack upon the racial desegregation of public schools that often, but not always, involves "busing." Large numbers of the children in the few studies cited by Armor attend desegregated schools without "busing." And we have noted that in his own METCO study many of his so-called "controls," who were supposed to be "unbused" and segregated, were in fact "bused" and desegregated. Furthermore, a check on his METCO sample finds that a substantial number were *not* bused. Armor was apparently aware of these problems, for he admitted in his court testimony for segregation in Detroit that "a more accurate title would be 'The Effects of Induced School Integration'."

To our knowledge, there is actually no evidence whatsoever that "busing" for desegregation harms children. This is fortunate, since over 40 percent of all school children in the United States are "bused" daily (though only three percent are "bused" for purposes of achieving racial desegregation).[77] Only one of the investigations mentioned in Armor's article actually utilized "busing" as an independent variable. It found, though this was also omitted, that black pupils in Evanston who were bused to desegregated schools attained significantly higher test score gains than those who either remained in or walked to desegregated schools.[78] This result may be an artifact of selection, but it at least indicates that "busing" *per se* did not impair achievement.

IV

*The Article's Basic Assumptions About
Racial Change Are Unjustified*

To this point, our critique has answered Armor's argument within the narrow confines of his view of the process of racial desegregation of the public schools. But here we wish to break out of these confines and to challenge the basic assumptions about racial change that undergird his entire article. Armor's thesis is predicated on viewing school desegregation as a technical matter, an inconvenient intervention whose merit must be judged solely by how well *black* children manage to adapt to it. Blacks are once again the "object" whose reactions should determine "what is good for them." The conditions faced by black children go unmeasured and ignored, and the whole context of

---

[77] Metropolitan Applied Research Center, *Fact Book on Pupil Transportation*, Document No. 2 (New York: MARC, 1972).
[78] Hsia, *Integration in Evanston*.

American race relations is conveniently forgotten. All interracial contact is assumed to constitute "integration." No mention whatsoever is made of white racism, individual and institutional, which the Kerner Commission maintained was at the root of the problem.[79] Nor is there any discussion of the strong argument that genuine integration is necessary primarily for its potential effects on *white* Americans and *their* racial attitudes.

Instead, the whole issue is portrayed as the creation of "liberal educators" who are "so intent on selling integration to reluctant white communities that they risk the danger of ignoring the opinion of the black community." [80] Forgotten is the fact that the issue was the creation of black America, from Charles Hamilton Houston to Roy Wilkins, and that it has been continuously opposed by white America with every conceivable means.

Data from the limited METCO sample are generalized to the whole black community.[81] The anti-busing resolution of the National Black Political Convention held in Gary, Indiana, in March 1972 is emphasized, but the paradoxical fact that the same Convention also passed a strong "pro-busing" resolution is not cited. While it is acknowledged that "many black leaders favor school integration . . ." and that "the *majority* of blacks *may still* endorse the *concept* of integration . . . ," [82] the full range of support for school integration (not merely desegregation) in the black community is never revealed. "Would you like to see the children in your family go to school with white children or not?" When asked this question at the time of the METCO research in 1969, 78 percent of a national sample of black Americans (*up* from 70 percent three years before) chose "go with whites," as opposed to 9 percent "not with whites" and 14 percent "unsure." [83] Thus not just a majority but an overwhelming portion of black America still opts for school integration. If any further evidence were needed, the immediate and hostile public reactions of many blacks to the initial newspaper stories concerning Armor's paper should have supplied it. This is not to deny that there are strong doubts among blacks, especially the young, as to whether white America

---

[79] National Advisory Commission on Civil Disorder, *Report* (Washington D.C.: U.S. Government Printing Office, 1968).

[80] Armor, "Evidence on Busing," p. 115.

[81] *Ibid.*, p. 113.

[82] *Ibid.*, pp. 112, 115 (italics added).

[83] Goldman, *Report from Black America*. Armor's data on black attitudes toward "busing" in his footnote 42 are outdated. By March 1972, blacks favored "busing" for integration by 54 percent to 34 percent (Louis Harris, "Antibusing Attitudes Harden," *The Boston Globe*, April 10, 1972).

will ever allow genuine integration to become the national norm, doubts that are only reinforced by the assumptions upon which Armor's article is based.

Armor asserts that the burden must fall upon those who support school integration to prove that it works. Given America's unhappy racial history, we believe that the burden of proof rests with those who wish to maintain racial segregation. But actually such contentions miss the point. The courts' interpretation of the 14th Amendment of the United States Constitution, and not social scientists' opinions about black responses, ultimately governs the racial desegregation of the public schools and court-ordered transporation which may be needed to achieve it. This fundamental fact was dramatically demonstrated by the judicial reaction to Armor's deposition in the Detroit school case, a deposition based on an earlier draft of "The Evidence on Busing." On June 12, 1972, U.S. District Court Judge Stephen H. Roth ruled the deposition inadmissible as evidence on the grounds of irrelevancy. The deposition, in Judge Roth's view, represented "a new rationale for a return to the discredited 'separate but equal' policy. . . ."

The Double Double Standard: a Reply

DAVID J. ARMOR

David J. Armor is the author of "The Evidence on Busing," reprinted above. The present article is his reply to Thomas Pettigrew et al., "Busing: A Review of 'The Evidence'."

Thomas Pettigrew and his associates have missed the essential point of my study. As a consequence, their comments shed little light on the current public controversy over busing. Indeed, their critique further promulgates the ambiguities and confusions that have prevailed in the field of race relations since Myrdal's *An American Dilemma*.

The essential requirement for sound reasoning in this matter is observance of the distinction among the findings of science, the results of policy, and the dictates of law or morality. I studied the results of existing policies of induced school integration (all of which used, of necessity, varying amounts of busing). I was *not* studying the scientific issue of what *might* happen under various conditions (other than those in effect in the programs studied), nor the legal question of whether it *should* have happened according to various constitutional interpretations. My task was far simpler. I asked only the question: What *has* happened? My critics have confused the *has* with the *might* and the *should*. This confusion is further compounded by their application of two double standards for the evaluation and use of the evidence on busing.

I am accused of having too severe standards and unrealistic ex-

---

David J. Armor, "The Double Double Standard: A Reply," *The Public Interest*, No. 30 (Winter 1973), pp. 119–131. Copyright © National Affairs Inc., 1973.

pectations about the benefits of induced school integration (which I will hereafter abbreviate as "busing"). But *I* did not formulate these standards and expectations. They come from the programs themselves, buttressed by several noteworthy studies, particularly the Coleman report and the 1967 report of the U.S. Commission on Civil Rights. I do not doubt that existing busing programs are also based upon moral and legal principles, especially the 1954 Supreme Court doctrine that "separate is unequal." But even in the 1954 decision social science findings are cited as "authority" and hence become entangled with constitutional issues.

One expectation stands out above all others: Integrated education will enhance the academic achievement of minority groups, and thereby close (or at least substantially reduce) the achievement gap. There is good reason for the prominence of this belief. The Coleman study revealed a large and consistent achievement gap between white students and most minority groups (with the notable exception of Oriental students). The gap between black and white students averages about 33 percentile points. This means that for any black child and white child drawn at random from the general population, we can expect the black child's scores to average about 33 percentile points below the white child's. This achievement gap became the main argument against segregated education and the yardstick by which to measure progress. It is unlikely that de facto segregated education would ever have become such a major issue, or that so many communities would have voluntarily initiated busing programs, without this evidence.

This is also the central issue in the critique. The critique makes the incredible claim that looking at black and white achievement differentials is not appropriate, since *both* groups may gain under integration. Not only is there little evidence in support of this claim, but even if it were true there is no way we could conclude from it that integration would solve the educational deprivation of minorities. Would we solve the economic problems of minorities if we raised *everyone's* annual salary by $3,500? Of course not. Such a gain was in fact registered by both whites and non-whites between the 1960 and the 1970 census, but there has been no lessening of the clamor over economic inequality. But money at least has some meaning in absolute terms; this is not the case for academic achievement as measured by testing. As any educational specialist knows, there is no "zeropoint" on an achievement test, and progress is always measured on a *relative* basis (i.e., a student's progress relative to a national or local norm). Thus if the black/white achievement gap does not change, there is no way one could conclude that busing is beneficial for minority groups.

I am accused of selecting only "negative" studies and leaving out seven other adequately-designed studies that were more "positive." In fact, I looked at all the studies that I could obtain at the time. Their results were so consistent that I was quite confident about my conclusions. I have now looked at these seven reports (only four of which meet the technical requirements for an adequate study) and have no reason to change my conclusions; nor do I see much evidence to support the authors' optimism.

The only way to settle this issue is to look at some of the findings. I have selected a number of studies that were not in my original review, including some that are cited by Pettigrew and his colleagues. The only criteria I used for my choices were the comprehensiveness of the data and the presence of some of the conditions my critics claim are important for achievement gains (i.e., two-way busing, classroom integration, duration, etc.). I will focus on reading achievement, since this is about the only academic skill which is measured in all of the studies.

The first example is drawn from the Evanston study, which in my opinion is technically one of the best. Also, it fulfills most of the important conditions cited in the critique: A sizable proportion of the students were black (about 20 percent); almost all classrooms were racially balanced; faculties were integrated (about 10 percent black); and the duration of the integration experience was three years. The performance of the fourth-grade cohort is typical (see Table 1). The black/white gap is 16 points before integration, or just about one standard deviation (almost identical to Coleman's finding for the sixth grade nationally). After three years of integration the gap has increased to 25 points, and we can see that the *black students in grade seven are performing at the same level that the white students were at in the fourth grade.* In other words, in the seventh grade the black children are three years behind white children in reading achievement. Similar results were found for cohorts starting at grades one and five and for performance on arithmetic achievement tests. We do not know whether the achievement of *both* groups might have been

TABLE 1. READING ACHIEVEMENT IN EVANSTON.[a]

Race	Before Integration (Grade 4—1967)	After Integration (Grade 7—1970)
White (N = 606)	253	278
Black (N = 185)	237	253
Gap	16	25

[a] Adapted from Jayjia Hsia, *Integration in Evanston* (Evanston: Education Testing Service, 1971), Table 11. Scores are based on the STEP reading test; the standard deviation is approximately 15.

TABLE 2. READING ACHIEVEMENT IN BERKELEY.[a]

Race	Before Integration (Grade 1—1967)	One Year of Integration (Grade 2—1968)	Two Years of Integration (Grade 3—1969)
White (N = 500+)	1.9	3.1	4.1
Black (N = 400+)	1.6	2.2	2.8
Gap	.3	.9	1.3

[a] Adapted from Arther D. Dambacker, "Comparison of Achievement Test Scores Made by Berkeley Elementary Students Pre and Post Integration" (unpublished report, Berkeley Unified School District, 1971), Table 7. Scores are grade equivalents based on the same test—the Stanford Achievement Test (administered in May each year).

enhanced; but what difference would that make in terms of the possible harmful effects on the black children in Evanston who are forced to compete for academic rewards at so large a disadvantage?

The Berkeley data also afford a good example, for the Berkeley program employed two-way busing (whites to previously majority-black schools and vice versa) and integrated faculties and classrooms. Although the study was cross-sectional, data were presented over a four-year period for six grade levels; thus it is possible to construct a first-grade cohort and follow that same grade (if not exactly the same students) through two years of integration experience (see Table 2). We can make inferences about these data if the student turnover rate is not too high, which is a reasonable assumption. In each year the gap increases, so that after two years of integration the gap is more than one grade level. Again, it is clear that integration has not closed the achievement gap in Berkeley, and the black students are competing at a large disadvantage.

Sacramento is one of the integration programs cited by the authors as indicating positive effects of integration. While it is true that there are some positive results reported for *some* tests, the black/white gap does not change. The data in Table 3 are the first-grade cohort. The resemblances to the Berkeley data are striking. Again we see that while the gap has not widened, it exceeds a whole grade level by the end of the third grade. Sacramento has also reported some interesting data which allow comparison of segregated minority students receiving intensive compensatory services with integrated minority students. Averaging over the Stanford Reading Test in grades one to six, we find that the compensated segregated students gained about 1.1 years, while the integrated students gained about 1.0 years. In other words, it is possible that the slight improvements Sacramento observed in achievement of integrated students com-

TABLE 3. READING ACHIEVEMENT IN SACRAMENTO.[a]

Group	Before Integration (May 1966)	After Integration (May 1967)	After Integration (May 1968)
Majority (N = 221)	2.1	3.2	4.1
Minority (N = 35)	1.6	2.0	2.9
Gap	.5	1.2	1.2

[a] Adapted from Albert J. Sessarego, "A Summary of the Assessments of the District's Intergration Programs, 1964–71" (unpublished report, Sacramento City Unified School District, 1971). Scores are grade equivalents based upon the Stanford Reading Test. Minority group includes both black and Mexican-American students.

pared to *non-compensated* segregated students (for some grades on some tests) are due to differences in the services of instruction received at the integrated schools and not to integration per se. While Coleman found that school facilities and staff were not major contributors to achievement differentials, he did not say that they had *no* effect whatsoever.

Another "positive" example cited by the critique is a study of integration via school "pairing" in New York City in 1965. This study is particularly interesting in that an attempt is made to compare integrated students with both black and white segregated students. While the study gives no indication about classroom or faculty integration (which are important for educational benefits, according to my critics), and while the paired school is not majority-white (another supposedly crucial condition), it does afford us a look at the black/white gap in reading achievement for a fifth-grade cohort. As can clearly be seen in Table 4, for the integrated students the achievement gap is large (starting at almost three grade levels) and increases (to almost three and one-half grade levels) after one year of integration. The "positive" result in this study is that the integrated black students gained 1.1 grades (or 11 months) while the segregated black students gained .9 (or nine months). It does not seem to me that this difference provides much ground for optimism, particularly since the segregated white students also gained about two months less than the integrated white students. That is, the slight difference we observe might be due to differences in instruction content or style and not due to the effect of integration.

The argument of Pettigrew and his colleagues that perhaps white students also gain in achievement from the integration experience per se demands close scrutiny. While it makes sense to argue that black students might gain by being in a classroom environment with

TABLE 4.   READING ACHIEVEMENT IN NEW YORK.[a]

School	Race	Before Integration (April 1965)	After Integration (May 1966)	Gain
Integrated,	White (N = 30)	6.8	8.5	1.7
paired school	Black (N = 32)	4.0	5.1	1.1
	Gap	2.8	3.4	
Segregated	White (N = 57)	5.7	7.2	1.5
schools	Black (N = 80)	3.5	4.4	.9
	Gap	2.2	2.8	

[a] Adapted from I. W. Stone, *The Effects of One School Pairing on Pupil Achievement* (unpublished Ph.D. Thesis, New York University, 1968), Tables 18 and 20. Scores are grade equivalents on the Metropolitan Achievement Reading Test.

higher-achieving white students (the so-called "peer" effect prominent in the Coleman study), it makes no sense at all to argue that white students will gain by being in a classroom environment with lower-achieving black students. What mechanism could possibly be operating that produces *opposite* peer effects for the two groups? It seems to me that my critics' reasoning is getting fuzzy here.

But this is not the crucial issue anyway. One of the main points of my study was to show that black achievement is not being helped in any significant way by busing, and that therefore we have to raise the possibility of harmful psychological effects due to the achievement gap. The small gain of two months for the paired black students in New York is little consolation for their being placed in an environment where they must compete for grades with students *three years ahead* of them in academic growth. The authors completely ignore this issue throughout their critique.

The critique cites another, more recent study of Project Concern (Hartford and New Haven) that shows more positive results. I originally described the Project Concern studies as showing "mixed" results. The new study does not change my view; in fact, it bears great similarity to the other studies presented here. Like the New York study, it presents results for both races in both integrated and segregated environments. It is a particularly good example in that the bused pupils received a variety of compensatory services (such as minority teachers and aides recruited from the sending schools). The results for the second grade are typical (see Table 5). Again, we can see that the achievement gap increases for the integrated students, starting out at 13 months and ending at almost two years. We have very much the same situation as in the New York pairing study; the integrated black students gain slightly more than the segregated black students (two

TABLE 5.   READING ACHIEVEMENT IN PROJECT CONCERN.[a]

School	Race	Before Integration (1971)	After Integration (1972)	Gain
Integrated school	White (N = 22)	3.4	4.7	1.3
	Black (N = 9)	2.1	2.9	.8
	Gap	1.3	1.8	
Segregated schools	White (N = 20)	3.9	5.2	1.3
	Black (N = 16)	1.8[*]	2.4[*]	.6[*]
	Gap	2.1	2.8	

[a] Adapted from Barbara R. Heller, *et al.*, "Project Concern, Westport, Connecticut" (New York: Center for Urban Education, 1972), Table 3. Scores are grade equivalents on the Metropolitan Achievement Reading Test. The asterisks indicate that the scores for the segregated black students have been adjusted to reflect a shorter testing period.

months), but the achievement differential is still large and increases over the year. Notice, however, that in this case the segregated white students gain as much as the integrated white students.

My critics cite other studies not presented here. As I have already said, three of them (Rochester, Goldsboro, N. C., and Newark) did not qualify according to my criteria for an adequate study; they did not use the same achievement tests both before and after integration. The Philadelphia study is of limited utility since it dealt only with black students with very high I.Q.'s. The Buffalo study showed mixed results, with one grade showing greater gains for integrated, one grade showing greater gains for segregated, and a third grade showing a small (two months) gain for integrated black students. But in all three grades the white integrated students showed even greater gains, indicating the same increasing achievement gap seen in the other studies.

In view of all of these studies, I can see no reason to change my conclusion that "to date there is no published report of *any* strictly education reform which has been proven substantially to affect academic achievement; school integration programs are no exception." It was my purpose to show that existing programs have not demonstrated a consistent and important effect on various expected benefits (especially achievement). It was not my intention to *prove* that achievement *could not* be affected, only to show that it *has not* been affected by *existing* programs. Therefore, my critics' argument that the programs I looked at did not fulfill the proper conditions for integration is beside the point. But I will go further than that: They have presented no convincing evidence that any programs—

even those fulfilling their conditions—are having an important effect. There is no clear evidence in the studies mentioned that they fulfilled their conditions, nor is there *any* evidence in these studies—regardless of the conditions—that school integration will close the achievement gap by "approximately a fourth." Of course, it is still true that, under some conditions, integration *might* have an effect. But those who believe this premise will have to produce far better evidence than is currently available.

The methodological critique of the Boston METCO study is equally irrelevant to my conclusions and recommendations. I would never have made policy statements based on the METCO research without seeing a considerable amount of supporting evidence. I think the reader can see from what has been presented that there is, indeed, a great deal of corroboration. Methodological critiques are always liable to a common fallacy: The existence of technical weaknesses in a study does not prove the converse of its findings. I believe in the METCO findings because they were consistent with many other studies, not because the METCO research was infallible. I am certainly cognizant of some of the limitations of the METCO research pointed out by the critique. Any single social science study could be given a similar treatment. Research conditions in policy evaluation studies are seldom ideal; this is why a social scientist must look for consistency across many studies before coming to any conclusions.

I do not agree with all of the criticisms of the METCO study made by Pettigrew and his associates. In particular, I take issue with their statement that many of the METCO control group students attended integrated schools and therefore were not a proper comparison group. Our control groups were screened for attendance at Boston public schools in the black community, most of which are predominantly black (particularly the elementary schools). Moreover, even those few control group students whose neighborhood school is majority-white still provide a proper comparison, not only because the proportions of minority and lower-class white students are higher in these schools, but also because the Boston schools are presumed unable to provide the kind of quality education found in middle-class suburban schools. After all, this is the whole rationale behind METCO and similar programs, and it must be the belief of many black parents who participate in METCO even though their children could go to majority-white neighborhood schools in Boston.

But the data presented in Table 2 of the critique are misleading in other respects. First, the authors did not use the complete METCO research records to identify schools attended by the control sample; instead, they tried to track down students using incomplete listings of students in a Boston public school register. Not surprisingly, then, they have no data on many of the control students—particularly those in the critical elementary grades. Second, it is not stressed that many of the secondary school control students were in transitional neighborhood schools with large and growing proportions of minority students. For example, of the 10 senior high students listed as integrated, four attended a "border-area" high school with an increasing minority enrolment of 27 percent in 1968 and 34 percent in 1969; another attended a high school whose minority enrolment increased from 42 to 64 percent during these two years; and two others attended a school with a 43 percent minority enrolment.

I undertook a complete examination of the original research records using questionnaires filled out by METCO parents in 1970 just prior to the second year of the research. Of the 36 (out of 41) elementary control students for whom there were reliable data, only 13 can be identified as attending predominantly white schools. Of the 23 students attending majority-black schools, only five attended schools with a substantial proportion of white students (all of whom were in one school whose minority enrolment increased from 53 percent in 1968 to 64 percent in 1969). In other words, in the elementary grades—which are, according to the critique, the more crucial years for achievement changes—complete records indicate that nearly two thirds of the control students attended segregated schools.

What is especially misleading (if not irresponsible) about all this is the authors' use of their incomplete data to conclude that it "renders [my] METCO research of no scientific interest in the study of busing and school desegregation." The clear implication here is that the control group students who went to predominantly white schools might have made large achievement gains which overshadowed lesser gains made by control group students in segregated schools. This would, in turn, make the control group gains spuriously high, perhaps even to the point of masking gains made by METCO students. But we do not have to engage in a lot of verbiage and speculation about this; we can examine the relevant elementary data directly (see Table 6). The data show clearly that the segregated control students do not differ in any important and consistent way from the full control sample (or the METCO sample, for that matter). A similar result also occurred for the junior high students; the high school student sample was too small to make any certain conclusion. What this means, then, is that *my original conclusion—that METCO achievement gains are not consistently larger than the control group—also holds when the control group consists only of those students attending inner-city segregated schools.* As has been so often the case throughout this discussion, when

TABLE 6.   READING ACHIEVEMENT GAINS FOR METCO AND CONTROL
            STUDENTS IN THE ELEMENTARY GRADES.[a]

Group	Grades 3 and 4	Grades 5 and 6
Control students in segregated schools (N's = 8 and 10)	.2	.8
Full control sample in original study (N's = 14 and 27)	.3	.7
METCO as reported in original study (N's = 88 and 59)	.4	.5

[a] All figures are achievement gains in grade equivalents. For the fifth and sixth
grade group, the five students attending the 53 per cent minority school have been
excluded for the sake of purity; if they are included, the average gain for the controls in segregated schools actually drops to .7 years.

rhetoric is replaced by hard, objective data, there does not appear to
be very much of substance in my critics' arguments.

The other major finding with which the critique finds fault is
that race relations seem to worsen as a result of induced school integration. Pettigrew and his colleagues seem to be somewhat am-
bivalent on this point. On the one hand, they criticize my conclusion
on methodological grounds, such as the fact that the third-wave
questionnaire was given in the white school for the METCO students
and at home for the control students. (They ignore that fact that
the second wave—which was given under the same conditions as
the first wave—already revealed the trend of increased separatism
among METCO students.) This would make one think they believe
that contact does not increase racial prejudice and hostility. But at
the same time they argue that the various indicators I used actually
reflect "positive" changes in black self-respect—and therefore do not
run counter to the expectations fostered by the integration policy
model. Let me take up these two different perspectives in order.

My conclusions on race relations, like those on achievement, were
not based only on METCO data. There was support from both the
Useem and Riverside studies; but more important, an entirely distinct study of school integration, using the identical separatism index
that was employed in the METCO research, gave strong supporting
evidence. This study was a cross-sectional evaluation of "A Better
Chance" (ABC), a program that places talented black high school
students in white prep schools. Its data were not ready in time for
use in my original article, but I can report the relevant figures now
(see Table 7). We see that the twelfth-grade ABC students (most of
whom started in the tenth grade) score 1.7 on the index while their

TABLE 7. BLACK SEPARATISM IN THE ABC PROGRAM.[a]

Grade	Black ABC Prep School Students	Black Segregated School Students	White Prep School Students
Tenth grades (N = 135, 130, 134)	1.4	1.3	1.1
Twelfth graders (N = 125, 137, 103)	1.7	1.0	1.0

[a] Adapted from George Perry. Scores are from a separatism index ranging from 0 to 4, where 4 means most separatist. The difference between the black ABC and public school students is not significant in the tenth grade, but is significant at beyond the .001 level for the twelfth graders. The vast majority of black ABC students joined the program in the tenth grade.

tenth-grade counterparts score 1.4. The black control groups (almost all of whom attend predominantly black schools) actually show the *opposite* trend from 1.3 at the tenth grade to 1.0 at the twelfth grade. The data are cross-sectional (that is, the twelfth graders are not the same group as the tenth graders), so we cannot claim a causal confirmation from this study alone. Nonetheless, the ABC tenth and twelfth graders are very similar in most important respects, and the public school control sample consists of black students matched with the ABC students on important characteristics such as ability and family background. Therefore, given the identical findings in the METCO research, I must conclude that there is a strong likelihood that induced school integration enhances separatist ideology as measured by my index.

But is this convergence invalidated by technical weaknesses in the METCO study? The critique is correct in pointing out that the attitude questionnaires were given to the METCO and control students under different conditions in the second year of the study. It also calls attention to the fact that a substantial portion of the control students at the junior and senior high levels (the only levels to take the attitude tests) attended majority-white schools. But the critique fails to note that this "weakness" of the original study can actually be used to further test contact theory by comparing integrated control group students with segregated control group students—both groups having filled out questionnaires under identical conditions (see Table 8). In my original study, I reported an over-all gain for the control group of .1. It can now be seen that the slight increase in separatism for the control group was actually due to the subgroup of students in inner-city integrated schools; their gain of .3 is almost as large as the .4 gain recorded for the METCO students. The segregated black students actually *declined* in their separatism scores—much as would

TABLE 8.   BLACK SEPARATISM GAINS FOR METCO AND CONTROL
           STUDENTS IN THE SECONDARY GRADES.[a]

	Control Students in Majority- Black Schools	Control Students in Majority- White Schools	METCO Students
Gain	−.1	.3	.4
N	(17)	(16)	(135)

[a] Gain scores for the separatism index reported in the original study for a two-year period. The negative change means that separatist attitudes declined.

be predicted by the ABC data presented earlier. Whatever interpretation one wishes to apply to these results, it seems clear that the METCO finding reported in the original study is not simply an artifact of questionnaire administration or of a faulty control group.

The available evidence supports the conclusion that induced school integration, by enhancing black identity and solidarity, may increase separatism and racial hostility; no evidence is presented by the critique that shows the converse. But is this a negative finding? I admitted in my original study that it might not be interpreted as such; on this point I obviously have no quarrel with my critics. I do, however, maintain that *this is not an expected finding,* either according to social science (which has long held to the Allport thesis that contact will reduce prejudice) or according to educational policy makers, most of whom stress the beneficial contribution of contact to racial understanding and harmony. And if it is contrary to expectations, it seems to me that this has very definite policy implications. Although the Supreme Court intended its 1954 ruling in favor of school integration to improve the self-concept of black people, it is highly doubtful that it expected this to be done at the expense of an increase in black hostility toward whites or white hostility toward blacks.

It seems clear that the biggest difference between my perspective and that of the critique is in regard to the policy implications of all this research. They have failed to show that the findings in my original five-city study were untrue; they have not provided convincing evidence that other programs have succeeded where these have failed; they have ignored the possibility of harmful effects. In short, their opposition to my recommendation against mandatory busing is based mainly upon the *possibility* that under certain conditions induced school integration *might* have substantial beneficial effects on minority students. In this regard, given Pettigrew's well-known use of social science findings in support of integration, their conclusions rely heavily upon the application of a double double standard.

Their belief in the possibility of educational benefits rests upon their highly questionable rejection of black and white achievement comparisons and upon a variety of small and inconsistent fluctuations in the achievement of bused students. This leads them to hold that my "firm policy conclusion against 'mandatory busing' is not substantiated by the evidence presented." Apparently, then, their view is that mandatory busing (or induced integration), whether ordered by the courts or by a local school board, is strictly a moral and constitutional issue and does not require any justification involving educational benefits. They have therefore placed the burden of proof not upon those who back the social intervention but upon those who object to the intervention.

I cannot agree with the assumptions behind this reasoning, with the kind of morality it represents, or with the implicit suggestion that social science should be used only when it favors the values of the social scientist. There is no doubt in my mind that our democratic values prohibit laws or actions that force the separation of racial or ethnic groups; I believe that the 1954 decision of the Supreme Court aimed to eliminate this compulsory separation of the races in the schools. But I also believe that compulsory integration—in the absence of clear evidence that the segregation was itself purposive and mandatory—gains little support from these same democratic principles. This is why most legal decisions and policy actions in the school desegregation movement have rested very heavily upon the assumed educational benefits of integration. In the absence of a clear constitutional or moral mandate to force racial balance in regions of de facto segregation, supporters of school integration turned to social science —where there was an unending (and unquestioned) supply of documentation of both the damage from racial segregation and the benefits of integration. This was the case in the 1954 decision (even though forced segregation was at issue); I believe it was true for the 1967 report of the U.S. Commission on Civil Rights, as exemplified in its summary statement that the "conclusions drawn by the U.S. Supreme Court about the impact upon children of segregation compelled by law . . . applies to segregation not compelled by law"; and I believe it is true for the present critique, which tries very hard—but without success—to challenge the findings of current research on induced integration.

But it follows that if the current research does not support the thesis of educational benefits, the policy must be questioned. Since the intervention has been based upon what I would call "preliminary" social science findings (very little of the data until recently was based on studies of *actual* induced integration), the burden of proof must fall upon those policy makers who support mandatory busing. The first double standard of the critique, then, is the burden of proof: To initiate the action one can use any type of social science data, whether or not it directly tests the policy in question and regardless of its technical adequacy. But once the integration policy is in full force, it cannot be questioned unless one can *conclusively prove* that school integration *cannot* have an effect on educational benefits. As far as I am concerned, the current data are far more adequate to test the efficacy of integration than was the research that existed prior to induced integration programs. Since it can in no way be concluded that the original research *proved* the existence of educational benefits, my critics clearly apply a double standard when they claim that the absence of benefits has not been proven and therefore we should not decide against mandatory busing.

The second double standard is applied by the critique's assertion that the whole matter is really a constitutional issue, to be decided by "the Court's interpretation of the 14th Amendment." The double standard here is obvious. One willingly applies social science findings to public policy if they are in accordance with one's values, but declares them irrelevant if they contradict one's values. Pettigrew's resort to this tactic recalls a press conference reported in *The New York Times* on June 11, 1972, in which Dr. Kenneth Clark—whose scientific research and assistance was so important in the 1954 Supreme Court decision— was quoted as saying that "courts and political bodies should decide questions of school spending and integration, not on the basis of un- certain research findings, but on the basis of the constitutional and equity rights of human beings." The double standard could not be expressed more graphically.

It will be disastrous for the social sciences if they allow themselves to be used in this way. We social scientists depend upon society for our existence; our credibility is undermined if we do not present and use our findings in a consistent manner. The responsible use of social science in policy matters requires that we state the facts as they occur, no matter how painful their implications. And if we are willing to use facts to initiate policy reform, we must likewise use them to question existing policy. I believe that in the long run society will benefit more from decisions based on facts than from ideology contradicted by facts.

I do not want to imply that we should engage in social interven- tion only when it is supported by social science or stop any social intervention when the findings of science question its support. Social science cannot be brought to bear on all issues of policy, sometimes for technical reasons and sometimes for ethical reasons. Some policies can- not be researched, and some policies are demanded by constitutional principles or by common morality. But when policies are based upon empirical considerations that social science can study, there is a way that policy and science can proceed in concert. That way utilizes the method of social experimentation and evaluation—a method that has long been prominent in the medical sciences. We would not think of prescribing a new drug without first obtaining sound evidence of both its efficiency and its harmlessness by experimental evaluation of its actual effects on human subjects (usually volunteers). Why should not a similar standard be applied to proposed remedies for curing social ills? Our assumptions about social behavior have been proven wrong in the past, and they will be proven wrong in the future. The only way to make reasonably sure that the remedy is not worse than the malady is to engage in careful research under realistic conditions. That our government is beginning to adopt the principle of social experimentation is shown by Congress's recent decision to perform a large-scale, long-term experiment to test the efficiency of a guaranteed income plan before implementing it for the whole nation. This is a welcome sign for those who want to see a closer connection between social science and public policy.

It is this kind of philosophy that led me to favor voluntary busing programs, not any evidence that voluntary busing is more efficacious than mandatory busing. I do not think the evidence pointing to an absence of educational benefits or the evidence for possible harmful effects is strong enough to justify a prohibition of busing for those families and communities that desire it—regardless of their motives. On the contrary, I would like to see more voluntary busing on a controlled, experimental basis accompanied by a careful research and evaluation effort. This is the only responsible way to resolve the controversy and to establish sound guidelines for policy makers.

Statement to the Senate Education Subcommittee

ELLIOT L. RICHARDSON

Elliot L. Richardson held three different cabinet posts in the Nixon administration before resigning as Attorney General to protest the firing of Watergate prosecutor Archibald Cox. Prior to Watergate, Richardson was Secretary of Defense. He is quoted here from testimony given in a March 24, 1972, appearance before the Senate Education Subcommittee, when he was Secretary of Health, Education, and Welfare.

Our national quest for equal educational opportunity is now at a crossroads. Some would describe the divisive debate on the busing of school children for desegregation purposes as a national crisis. Surely few issues of domestic policy have produced so much heat and so little light.

The fabric of the body politic can withstand, on any given set of issues at one time, just so much strain and no more. In our judgment, we have reached that point on the issues now subsumed under the heading of "busing."

We must rechart our national course. If one thing is clear, it is that we cannot continue the current degree of pressure on our school systems. As the President said two years ago:

One of the mistakes of past policy has been to demand too much of our schools: They have been expected not only to educate, but also to accomplish a social transformation. Children in many instances have not been served, but used—in what all too often has proved a tragically futile effort to achieve in the schools the kind of a multiracial society which the adult community has failed to achieve for itself.

If we are to be realists, we must recognize that in a free society there are limits to the amount of Government coercion that can reason-

174

ably be used; that in achieving desegregation we must proceed with
the least possible disruption of the education of the Nation's children;
and that our children are highly sensitive to conflict, and highly vulnerable to lasting psychic injury.

But to rechart our course is not to abandon it, nor to lose sight of
our fundamental objectives, nor to break faith with the progress
achieved since *Brown v. Board of Education* was decided, some
eighteen years ago.

The problems of achieving equal educational opportunity have
themselves changed during those eighteen years, because the dual
school systems in our Southern States have now been substantially disestablished.

Let us put aside the question of who deserves the credit for this
progress. The facts are that in the eleven Southern States since 1968,
the percentage of black children in all-black schools has dropped from
68 percent to 9.2 percent and the percentage of black children in
majority white schools has increased from 18.4 percent to 43.9 percent.
More of the minority children in the South now attend effectively integrated schools than those in the North.

Now, in looking at the distance we have yet to travel, we find a
whole complex of problems which face us at the end of the road that
began with *Brown* eighteen years ago. We face the vast ghettos in our
large cities, the occasional problems of in-school discrimination, the
few districts that still operate *de jure* segregated systems, the widespread belief that remedies have been imposed that harm more than
they help, and, above all, the enormous educational disadvantages
afflicting our poor and minority children.

As we look to the future, we must now focus much more specifically on education itself: on assuring that the opportunity is not only
equal, but adequate, and that in those remaining cases in which desegregation has not yet been completed it be achieved with a greater
sensitivity to educational needs.

The parents of all children—black and white alike—are demanding more and better education from our school systems.

To put it another way, there is a belief abroad in the land that,
in enforcing the guarantees of the Fourteenth Amendment, we have
forgotten this basic objective.

There is a belief abroad in the land that our courts are busing
children to achieve a racial balance, or busing children without regard
to any set of rational educational values.

There are legitimate concerns that the results in some cases are
not educationally sound for at least some of the children involved.

The perceptions of our citizens form real parameters for action by their Government.

We must reestablish by action, not words alone, the primacy of the educational objectives which underlie the original *Brown* cases. We must downgrade our reliance on the transportation of students between schools or school systems as our primary tool to achieve equal educational opportunity. Transportation can never do the whole job. It can never reach the core areas of our cities where education deprivation is the greatest.

Father Hesburgh's Program for Racial Justice

THEODORE M. HESBURGH

The Reverend Theodore M. Hesburgh is President of
Notre Dame University and past Chairman of the
United States Commission on Civil Rights. His comments on busing and integration are from a longer
article on social justice in America.

When one tries to find an effective approach to the total problem of
racial justice, education is by all odds the best. View the vicious circle:
A black youngster is generally born into an atmosphere of poverty
and failure. He grows up in a poor house in a poor neighborhood.
He has a 30 percent chance of not having a father at home to guide
him, and, if so, his mother must often work to support him, which
deprives him of the parental education that most white youngsters take
for granted. Then he must go to a dismal ghetto school which re-
sembles a jail more than a school and, often enough, functions as a
custodial rather than an educational institution. All around him the
atmosphere is polluted, not just bad air and water, but a bad human
situation in which to grow up: failure, violence, drugs, prostitution,
stealing, unemployment, aimlessness, hopelessness.

Our black youngster may be bright, but no matter. Many of our
eager politicians of both parties, lusting for office, obliterate whatever
hope he might have of leaving this impossible situation. Even if busing
is the only way out, and the courts find that he is indeed being de-

---

prived of his Fourteenth Amendment rights to equal opportunity in education, busing will not be available to him as a means of redressing his inequality, if these politicians have their way. If good white neighborhood schools are good for whites in the suburbs, then bad blacks neighborhood schools are in no way good for blacks in the ghetto. But no matter: Blacks should not be allowed to contaminate our nice white schools, or neighborhoods, or businesses, and they don't have enough political power to challenge the white majority anyway. So prejudice speaks.

Mind you, I am not proposing that white children go to bad ghetto schools. I am making the opposite point: that unless black children are given a chance to get out of, and away from, these schools we now finally see as so bad (since white children might have to attend them), then we have destroyed the last bridge out of the ghetto, which we also created by prejudice and often by Government-financed housing policies.

Without a real educational opportunity (which for a black often means a non-ghetto school), the black youngster will never eventually matriculate at a first-rate college or university, will never qualify for a profession or even a decent job, will never be able to support his family, will often drop out of the only dismal school available and become a troublesome, costly and nonproductive member of society. This isn't much fun for him either, so he will also often be frustrated, aggressive, violent.

There is no escape in trying to put the blame for such educational deprivation on inherent lack of talent or virtue. There are too many telling examples of those few given an equal chance measuring up and even excelling. It would be like accusing blacks of lack of physical courage to compete when they were excluded from competition in professional sports, as they were excluded during our apartheid years. Once allowed to compete, they not only excelled, they dominated, despite their being a minority. The same is true in other fields.

There will always be inequality of performance among men and women of every country. Some will be more virtuous, work harder, accomplish more. But it is in the nature of *our* national commitment that here in America all will start equal, all will have equality of opportunity. As long as equality of opportunity is not a reality for all, we have no right to criticize bad performance. And it is not a reality today.

I am not saying here that blacks can get a good education only in the company of whites, but I am saying that most predominantly white schools are much better than most predominantly black schools in a society where the majority is white and the political power of the purse is white, where most whites live in good neighborhoods and most blacks in the worst neighborhoods—those discarded by whites. I am saying that in America, North and South, East and West, white children educated in predominantly white schools have historically had a better education than black children educated in predominantly black schools. There have been ample studies to document this.

Some say improve the ghetto schools, but for long decades we whites have been unconcerned about black education and blacks are rightly dubious about another empty promise. Meanwhile, another generation of young blacks and other colored minorities is condemned to another round of human hopelessness.

One final point: Ever since there have been buses, white parents have been busing their children to where the best education was—as black children were bused only to inferior schools, away from whites. It was only when it looked as if the process might be reversed that the furor began.

Moving the Constitution to the Back of the Bus

I. F. STONE

I. F. Stone is a contributing editor of *The New York Review of Books*. He was formerly editor and publisher of *I. F. Stone's Weekly*. His books include *The Truman Era, The Haunted Fifties*, and *In a Time of Torment*.

During Reconstruction, when the Southern states were still under military occupation, a Mississippi editor who was an "unreconstructed rebel" published an editorial in the Vicksburg *Times* called "The Scoundrelism of Satraps." It severely criticized the Yankee general in command of that area. The editor was arrested and held for trial before a military commission under the Reconstruction Acts. He sought his freedom on a writ of habeas corpus, and when this was denied by the circuit court, appealed to the Supreme Court.

The radicals in Congress, fearing that he would win and that the Court might hold the Reconstruction Acts unconstitutional, as indeed a majority seemed about to do, took an extraordinary step. Though the Court had already taken jurisdiction and heard argument in the case, Congress over President Johnson's veto passed a rider amending the Judiciary Act of 1789 to withdraw jurisdiction in habeas corpus appeals from the Supreme Court. Thereupon in *Ex Parte McCardle* (7

I. F. Stone, "Moving the Constitution to the Back of the Bus," *The New York Review of Books*, April 20, 1972. Reprinted with permission from *The New York Review of Books*. Copyright © 1972, New York Review Inc.

Wall. 506) the Court, in 1869, regretfully dismissed the editor's appeal on the ground that authority to hear it had been withdrawn.

This obscure, dubious, and difficult case is the nearest thing to a precedent in American constitutional law for a bill Nixon has submitted to Congress. This declares a "moratorium" on all busing decisions by the federal courts until July 1 of 1973 or until the passage of its companion measure in his anti-busing program, the "Equal Opportunities Educational Act of 1972," if that should be passed earlier. The effect of *Ex Parte McCardle* was to prevent the Supreme Court from enforcing a basic constitutional right, that of habeas corpus. The purpose of "The Student Transportation Moratorium Act of 1972," as submitted to Congress by Nixon, is to prevent the Supreme Court and the lower federal courts for a time from enforcing, as they deem necessary, the constitutional right of blacks and other minorities to nonsegregated schools under the "equal protection" clause of the Fourteenth Amendment.

The constitutional question raised in both cases could hardly be more fundamental. Can Congress by legislation block the courts from enforcing fundamental rights? This casts a shadow far beyond the issues of school desegregation or of busing as one means of implementing it.

This is the second time in less than a decade that the Republicans have put forward this particular ploy to undercut Supreme Court decisions they disliked. In August 1964, the late Senator Dirksen, then minority leader of the Senate, offered a similar "moratorium" rider to suspend for two to four years the historic "one man, one vote" reapportionment decision of the Supreme Court two months earlier. This brought a sharp protest from fifteen of the country's most prestigious law school deans and law school professors, including Erwin N. Griswold, then dean of Harvard Law School and now solicitor general.[1]

What they said then of the Dirksen rider applies equally to the busing "moratorium" rider the Administration is now seeking. They said the effect is not merely "to limit the jurisdiction of the federal courts." It is "to declare by statute, without constitutional amendment, that for a period of time certain constitutional rights may not be vindicated in any court, state or federal." Only once before in our history, the law professors said, citing the *McCardle* case, had Con-

---

[1] The list of signers and the full text may be found in *The New York Times* for August 10, 1964. Also see the discussion on pp. 387–8 of *The Constitution and the Supreme Court: A Documentary History*, Vol. II, edited by Louis H. Pollak (World, 1966).

gress "acted to prevent a constitutional decision which it anticipated." Most historians and legal analysts, they went on, "have regarded the McCardle case as an unfortunate episode in our history" which "ought not to be repeated in this even more drastic form." [2]

What happened in *McCardle* and what Nixon proposes now are linked in the painful history of the attempt to achieve full emancipation from slavery. The difference is that then a radical majority sought to enforce the rights of the freedman. Now a conservative white majority under Nixon's leadership seeks to hand his descendants a setback. For the issue is not busing—busing for better white schools and busing for segregated black schools are accepted and familiar devices. *The issue is not to have to go to school with slum children, black, brown, or white.* As an outraged white resident of Coy, Alabama, put it to a reporter for the *Wall Street Journal* (see the article by Neil Maxwell, March 20), "As long as we don't have niggers on there, it's not busing. Busing is making white children get on with niggers." That is the naked issue and that is the real feeling to which Nixon, Wallace, and Democratic opportunists like Humphrey have been pandering.

A constitutional, a moral, a racial, and an educational crisis are intertwined in the controversy Nixon has precipitated by his anti-busing program. It comes at a time when he has been engaged for several years in shaping a new Supreme Court majority which will be as mediocre and compliant as the choices he can get past the Senate. It comes when the Senate is even now wrestling with the question of whether to confirm as attorney general a Goldwaterite Republican indifferent both to civil liberties and minority rights.

A sketch of Richard Kleindienst in the *Harvard Law Record* of March 3 (he was graduated from Harvard Law School in 1950) recalls that in November 1969, when 300,000 people were expected in Washington to protest the war, Kleindienst in a planning session advocated mass arrests in case of violence. "When questioned about the constitutionality of his plan, he brusquely replied," says the account in the *Record*, " 'We'll worry about the Constitution later.' " That seems to be his attitude still as the President's acting attorney general in formulating this new anti-busing program.

At the White House press briefing on March 17, the acting attorney general showed the same lack of candor and the same talent for the disingenuous that he has demonstrated so fully before the Senate

---

[2] "There is a serious question," Justice Douglas wrote for himself and Justice Black in *Glidden v. Zdanok* (370 U.S. 530), "whether the McCardle case could command a majority view today."

Judiciary Committee. He was asked at the briefing to address himself "to the overall question of constitutionality and particularly the constitutionality of the moratorium legislation." Instead of beginning with an honest admission of the constitutional complexities and of the fact that even *Ex Parte McCardle* isn't precedent enough, he began by trying to give the impression that there was no difficulty whatsoever. Only slowly and reluctantly did he admit some of the truth.

This was his progression from bland misrepresentation to damaging admission: First he said that "there can be no legitimate doubt whatsoever" that Congress under Section 5 of the Fourteenth Amendment and Article III of the Constitution had the power to enact the new anti-busing legislation. This can only be described as the most whopping oversimplification of the year. He said that "many constitutional lawyers had been consulted" and "the opinion of all that I know" agreed that when the moratorium bill was combined with the longer range "equal educational opportunities act" Congress "certainly . . . has the power."

All one can conclude from this is that the acting attorney general's acquaintance among constitutional lawyers must be extremely limited. Section 5 of the Fourteenth Amendment gives the Congress power "by appropriate legislation" to "enforce" the amendment's grant of equal protection. But any legislation framed not to enforce but to undercut its great purposes would be held unconstitutional by any Supreme Court that did its duty. As recently as 1965 in *Katzenbach v. Morgan* (384 U.S. 641), the Court, speaking through Mr. Justice Brennan, said that Section 5 "does not grant Congress power to restrict, abrogate or dilute" the amendment's guarantees of equal protection and due process.

Nor can Article III readily be used for the purpose Kleindienst would assign to it. Article III says the Supreme Court, aside from certain enumerated types of cases, "shall have appellate jurisdiction, both as to Law and Fact, with such Exceptions and under such Regulations as the Congress shall make." But few if any constitutional lawyers today would agree that this regulatory power can be used by Congress, as in *Ex Parte McCardle,* to prevent the Supreme Court from enforcing fundamental rights guaranteed by the Constitution or from operating as an independent check on the legislative and executive branches of the government. If it could, we would have parliamentary supremacy, as in England, rather than a government of separation of powers with "checks and balances." In that case minorities would have no judicial protection against majorities.

The real meaning of Article III and the extent to which it may give Congress power over constitutional adjudication is a recurrent subject of controversy whenever Supreme Court decisions displease a substantial body of opinion. In the Thirties radical New Dealers, myself among them, looked to Article III and re-examined *Ex Parte McCardle* to see if these offered any hope of curbing the "nine old men" of the Supreme Court who were striking down one New Deal reform after another.[3] FDR tried his "court packing" plan as a remedy when it became all too obvious that the "exceptions" clause of Article III and *Ex Parte McCardle* were wan hopes. How wan they remain today was demonstrated just before the White House briefing in which Kleindienst participated.

If he had indeed consulted "many constitutional lawyers" and obtained their advance approval, who and where were they? Why were they not produced to back him up at the White House briefing? Two law professors, Robert Bork of Yale and Charles Alan Wright of the University of Texas, were on hand to give their views but ducked out when told they would be talking on the record with two dozen reporters. They had been told they would be talking only off the record and to a picked few. If the constitutionality of the Nixon anti-busing program is as clear as Kleindienst says it is, one wonders why the only two professors he could marshal refused to say so in public.[4]

The full flavor of Kleindienst's presentation is best savored from the climactic portion in the transcript. After he told of the lawyers he had consulted, he was asked a plain question but tried his best to evade a plain answer:

---

[3] For the most comprehensive argument along these lines see Louis B. Boudin's *Government by Judiciary* (1932, reprinted by Russell & Russell, 1968), a two-volume work of enormous scholarship by a man who was in his time a distinguished Marxist scholar and a leading New York labor lawyer. The most recent study of the problem is *Congress v. The Supreme Court* by Raoul Berger (Harvard University Press, 1969), which is written with distinction. He concludes that the framers intended the Supreme Court to wield the ultimate weapon of the judicial veto and that they never intended the "exceptions" clause of Article III to become a Congressional "check on the Court's constitutional decisions."

I now agree with Berger but perhaps that is because circumstances have changed. Constitutional exegesis, too, depends on whose ox is being gored. The radical Republicans a century ago argued that the Reconstruction of the rebel states to ensure full equality for the freed blacks was a political and not a judical problem. This was also Dirksen's view of one man, one vote reapportionment. This is, in part, a semantic dodge when the Supreme Court disagrees with one's "politics."

[4] According to John P. MacKenzie in the Washington *Post*, March 18, 1972, Bork's colleague at Yale, Alexander Bickel, recently told the House Judiciary Committee that a bill similar to the Administration's would fail a modern test. Congress "can assign large tasks to the Federal courts" under Article III "and take the tasks away," Bickel said. But he acknowledged that it can't "pick and choose" by stripping power when it doesn't like what the courts have done.

Q. Is there a precedent in case law for this kind of action?

Mr. Kleindienst: The Congress has dealt with the question of remedy in the courts going clear back to 1793 in one way or another. So, to that extent, there is a precedent, and that, I think, is what permits constitutional lawyers to say that Congress has that power. *There is no precedent in exactly this kind of situation.* . . . [Emphasis added.]

Even after that admission, he fuzzed the picture and tried to mislead the reporters by going on to say, ". . . but the Congress, for instance, in the National Labor Relations Act, determined a national policy that was to apply between employees and employers in representation. That, again, is a question of remedy. The Supreme Court has said what the remedy would be under certain circumstances. So, constitutionally, I think there is ample precedent."

This confuses statutory with constitutional rights. The National Labor Relations Act established certain statutory rights and the remedies to enforce them. In representation cases appeals to the courts are restricted to protect the rights of workers and the authority of the National Labor Relations Board from interminable interference by injunction.[5] When Congress establishes statutory rights, it can provide, change, or withdraw not only the remedies but the rights themselves. But rights created by the Constitution are not subject to restriction or withdrawal by Congress. Constitutionally the precedents for what Nixon is trying to do are not only *not* "ample," to use Kleindienst's word, they are nonexistent. Even *Ex Parte McCardle* didn't withdraw the right of habeas corpus from that Confederate editor. He appealed for the writ in the circuit court and lost. All Congress did *on the face of it* was to withdraw the Supreme Court's appellate jurisdiction so he could not get a reversal in the Supreme Court. The radicals could argue that neither the right to habeas

---

[5] Kleindienst's labor law is also deceptive. The predecessor labor board, established by executive order, had never been able to bring about a labor representation election where the employers balked because they found it so easy to enjoin the board in the courts. The hearings on what became the Wager Act show that Congress restricted appeals from orders for representation elections to remedy this situation. Appeals to the courts were provided only where an employer, after such an election, refuses to bargain. He can then be hailed into court by the board for an enforcement order and thus obtain a judicial review indirectly.

Even here, however, the courts have provided their own remedies outside the statute by holding in a few cases that the board could not enforce its orders if evidence showed that it had clearly exceeded its statutory authority. This is the meaning of Kleindienst's opaque reference to the fact that "under certain circumstances" the Supreme Court "has said what the remedy would be." How much greater is the Court's power to apply its own remedies, like busing, to enforce constitutional rights!

corpus nor the remedy was withdrawn. Kleindienst was mumbling through his hat.

This is where the constitutional problems begin with Nixon's long-range measure, his "equal educational opportunities" bill. In some ways the unconstitutionality of this bill is even plainer than his other bill for a temporary "moratorium." For the longer range measure seeks to restrict the remedies the courts may apply in school desegregation, especially busing, and thus nullify their power to enforce constitutional rights created by the "equal protection" clause of the Fourteenth Amendment.

But before we go into the legalities, I would like to call attention to the vagueness of the factual presentation on busing in the White House briefing. If the Administration were going into the Supreme Court in a plea against busing, the first requirement would be evidence for Nixon's TV assertion that busing had reached "massive" and unreasonable proportions. In this respect the briefing was not only unsatisfactory but confusing. At one point toward the end the question was asked:

> If, as the experts have testified here, we do not even know the extent of busing involved in the desegregation process, then what is the hard evidence that supports a Presidential call for a moratorium on busing?

To this Mr. Ehrlichman could only furnish a long, emotional but inconclusive answer the gist of which was, "Every place you go around this country" this is "the front-burner issue in most local communities." But there *are* some figures and they do not support the hysteria whipped up during and since the Florida primary.

The latest issue available of the *Digest of Educational Statistics* [6] carries a table on the number and percent of public school pupils transported at public expense. This shows a sharp rate of increase in public transportation in the quarter century before the school desegregation decision in 1954. The percentage transported was 7.4 percent in 1929. In the next ten years it more than doubled to 16.3 percent in 1939. In the next decade it went up by three-quarters to 27.7 percent in 1949. In the school year of the *Brown* decision, 1954-54, it had risen to 32.8 percent. In all those years there was no outcry against busing. Busing made possible the transition from the one-room schoolhouse to the consolidated school. The outcry against

---

[6] Publication No. OE 10024-70 (Department of Health, Education and Welfare, 1970). See Table 46, p. 36.

busing only began when it was used to mix white with colored, affluent with poor.

In the years since *Brown,* the percentage of bused schoolchildren has risen to almost 45 percent. But *less than 3 percent* of the total, according to a speech in the House on March 22 by Congressman Stokes (D., Ohio), chairman of the Black Caucus, "are bused for purposes of desegregation."

The figure is startling and it is up to the Nixon Administration to rebut it. It begins to seem less startling when one looks at the statistical tables that accompanied the Stokes speech. These originated with an HEW release of last June 13 on the progress made in desegregating schools. The figures show that in 1970, 71.8 percent of all black pupils were in schools where 80 to 100 percent belonged to a minority race. The percentage of black pupils going to schools where more than half the students were black or brown was 83.9 percent. The figures show that Nixon was, as Stokes said, "tragically and grossly incorrect" when he declared in his TV address on busing that "the dismantling of the old dual system has been substantially completed." Only 16.1 percent of all black pupils were in schools where more than half the pupils were white.

Busing may be far from satisfactory but the courts have been driven to it by years of skillful evasion of desegregation decisions. To abandon it in the absence of better remedies is to risk a deepening of racial disillusion and bitterness. The new Nixon legislation, under cover of the anti-busing hysteria, would invite *re*segregation. At the White House briefing the press was assured that no "rollback" was intended, but that is exactly what Section 406 of Nixon's "equal opportunities" bill invites. It says:

> On the application of an educational agency, court orders or desegregation plans under Title VI of the Civil Rights Act of 1964 in effect on the date of enactment of this Act and intended to end segregation of students on the basis of race, color or national origin shall be reopened and modified to comply with the provisions of this Act.

Just to make the purpose clear to the least discerning, this provision carries the heading "Reopening Proceedings." Segregationists and white supremacists will be down like a swarm of hornets on any school board that does not take advantage of these provisions. The proposed act holds multiple attractions for those who would like to turn back the clock. Title IV, Section 402, "Remedies," spells out all the old dodges school boards have used since *Brown* to avoid integration and provides that no busing may be ordered by a court "until it is demonstrated by clear and convincing evidence" [7] that "no other method set out in Section 402 will provide an adequate remedy." Since one of the methods spelled out is "the construction of new schools," this is another route to "separate but equal," the old *Plessy v. Ferguson* Jim Crow doctrine the *Brown* decision in 1954 was supposed to have outlawed.

Nixon's bill would upset almost two decades of adjudication and sprinkle the path of integration with new legal pitfalls. An example is in Section 401, which says that a court can impose "only such remedies as are essential to correct particular denials of equal educational opportunity." What does "particular" mean? It might mean that each separate "denial" would require separate judicial action.

Looked at as a whole the two new bills clearly represent an attempt to turn back the clock and to override the Court's authority in enforcing constitutional rights. It would take a Supreme Court packed with lawyers like Carswell, Rehnquist, and Kleindienst to rubber stamp this program as constitutional. Certainly Nixon must go far to the right of his own Chief Justice Burger and his own appointee Blackmun to obtain judicial approval. For Burger wrote, and Blackmun joined in, the unanimous opinion last April 20, 1971, *Swann v. Charlotte-Mecklenburg Board of Education,* which for the first time explicitly approved busing as a tool of integration and unleashed the white racist hysteria to which Wallace, Nixon, Humphrey, and many others who know better have been pandering.

Nixon's own chief justice seems to be replacing Warren as the target of rightist slander. When Nixon, with sly demagogy, talked in his TV address of March 16 about busing children "across a city to an inferior school just to meet some social planner's concept of what is considered to be the correct racial balance," he was caricaturing and distorting Burger's decision in *Swann.* The below-the-belt quality of Nixon's rhetoric is brought into sharp focus when one recalls that the chief justice explicitly rejected the idea of a "correct racial balance" in favor of a pragmatic and flexible approach.

"The constitutional command to desegregate schools," Burger ruled in *Swann,* "does not mean that every school in every community must always reflect the racial composition of the school system as a whole." It would be amusing to know what the chief justice muttered to Mrs. Burger at this point in Nixon's TV address.

In all Nixon's career there has rarely been a trickier performance

---

[7] This, the standard proof required for fraud in civil cases, is far more strict than any of the more familiar standards for regulatory agencies. It represents another hurdle to successful integration suits.

than in the presentation of his anti-busing program. Its unveiling on TV was misleading, its offer of new funds for "quality education" was deceptive, the gap between his presentation and the fine print in his legislative program becomes deeper the longer it is studied. "Mr. Nixon," Congressman Conyers of Detroit told the House on March 22, "is playing a game which threatens to tear at the already delicate legal and social balance in this country. He has chosen to cater to the fear of the powerless and to manipulate the power of the fearful." To the President's untrustworthy promises of quality education in the ghettos, this leading spokesman for the Black Caucus replied that even if Nixon were really offering new and adequate funding (which he is not):

> Quality education is more than airy classrooms, well-paid teachers, and lots of books. There can be no quality education without integration. Quality education means an educational experience which will lay the foundation for intelligent participation in a democratic society. Children who are raised in isolation can hardly be expected to understand their society and its workings.

Integration has its hardships. Black as well as white children do suffer in adjusting to it. But these are the pains of movement toward multi-racialism. To stop the progress after so much sacrifice and disruption, to move back toward the past, to play on people's worst instincts is to risk America's future for the lowest kind of politics. The problems of education in our society are complex and appallingly difficult. No one has a full, much less an easy, answer. But the way toward it will not be found by diverting emotion and energy to the false and peripheral problem of busing. The price of failure is to drift further toward a country irreconcilably split into two hostile nations, a giant Ulster bound sooner or later to erupt.

Is Busing Necessary?

NATHAN GLAZER

Nathan Glazer is professor of education and social structure at Harvard University. His books include *The Lonely Crowd* (with David Riesman and Reuel Denney), *Beyond the Melting Pot* (with Daniel Moynihan), and *Remembering the Answers: Essays on the American Student Revolt*.

I

It is the fate of any social reform in the United States—perhaps anywhere—that, instituted by enthusiasts, men of vision, politicians, statesmen, it is soon put into the keeping of full-time professionals. This has two consequences. On the one hand, the job is done well. The enthusiasts move on to new causes while the professionals continue working in the area of reform left behind by public attention. But there is a second consequence. The professionals, concentrating exclusively on their area of reform, may become more and more remote from public opinion, and indeed from common sense. They end up at a point that seems perfectly logical and necessary to them—but which seems perfectly outrageous to almost everyone else. This is the story of school desegregation in the United States.

For ten years after the 1954 Supreme Court decision in *Brown*, little was done to desegregate the schools of the South. But professionals were at work on the problem. The NAACP Legal Defense Fund continued to bring case after case into court to circumvent the endless forms of resistance to a full and complete desegregation of the dual school systems of the South. The federal courts, having started on this journey in 1954, became educated in all the techniques of subterfuge and evasion, and in their methodical way struck them down one by one. The federal executive establishment, reluctant to enter the battle of school desegregation, became more and more involved.

The critical moment came with the passage of the Civil Rights Act in 1964, in the wake of the assassination of a President and the exposure on television of the violent lengths to which Southern government would go in denying constitutional rights to Negroes. Under Title IV of the Civil Rights Act, the Department of Justice could bring suits against school districts maintaining segregation. Under Title VI, no federal funds under any program were to go to districts that practiced segregation. With the passage of the Elementary and Secondary Education Act in 1965, which made large federal funds available to schools, the club of federal withdrawal of funds became effective. In the Department of Justice and in the Department of Health, Education, and Welfare, bureaucracies rapidly grew up to enforce the law. Desegregation no longer progressed painfully from test case to test case, endlessly appealed. It moved rapidly as every school district in the South was required to comply with federal requirements. HEW's guidelines for compliance steadily tightened, as the South roared and the North remained relatively indifferent. The Department of Justice, HEW, and the federal courts moved in tandem. What the courts declared was segregation became what HEW declared was segregation. After 1969, when the Supreme Court ordered, against the new administration's opposition, the immediate implementation of desegregation plans in Mississippi, no further delay was to be allowed.

The federal government and its agencies were under continual attack by the civil-rights organizations for an attitude of moderation in the enforcement of both court orders and legal requirements. Nevertheless, as compared with the rate of change in the years 1954 to 1964, the years since 1964 have seen an astonishing speeding-up in the process of desegregating the schools of the South.

Writing during the Presidential campaign of 1968, Gary Orfield, in his massive study, *The Reconstruction of Southern Education,* stated:

> To understand the magnitude of the social transformation in the South since 1964, that portrait of hate [of black students walking into Little Rock High School under the protection of paratroopers' bayonets] must be compared to a new image of tense but peaceful change. Even in the stagnant red clay counties in rural backwaters, where racial attitudes have not changed much for a century, dozens or even hundreds of black children have recently crossed rigid caste lines to enter white schools. Counties with well-attended Ku Klux Klan cross-burnings have

seen the novel and amazing spectacle of Negro teachers instructing white classes. It has been a social transmutation more profound and rapid than any other in peacetime American history.

This is a revolution whose manifesto is a court decision and whose heroes are bureaucrats, judges, and civil-rights lawyers. . . .

Mr. Orfield thought that it was all coming to an end. With Nixon attacking the guidelines that had brought such progress, and with the civil-rights coalition coming apart in the fires of the cities of the North, Mr. Orfield wrote, "A clear electoral verdict against racial reconciliation [that is, the election of Mr. Nixon] could mean that the episode of the school guidelines may recede into history as an interesting but futile experiment." Mr. Orfield underestimated the bureaucrats, the courts, and the overall American commitment to the desegregation of Southern schools. While Mr. Nixon's appointees were suffering the same abuse as Mr. Johnson's before them for insufficient zeal, the desegregation of the racially divided school systems of the South proceeded. Thus the Director of the HEW Office of Civil Rights, J. Stanley Pottinger, could summarize some of the key statistics as of 1970 in the following terms:

> When school opened in the fall of 1968, only 18 percent of the 2.9 million Negro children in the Southern states attended schools which were predominantly white in their student enrolments. In the fall of 1970, that figure had more than doubled to 39 percent . . . [and] the percentage of Negroes attending 100 percent black schools dropped . . . from 68 percent to 14 percent. In 1968, almost no districts composed of majority Negro (and other minority) children were the subject of federal enforcement action. It was thought . . . that the limited resources of government ought to be focused primarily on the districts which had a majority of white pupils, where the greatest educational gains might be made, and where actual desegregation was not as likely to induce white pupils to flee the system. . . . 40 percent of all the Negro children in the South live in [such] systems. . . . Obviously, the greater the amount of desegregation in majority black districts, the fewer will be the number of black children . . . who will be counted as "desegregated" under a standard which measures only those minority children who attend majority white schools.
>
> In order to account for this recent anomaly, HEW has begun to extract from its figures the number of minority children who live in mostly white districts and who attend mostly white schools. Last year, approximately 54 percent of the Negro children in the South who live in such districts attended majority white schools. Conversely, nearly 40 percent of the 2.3 million white children who live in mostly black (or minority) districts, now attend mostly black (or minority) schools.[1]

---

[1] In *Inequality in Education*, Center for Law and Education, Harvard University, August 3, 1971.

There has been further progress since, and if one uses as the measure the number of blacks going to schools with a majority of white children, the South is now considerably more integrated than the North.

Yet the desegregation of schools is once again the most divisive of American domestic issues. Two large points of view can be discerned as to how this has happened. To the reformers and professionals who have fought this hard fight—the civil-rights lawyers, the civil-rights organizations, the government officials, the judges—the fight is far from over, and even to review the statistics of change may seem an act of treason in the war against evil. Indeed, if one is to take committed supporters of civil rights at their word, there is nothing to celebrate. A year ago the Civil Rights Commission, the independent agency created by the Civil Rights Act of 1957 to review the state of civil rights, attacked the government in a massive report on the civil rights enforcement effort. "Measured by a realistic standard of results, progress in ending inequity has been disappointing. . . . In many areas in which civil-rights laws afford pervasive legal protection—education, employment, housing—discrimination persists, and the goal of equal opportunity is far from achievement." And the report sums up the gloomy picture of Southern school segregation, 16 years after *Brown:* "Despite some progress in Southern school desegregation . . . a substantial majority of black school children in the South still attend segregated schools." [2] Presumably, then, when a majority of Negro children attended schools in which whites were the majority, success by one measure should have been reported. But in its follow-up report one year later, this measure of success in Southern school desegregation was not even mentioned. The civil-rights enforcement effort in elementary and secondary schools, given a low "marginal" score for November 1970 (out of four possibilities, "poor," "marginal," "adequate," and "good"), is shown as having regressed to an even *lower* "marginal" score by May 1971, after HEW's most successful year in advancing school integration!

But from the point of view of civil-rights advocates, desegregation as such in the South is receding as a focus of attention. A second generation of problems has come increasingly to the fore: dismissal or demotion of black school principals and teachers as integration progresses and their jobs are to be given to whites; expulsions of black students for disciplinary reasons; the use of provocative symbols (the Confederate flag, the singing of "Dixie"); segregation within individual schools based on tests and ability grouping; and the rise of private schools in which whites can escape desegregation.

---

[2] *Federal Civil Rights Enforcement Effort,* 1970, p. 14.

But alongside these new issues, there is the reality that the blacks of the North and West are also segregated, not to mention the Puerto Ricans, Mexican Americans, and others. The civil-rights movement sees that minorities are concentrated in schools that may be all or largely minority, sees an enormous agenda of desegregation before it, and cannot pause to consider a success which is already in its mind paltry and inconclusive. The struggle must still be fought, as bitterly as ever.

There is a second point of view as to why desegregation, despite its apparent success, is no success. This is the Southern point of view, and now increasingly the Northern point of view. It argues that a legitimate, moral, and Constitutional effort to eliminate the unconstitutional separation of the races (most Southerners now agree with this judgment of *Brown*), has been turned into something else—an intrusive, costly, painful, and futile effort to regroup the races in education by elaborate transportation schemes. The Southern Congressmen who for so long tried to get others to listen to their complaints now watch with grim satisfaction the agonies of Northern Congressmen faced with the crisis of mandatory, court-imposed transportation for desegregation. On the night of November 4, 1971, as a desperate House passed amendment after amendment in a futile effort to stop busing, Congressman Edwards of Alabama said:

> Mr. Chairman, this will come as a shock to some of my colleagues. I am opposing this amendment. I will tell you why. I look at it from a rather cold standpoint. We are busing all over the First District of Alabama, as far as you can imagine. Buses are everywhere . . . people say to me, "How in the world are we ever going to stop this madness?" I say, "It will stop the day it starts taking place across the country, in the North, in the East, in the West, and yes, even in Michigan."

And indeed, one of the amendments had been offered by Michigan Congressmen, long-time supporters of desegregation, because what had been decreed for Charlotte, North Carolina, Mobile, Alabama, and endless other Southern cities was now on the way to becoming law in Detroit and its suburbs.

As a massive wave of antagonism to transportation for desegregation sweeps the country, the liberal Congressmen and Democratic Presidential aspirants who have for so long fought for desegregation ask themselves whether there is any third point of view: whether they must join with the activists who say that the struggle is endless and they must not flag, even now; or whether they must join with the Southerners. To stand with the courts in their latest decisions is, for liberal Congressmen, political suicide. A Gallup survey last October revealed that 76 percent of respondents opposed busing, almost as many in the East (71 percent), Midwest (77 percent), and West (72 percent), as in the South (82 percent); a majority of Muskie supporters (65 percent) as well as a majority of Nixon supporters (85 percent). Even more blacks oppose busing than support it (47 to 45 percent). But if to stand with the further extension to all the Northern cities and suburbs of transportation for desegregation is suicide, how can the liberal Congressmen join with the South and with what they view as Northern bigotry in opposing busing? Is there a third position, something which responds to the wave of frustration at court orders, and which does not mean the abandonment of hope for an integrated society?

How have we come from a great national effort to repair a monstrous wrong to a situation in which the sense of right of great majorities is offended by policies which seem continuous with that once noble effort? In order to answer this question, it is necessary to be clear on how the Southern issue became a national issue.

After the passage of the Civil Rights Act of 1964, the first attempt of the South to respond to the massive federal effort to impose desegregation upon it was "fredom of choice." There still existed the black schools and the white schools of a dual school system. But now whites could go to black schools (none did) and the blacks could go to white schools (few dared). It was perfectly clear that throughout the South "freedom of choice" was a means of maintaining the dual school system. In 1966 HEW began the process of demanding statistical proof that substantially more blacks were going to school with whites each year. The screw was tightened regularly, by the courts and HEW, and finally, in 1968, the Supreme Court gave the *coup de grâce,* insisting that dual school systems be eliminated completely. There must henceforth be no identifiable black schools and white schools, only schools.

But one major issue remained as far as statistical desegregation was concerned: the large cities of the South. For the fact was that the degree of segregation in the big-city Southern schools was by now no longer simply attributable to the dual school systems they, too, had once maintained; in some instances, indeed, these schools had even been "satisfactorily" (by some federal or court standard) desegregated years before. What did it mean to say that their dual school systems must also be dismantled "forthwith"?

Contrast, as a concrete instance, the case of rural New Kent County in Virginia, where the Supreme Court declared in 1968 that "freedom of choice" would not be accepted as a means of desegregating a dual school system. Blacks and whites lived throughout the county.

There were two schools, the historic black school and the historic white school. Under "freedom of choice," some blacks attended the white school, and no whites attended the black school. There was a simple solution to desegregation, here and throughout the rural and small-town South, and the Supreme Court insisted in 1968, fourteen years after *Brown,* that the school systems adopt it: to draw a line which simply made two school districts, one for the former black school, and one for the former white school, and to require all children in one district, white and black, to attend the former black school, and all children in the other, white and black, to attend the former white school.

But what now of Charlotte, Mobile, Nashville, and Norfolk? To draw geographical lines around the schools of these cities, which had been done, meant that many white schools remained all white, and many black schools remained all black. Some schools that had been "desegregated" in the past—that is, had experienced some mix of black and white—had already become "resegregated"—that is, largely black or all black as a result of population movements rather than any official action.

If there were to be no black schools and no white schools in the city, one thing at least was necessary: massive transportation of the children to achieve a proper mix. There was no solution in the form of geographical zoning.

But if this was the case, in what way was their situation different from that of Northern cities? In only one respect: the Southern cities had once had dual school systems, and the Northern cities had not. (Even this was not necessarily a decisive difference, for cities outside the Old South had also maintained dual systems until 1954. Indiana had a law permitting them until the late 1940's, and other cities had maintained dual systems somewhat earlier.) Almost everything else was the same. The dynamics of population change were the same. Blacks moved into the central city, whites moved out to the suburbs. Blacks were concentrated in certain areas, owing to a mixture of formal or informal residential discrimination, past or present, economic incapacity, and taste, and these areas of black population became larger and larger, making full desegregation by contiguous geographical zoning imposible. Even the political structures of Southern and Northern cities were becoming more alike. Southern blacks were voting, liberal candidates appealed to them, Southern blacks sat on city councils and school boards. If one required the full desegregation of Southern cities by busing, then why should one not require the full desegregation of Northern cities by busing?

Busing has often been denounced as a false issue. Until busing was decreed for the desegregation of Southern cities, it was. As has been pointed out again and again, buses in the South regularly carried black children past white schools to black schools, and white children past black schools to white schools. When "freedom of choice" failed to achieve desegregation and geographical zoning was imposed, busing sometimes actually declined. In any case, when the school systems were no longer allowed to have buses for blacks and buses for whites, certainly the busing system became more efficient. After 1970, busing for desegregation replaced the busing for segregation.

But this was not true when busing came to Charlotte, North Carolina, and many other cities of the South, in 1971, after the key Supreme Court decision in *Swann v. Charlotte-Mecklenburg County Board of Education.* The City of Charlotte is 64 square miles, larger than Washington, D.C., but it is a part of Mecklenburg County, with which it forms a single school district of 550 square miles, which is almost twice the size of New York City. Many other Southern cities (Mobile, Nashville, Tampa) also form part of exceptionally large school districts. While 29 percent of the schoolchildren of Mecklenburg County are black, almost all live in Charlotte. Owing to the size of the county, 24,000 of 84,500 children were bused, for the purpose of getting children to schools beyond walking distance. School zones were formed geographically, and the issue was, could all-black and all-white schools exist in Mecklenburg County, if a principle of neighborhood school districting meant they would be so constituted?

The Supreme Court ruled they could not, and transportation could be used to eliminate black and white schools. The Court did not argue that there was a segregative intent in the creation of geographical zones —or that there was not—and referred to only one piece of evidence suggesting an effort to maintain segregation, free transfer. There are situations in which free transfer is used by white children to get out of mostly black schools, but if this had been the problem, the Court could have required a majority-to-minority transfer only (in which one can only transfer from a school in which one's race is a majority, and to a school in which one's race is a minority), as is often stipulated in desegregation plans. Instead the Court approved a plan which involved the busing of some 20,000 additional children, some for distances of up to 15 miles, from the center of the city to the outer limits of the county, and vice versa.

Two implications of the decision remain uncertain, but they may lead to a reorganization of all American education. If Charlotte, because it is part of the school district of Mecklenburg County, can be totally desegregated with each school having a roughly 71–29 white-black proportion, should not city boundaries be disregarded in other places and larger school districts of the Mecklenburg County scale be created wherever such action would make integration possible? A district judge has already answered this question in the affirmative for Richmond, Virginia.

But the second implication is: If Charlotte is—except for the background of a dual school system—socially similar to many Northern cities, and if radical measures can be prescribed to change the pattern that exists in Charlotte, should they not also be prescribed in the North? And to that question also a federal judge, ruling in a San Francisco case, has returned an affirmative answer.

San Francisco has a larger measure of integration probably than most Northern cities. Nevertheless *de facto* segregation—the segregation arising not from formal decisions to divide the races as in the South, but from other causes, presumed to be social and demographic —has long been an issue in San Francisco. In 1962, the NAACP filed suit against the school board, charging it with "affording, operating, and maintaining a racially segregated school system within the San Francisco Unified School District, contrary to and in violation of the equal protection and due process clause of the Fourteenth Amendment of the Constitution of the United States." As John Kaplan has written:

> The history of this suit is a short and strange one. The Board of Education retained for its defense a distinguished local attorney, Joseph Alioto [now the mayor], who was primarily an anti-trust specialist. Alioto started discovery proceedings and the heart seemed to go out of the plaintiffs.
>
> In any case, after admitting in depositions that the Board had no intention to produce a condition of racial imbalance; that it took no steps to bring about such a condition; that its lines were not drawn for the purpose of creating or maintaining racial imbalance; that there was no gerrymandering; and finally that the Board was under no obligation to relieve the situation by transporting students from their neighborhoods to other districts, the plaintiffs' attorney allowed the suit to be dismissed for want of prosecution on December 2, 1964.

It was assumed that this disposed of the legal issue. Meanwhile the San Francisco school system continued to struggle with the problem. After a long series of censuses, disputes, and studies, the school board proposed to set up two new integrated complexes, using transportation to integrate, one North and one South of Golden Gate Park. They were to open in 1970. When, however, one was postponed because of money problems, suit was brought once again by integration-minded parents, this time charging *de jure* segregation on the ground that the school board's failure to implement the two integrated school complexes amounted to an official act maintaining the schools in their presently segregated state.

Judge Stanley Weigel, before whom the matter was argued, very sensibly decided to wait for the Supreme Court's ruling in the Charlotte-Mecklenburg County case which, he and many others thought, might once and for all settle the question of whether *de facto* segregation was no less unconstitutional than *de jure* segregation. Although one may doubt from certain passages in the Charlotte-Mecklenburg decision that the Supreme Court did indeed mean to outlaw *de facto* segregation, Judge Weigel seems to have decided that it did. "The law is settled," he declared, "that school authorities violate the constitutional rights of children by establishing school attendance boundary lines knowing that the result is to continue or increase substantial racial imbalance."

But in ordering the desegregation of the San Francisco schools by transportation, Judge Weigel did not simply rest the matter on *de facto* segregation; he also listed acts of commission and omission which he believed amounted to *de jure* school segregation.

Now one can well imagine that a school board which does not or did not recently operate under state laws that required or permitted segregation could nevertheless through covert acts—which are equally acts under state authority—foster segregation. It could, for example, change school-zone lines, so as to confine black children in one school and permit white children to go to another school. It could build schools and expand them so that they served an all-black or all-white population. It could permit a transfer policy whereby white children could escape from black schools while blacks could not. It could assign black teachers to black schools and white teachers to white schools.

Judge Weigel charged all these things. The record—a record made by a liberal school board, appointed by a liberal mayor, in a liberal city, with a black president of the school board—does not, in this layman's opinion, bear him out, unless one is to argue that any action of a school board in construction policy or zone-setting or teacher assignment that precedes a situation in which there are some almost all-black schools (there were no all-black schools in San Francisco) and some almost all-white schools (there were no all-white schools in San Francisco) can be considered *de jure* segregation.

Under Judge Weigel's interpretation, there is no such thing as *de facto* segregation. All racial imbalance is the result of state actions, either taken or not taken. If not taken, they should have been taken. *De facto* disappears as a category requiring any less action than *de jure*.

This is the position of many lawyers who are arguing these varied cases. I have described the San Francisco case because it led to a legal order requiring desegregation by transportation of the largest Northern or Western system so far affected by such an order. But massive desegregation had also been required by a district judge in Denver, who had then had his judgment limited by the Circuit Court of Appeals. It is this Denver case that will become the first case on Northern or Western *de facto* school segregation—if we still allow the term some meaning—to be heard by the Supreme Court. What the Supreme Court will have to decide is whether the historical difference between Charlotte and Denver permits Denver or any other city to do any less than Charlotte has been required to do in order to integrate its schools.

Simultaneously, Detroit and the surrounding counties and the state of Michigan are under court order to come up with a plan that permits the desegregation of the schoolchildren of Detroit by busing to the neighboring suburbs, and a federal judge is moving toward the same result in Indianapolis. If the Supreme Court should uphold the district judge's ruling in the Richmond case, it will then similarly have to decide whether anything in the history or practices of Detroit and Indianapolis justifies ordering less in those cities than has been ordered in the city of Richmond.

The hardy band of civil-rights lawyers now glimpses—or glimpsed, before the two latest appointments to the Supreme Court—a complete victory, based on the idea that there is no difference between *de facto* and *de jure* segregation, an idea which is itself based on the larger idea that there is no difference between North and South. What is imposed on the South must be imposed on the North. As Ramsey Clark, a former Attorney General of the United States, puts it, echoing a widely shared view:

> In fact, there is no *de facto* segregation. All segregation reflects some past actions of our governments. The FHA itself required racially restrictive covenants until 1948. But, that aside, the consequences of segregated schooling are the same whatever the cause. Segregated schools are inherently unequal however they come to be and the law must prohibit them whatever the reason for their existence.

In other words, whatever exists is the result of state action. If what exists is wrong, state action must undo it. If segregated schools were not made so by official decisions directly affecting the schools, then they were made so by other official decisions—Clark, for example, points to an FHA policy in effect until 1948—that encouraged residential segregation. Behind this argument rests the assumption, now part of the liberal creed, that racism in the North is different, if at all, from racism in the South only in being more hypocritical. All segregation arises from the same evil causes, and all segregation must be struck down. This is the position that many federal judges are now taking in the North—even if, as Judge Weigel did, they try to protect themselves by pointing to *some* action by the school board that they think might make the situation *de jure* in the earlier sense as well.

II

I believe that three questions are critical here. First, do basic human rights, as guaranteed by the Constitution, require that the student population of every school be racially balanced according to some specified proportion, and that no school be permitted a black majority? Second, whether or not this is required by the Constitution, is it the only way to improve the education of black children? Third, whether or not this is required by the Constitution, and whether or not it improves the education of black children, is it the only way to improve relations between the races?

These questions are in practice closely linked. What the Court decides is constitutional is very much affected by what it thinks is good for the nation. If it thinks that the education of black children can only be improved in schools with black minorities, it will be very much inclined to see situations in which there are schools with black majorities as unconstitutional. If it thinks race relations can only be improved if all children attend schools which are racially balanced, it will be inclined to find constitutional a requirement to have racial balance.

This is not to say that the courts do not need authority in the Constitution for what they decide. But this authority is broad indeed and it depends on a doctrine of judicial restraint—which has not been characteristic of the Supreme Court and subordinate federal courts in recent years—to limit judges in demanding what they think is right as well as what they believe to be within the Constitution. Indeed, it was in part because the Supreme Court believed that Negro children *were* being deprived educationally that it ruled as it did in *Brown*. They were being deprived because the schools were very far from "separate and equal." But even if they were "equal," their being "separate" would have been sufficient to make them unconstitutional: "To separate them from others of similar age and qualifications simply because of their race generates a feeling of inferiority as to their race and status in the community that may affect their hearts and minds in a way unlikely ever to be undone."

While much has been made of the point that the Court ruled

as it did because of the evidence and views of social scientists as to the effects of segregation on the capacity of black children to learn, the fact is that the basis of the decision was that distinctions by race had no place in American law and public practice, neither in the schools, nor, as subsequent rulings asserted, in any other area, whether in waiting rooms or golf courses. This was clearly a matter of the "equal protection of the laws." It was more problematic as to what should be done to insure the "equal protection of the laws" when such protection had been denied for so long by dual school systems. But remedies were eventually agreed upon, and the Court has continued to rule unanimously—as it did in *Brown*—on these remedies down through *Swann v. Charlotte-Mecklenburg Board of Education.*

Inevitably, however, the resulting increase in the freedom of black children—the freedom to attend the schools they wished—entailed a restriction on the freedom of others. In "freedom of choice," the freedom of white children was in no way limited. In geographical zoning to achieve integration, it was limited, but no more than that of black children. But in busing to distant schools, white children were in effect being conscripted to create an environment which, it had been decided, was required to provide equality of educational opportunity for black children. It was perhaps one thing to do this when the whites in question were the children or grandchildren of those who had deprived black children of their freedom in the past. But when a district judge in San Francisco ruled that not only white children but Chinese children and Spanish-speaking children must be conscripted to create an environment which, he believed, would provide equality of educational opportunity for black children, there was good reason for wondering whether "equal protection of the laws" was once again being violated, this time from the other side.

We are engaged here in a great enterprise to determine what the "equal protection of the laws" should concretely mean in a multi-racial and multi-ethnic society, and one in which various groups have suffered differing measures of deprivation. The blacks have certainly suffered the most, but the Chinese have suffered too, as have the Spanish-speaking groups, and some of the white ethnic groups. Is it "equal protection of the laws" to prevent Chinese-American children from attending nearby schools in their own community, conveniently adjacent to the afternoon schools they also attend? Is it "equal protection of the laws" to keep Spanish-speaking children from attending school in which their numerical dominance has led to bilingual classes and specially trained teachers? Can the Constitution possibly mean that?

One understands that the people do not vote on what the Constitution means. The judges decide. But it is one thing for the Constitution to say that, despite how the majority feels, it must allow black children into the public schools of their choice; and it is quite another for the Constitution to say, in the words of its interpreters, that some children, owing to their race or ethnic group alone, may not be allowed to attend the schools of their choice, even if their choice has nothing to do with the desire to discriminate racially. When, starting with the first proposition, one ends up with the second, as one has in San Francisco, one wonders if the Constitution can possibly have been interpreted correctly.

Again and again, reading the briefs and the transcripts and the analyses, one finds the words "escape" and "flee." The whites must not escape. They must not flee. Constitutional law often moves through strange and circuitous paths, but perhaps the strangest yet has been the one whereby, beginning with an effort to expand freedom—no Negro child shall be excluded from any public school because of his race—the law has ended up with as drastic a restriction of freedom as we have seen in this country in recent years. No child, of any race or group, may "escape" or "flee" the experience of integration. No school district may facilitate such an escape. Nor may it even (in the Detroit decision) fail to take action to close the loopholes permitting anyone to escape.

Let me suggest that, even though the civil-rights lawyers may feel that in advocating measures like these they are in the direct line of *Brown,* something very peculiar has happened when the main import of an argument changes from an effort to expand freedom to an effort to restrict freedom. Admittedly the first effort concerned the freedom of blacks, the second in large measure concerns the freedom of whites (but not entirely, as we have seen from the many instances in the South where blacks have resisted the elimination of black schools, and in the North where they have fought for community-controlled schools). Nevertheless, the tone of civil-rights cases has turned from one in which the main note is the expansion of freedom, into one in which the main note is the imposition of restrictions. It is ironic to read in Judge Stanley Weigel's decision, following which every child in the San Francisco elementary schools was placed in one of four ethnic or racial categories and made subject to transportation to provide an average mix of each in every school, an approving quotation from Judge Skelly Wright:

> The problem of changing a people's mores, particularly those with an emotional overlay, is not to be taken lightly. It is a problem which will require the utmost patience, understanding, generosity, and forbearance from all of us, of whatever race. But the principle is that we are, all of us, freeborn Americans, with a right to make our way, unfettered by sanctions imposed by man because of the work of God.

That was the language of 1956. One finds very little "patience, understanding," etc., in Judge Weigel's own decision, which required the San Francisco School District to prepare a plan to meet the following objectives:

> Full integration of all public elementary schools so that the ratio of black children to white children will then be and thereafter continue to be substantially the same in each school. To accomplish these objectives the plans may include:
> a. Use of non-discriminatory busing if, as apppears now to be clear, at least some busing will be necessary for compliance with the law.
> b. Changing attendance zones whenever necessary to head off racial segregation.

According to Judge Weigel, the law even requires:

> Avoidance of the use of tracking systems or other educational techniques or innovations without provision for safeguard against racial segregation as a consequence.

Can all this be in the Constitution too?

A second issue that would seem to have some constitutional bearing is whether those who are to provide the children for a minority black environment are being conscripted only on the basis of income. The prosperous and the rich can avail themselves of private schooling, or they can "flee" to the suburbs. And if the Richmond and Detroit rulings should be sustained, making it impossible to "escape" by going to the suburbs, the class character of the decisions would become even more pronounced. For while many working-class and lower-middle class people can afford to live in suburbs, very few can afford the costs of private education.

Some observers have pointed out that leading advocates of transportation for integration—journalists, political figures, and judges—themselves send their children to private schools which escape the consequences of these legal decisions. But even without being *ad hominem*, one may raise a moral question: if the judges who are imposing such decisions, the lawyers who argue for them (including brilliant young lawyers from the best law schools employed by federal poverty funds to do the arguing) would not themselves send their children to the schools their decisions bring into being, how can they insist that others poorer and less mobile than they are do so? Clearly those not subject to a certain condition are insisting that others submit themselves to it, which offends the basic rule of morality in both the Jewish and Christian traditions. I assume there must be a place for this rule in the Constitution.

A key constitutional question with which the Supreme Court will now finally have to do deal is whether *de facto* segregation is really different from *de jure* segregation, and if so, whether lesser remedies can be required to eradicate it.

Is there really a meaningful difference between a 100 percent black school under a law that prohibits blacks from going to school with whites, and a 100 percent black school that is created by residential segregation? The question has become even subtler: is there a difference between a majority black school in a city which once had *de jure* segregation, and such a school in a city which did not? I believe that the answer to the second question is no. But in the first case the distinction was meaningful when the Supreme Court handed down *Brown* and is meaningful today. In the *de facto* situation, to begin with, not all schools are 100 percent segregated. Indeed, none may be. A child's observation alone may demonstrate that there are many opportunities to attend integrated schools. The family may have an opportunity to move, the city may have open enrolment, it may have a voluntary city-to-suburb busing program. The child may conclude that if one's parents wished, one could attend another school, or that one could if one lived in another neighborhood—not all are inaccessible economically or because of discrimination—or could conclude that the presence of a few whites indicated that the school was not segregated.

Admittedly social perception is a complicated thing. The child in a 100 percent black school as a result of residential concentration and strict zoning may see his situation as identical to that of a child in a 100 percent black school because of state law requiring separation of the races. But the fact is that a black child in a school more than 47 percent black (the San Francisco definition of "segregation") may also see himself as unfairly deprived. Or any black child at all, in view of his history, and the currently prevailing interpretation of his position, even if he is the only black child in a white school, may so conclude. Perception is not only based on reality, a reality which to me makes the *de facto* segregated school a very different thing from the *de jure* segregated school. Perception can turn the lovely campuses of the West Coast into "jails" which confine young people, and can turn those incarcerated by courts for any crime into political prisoners. If we feel a perception is wrong, one of our duties is to try to correct it, rather than to assume that the perception of being a victim must alone dictate the action to be taken. False perceptions are to be responded to sympathetically, but not as if they were true.

If one finds segregation of apparently *de facto* origin, what is the proper remedy?

In some cases, one can show that it is not really *de facto* by pointing to actions that the school board took with a segregatory intent—for example, changing a school-zone line when blacks moved into an area to keep a school all or mostly black or another one all or mostly white. I do not think this was demonstrated in the case of San Francisco, but it was the crucial issue in the first Northern school desegregation case, that of New Rochelle, which was never reviewed by the Supreme Court, and in Pontiac, Michigan, and for some schools in Denver. In districts with a hundred or more schools and a long history, with perhaps scores of school-zone lines changed every year, it would be unlikely if one could not come up with some cases that seemed to show this. Sometimes it was done under pressure of local white parents. Finding this, a court might require something as simple as that the zone line be changed back (this, of course, by the time it came to court would hardly matter since the black residential area would almost certainly have expanded and both zone lines would probably be irrelevant). Or it might require that no zone line be set in the future which had the effect of maintaining segregation. Or that no parental wishes of this sort be taken into account. In cases where segregatory zone lines were commonly or regularly set (Pontiac) more radical relief would be more appropriate.

But there is a basic and troubling question here. School boards are either elected, or appointed by elected officials. They are thus directly or indirectly responsible to citizens. One can well understand the constitutional doctrine which asserts that no elected or appointed board, no governmental official, may deny constitutional rights—e.g., allowing a Communist to speak in a school building—regardless of the wishes of its constituency. But in the case of schooling and school-zone boundary-setting, a host of issues is involved: convenience of access, quality of building, assumed quality of teaching staff, racial composition of students, etc. A board is subject to a hundred influences in making such a decision. It is not as simple a matter as proving this Communist was not allowed to speak because of mass pressure. Nor is the motivation of parents and boards ever unmixed.

In Boston, the school board opened a new school in a black section. It tried to save the state aid that would be lost if it did not take some action to desegregate, and it zoned children living at some distance away into the new school. The white parents protested and eventually the board succumbed to their pressure and allowed them to send their children to their old nearby schools. To the minds of most enforcers of school desegregation, state and national, the board condemned itself for a segregatory act. One of the things the boycotting parents said was that they were afraid their children would get beaten up going through the area they had to traverse in order to get to school. Who is to say that this was pure fantasy, in the conditions of the modern city, and that what the white parents really meant was that they did not want their children to go to a mostly black school? It is this kind of determination on the intent and effect of hundreds of school-board decisions that judges are now required to make. When one reads cases such as those in Indianapolis, Detroit, and elsewhere, the mind reels with the complexity of numerous school-zoning and construction decisions. Briefs, hearing transcripts, exhibits run to thousands of pages. And at least one conclusion that this reader comes to is that no judge can or ought to have to make decisions on such issues, and the chances are that whatever decision he makes will be based on inadequately analyzed information.

Is it the law—and, not being a lawyer, I do not know—that if a segregatory intent pays *any* part in school decisions, then *every* measure of relief, no matter how extensive, is justified? If so, from a non-legal point of view it seems odd that one uncertain act with an uncertain effect on the social and racial patterns of an entire city should justify massive measures to reconstruct a school system.

Perhaps the most serious constitutional issue in a line of cases erasing the distinction between *de jure* and *de facto* segregation and also erasing the political boundaries between school districts in order to achieve a racial balance in which every black student is in a minority in every school (and presumably, as the cases develop, every Spanish-speaking student, and so on), is that all this makes impossible one kind of organization that a democratic society may wish to choose for its schools: the kind of organization in which the schools are the expression of a geographically defined community of small scale and regulated in accordance with the democratically expressed views of that community. This is the point Alexander Bickel has argued so forcefully. We have had a good deal of discussion in recent years of "decentralization," "community control," and "parental control" of schools. There were reasons for "community control" long before the issue exploded in New York in the late 1960's, and there were reasons for "parental control" long before the educational voucher scheme was proposed. Now the new line of cases makes the school ever more distant from the community in which it is located and from the parents who send their children to it.

While busing schemes vary, in some, children from a number of different areas are sent to a single school and children from one area are sent to a number of schools. It becomes hard for parental or community concerns to be exercised on the particular school to which one's children go. Thus, in San Francisco, in the Mission district, owing to the effective work of the Mission Coalition (an Alinsky-style community organization), the local community has considerable influence on public programs in the area. With a wide base of membership, this organization can help determine what is most effective in the local schools. But if it wants to create an atmosphere in the school best suited to the education of Spanish-speaking children, what sense does this make when the schools are filled with children from distant areas? And how can it influence the education the Mission children receive in the distant schools to which many of them are now sent?

In effect, the new line of cases gives enormous control to central school bureaucracies, who will make decisions subject only to the courts and the federal government on the one hand, and the mass opinion of a large area dominated by the inevitable slogans which can create majorities on the other. Clearly this is one way of reducing the influence of people over their own environment and their own fate. I believe indeed that the worst effect of the current crisis is that people already reduced to frustration by their inability to affect a complex society and a government moving in ways many of them find incomprehensible and undesirable, must now see one of the last areas of local influence taken from them in order to achieve a single goal, that of racial balance.

The one reason for community control that has recently been considered most persuasive is that the inadequate education of black children may be improved under a greater measure of black community control. This may or may not be the case, but I believe that all people, black and white, have the right to control as much of their lives as is possible in a complex society, and the schools are very likely the only major function of government which would not suffer—and might even benefit—from a greater measure of local control. In education, there are few "economies of scale." It has always seemed fantastic that educators, in proposing "complexes" for 20,000 elementary-school children for purposes of desegregation, could also argue that schools of that size would also be more "efficient." Interestingly, lawyers and judges, in their effort to find de jure segregatory intent in the acts of Northern school boards, will sometimes claim that schools were deliberately made small to lessen the chances of integration. Thus in Detroit, one charge against the school board, accepted by Judge Roth, was that the board built small schools of 300 in order to contain the population and make desegregation more difficult. Paul Goodman and many others would argue that even schools of 300 are probably too large. In San Francisco, on the other hand, the argument was that schools were expanded to "contain" the black and white population. The Detroit judge, it seems, would have preferred the large San Francisco schools, and the San Francisco judge would have preferred the small Detroit schools, if one takes their arguments at face value. But one may be allowed to suspect that if the situations had been reversed, they would still both have found "*de jure*" segregation in their respective cities.

One consequence of this transfer of power to the center when one transports for racial balance is that there is no local pressure to build a school to serve a local population, since one cannot know what the effect of any local school will be. Thus all decisions on school building revert to the hands of the central school authorities, only affected, as I have already pointed out, by judges and the federal government on the one hand, and a mass opinion unrelated to local district needs on the other. I am skeptical as to whether this will improve school-construction policies. Federal civil-rights agencies and judges have not as yet shown themselves very perceptive in their criticism of local school-construction policies. One piece of evidence of *de jure* segregation, cited by the San Francisco judge, was the building of a new school in Hunter's Point, a black area. The school authorities had resisted building there. The local people insisted on a new school. Just about everyone who supports desegregation in San Francisco supported the local people, even though they knew that the school would be segregated. The local NAACP also supported the building of the new school. The judge, in his decision, cited the building of this school as a sign of the "segregatory" policies of the San Francisco school authorities. To the judge, the black people of Hunter's Point were being "contained," when they should have been sent off elsewhere, leaving their own area devoid of schools (or perhaps any other facilities). But for the people of the area who demanded the school, they were being served. That their school would be, to a federal judge's mind, "segregated" did not seem to them a good reason for all city facilities to be built only in white or Spanish-speaking or Chinese areas.

The attempt of judges and civil-rights lawyers to argue that this or that school was built to be "segregated" for whites or blacks is in any case often naive. The dynamics of population movements in the cities have been too rapid (the black population of San Francisco increased from 5,000 in 1940 to 96,000 in 1970) and the process of school-building too slow, for any such intention to be easily demonstrated or realized in Northern cities. One of the schools cited in the San Francisco case as "segregated" black (64 percent black in 1964), had been cited as recently as 1967 in the Civil Rights Commission's report on *Racial Isolation in the Public Schools* as having been built in order to foster the "segregation" of whites, since it had opened in 1954 with a student body that was almost all white. Presumably, at least for the intervening period, it must have been integrated.

The crucial point is: do federal courts have the right to impose a school policy that would deprive local communities and groups, white and black, of power over their schools? Some of them seem quite sure that they do. Judge Roth in Detroit is critical of the blacks of that city for contributing to what he considers "segregation" by demanding black principals and teachers:

> In the most realistic sense, if fault or blame is to be found it is that of the community as a whole, including of course the black components. We need not minimize the effect of the actions of federal, state, and local governmental officers and agencies . . . to observe that blacks, like ethnic groups in the past, have tended to separate from the larger group and associate together. The ghetto is a place of confinement and a place of refuge. There is enough blame for everyone to share.

We would all agree with Judge Roth that the ghetto must not be a place of confinement and that everything possible must be done to make it as easy for blacks to live where they wish as it is for anyone else. But why should it be the duty or the right of the federal government and the federal judiciary to destroy the ghetto as a place of refuge if that is what some blacks want? Judge Roth is trying to read into the Constitution the crude Americanizing and homogenizing which is certainly one part of the American experience, but which is just as certainly not the main way we in this country have responded to the facts of a multi-ethnic society. The doctrines to which Judge Roth lends his authority would deny not only to blacks, but to any other group, a right of refuge which is quite properly theirs in a multi-ethnic society built on democratic and pluralist principles.

I do not speak here of limiting what communities may freely choose to do in order to integrate their schools. I speak only of the judicial insistence that they *must* do certain things. Much busing for desegregation is engaged in by school boards independently of court decisions, because the board feels this is good for education; or because it is under pressure from blacks and white liberal citizens who demand such measures; or because it is required or is under pressure to do so from state education authorities—who, in the major Northern and Western states, and in particular in Massachusetts, New York, Pennsylvania, and California, require local school districts to eliminate racial imbalance defined in various ways. More than 50 percent black is racial imbalance in Massachusetts, and 15 percent more or less of each group in each school than the proportion of that group in the entire district is racial imbalance in California. (It was on the basis of the 15 percent rule that more than 47 percent black was considered segregated in San Francisco, for the proportion of black students in the schools was 32 percent.) Thus, the City of Berkeley has been transporting its children to achieve integration for three years now, without any court or federal action. Riverside has done the same. Many cities have implemented, independently of court action, some degree of transportation for integration. Many of these actions have been attacked in the courts from the other side—that is, by white parents charging that for racial reasons alone they were being assigned to schools far from their homes. All these challenges have been struck down in the courts, in spite of state laws (such as New York's) which declare transportation for desegregation illegal. Interestingly enough, while the San Francisco school board was under attack from one side for having failed to implement one of its integration-through-busing school complexes, it was under attack from the other side for having implemented the one it had. It was of course the first of the two attacks that was supported by the district judge.

It is not this kind of action-to-integrate—undertaken by elected school boards, or by school boards appointed by elected officials, for educational or political reasons—that is under discussion here. Unless a political decision is clearly unconstitutional it should stand. Indeed, it is very likely that decisions to achieve racial balance taken by school boards not under judicial or federal order but because the political forces in that district demand it, have better effects than those undertaken under court order by resentful school administrations. In the first case, the methods of reducing racial imbalance have been worked out through the processes of political give-and-take, the community and teachers and administrators have been prepared for the change by the political process, the parents who oppose it have lost in what they themselves consider a fair fight. The characteristics of judge-imposed decisions are quite different.

III

There is, then, considerable room for doubt as to whether the Constitution actually mandates a system whereby every school shall have a black minority and no school shall have a black majority. Nevertheless present-day judges, with whom the doctrine of judicial restraint is not especially popular, seem able to find constitutional warrant for whatever policies they feel are best for the society. And so we come to the other crucial questions raised by the new line of cases: Is school desegregation the only way to improve the education of black children and/or the relations between the races?

Without rehearsing the terrible facts in detail, we know that blacks finish high school in the North three or more years behind whites in achievement. We also know with fair confidence that this huge gap is not caused by differential expenditures of money. Just about as much is spent on predominantly black schools outside the South as on predominantly white ones. Classes in black schools will often be smaller than classes in white ones—because the black schools tend to be located in old areas with many school buildings, while white schools tend to be in newer areas with fewer and more crowded school buildings. Blacks will often have more professional personnel assigned, owing to various federal and other programs. There are, to be sure, lower teacher salaries in the predominantly black schools, because they usually have younger teachers with less seniority and fewer degrees. Anyone who believes this is a serious disadvantage for a teacher has a faith in experience and degrees which is justified by no known evidence. (It is quite true that the big cities spend much less on their schools, white and black, than the surrounding suburban areas, which are almost entirely white. Regardless of the fact that spending more is unlikely to do much to improve education—it tends mostly to improve teachers' salaries and fringe benefits—it is quite unconscionable that more public money should be spent on the education of those from prosperous backgrounds than on those from poorer families. But this is quite separate from the issue of whether within present school districts less is spent on the education of black children, and whether spending more would reduce the gap in achievement.)

If money is not the decisive element in the gap between white and black, what is? In 1966 the Coleman report on *Equality of Educational Opportunity* reviewed the achievement of hundreds of thousands of American school children, black and white, and related it to social and economic background, to various factors within the schools, and to integration. In 1967, another study, *Racial Isolation in the Public Schools,* analyzed the effects of compensatory-education programs and reviewed the data on integration. Both studies—as well as subsequent experience and research—suggested that if anything could be counted on to affect the education of black children, it was integration. However, the operative element was not race but social class. The conclusion of the Coleman report still seems the best statement of the case:

> . . the apparent beneficial effect of a student body with a high proportion of white students comes not from racial composition per se, but from the better educational background and higher educational aspirations that are, on the average, found among white students.

On the other hand, if such integration did have an effect, it was not very great. The most intense reanalysis of Coleman's data [3] concludes:

Our findings on the school racial composition issue, then, are mixed . . . the initial *Equality of Educational Opportunity* survey overstressed the impact of school social class. . . . When the issue is probed at grade 6, a small independent effect of schools' racial composition appeared, but its significance for educational policy seems slight.

The study of these issues has reached a Talmudic complexity. The finding that integration of different socioeconomic groups favors the achievement of lower socioeconomic groups apparently stands up, but the effect is not large. One thing, however, does seem clear: integrating the hapless and generally lower-income whites of the central city with lower-income blacks, particularly under conditions of resentment and conflict, as in San Francisco, is likely to achieve nothing, in educational terms.

In San Francisco, the number of children enrolled in elementary schools dropped 6,519 against a projected drop of 1,508 (a 13 percent decline against a projected 3 percent decline) in response to Judge Weigel's decision. The junior-high-school enrolment, not yet subjected to full-scale busing, declined only 1 percent, and high-school enrolment remained the same. In Pasadena, California, there was a 22 percent drop in the number of white students in the school system between 1969—before court-imposed busing—and 1971. In Norfolk, Virginia, court-imposed busing brought a drop of 20 percent. If, as seems probable, it is the somewhat better-off and more mobile who leave the public-school system when busing is imposed, the effect on the achievement of black children is further reduced.

It is in response to such facts as these and in the light of such findings as Coleman's that judges in Detroit and Indianapolis and elsewhere now call for combining the central city and the suburb into unified school districts. But if this elaborate reorganization of the schools is being undertaken so that the presumed achievement-raising effect of socioeconomic integration may occur, we are likely to be cruelly disappointed. There is little if any encouragement to be derived from studies, published and unpublished, of voluntary busing programs even though such busing takes place under the most favorable cir-

---

[3] David K. Cohen, Thomas F. Pettigrew, and Robert S. Riley, "Race and the Outcomes of Schooling," in Frederick Mosteller and Daniel P. Moynihan (Eds.), *On Equality of Educational Opportunity* (New York: Random House, 1972).

cumstances (with motivated volunteers, from motivated families, and with schools acting freely and enthusiastically). Indeed, much integration through transportation has been so disappointing in terms of raising achievement that it may well lead to a revaluation of the earlier research whose somewhat tenuous results raised what begin to look like false hopes as to the educational effects of socioeconomic integration.

IV

There is yet a final argument. One will hear it in Berkeley, which underwent full desegregation by busing three years ago, and which has seen no particular reduction of the white-black achievement gap. The argument is that school integration will improve relations between the races and that in view of the extremity of interracial tensions in this county, anything that improves these relations must be done. In Berkeley, a liberal community with an elected school board which voluntarily introduced transportation for racial balance and was not turned out for doing so, one can perhaps make this argument. But race relations are not ideal even in Berkeley, as Senator Mondale's committee discovered last year when it conducted hearings there on the most successful American case of racial balance through transportation.

The Mondale committee discovered, for example, that after the schools were fully integrated, a special program for blacks—Black House—was established at the high-school level from which non-black students and teachers were excluded. (Berkeley High School, the only one in the city, has always been integrated.) The committee discovered, when it spoke to students—selected, one assumes, by the school authorities because they would give the best picture of integration—that students of different groups had little to do with one another. The black president of the senior class said: ". . . the only true existence of integration of Berkeley High is in the hallways when the bell rang everybody, you know, pass [sic] through the hallways, that is the only time I see true integration in Berkeley High." Senator Brooke probed deeper. Since the young man was black and a majority of his classmates were white, had they not voted for him? "The whites didn't even participate in voting. . . . They felt the student government was a farce." (The opposing candidate was also black.) What about social activities? "Like we have dances, if there is a good turnout you see two or three whites at the dances. . . ." Intramural sports? "The basketball team is pretty integrated, the crew team is mainly white, soccer team mainly white, tennis team mainly white." Did this mean, Senator Brooke asked, "that blacks don't go out for these teams that are white and whites don't go out for those teams that are all black?" The class president guessed that "whites like to play tennis and blacks like to play basketball better." Still, he did think integration was a good idea, as did a Japanese girl who told the Senators: "I think like the Asian kids at Berkeley High go around with Asian kids."

A Chicano student testified:

I think the integration plan is working, started to work in junior high, it is different levels, the sixth graders go up to seventh grade now. I think now the Chicanos and blacks, they do hang around in groups. Usually some don't, I admit, like I myself hang around with all Chicanos but I am not prejudiced. I do it because I grew up with them, because they were my school buddies when there were segregated schools.

A black girl in elementary school said: "About integration, I don't think it is too integrated, but it is pretty well integrated. I have a lot of white friends. . . ." She lives in an integrated neighborhood. A white girl from the high school testified:

Integration, ideally, as far as I can see it isn't working. I mean like as far as everybody doing things together . . . I have one class where there are only two whites in it, I being one of them, you know, like I don't have any problems there, but outside . . . [with other blacks] we just do different things. I am not interested in games. I couldn't care less. I don't know anything about Berkeley as far as the athletics go. . . . I wear very short skirts and walking down the halls I get hassled enough by all the black Dukes, you know. . . .

Senator Brooke was surprised she wasn't hassled by the white boys too and suggested that they might use a different technique.

This is about the most positive report one can make on school integration. Why should anyone be surprised? There is a good deal of hanging around in groups, and there is some contact across racial lines, but the groups seem to have different interests and different social styles. The younger children have more in common than the older ones. It would be hard to say whether this commonality of interest will continue through high school—a popular Berkeley theory— or whether differences will assert themselves as the children grow older even though they were exposed to integration earlier than those now in high school. In other communities which have been studied, black children who are bused tend to become more anti-white than those who are not bused. One can think of a number of reasons for this.

If, then, the judges are moving toward a forcible reorganization of American education because they believe this will improve relations between the races, they are acting neither on evidence nor on experience but on faith. And in so acting on faith they are pushing against many legitimate interests: the interests in using tax money for education rather than transportation; the interest of the working and lower-middle classes in attending schools near their homes; the interest of all groups, including black groups, in developing some measure of control over the institutions which affect their lives; the interest of all people in retaining freedom of choice wherever this is possible.

There is unfortunately a widespread feeling, strong among liberals who have fought so long against the evil of racial segregation, that to stop now—before busing and expanded school districts are imposed on every city in the country—would be to betray the struggle for an integrated society. They are quite wrong. They have been misled by the professionals and specialists—in this instance, the government officials, the civil-rights lawyers, and the judges—as to what integration truly demands, and how it is coming about. Professionals and specialists inevitably overreach themselves, and there is no exception here.

It would be a terrible error to consider opposition to the recent judicial decisions on school integration as a betrayal of the promise of *Brown*. The promise of *Brown* is being realized. Black children may not be denied admittance to any school on account of their race (except for the cases in which courts and federal officials insist that they are to be denied admittance to schools with a black majority simply because they are black). The school systems of the South are desegregated. But more than that, integration in general has made enormous advances since 1954. It has been advanced by the hundreds of thousands of blacks in Northern and Western colleges. It has been advanced by the hundreds of thousands of blacks who have moved into professional and white-collar jobs in government, in the universities, in the school systems, in business. It has been advanced by the steady rise in black income which offers many blacks the opportunity to live in integrated areas. Most significantly, it has been advanced because millions of blacks now vote—in the South as well as the North—and because hundreds of blacks have been elected to school committees, city councils, state legislatures, the Congress. This is what is creating an integrated society in the United States.

We are far from this necessary and desirable goal. It would be a tragedy if the progress we made in achieving integration in the 1960's were not continued through the 70's. We can now foresee within a reasonable time the closing of many gaps between white and black. But I doubt that mandatory transportation of schoolchildren for integration will advance this process.

For, so far as the schools in particular are concerned, the increase in black political power means that blacks—like all other groups—can now negotiate, on the basis of their own power, and to the extent of their own power, over what kind of school systems should exist, and involving what measure of transportation and racial balance. In the varied settings of American life there will be many different answers to these questions. What Berkeley has done is not what New York City has done, and there is no reason why it should be. But everywhere black political power is present and contributing to the development of solutions.

There is a third path for liberals now agonized between the steady imposition of racial and ethnic group quotas on every school in the country—a path of pointlessly expensive and destructive homogenization—and surrender to the South. It is a perfectly sound American path, one which assumes that groups are different and will have their own interests and orientations, but which insists that no one be penalized because of group membership, and that a common base of experience be demanded of all Americans. It is the path that made possible the growth of the parochial schools, not as a challenge to a common American society, but as one variant within it. It is a path that, to my mind, legitimizes such developments as community control of schools and educational vouchers permitting the free choice of schools. There are as many problems in working out the details of this path as of the other two, but it has one thing to commend it as against the other two: it expands individual freedom, rather than restricts it.

One understands that the Constitution sets limits to the process of negotiation and bargaining even in a multi-racial and multi-ethnic setting. But the judges have gone far beyond what the Constitution can reasonably be thought to allow or require in the operation of this complex process. The judges should now stand back, and allow the forces of political democracy in a pluralist society to do their proper work.

Busing in Perspective

WALTER F. MONDALE

Walter F. Mondale has been United States Senator
from Minnesota since 1964. Before that, he was Minnesota Attorney General. He is currently chairman of the
Senate Subcommittee on Children and Youth, which
he also helped create.

School desegregation is a fact of American educational life. The law
of the land is clear, and it will not change. Officially imposed school
segregation—whether the result of state law or covert policy—must
be overcome. A unanimous Supreme Court resolved any lingering
doubts last April with Chief Justice Burger's decision in *Swann v.
Charlotte-Mecklenberg*. A racial balance is not required. All-white or
all-black schools may remain after all reasonable steps have been taken.
But every reasonable effort must be made to overcome the results of
officially approved school segregation: "School authorities should
make every effort to achieve the greatest possible degree of actual
desegregation . . . ." And reasonable transportation will be required
where necessary to defeat the results of racially discriminatory student
assignment policies. ". . . We find no basis for holding that the local
school authorities may not be required to employ bus transportation
as one tool of school desegregation. Desegregation plans cannot be
limited to the walk-in school."

There has been legitimate criticism of the process of school desegregation: court orders have at times been arbitrary; student transportation has in a few cases worked unnecessary hardships; some
federal administrators have been overbearing and rigid. There are

---

Walter F. Mondale, "School Busing in Perspective," *The New Republic*, March 4,
1972. Reprinted by permission of *The New Republic*, © 1972, Harrison-Blaine
of New Jersey, Inc.

other equally legitimate criticisms which we have heard less often: thousands of qualified black teachers and administrators have been demoted or dismissed; black children have been subjected to abuse by fellow students, by teachers and by school administrators; the wealthy have fled to suburbs or placed their children in private schools, so that desegregation has affected only the poor.

But we will not answer these criticisms by refusing the federal support needed to make school desegregation educationally successful, or by withdrawing the federal government from enforcement of the Fourteenth Amendment. The choice is not between blind acceptance of "massive busing for racial balance" or total rejection of support for any transportation to achieve school desegregation. Busing is one means—and at times the only means—by which segregation in public education can be reduced. In itself, busing can be either helpful or harmful. It can be the safest, most reasonable way for children to reach the integrated schools of high quality. Or it can be used to uproot stable communities and destroy the one chance that parents have to provide the best for their children.

Like the President, I do not support "unnecessary transportation to achieve an arbitrary racial balance," and none of the hundreds of educators with whom I have talked in the past two years supports this kind of effort. The Supreme Court has made it very clear that busing will be required only where it is reasonable and does not place undue burdens on school children: "Busing will not be allowed to significantly impinge on the educational process." Thus, educationally advantaged students should not be bused to schools where they will be over-whelmed by a majority of students from the poorest and most disadvantaged backgrounds. All the evidence we have collected indicates that this kind of "desegregation" helps no one at all.

But if we bar the use of reasonable transportation as one tool for achieving desegregation, we will set in concrete much school segregation which is the clear and direct product of intentional government policy—segregation which would not exist if racially neutral policies had been followed.

In South Holland, Illinois, for instance, a U.S. district court found public agencies deeply involved in fostering school segregation. The schools were located in the center rather than at the boundaries of segregated residential areas in order to achieve school segregation. School assignment policies were adopted under which black children living nearer to white schools attended black schools, and white children living nearer to black schools attended white schools. School buses were used to transport students out of their "neighborhoods" in order to achieve segregation. Finally, teachers were assigned on a racial basis. If transportation to achieve desegregation is prohibited, public school segregation in South Holland will continue.

The courts have found virtually identical conditions in Norfolk, Virginia; Pasadena, California; Charlotte, North Carolina; Denver, Colorado and countless other communities.

Contrary to popular impression, courts have not generally ordered excessive busing or engaged in indiscriminate "racial balancing." The proportion of children riding buses to school in the Deep South is less than three percent above the national average, and barely seven percent above the average for the northern and western states. Recent HEW studies show that aggregate busing has not increased as a result of desegregation. In Louisiana and Florida, although the total number of students bused has increased, the average distance traveled has decreased substantially. And in the South's 25 largest school districts this year, 33 percent of the total black enrolment attended virtually all-black schools. This hardly indicates overzealous "racial balancing."

For nearly two years, I have served as Chairman of the Select Committee on Equal Educational Opportunity in the Senate. It has been a painful two years, and I am left with a deep conviction that American education is failing children who are born black, brown or simply poor. In Hartford, Connecticut, the median IQ level of black elementary school students is perilously close to eligibility for special schools for the mentally retarded; in rural Appalachia, fewer than 50 of every 100 fifth graders graduate from high school; in New York City, the dropout rate of Puerto Rican children between grades 10 and 12 is 56.7 percent; 50 percent of American Indian students never complete high school.

What are we to do? Those who want us to abandon school integration say all our energies should be devoted to improving the quality of education in racially and economically isolated schools. They rightly point out that thousands of children attend schools that will not be integrated—racially or economically—in the next decade, and that ways must be found to provide better education in schools serving only the disadvantaged. But we have not found those ways! With few exceptions, an annual federal investment of $1.5 billion in "compensatory" education has little perceptible impact on mounting educational disadvantage. We must increase our efforts, but success is far from certain. At the same time, we cannot afford to abandon other hopeful approaches. And it has been demonstrated that integrated education— sensitively conducted and with community support—can be better education for all children, white as well as black, rich as well as poor. It has been tried and is working.

Nearly 1000 minority group students, selected on a random basis, are bused each day from the Hartford, Connecticut ghetto to suburban schools, as part of Project Concern. Extensive testing of these children since the inception of the project in 1966 shows that time spent in the suburban schools has a dramatic impact on achievement. Fifth graders who have been in the program two years are five months ahead of those who have been in the project only one year. Those who have spent three years in the project in turn scored another four months ahead of the two-year group or a full academic year ahead of the first group. The chances for a significant gain in basic reading and arithmetic skills have been increased three-fold. In Berkeley, California, where a major effort has been made to record the educational impact of integration, average achievement of black students increased by 60 percent while the achievement rate for white students also rose. Similar results emerge from less comprehensive testing programs in Sacramento, California, and White Plains and Rochester, New York.

Hoke County is a small rural community of 18,000 in eastern North Carolina. Its schools serve 4850 children: 50 percent black, 35 percent white and 15 percent Lumbee Indian. The county had separate schools and classes for each group and a triple transportation system. Then in 1968 and 1969, Hoke County established a unitary system under which each school reflected the county-wide population distribution. They didn't just mix the children together and forget them once they entered the schoolhouse door. They tested every child to determine his level of achievement and took account of the low achieving students' special needs. They made sure that no teachers or principals were displaced or demoted—in fact, Indian and black personnel were promoted. They talked with fearful parents and counseled apprehensive students; they integrated all extracurricular activities so that every school-sponsored organization had representatives of all races in both its membership and its leadership.

Here's a school system which is 65 percent minority and it's making integration work. How? By being human about it and by focusing on what happens at the end of the bus ride. Before integration, white sixth graders were a year ahead of their Indian and black counterparts. By twelfth grade the gap was two full years. At the end of the first year of integration, white students continued to progress as before. Black students gained a year and a half; their rate of achievement was more than 50 percent better than before. Could this have happened without integration? The superintendent thought not: "I don't think it would ever happen," he said, "if we kept the schools segregated and kept pouring in money for compensatory education in segregated schools.

But I believe in an integrated system that we will eventually work it out."

The Hoke County children ride to school on buses 15 fewer minutes each day to integrated schools than they did under the segregated school system. The five-member local school board provided the kind of positive leadership necessary to make integration successful. It never reneged, publicly or privately, on its commitment to integration and it was reelected. The candidate who thought the system moved too fast toward integration finished last in a field of nine candidates.

Hoke County is not unique. Nor is Berkeley, California, the largest city in the nation to integrate its entire school system voluntarily. Berkeley is 45 precent white, 44 percent black and 11 percent Asian and Spanish-surnamed. Its schools were integrated more than three years ago, and they are building a quality, integrated system, because everyone is involved. Anglo youngsters' achievement rates are accelerating and those that are growing the fastest are those of students who have been in integrated classes longest. White third graders who have been in integrated classes for two years gained four months over those third graders who have been in integrated classes for one year. At the same time, black student achievement has increased from half to eight-tenths of a year's growth per year.

Berkeley is a university town with a high tax base, well above average in per pupil expenditure. Baldwin, Michigan, on the other hand has a low tax base, a low per pupil expenditure, a school operating budget deficit of $100,000 a year and dismally low achievement levels. Its schools are the second worst academically in Michigan. Twelve percent of Baldwin's working force is unemployed; 40 percent of its families have incomes under $3000 per year; 53 percent of its people have less than nine years of formal education. Baldwin has its problems. But "busing" and "racial balance" are not among them. Every child is in an integrated class. More than 80 percent of its 1041 students are bused. Some students board their buses as early as 7 a.m. and travel 60 miles to arrive at school at 8:20. The shortest one-way bus ride in this 370 square mile school district is 20 miles. The superintendent told our select committee: "We are proud of the fact that we are an integrated school system. In fact this year during our football season we came up with a little pin that really exemplifies what we are talking about. I would like to leave this with you. It says, 'Baldwin has Soul.'"

I asked him whether there was any opposition to busing. He said: "Our neighbors in Cadillac, Luddington, Big Rapids, etc., are pretty shook up over there. They think we are going to bus some of our black children over to their schools. So busing is an issue in Baldwin only as far as our neighbors are concerned."

Let's be candid: busing is the way the overwhelming majority of school children outside our central cities get to school. Twenty million elementary and secondary school children are bused. They rode 256,000 yellow buses 2.2 billion miles last year, at a cost of $1.5 billion. Forty percent of our school children—65 percent when those riding public transportation are included—ride to school every day for reasons that have nothing at all to do with school desegregation. So the issue is not, to bus or not to bus; it is whether we will build on successful examples to make school desegregation work; whether we will help the courts to avoid educational mistakes—or leave them to face the complexities of school desegregation alone.

And there are complexities. Court-ordered desegregation is costing Pontiac, Michigan, $700,000 and Pontiac has had to cut educational programs to meet these costs. The superintendent and chairman of the school board in Dade County, Florida testified last June that, "The financial impact of desegregation is placing severe demands and burdens on the affected school systems." School desegregation in Dade County, which has a $250-million school budget, cost an additional $1.5 million in just six months. Additional transportation is costing $670,000 a year. Pasadena, California is spending $300,000 in Federal Aid for Impacted Areas which would otherwise be used for instructional programs. Pasadena is implementing a federal desegregation court order. In Harrisburg, Pennsylvania, which is desegregating under state administrative procedures, additional transportation expenses are more than $500,000 a year. Harrisburg has had to cut additional programs to pay for busing. In Nashville, Tennessee, because of an inadequate number of school buses, opening times for schools have been staggered so that some children start school as early as 7:00 a.m., and others arrive home after dark. The inconvenience this has caused threatens public support for education in Nashville.

And yet . . . the Department of Health, Education, and Welfare has refused to allow expenditures of any of the $65 million in emergency desegregation funds appropriated by Congress this year to support transportation.

No one has suggested that every school can—or should—be integrated tomorrow. No one is requiring that. Segregated schools remain in Atlanta under federal court order; segregated schools will continue in the great urban centers of the North despite our best efforts. But if we abandon support for school integration where it can be accomplished, if we refuse to support the essential remedy, which busing so often is, and if we destroy the public goodwill necessary to make desegregation successful once it has taken place—we will work tragic harm. We're at a crossroads. School desegregation in the South is largely completed. But we from the North are now beginning to feel the pressure to abandon the course set by the Fourteenth Amendment. If we do, in the name of anti-busing, we will deal a blow to public education in the North and in the South from which it may never recover.

Two Letters on "The Coleman Report"

JAMES S. COLEMAN

James S. Coleman, professor of sociology at the University of Chicago, is principal author of "Equality of Educational Opportunity," more commonly known as the "Coleman Report." The "Report," commissioned by the Department of Health, Education, and Welfare, was a massive study of the lack of equal educational opportunity in the United States. Its findings have been constantly referred to by the courts and by scholars in the debate over busing. The first letter included here, which Professor Coleman sent to *The New York Times*, was not printed there because *The Times* could not find space for it. The letter did appear in *The Public Interest* in the summer of 1972.

TO *THE NEW YORK TIMES*
(April 13, 1972)

Although I make it a practice to stay away from reporters, some statements of mine were printed in Sunday's (April 9) *Times*. I want to clarify several things concerning the findings of the so-called "Coleman Report," and the use of those findings by governmental institutions, including the courts:

1. The Report found, as I have testified in various court cases, and

James S. Coleman, "Coleman on 'The Coleman Report'," *The Public Interest*, No. 28 (Summer 1972), pp. 127–128. Copyright © National Affairs Inc., 1972. James S. Coleman, "Letter to the Editor," *The Baltimore Sun*, April 23, 1972. Used by permission of The Baltimore Sunpapers.

as has been confirmed by numerous further analyses of those same data, that the academic achievement of children from lower socio-economic backgrounds (black or white) was benefited by being in schools with children from higher socio-economic backgrounds (black or white).

2. This achievement increment is not nearly sufficient to overcome the educational disadvantage of children from lower socio-economic backgrounds.

3. This effect, however, was greater than those of other school resources of the kind ordinarily added by compensatory programs. The effects of these resources on achievement can hardly be found at all.

My opinion, with which others who have more experience in constitutional law than I may disagree, is that the results stated in 1 and 3 above have been used inappropriately by the courts to support the premise that equal protection for black children is not provided unless racial balance is achieved in schools. I believe it is necessary to recognize that equal protection, in the sense of equal educational opportunity, cannot be provided by the State. Most of the inequality of opportunity originates in the home, through loving care and attention by parents— but differential care and attention, since parents differ—and the State can hope only to add opportunity in such a way that these inequalities are not increased but reduced. This does mean, of course, that actions of the State that have increased racial or socio-economic segregation should be corrected by the courts, but not on the mistaken assumption that they are thereby creating equal educational opportunity.

While the issue of racial integration in schools does not, I believe, involve constitutional questions of equal protection for black children conditional upon increased achievement in integrated schools, it is a matter on which school boards and governmental authorities have a responsibility to take affirmative action—action with a less punitive and blunt quality than some court decisions, but affirmative action nevertheless. In the past 20 years, there has been an increasing self-segregation into homogeneous communities by those families that have greatest freedom to move. The result is an increasing social and economic segregation in the schools, which makes a mockery of the classic American conception of the common school attended by children of all social groups.

Probably the most cogent recent statement on this issue is that made by the New York Board of Regents on March 24, in reaffirming its stand on school integration. The Board of Regents did not mention constitutional equal protection of black students because of greater achievement in integrated schools, but said rather, "This Board cannot foresee any but the most sullen and corrosive scenarios of the future if the multi-colored and multicultured children of this state and nation are not permitted to get to know one another as individuals."

TO *THE BALTIMORE SUN*
(April 23, 1972)

In 1966, I and others authored a U.S. Office of Education report to Congress and the President on the nature and sources of inequalities of educational opportunity by race. The report was titled "Equality of Educational Opportunity," and commonly known as the "Coleman Report." Soon after that, external pressures on local school boards began in earnest in the South to desegregate their schools. These pressures, from court suits, from state governments, and from the Federal Government, initally were limited to abolition of the dual school system by instituting a single set of attendance zones. This is what desegregation meant for those school systems, like Baltimore, Washington, and other boarder-state systems that desegregated in the years following the 1954 Supreme Court decision in *Brown v. Board of Education.* But recalcitrant districts dodged desegregation, and in the late 1960's, the battle between the courts and school boards escalated. In this battle, the idea of racial balance emerged in court decisions, as the only sure way the court could find to keep the school districts honest in desegregation. With this, the issue of school desegregation changed from eliminating enforced racial segregation in the schools to instituting affirmative racial integration. This new goal found strong supporters among moderate blacks and whites, and opponents among conservative whites and separatist blacks. The central motivating force among the moderates was probably no longer injustices perpetrated upon black children, but the desire to create an integrated society, a desire heightened by the central-city riots of the late 1960's.

But the arena of battle in this issue was the courts, and the courts are not designed so much to promote the public good (for example, an integrated society) as to protect against bads (for example, unequal protection before the law). There was no direct way the courts could work toward the integration of races in society, except under the guise of implementing constitutionally guaranteed protections. Thus when affirmative school integration became the issue, with racial balance in schools as the goal of black and white moderates, then protection of black students, under the Fourteenth Amendment to the Constitution, remained the overt issue in the courts. And this is when evidence about the effects of integrated schools on achievement of black students begin to be important to the courts (in calendar time, about 1968). The so-called "Coleman Report" showed that the performance of children from disadvantaged backgrounds was higher in schools with high proportions of children from advantaged backgrounds—and, on the other hand, the effects of other school resources in racially or socially homogeneous schools was very small. This implied that for increasing the achievement of black children, integration of schools was likely to be more effective than compensatory programs which increased the physical and teaching resources in black schools. These results were used by the courts to help sustain the argument that equal protection under the Constitution was not provided for black children except in integrated schools, and thus that school districts— North and South—had constitutional responsibility to repair any previous administrative or legal acts that increased segregation by full affirmative action to create racial balance in their schools.

Viewed in this way, it may appear that the courts were mistaken, attempting to increase racial integration of the society under the guise of equal protection for black students. But all this must be viewed against a backdrop of social changes. These changes consisted of increasing private affluence, the growth of automobile transportation, and the movement from farm to town, town to city, and city to suburb, all together increasing the racial and economic segregation of residential areas. This radical change in the ecology of society has threatened to destroy the traditional American conception of the "common school," where children from all economic levels and all ethnic groups mixed and became fully Americans. America was the first nation to implement a conception of the common school for all citizens rather than a two-tier system with a set of elite schools for the higher classes. Insofar as the "common school" provided equal protection under the Fourteenth Amendment, it is clear that the increasing homogenization of residential areas, which creates elite schools in elite suburbs, is threatening that equal protection. Thus it may well be that the courts are correct in arguing that equal protection requires affirmative integration of schools.

But if they are correct, then they are correct on somewhat different grounds than are usually given in judges' decisions. They are not correct because some legal actions in the past have increased racial segregation, but because the law has allowed private affluence and social change to destroy the common school and replace it by "elite schools" in some suburbs and "ordinary schools" in other suburbs and central cities. And they are correct because the absence of a "common school" means segregation by economic level as well as by race.

Further, the different grounds imply different remedies than those of "racial balance in the schools" that the courts have attempted to impose. The extent of social change has probably made impossible the rescuscitation of the common school in its old form, and mechanical solutions imposed by courts in the attempt to do this will probably not long endure. What is necessary is positive action to bring back, through auxiliary institutions, the equal protection that the common school once provided through its social mixing. It means the community, or the state, has a responsibility to insure that such social mixing of children takes place, possibly in the schools but possibly in new institutions: in joint endeavors among children from different schools, in heterogeneous summer camps, day camps, part schools, work experiences. Since the aim is a certain kind of experience toward American citizenship that is no longer provided by homogeneous schools, efforts can be directed not toward a full revision to the past, but toward institutions that bring about such experience in constructive ways. Such institutions could bring together black and white children, rich and poor, in activities which were threatening to no group, which formed lasting ties through common experience and organized programs—but without a full reorganization of the schools to overcome residential segregation. Where it is feasible to build such relationships through racially and socially integrated schools, that is the simplest way. But the point is that it is not the only way. The community has taken responsibility for public education of its members' children; where a certain portion of that education cannot be feasibly provided in the schools due to residential segregation, then the responsibility neither vanishes nor implies a reversion to the socially mixed common school. It lies instead in providing adjuncts to the schools, at public expense, to provide that experience in settings that would create strong integration forces between blacks and whites, and between different socio-economic levels.

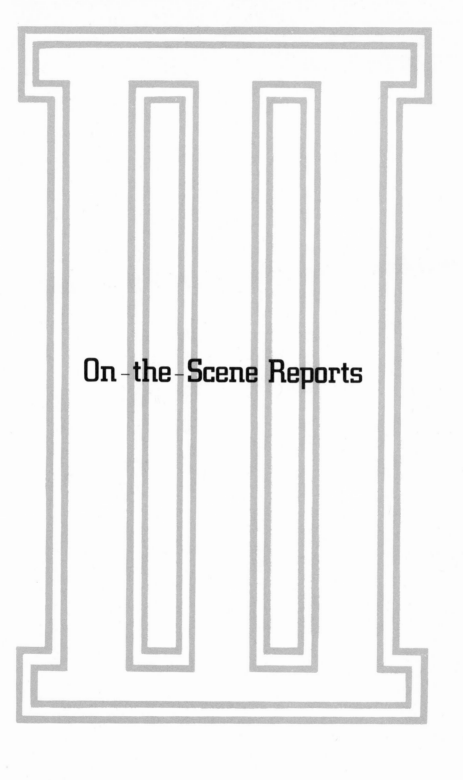

On-the-Scene Reports

Billy's Bus Driver

ROBERT COLES

Robert Coles is a child psychiatrist with the Harvard
University health services. Among his recent books are
Erik H. Erikson: The Growth of His Work and *The
Middle Americans.* He is currently completing a four-
volume work, *Children of Crisis.* "Billy's Bus Driver"
is taken from the third volume of that study, *The
South Goes North.*

Billy's bus driver is a leader of sorts, a hero to Billy and the many
other children who ride that bus; but the man is also a follower, a
self-declared admirer of the children he drives to school—which
means one who looks up to them and mixes generously his admiration
with any envy he feels and from time to time puts into words. He does
envy them. He wishes he had the "chances" they have. What are
those chances? Oh, they defy mention and enumeration. They are so
obvious. Why even ask about the most evident of things—the splendid
school building, the gym the boys talk about, the "beautiful cafeteria"
the girls mention, and on and on? Most of all, he insists, there are all
those rich, well-born and lucky white children, who have quite a
future ahead of them. He is sure they will inspire the black children
now in the same school; he is sure that in the long run the inconvenience of bus travel "will more than pay off."

He never used to be much for "integration of education," or even
for any kind of education as a way out for black children: "I was born
right here in this city, and I've lived here all my life. No one has anything to teach me about white people. I know them. For years I

Robert Coles, "Billy's Bus Driver," *The South Goes North,* Volume III of *Children
of Crisis* (Boston: Atlantic–Little, Brown and Co., 1972), pp. 96–102. Copyright
© 1971 by Robert Coles.

worked in buildings where they live. I took care of their garbage and
I went on errands for them and I listened in on their goddam fights.
I learned what they're all about. They're a bunch of fakers and frauds,
like I guess a lot of my own people are! I'd come home and I'd go have
a beer, and my buddies would ask me about the white man, the white
man. I'd say who the Hell do you think the white man is? I'd tell them
all I'd pick up there in those swank, luxury apartments: the women
playing around with other men, the men cheating on their wives, the
bottles of liquor I'd have to get rid of, and one guy, he went to prison
for cheating the government out of taxes, and I heard there was a total
of a million dollars he'd never even put down. But they caught him.
You know what I heard his wife say? I was cleaning out her damn
sink. She'd blocked it up. She was on the phone and she said her husband would do it again, because he still came out ahead. That's what
she said. I heard that he went to some prison for 'nice people.' I
would come home and tell my wife: it's not whether you go and break
the law that counts, but who you are when you break the law. I took
a few things myself when I worked in one of those buildings. I'll
admit it. I'm not ashamed of it: a bottle of booze now and then, and
a pair of shoes for the wife. What are you supposed to do when you're
in an apartment and the lady has so many shoes you think you're in
a shoe store? They never miss stuff like that—so long as you don't
take too much at once. But I got sick, and I had to quit being a
janitor. The doctor said I was working too hard, and my heart couldn't
take it. So, this job has been perfect for me. Besides driving the bus
I drive a cab for a few hours, too. I'm on wheels most all the time now,
it seems. I get up and I'm driving the bus. Then I drive the cab for a
few hours. Then I get the bus and go pick up the kids. I see the white
man's world and I see the black man's; and let me tell you, they're not
the same."

He is in his fifties, a man scarred by a difficult life. His heart has
never been quite right; years of troubles as a result of the damage
rheumatic fever did to the organ's valves have now been followed by
coronary insufficiency. His wife has had cancer of the breast and also
has a cardiac problem. His one daughter died from pneumonia at the
age of five. He has a son who is somewhat retarded and lives with his
parents. Nevertheless, the man is a friendly, optimistic person who
swears much more often than I will reveal here, who provides for his
family, who is gentle and tender with his son and nostalgic about
the joys of fatherhood he experienced for the few years his daughter
lived, who loves his wife very much, who can be brusque and even
rude with a visitor, only to turn around and shower him with advice,
counsel, information, opinions, and the "common sense" he particu-

larly tries to find for himself and have available for others. Moreover, he is a flexible man, unconcerned with useless conventions, interested in the changes taking place around him, willing to acknowledge his own errors and limitations, anxious to have others take up where he feels he and his generation failed: "When a guy gets to be my age, he looks at a boy like that Billy you go and see—and he's glad. He's glad the world won't stop with him and all he's failed to do. Mind you, I'm no failure, not in my eyes. It's just that I could have been a lot more than I've turned out to be. I may sound conceited to you, saying that, but it's true.

"After all, I was born in this city, and so were my parents. We're not the kind of Negroes that have come up here from the South in the last few years. There's nothing wrong with them. I'm not saying a word against them. It's just that they have one Hell of a time getting used to the city, whereas I'm onto things here. Why, I almost graduated from high school. If it hadn't been for the goddam depression I would have graduated. Poverty they call it today; well, in the thirties no one talked about poverty. We were just plain poor, every one of us was. But even though I was poor, I never lost my self-respect. I went to the library and I read. I'd sit there on a Saturday afternoon and it would be a Hell of a lot warmer than in my house, and I'd read the magazines and look into a book or two. I won't say I read them from cover to cover, but I got a lot of the messages in them, I know I did."

In fact he speaks like a Bostonian; on tape he would not impress most listeners as a black man. His ancestors lived in Pennsylvania before they came to Massachusetts—and when he talks about the Georgia from which his family "originally came," he is like the American of English or German stock who is going back, way back to a past that is unreal for him and is more a part of the nation's history than his particular family's. He has his own version of the old-timer's pride —again, it is not purchased at anyone else's expense. He can describe Boston "before a lot of Negroes lived here." He can talk about the Negro families that used to live way out in the country, had small farms, were independent and "all but white." He can talk about the Negroes who have lived on Cape Cod for a long time, or up in New Hampshire and Maine. They were pioneers, willing and able to go places their racial brothers had not gone, would not make a habit of seeking out. But maybe such boldness and industry and ingenuity and self-sufficiency is not enough, not if millions of black children like Billy are to find *their* destiny: "You see, Billy lives right here in the city, and even if his family has been around a little longer than most, they're not going to be able to find a quiet little place somewhere out in the country, because they're city people. I am, too. There are some from my background who are pretty well-off, you know. They became doctors and lawyers and all that. A few of them have even gone out to the suburbs. They can usually find a good home where the Jews live. The Jews will take a few Negroes, provided there aren't too many of them ready to follow. The Jews pride themselves on being progressive. But most of us have to stay right here—and that's why I say it's fellows like that little Billy who are going to be pointing the way for us. He'll never be a crazy type; they're full of noise, a lot of talk and nothing else. I guess they'd call me an Uncle Tom, but who cares!

"No, Billy will go right through school and learn all he can; then he'll be a credit to his people, his race. And Billy won't have to move into some white neighborhood just to prove he's as good as the whites. He'll have them wishing they were living near him! You know why I say that? Let me tell you. A few years ago I never would have believed I'd be talking like this. I watch that boy get off the bus, and sure enough, it doesn't take but a minute before there are some white kids coming up to him and they practically fight each other to get a word with him. I know he won't tell you that. He won't tell his parents, either. Don't you see, a boy like that has pride. That's *real* 'black pride,' the kind he has. He isn't going to go bragging that he's popular with the white ones. No sir, he doesn't even see it that way, because as a matter of fact he's not trying to be popular with anyone. He's just Billy, a damn smart kid who knows the score and isn't going to be tricked by the white man.

"I don't believe those white ones even think of him as a colored kid, a Negro. I've about stopped thinking of all the kids as Negro kids. When they get off my bus, they're just kids. Oh, I don't really mean that, I guess. Can you ever forget? I think Billy probably comes nearer to forgetting than any of us—even if it's always there in the back of his mind, the idea that he's a Negro. You can never quite trust a white man to be above prejudice, even when he swears up and down on every Bible he can get his pale little hands on that he's not prejudiced, he's not, he's not. I remember one man whose apartment was on the top floor of the apartment house where I worked as a janitor. He kept on telling me that he treated Negroes like other people, and he liked them, and everyone is equal and all that. Once I heard him in the hall talking about 'jazz-bos.' I didn't even know what he meant at first. I swear it. Then I figured it out, what he was getting at. He thought that he was being funny and smart: 'The jazz-bos are trying, but there's just so far they can push themselves with the raw material they've got.' That's what he was saying—my friend! I'll bet there are other whites who wouldn't ever talk like that—but they're still as prejudiced when you get down to it as he is.

"Now Billy, he's onto all that. He'll never go around trusting white people; but he'll have them trusting him. And like I keep on saying, he'll be a credit to us. We need our leaders, you know. Up here in the North we need the kind of man Dr. King was, only a northern kind of Dr. King—and that means not a minister, probably, but a lawyer or a businessman, something like that. We're still a pretty religious people, I'd say, but not the way the southern Negro is, from what I can tell. I've never been farther south than Washington, D.C., and that was plenty south for me! We're probably the most religious group of people in America, the most Christian. I have a sister and she once said something to me I'll never forget as long as I live. She said it must be real strange for Jesus up there in Heaven. He had all those white people on His side a long time ago, and they were trying to conquer the world for Him. They brought us here, and they told us to worship Him, and we did. Now they've left Him, most of them, and we're sticking closer to Him than they are. When she told me that I thought to myself that this country is a strange, strange place."

He goes on to remind me that the churches are full every Sunday with black families—even though Jesus is still represented as white in many of those churches. He insists that prayer and churchgoing are quite necessary for black people in Roxbury, in Harlem, in Cleveland's Hough section and Chicago's South Side and West Side. "We haven't too much to lean on, or too many friends we can trust," he says. Then, sarcastically but also with real sincerity, he calls Jesus Christ a friend, one of the few the black people have—though he for one catches himself thinking this as he drives the bus past one black church after another: "Where is He? Why does He allow all of this? He must be disgusted with the way things are, but He doesn't do anything. And meanwhile my people go all the time to those churches and they carry on—do they!—and they come out believing, really believing. I wonder. I really wonder!"

In contrast, he has no doubts about the value of the bus. He has seen the children get accustomed to a first-rate school. He has seen them become involved in learning as never before. He has seen his own contribution: he is a strong, well-spoken, active man whom the children admire and talk to all the time, and find it a real pleasure to know. I have often thought as I rode with him that he runs a kind of school on that bus of his. He points things out to the children. He asks them questions. They huddle close to his seat and listen to his stories, his jokes, his clever remarks, full of irony and vigorous social satire. They are allowed to move about, change seats, even scrap a little—and here is why a man with no degrees to his name and no experience as a teacher justifies such an approach: "I don't want to sit hard on these kids and teach them that the only thing they can do is sit, sit, sit, and stay in their place and move nowhere. Hell, I like them to move around and show some fight in them. I tell them they can scrap, but no one is to get hurt, and if a kid says, 'Enough,' the kid he's fighting with has to stop—*or else.* That way, they get the mischief out of their system here on the bus. That way, they're quieted down and ready for school when we get there. 'Give 'em Hell,' I call to them when they get off. And I believe they listen to me."

He next asks me what I think, and I tell him that I think he is right. I tell him that to those children he is an intelligent man, a wise man, a man they can really feel close to and fall back upon twice a day. He is surprised, or seems to be surprised. Actually, he is not surprised at all. Yes, he eventually admits, he knows that; and yes, he is glad he can do a little for those children. What else better, he asks me, can anyone do in the few years we are given here on this earth?

Bunkerism in Canarsie: Out of the family and into the street

DALTON JAMES

Dalton James writes for *The Village Voice.*

"Look, you gotta admit that Negroes got this criminal tendency. . . ."
I'm driving through Canarsie and I say to myself this must be one
of the last bastions of redneck defense in the borough of Brooklyn.
A perennial white sale!

But what are they selling in this Jewish-Italian fortress placarded
with Republicanixon politics—a nicely laundered jungle of elephantile
images and infantile messages? "Prejudice, brother," an eighth grade
white boy would answer me later, offering to soulshake my hand.

At East 100th and Avenue J, perilously close to the domed green
and black armored cars belonging to Junior High School 211, and in
uncomfortable range of New York's finest troops lacing the area like
long combat boots, I see a platoon of angry whites ramming rhetoric
down the ears of a muscular black. The view from my windshield is
too distant and I abandon it to join the group.

The black man of periscopic height has the demeanor of a First
Cav infantry officer and he's looking over the Caucasian wave and
pointing to the target of 211 as I sneak up. The treeline of patrol cars
in that direction is impressive and impregnable.

The noisy rotors of a police helicopter overhead are stifling the

Dalton James, "Bunkerism in Canarsie: Out of the Family and into the Street,"
The Village Voice, November 9, 1972. Reprinted by permission of *The Village
Voice.* Copyrighted by The Village Voice, Inc., 1972.

effect of his voice. They whirl not unlike hummingbird wings, pro-
pelling the beast like a gunship in the Hobo Woods. Often they dip
in the sky, slashing the voices of the group to make tight corners and
daring the occupants on the ground side to fall out and spatter the
street corner debacle. Sometimes they level off to strafe the area with
ear pollution. Mission: unknown.

"You people cannot be real," the black is saying.

"Of course, we are," a young mother retorts. "We're certainly not
racists like you claim we are, but just mothers concerned about our
children." The 30-ish woman looks up at the man through square-
shaped lenses, her blonde hair combed back to reveal a round mother-
of-two-at-211 face stippled with freckles and anxiety. "Tell me, why
would you want your child to come to school all the way over here?"
She is speaking, rather shouting, again.

"Because the education people says the schools in the black neighborhoods are crowded and there is need to bus 31 little black children
to a school in this area. Simple, lady. This is not my doing. We are only
following the dictates of the education department, and I can't see
why all this demonstration against innocent black kids."

The black is heavily mustachioed, and he looks like a trainman
in the furniture business. An engineer's cap almost smothers his afro
and the words "American Chair" smear his left breast. He's wearing
hardhat boots and a serious mood. She's responsible for "Vote for
Andreassi" and "Nixon Now or Never" buttons on her black coat, on
which is sewn an Italian Civil Defense League patch. They glare at
each other through the noise of the chopper, and the word "Bunkerism"
escapes his lips. "Nothing but racists," he extends.

A high school student crashes into the argument and reveals that
last year he attended 211 and the blacks there at the time were belliger-
ent toward the white kids. A few blacks terrorized the whole school.
Mean cats, they'd extort money from the sons of Italy heritage in a
violent battle and the Civil Defense patches would mean nothing to
their fathers.

"You expect me to believe that?" the black asks stonily.

"Goddam right! I've been beaten several times in that cafeteria.
Sometimes you'd walk into the cafeteria and it looks like a zoo. The
black guys are all there waiting for us to come and eat so they can
beat us up for our 40 cents. Now don't think I'm a racist, mister, because one of my best friends is black."

The man looks at him in an oh-yeah-so-what-else-is-new manner.
But the kid continues to speak.

"His name's Bruce, he lives in that house over there. When he first
came on this block, he stayed inside for two months because he was

scared we'd beat him up. But when he finally came out and we rapped together, it was so different, I mean he was so nice."

A short, bony-faced, eagle-nosed man whose family was "oppressed in Europe more than you people" cuts in with an explanation that could force Cleaver out of his Algerian retirement. "You asked earlier why we oppose this school thing. You you want to know the real reason?" He's stumbling over his words, trying to get them across the hurdle of his speech impediment. He hasn't shaved since Kissinger's last return from Saigon.

"Look, let's let's not doubt this this fact. You you people are criminal by nature. I mean I mean there's evidence all all over to support this. Look at Harlem and Bedford Stuy Stuy Stuyvesant. All that that crime in the streets. All those those robberies and murders and dope. All those jails crammed with with black people, you you see what I mean. I mean we don't don't want to see the area turned into a dope scene. And blacks beating up whites. You see? I'm not saying all all your people are criminals, but but the percentage is is so high you can't really blame blame us, you see what I mean?"

I cannot see what this dumb whitey means and I look at the American Chair and he's breaking to throw himself at the bigot. The other whites are happy to hear their emotions poured out of their brother's mouth, and they begin to congratulate him with "that's right!"

I can't stand it. "You must be crazy, Jack," I say. "Who's more criminal than the Mafia?" (I strengthen the last word.) "Who's really directing the dope traffic? Who created Super Fly? Who's more criminal than the President, the cops, your own people cheating the poor in the supermarkets? You ever checked out why some jails are nearly all black, why we are there in the first place? Why we can't bribe cops and judges the way whites do?"

"Look, that's that's not the point. You gotta admit that Negroes got this criminal tendency, and and when you put 31 more in that school, this neighborhood would would be destroyed," the bigot strikes back weakly.

The corner scene is now a cauldron of epithets and cheap Agnewisms. It is boiling. Three heavy duty white men, one with a megaphone, another with thick glasses riding his nose bridge, and the third with meaty hands and a big gut, crawl out of a compact as if on cue. The gunship is still up there as they rush up to tend to the fire.

"Any trouble here?" asks the big gut. He repeats it, stoking the embers in typical celluloid fashion.

A woman answers that everything is taken care of. Not to worry. She remembers the morning battle.

"They let the goddam kid out of jail" (referring to a black arrested earlier in the racial confrontation). "Sure there's no trouble?" he asks again, riveting his eyes on the two blacks in the huddle. He wants to start something. The other two are flanking him like concrete.

I peel off and walk under a banner stretched across Avenue J. "Black or White, Canarsie Children for Canarsie Schools," it tells the cold wind gnawing at its untruth, for the black projects a mile away stand firmly in Canarsie territory. And the blacks are not in exile. Not any more.

Pressing Decisions

JAMES A. MICHENER

James A. Michener is the author of sixteen books; among them are *Tales of the South Pacific* (which won the Pulitzer Prize for Fiction in 1947), *Return to Paradise, Hawaii,* and *Kent State.* "Pressing Decisions" is an excerpt from a longer article, "The Red Kimono."

As I grow older I am constantly surprised at how little I know. I look at the evidence. I listen to debate. And I try to think for myself. Yet time after time I wind up ignorant, having missed the nub of the question.

In my hometown we have had busing for the last 60 years. (In my day it was done by trolleys.) Today, each morning down my road, the yellow buses come at 7:15, and although some parents have thought that this was a little early for children eight and nine to be waiting in the cold, everyone so far as I know applauds the idea of taking our children to central schools many miles away.

I had supposed that my community must be in favor of a process which had worked so long and with such good results, and I did not pay attention when my neighbors began protesting against the whole concept of busing. I heard some violent things said, but I dismissed them as irrelevant. It was inconceivable to me that people who had supported busing for 60 years were now turning against it.

But the other day, after bridge with friends I have known intimately for many years, someone raised the question of busing, and the argument became so heated—six vigorously against and two in favor—that after a while a sagacious woman said, "Enough! We've reached a point where sensible comment is no longer possible."

We have no blacks in our community. We are not faced with the problem of either sending our children out of our district or admitting black children from some other district. But the fury that can be generated even in our town by the abstract problem of busing is extraordinary, and I knew nothing about it until it exploded in my face.

What has been happening across the United States is fairly clear. Pressure from blacks for a just place in our society has had to be acknowledged publicly. Who could openly state that he was against equal educational opportunity for an attractive little black girl of eight? No one I know. Who can openly state that he thinks it all right for the construction industry to exclude blacks, no matter how hard they try to qualify themselves? No one in my circle of friends.

We are all for the inescapable adjustments needed to insure equality, but inwardly we fight against any further concession to the blacks. This intransigence, especially among older whites, is a terrible thing. It is insensitive, and it infuriates blacks. Black leaders, caught up in desperation, are goaded into making inflammatory statements of the most stupid kind. The whites make note of the threats and take consolation in the fact that the blacks were that way all along.

We are caught in a dreadful whirlpool, out of which only the whites over the age of 60 can rescue us. Because of our age, we will not lose much if America cracks apart on this issue. Our lives and our destinies within this nation are by now fairly well determined, and revolution cannot harm us for long. Therefore we should feel free to speak, to lead our countrymen from the folly in which they are engaged.

Busing seems not the way to achieve what we are after and ought to be dropped. The best argument against it was given by a neighbor: "You forget, Michener, that when we came to school on the trolley car we were coming to a *better* school. So that any expense of time or money was justified. But if you bus our children into Philadelphia, they will be going to a worse school. And for that there can be no justification."

But I am appalled when my friends chortle, "See! At their convention in Gary, even the blacks came out against busing." They do not stop to inspect what the Gary convention wanted in place of busing. All-black schools in all-black communities. All-black teachers. An all-black curriculum. And since the black urban community has only a small tax base to support its schools, funds will have to be contributed by the white suburbs and controlled by all-black school boards and all-black administrators.

Does America really think that this is a viable improvement upon busing? Something in between is needed. We need to foster integration by assuring equal access to jobs and to homes in the better neighborhoods. And we must upgrade the quality of all schools, though, alas, I see no evidence at present that this is going to be done.

Busing for Integration is Working Well in Central 7 School District—Knock Wood

WALTER GOODMAN

Walter Goodman lives in Greenburgh, New York, and his children attend public school there. He is the author of *The Committee: The Extraordinary Career of the House Committee on Un-American Activities, All Honorable Men,* and *Black Bondage.*

The word "busing" and all that goes with it, as well as much that does not necessarily go with it at all, has become a formidable force in the land. It drives housewives into the streets and politicians to shelter. It is influencing the race for the Presidency, and may, if the commotion persists, mar the U.S. Constitution. My subject here, however, is merely the way it has touched my life and the lives of others where I live.

My formative years in the Bronx were not affected by school busing, a mode of transportation which was reserved in my mind for the rich and the crippled. During my last three public-school years, a number of us did have to take a bus ride up the Grand Concourse to DeWitt Clinton High School, but nobody thought of himself as being bused; we were just taking the bus up the Grand Concourse.

My acquaintance with the subject was not much enlarged until late in 1955, when I did a report on school desegregation in the town of White Sulphur Springs, W. Va., which up to the 1954 Supreme Court decision and for some time thereafter, had 13 schools for white children and one for colored children. The latter, no matter where they might live, attended the one school, which was geared to provide staff for the famed Greenbrier Hotel, the town's major employer. The colored school offered no foreign language, no English above the sophomore level, no algebra. To reach this inferior school, many children were obliged to travel long distances. One of the longer daily round trips—108 miles—was endured by a boy who lived four blocks from a white school. He usually got home about eight in the evening, unless he stayed for football practice and missed the 20-year-old bus, warmed by a pot-bellied stove, that somehow managed the twice-a-day journey over the mountains. Then he reached home about 8 o'clock the following evening.

Although this case escaped the compassionate notice of the young Richard Nixon, everyone's attention at the time was naturally focused on schools in the South—and would continue to be so focused for a decade. Quite unknown to me, but of consequence for my family's future, was an effort at school desegregation, unforced by law, that had taken place in 1951 in the Westchester town of Greenburgh, about 25 miles from New York City. It had been carried out without riots, for reasons of economy and general educational upgrading of a poor system, as well as for racial balance. Thanks to the postwar white influx, by 1951 the district's white elementary school was overcrowded, whereas the newer black elementary school was half empty. Had the situation been reversed, desegregation might have had a dimmer prospect. In any case, Greenburgh did desegregate, and it all depended on busing.

In 1959, knowing little more about the district than the fact that a house was available in our price range and that the mortgage man at the bank had let drop a comment about lots of colored in the schools, we moved to Greenburgh—in time for my older son to enter kindergarten. In June he will be graduated, we hope, from high school. With the exception of a year spent in Chicago, he has never *not* been bused to school. His brother, now in the tenth grade, can make the same claim, along with millions of other American children. The experiment in Greenburgh is now 20 years old. Its failures and its accomplishments during that time suggest where busing for purposes of school integration is likely to work and what its working can mean for the people affected.

The Greenburgh Central 7 School District stretches over 8½

hilly square miles lying roughly between Scarsdale and White Plains on the Penn Central's Harlem line. It contains welfare recipients and exceedingly well-to-do businessmen, professors and illiterates; there are Catholics, Protestants and Jews in comparable quantities; our politics run from Concerned Democrat to concerned Conservative. Of the 3,700 children now in our schools about 34 per cent are black. Some of them come from the local ghetto known, naturally, as Fairview, which helps to disfigure State Route 119 near the border of Elmsford; others come from very comfortable black neighborhoods, from racially mixed neighborhoods and from predominantly white neighborhoods throughout the district. The white students cut across the whole range of that universe known as the middle class—from expensive homes in 99 per cent white Hartsdale, which was compelled to merge with us a few years ago despite the strenuous objections of most of its residents, to modest garden apartments near—ugh! —Central Avenue. Wherever they originate, in any given year, 9 out of 10 of the students are bused to school.

Our district has eight schools, three of them situated on the 160-acre Warburg Campus, a 1956 gift from Mrs. Frieda Schiff Warburg. The estate was reported to be worth around $1-million when the deed was transferred; to Central 7 its value has been inestimable. Under the so-called Princeton Plan, children are assigned to their schools without regard for where they live; an exception may be made for a child who lives directly across from a school, but not for one who lives two blocks away. For his first three grades, a child goes to one of three schools—two of them in white neighborhoods, one in a middle-class integrated neighborhood. For grades 4 through 6, he is moved to one of two schools, both in black neighborhoods. Thus, emphasizes Superintendent Thomas D. Wogaman, who came to us in 1969 from Berkeley, Calif., where he had taken part in integrating that school system, "the busing is a two-way process. That, for me, is philosophically *extremely* important. It demonstrates that integration is communitywide."

I can testify that our children never had a sense that they were being bused into "black schools" in fourth grade or that black children had been attending "our schools" before that. Within the schools, black interests as well as all manner of other interests are amply represented in classrooms and libraries as well as on bulletin boards. The entire seventh grade is housed in a single building, and everybody from eighth grade up—1,250 students and growing—attends Woodlands High School, which was built on the Warburg Campus in the early sixties.

To return to the early grades, the criteria for putting together classes are simple: Every class must have approximately two white pupils for every black one, thereby reflecting the district-wide ratio, and it must have about as many boys as girls. The law of random selection holds out the prospect that each class will have its share of rich and poor as well. Later, as the children become known, they are distributed so that no teacher gets burdened with all slow students or blessed with all bright ones, and so that each child, insofar as possible, gets the kind of teacher—strictly organized or free and easy—who seems to suit him best. So although a child can count on remaining in the same school from first to third grade, and then from fourth to sixth grade, his class will be shaken up each year. The two-to-one, white-black ratio, however, holds steady throughout.

Nearly all the children are taken to and from their schools by buses. Forced busing. Tom Wogaman observes: "Busing is a form of transportation. It's neither morally right nor morally wrong. It's what you do with busing that makes it right or wrong. It's what's at the end of the bus ride that counts."

We have had few accidents. Apart from weekly complaints about buses arriving late or not arriving at all, or being driven by madmen, there is not much of general interest to report about the system. Our most embarrassing logistical moment occurred several years ago when it was discovered that a bus from a black neighborhood was dropping off its occupants at the back door to one of the schools. That was quickly changed.

Though technically complicated, busing is in principle the simplest of operations. We bus those students, the vast majority, who live more than a half a mile from the elementary school to which they have been assigned or more than a mile from a secondary school. The cost last year was $262,863—90 per cent of which was paid for by the state. Given the spread-out nature of our district, its lack of sidewalks and wealth of busy throughfares, most of our children would be bused even if we reverted to neighborhood schools. Therefore, when criticism is directed at the cost of busing, one assumes that the critic is either unacquainted with the realities or is in fact opposing it for other reasons.

Yet the cost of running the schools of Central 7 is high, among the very highest in the county—higher per capita than Ardsley, higher even than Scarsdale. And since we are far from the richest per-capita school district in Westchester, we are feeling the pinch—as indicated by the difficulty in recent years in getting our school budgets passed. The cost is high in part because we have too many separate buildings for our size, including a couple of old and inefficient ones. (The administration is proposing the construction of a new "middle-school," grades 6 through 8, on the Warburg Campus, which would permit us to phase out the old schools and, incidentally, make a return to neighborhood schools that much more unlikely. The plan is meeting opposition.)

More to the point, education for children with exceedingly diverse abilities, problems and expectations is expensive. For example, a district like Ardsley, with its almost entirely college-bound student body, need not invest in as much expensive equipment for industrial arts, home economics, or business education—subjects in which Central 7 students can major. Yet since most of our graduates do go on to college, we may not neglect the academic subjects. Moreover, we have learned that a heterogeneous class should not be as large as a homogeneous one if the teacher is to be effective—and smaller classes mean higher costs.

In 1959, after several years in which Greenburgh had congratulated itself on being in advance of the Supreme Court with regard to school desegregation, standard achievement tests showed that median scores for all grades were just on or below the national norms— a discouraging set of figures for a school in Westchester County. As if that weren't bad enough, the achievement level of black students seemed to drop further behind the white level at each succeeding grade. In the fifth and sixth grades, especially, a group of unruly boys and girls—mostly black—were making classroom life difficult for everyone. Might it not be better, administrators asked, to violate the canons of integration and separate the problem children, for their sakes and the sakes of their classmates? Dr. Kenneth Clark, called in as a consultant, proved sparing with his advice: "I can't tell you what to do. It's your decision. If it were mine, I suppose I would set up the two special classes."

The classes were set up—but lasted only a year. They showed no signs of success, in part because of inadequate preparation, but also because the children were found to be "extremely depressed"—and many other people in the district were depressed, too. Our supervising principal at the time, Dr. George E. Fitch, did not solace himself with the reasoning, soon to become popular, that if test results are bad, there must be something the matter with the tests. He brought the problem to the school board: "The board has two policies on its books. The first policy states that the schools shall be integrated. The second policy states that the school programs shall be broad and flexible enough to meet the interests and needs and challenge and develop the abilities of each child. Can the second policy be fully implemented in a heterogeneous, integrated classroom or would any type of grouping—even temporary—which would segregate pupils be antithetical to the first policy?"

What does a school district do when faced with a problem? It calls in consultants. Our consultants arrived in the spring of 1961 from New York University's Center for School Services. At about the same time, the district received a Project Able grant from New York State for a program aimed at our "culturally deprived" children. Out of these studies began to emerge the district as it exists today—commited to integration, with the understanding that that commitment is part of a larger educational commitment.

Today, classes are kept relatively small—the generally met standard is fewer than 20 pupils in first grade and fewer than 25 thereafter. We have all manner of specialists, particularly for the teaching of reading, but also psychologists, social workers, a speech therapist, a "drug coordinator" to head our drug-education and counseling program, and all manner of paraprofessionals. During the great merger controversy of the mid-sixties, those in Hartsdale who were reluctant to join us took the existence of all those specialists as evidence of our depravity. Where there is help, they reasoned, there is trouble.

Of some 270 teachers and administrators, about 65 are black, a very high proportion as things go in Westchester. Our assistant superintendent for instruction, Dr. Robert Frelow, who worked with Tom Wogaman in Berkeley, holds one of the highest positions of any black school official in the land, and last year we hired a black former Olympics wrestler to be director of student activities, and a former University of Illinois All-American to be our (and the county's) first black football coach.

At the beginning, and again after the merger with Hartsdale, teachers who lacked experience or enthusiasm for dealing with black children or poor children posed considerable difficulties. In this respect, the years and the district's reputation at teachers' colleges have helped. Irving Miller, our assistant superintendent for administration, reports that we no longer solicit for teachers; young teachers who want to work here apply in sufficient numbers to enable us to select those who seem likely to be comfortable and useful in this untypical setting. In his interviews with applicants, Bob Frelow tries "to identify areas of flexibility—how the teacher feels about busing, about black studies, how much experience he's had with ethnic groups, Italian and Jewish as well as black." During the first year, every new teacher is enrolled in courses on community relations and Afro-American history. Our teachers are well-paid and turnover is not high.

Here, then, is the situation: A teacher, well-intentioned, well-equipped, is faced with a typical, highly diverse Central 7 elementary class. In my school days at P. S. 28, each grade was divided into three classes—smart, dumb and so-so. That kind of division is strictly forbidden at Central 7. Even within the class, grouping of children by ability is looked on with suspicion by district liberals as a foot-in-the-door to resegregation. But if the teacher is to teach, she must group—that is, she must separate children with like abilities or interests.

Ruth Norden has graced our district for eleven years; she had both my sons in second grade. Now she has a third-grade class. She does a lot of grouping—but never in a hard-and-fast way. There is a continual flow of pupils from group to group, with much changing of chairs. She resists putting children together simply for the sake of black-white balance, a gesture that seems to her hypocritical. Some children are good at measuring, others at multiplying. Whereas reading is grouped by ability, with "super-readers" and nonreaders separated, social studies and science can be grouped by interest.

Nothing is frozen—no Robins or Bluebirds. Projects at the elementary level benefit from combinations of different talents—the writer, the artist, the organizer, the social director. "We don't brand 7-year-olds as *genus* genius or *genus* stupid," says Tom Wogaman. The district-wide rule: Label the task—not the child.

No class is without its complement of slower readers, but even here, despite a disproportionate number of children from poor black families, the split is rarely complete. Of the six below-level readers in Ruth Norden's present class of 26, three are white, two are black and one is an Oriental child for whom English is a second language. The nine above-grade-level readers are all white, an unusual occurrence. For the past few years, the district has been making intensive efforts in the critical reading area. One of Mrs. Norden's slower readers is now getting 20 minutes of individual instruction with a reading specialist twice a week. Another is getting 40 minutes with a college volunteer.

How have we been doing? At the very least, the kind of unmanageable classroom disruption that faced the district in the late fifties seems to have been mastered, but we are still some way from the millenium. Tests made in 1967 showed considerable improvement in all areas over the 1959 scores, but half of our black children and a quarter of our white childern were still reading at below-grade level. Today, children from Fairview and from poorer white neighborhoods are still entering school with little of the preschool book experience of the more privileged—though Head Start, nursery school and day-care effort, not to mention television, seem to be reducing their numbers.

Some are still arriving at seventh grade unable to read well enough to hold down a decent job. The situation disturbs Tom Wogaman for other than strictly academic reasons: "Kids reach seventh grade and they're not able to cut it, after their parents have been assured, 'Don't worry. Johnny's doing fine.' That's an insult. What it means to the black community is that the teacher didn't expect much of Johnny to begin with."

Still, the results of standard tests on arithmetic and reading over the years are encouraging, if not spectacular. Our elementary pupils are now performing above the state average and at about the county average—which is high for the nation. White achievement levels remain higher than black levels; but whereas in the past the gap kept widening from grade to grade, now the annual gains of the two groups are about equal. Our experience seems to confirm the conclusions of others. The Superintendent sums up: "When minority youngsters, particularly from disadvantaged backgrounds, go to school in mixed company, their achievement tends to go up, and there is not a corresponding drop in the achievement of kids who are academically oriented. So, insofar as there is academic gain, it's net, not gross—not at the expense of anybody else."

The percentage of graduates who go on from Woodlands High School to higher education runs between 70 and 75 percent—not up to Scarsdale's 90 percent-plus, but eminently respectable among less affluent, less white districts. The percentage of black students going to four-year colleges is not far below the white percentage—54 percent as compared with 60 percent. Each year, we contribute one or more graduates to almost every Ivy League college, and follow-up studies indicate that their dropout rate is somewhat lower than the national average.

Heartening—yet the case for integration cannot stand on academic achievement alone. White parents know that all-white schools nearby do at least as well for their students in that regard, maybe better. On the other hand, William Brown Jr., a black data-processing manager with the First National City Bank, who is running for school board this spring, blames the unsatisfactory progress of numbers of black students on a lack of commitment by white teachers. He is not against neighborhood schools: "Busing for integration doesn't turn me on. Busing for education turns me on."

With the connection between integration and education as hazy as ever, our system reflects the somewhat tattered belief of integration-minded people that only by living together can we learn to live together, and that that goal is worth a price, if indeed there is one. For two of the three Christmases that he has been in Central 7, Tom Wogaman has invited recent graduates of Woodlands to his office to sit around and talk about their experiences at college. The consensus was that "academically they are right there, not particularly better, not particularly worse, but much better able than graduates of better known schools to get along in their new settings and with people of different backgrounds."

Integration, we have learned, creates strains of its own. It was easier for the children of liberal parents in premerger Hartsdale to grow up with their kindly impulses toward racial minorities intact. Although they may have encounted bullying whites, they had had no experience of being shoved by tough ghetto kids in the halls, being elbowed out of line in the cafeteria, being shaken down in the bathrooms. Here is a full-page headline which appeared a few weeks ago in our friendly local paper, over a report of a Central 7 board meeting: "EXTORTION, STEALING, BULLYING IN SCHOOLS OUTRAGE PARENTS." The subject comes up regularly, here as elsewhere.

But before the merger, the children in Hartsdale would have had no opportunity to be with black youths who do not do those disagreeable things. A moderately perceptive child must find it difficult to go through our schools without learning for himself the elementary lesson that racial generalizations are untrustworthy. I remember being taught that truism in school and desiring to believe it, but being obstructed by my personal experience, or want of experience. To that extent, I was deprived, like the youngsters in neighboring Ardsley. One of our elementary-school teachers who lives in neighboring Valhalla chooses to have her two children bused to Central 7 to avoid just such deprivation.

As a matter of fact, the most recent serious disturbance at our high school was set off not by blacks, but by a gang of white "non-achievers" from relatively low-income families, who started a fight with long-haired middle-class white seniors. At one point, a delegation of black and white students protested to the high-school principal efforts by some of the "ethnics" to declare a section of the campus off-limits to blacks.

Socio-economic tensions are evident among black students, too. During racial disturbances some years ago, Roy Campanella's son was roughed up by black youths angry over his association with whites. The complex challenges that face middle-class black boys and girls coming of age in America at this time deserve more attention, and more understanding, than they are likely to receive from observers whose pleasure it is to wax romantic about ghetto culture. In any event, our schools provide daily evidence that race is not the sole nor invariably the most significant factor in our society's animosities.

Some of our hopes—ingenuous, white liberal hopes—have been disappointed. Reporting on life in this district before the merger with Hartsdale, I wrote somewhat smugly: "Both my sons, nine and seven, visit and are visited by Negro friends. Recently, the younger one announced aboard the school bus that was carrying him and one such friend to our stop: 'See this kid—I'm taking him home with me, and I like him as much as anybody.' "

To judge by the experience of my children and that of others, the interracial friendships of the early grades do not often endure past junior high school. The reasons are not difficult to sort out: Our neighborhoods remain largely broken up into white and black; there is only one black family near us. Although the school administration has resisted any clear-cut "tracking" arrangement which would separate college-bound youngsters from others, high-school students are nonetheless divided by their postschool prospects; there is a single black student in my older son's advanced French course, whereas few whites opt for Swahili. "Any departure from heterogeneity must bear the burden of proof," declares Tom Wogaman, but he is not unsympathetic to the desires of parents for enrichment and honors courses, which tend to turn out largely white, or to black desires for black studies.

In extracurricular activities, too, there are divisions. My younger son plays on an all-white tennis team. The soccer team, too, is white, whereas the basketball team is nearly all black. On the other hand, track and baseball are pretty well mixed, and rooters at the major sports events are of all hues. The chorus is mostly, but not all, white; the band is mostly, but not all, white; the high-school theater group is talented and mixed. By high school, "life-styles" have begun to take shape; the possibility of interracial dating becomes a source of anxiety for students as well as parents. (A recent issue of the high-school newspaper was dominated by a debate on the subject, with black writers mostly anti.) The virus of "separatism" running through the land does not leave us untouched, as evidenced by color groupings in the Woodlands cafeteria.

And yet, along with the pull away from what many of us in a more innocent time dreamed of as an integrated society, high-school life in Greenburgh is not a matter of black or white for most students. So much is taken for granted here that is unavailable elsewhere. There are countless casual interracial contacts, there are collaborative efforts for specific causes, there are a few close friendships, and many friendly interludes; there is identification with Woodlands and so with one another, and there is the great fact of having gone to school together from kindergarten onward. The thoroughgoing nonparticipants of both races are mostly youths who would have difficulties in any school.

No one can be certain of what it will all mean, but if I may quote the mother of my children: "They're much less self-conscious about race than I was, more realistic and more easy-going. I don't think they're as likely to beat their breasts over it or to fall into condescension." Parhaps those early friendships are not altogether lost. As the son of a black friend assured his mother, "We're doing our own things now, but we're not mad at each other."

What are we to conclude from this confused picture? No prudent resident is about to declare that a bad incident or an increase in the national hate waves could not bring a racial outbreak of the sort that occurred at Woodlands after the murder of Martin Luther King and that has troubled many other school districts. "We had disturbances when other schools had them," notes Tom Wogaman. "Now, other schools seem apathetic and so does Central 7." He goes on. "We can't escape the country's polarization, but given the external stimuli, there's an amazingly low degree of racial antipathy here. There's more separatism than I'm happy with—but it's a benign separatism with few confrontations. The difference is we can have a fight that crosses race lines and have it regarded by students as a fight between individuals, not the beginnings of a race riot."

During the spring of the first year in the district, a serious fight broke out in the cafeteria between a couple of "big fellows"—black against white. It did not go beyond that. In the same week, there was a similar fight at White Plains High School—a larger school with a lower proportion of blacks than we have and a shorter, less thorough history of integration—that blew up into a major confrontation.

Again, last year, racial incidents at White Plains resulted in a school boycott. Some of our students asked the high-school principal, Colin Bentley, for permission to have blacks from White Plains address an assembly at Woodlands. Permission was granted. An administrator reports: "They came over. It was a pretty hairy situation. There were the usual four-letter words and the shouting—but despite great sympathy among our students for the kids from White Plains, they couldn't sell their wares. Our kids didn't join in the boycott." Why? In part, it may have been that most of the demands of the White Plains students, for such things as a bulletin board for black announcements, had long since been *de facto* here. More important, one would like to believe, was the general sense, certified by our busing arrangements over many years, that our schools are held in common, and are not white institutions which, out of generosity or coercion, are playing host to outside blacks. As Tom Wogaman phrases it: "The past is a bank account."

Among the district's adults, black participation in school affairs is substantial. Two of the present nine members of the school board are black, as is the current president of the P.-T.A. Bob Frelow, who has three boys of his own in the schools, observes: "The black community here doesn't feel powerless. They see political alternatives. They have realistic hopes for their kids. They know the kids won't be totally wiped out."

Our schools form the center of community life in Greenburgh, and as the husband of a recent P.-T.A. president, I can testify that the numerous and continuing contacts between black and white residents on school matters have an impact on social life—friendships have been formed, black families have moved into once-white neighborhoods without trauma, people who grew up on one or another side of the color bar have learned to deal with each other, and even get some fun out of it. I do not mean that all is roses between us: The gaps are wide, but we have discovered that they can be bridged for shared purposes. In a (thoroughly integrated) show that residents put on at Woodlands last year for the benefit of the American Field Service, one of the hit numbers, sung by a white P.-T.A. officer and a black teacher, was called, "I've Grown Accustomed to Your Race": "I've grown accustomed to the sight/Of you each Tuesday night,/Accustomed that you're white."

(The integration on school affairs does not cross economic boundaries. Low-income whites and blacks play little part here. And it is skewed by religion, as well, with Catholics participating in far lower proportions than their numbers in the town. Many Catholic families, of course, have their children bused to all-white parochial schools, and limit their public-school activity to voting against the budget. Despite the best efforts of our WASP's and public-school Catholics, P.-T.A. committees occasionally take on the appearance of a National Conference of Black Christians and Jews.)

Relationships nourished in school activities have moved outward to affect the town as a whole, a town run until every recently by as lackluster a clique of Republican politicos as the county holds. People who met first on one of Central 7's innumerable citizens committees or while campaigning in a school-board election or as nursery-school volunteers have become allies in lending support to a day-care center, an urgent need of working mothers in Fairview; in pressing for a teen-age recreation facility to serve black youths (and white ones, too, we hope) who have been generally slighted over the years by the town bureaucracy; in fighting for low-cost scatter housing despite local opposition and official foot-dragging. The busing of our children has broadened, enlivened and enriched the lives of us adults, and improved the town.

As the world goes, busing for purposes of school integration may be marked a success in Greenburgh. How applicable is our experience to other communities? Well, we are not your typical American town.

Our path has been eased by the existence here of a community-minded, well-educated, white, liberal element and a stable, active middle-class black element which, despite significant differences, have been solid forces for integration. (The main difference on school matters is as much generational as racial: the whites, fairly secure in the knowledge that their children will get into college and find a place for themselves afterward, tend to be more "permissive" regarding discipline, dress and general school organization; the middle-class blacks tend to place more value on rules for orderly behavior and on structured teaching methods. Recently, this has led to an alliance between some blacks and more conservative whites who have no history of engagement in black causes but are all for "structure" in the schools.)

Before Central 7 is taken as a model for New York City, some physical characteristics had best be acknowledged: Greenburgh lends itself to busing. I live at the edge of the district, close to the Ardsley line, yet my children have never had more than a 20-minute ride to any of their schools. It is not unusual to hear parents of kindergarten pupils, who are on a half-day schedule, complain that the bus makes such good time that scarcely have the little ones been taken off than they are back again and yelling.

So our experience is by no means generally applicable. The effort of liberals in Scarsdale to have a batch of black children from Mount Vernon bused into their estimable schools is indubitably well-intentioned, but the Mount Vernon children could scarcely fail to note that the schools were not truly theirs. They might conclude that they were being used as another educational resource for the fortunate children of Scarsdale. If Scarsdale is interested in integration, it might consider a merger with next-door Eastchester.

Nor does our experience have much to teach big cities, with their large ghettos and their ethnic enclaves. Partisan of busing though I am, I share the qualms of other parents, black as well as white, over having young children taken daily into tough neighborhoods or hostile ones. Louis Jones 3d, a black college administrator now running for our school board, is heartily in favor of integration. Yet he would rather have his children attend an all-black school than be bused to a place where they were not wanted. In that regard, he believes that Greenburgh is "a model to the nation"; he only regrets that the nation does not seem to be ready for Greenburgh.

As for busing children out of the inner cities to the suburbs, that seems to me feasible where distances are not too long, where arrangements can be made for the children and their parents to participate in the whole range of school activities, so many of which perforce occur in the evening. It is not enough that they be mere visitors to someone else's schools.

Those who have promoted busing as a solution for problems which it cannot solve, who have made it a point of doctrine in the ideological wars, must, I think, share some of the responsibility for the antibusing storm now raging across the land. But their responsibility is slight beside that of the politicians who are riding along with it. Governor Wallace we all know; Senator Jackson we are coming to know better all the time; the new Senator Humphrey scarcely seems to know himself from one day to the next; and the President, lest anyone forget, takes care to remind us of the kind of politician he has always been.

How will the furor affect Central 7? On his arrival here in July 1969, in the midst of one of our annual budget fights, Tom Wogaman "hit two or three coffees a night." At some of them, residents raised the possibility of saving a few dollars by modifying our busing arrangements to permit more elementary pupils to attend schools near their homes. His reply: "The day that this school district goes to a neighborhood system is the day I get on the airplane and fly out. It's not a negotiable question."

"Unless you go into the woodwork," reports Renee Hertz, a school-board member from Hartsdale, who bears the liberal stigma of having favored the merger, "people are too sophisticated to put their feelings in terms of integration. Around here that's gauche. Still, at coffees, you get innuendoes—'Wouldn't it be cheaper if my child walked to school? We live right down the street.'" Recently, she has encountered disenchantment with integration among a few black parents, a feeling that it might be better perhaps if black children were taught by black teachers. "We're used to being clobbered by conservatives," she says sadly. "But when, after all the painful and precious experience, you're hit full in the face by blacks for what you're trying to do, you don't know how to react." Tom Wogaman has no doubt that if we had kept neighborhood schools and never gone onto the Princeton Plan, any proposal to integrate in today's heated-up atmosphere would be beaten —"We'd be clawed to pieces."

Central 7 is not an island. But we have had school integration for 20 years, and despite a black-separatist voice here, a white-neighborhood-school voice there, the principle seems entrenched. Even with a conservative drift in recent school-board elections, no one has publicly proposed going back on our two-decade commitment. It has been four years since a school-board candidate—a Hartsdale man who had opposed the merger—suggested a return to neighborhood schools; he was soundly beaten. Jim Frank, the black member of the board who beat him, says: "We've come such a long way that the policy of integrated education will remain." Knock wood.

Perhaps when this election year's passions subside, parents and politicians around the country may permit themselves to study districts like Central 7 which made a choice for integration years ago and have been living with the consequences. They will find no racial or educational paradises, but they may find rewards they had not anticipated. Busing has helped to make this a place where one finds oneself developing the sort of school spirit that I never enjoyed in the days when I was walking to P. S. 28 or taking the bus up the Concourse to Clinton.

School Busing: Charlotte, N.C.

FRANK BARROWS

Frank Barrows is a newspaper reporter with an intimate knowledge of school busing in Charlotte as a
result of his work in *The Charlotte Observer.* He has
also written for *Atlantic Monthly* and *Golf Magazine.*

Gone from the thoroughfares of Charlotte, North Carolina, are the
thousands of NO FORCED BUSING bumper stickers which appeared
two years ago during the city's bitter but futile stand against a court
order demanding total desegregation of the public schools. On the
streets today a giant fleet of buses can be seen transporting white
students into the ghetto and black students into the suburbs calmly,
regularly, and efficiently.

The disappearance of protest slogans and the sight of children
laughing and shouting normally as they wait at the corner might lead
to the assumption that all eventually went well here, that indignation
has matured into consent, that the integrated classroom is an accomplished goal and the school bus ride an accepted fact.

SIGNS

Unfortunately, in the middle of a third full year of extensive busing,
Charlotte belies such facile judgment. Appearances aside, the vast
majority of those parents whose automobiles sported angry stickers still
think busing an outrageous injustice. But, tired and frustrated, they
have wearily resigned themselves to it. Moreover, in the schools, where
telephoned bomb threats are commonplace and overt white-black ten-

sion occasionally erupts into violence, teachers have discovered that neither educational nor racial problems are being solved by the mere reassignment of pupils.

Still, that bleak evidence is offset by some encouraging signs. Organized opposition has withered and died. In the latest school board elections, outspoken antibusing candidates fared poorly. A poll revealed that only 35 percent of the adults in Charlotte cite busing as the aspect of the schools that most bothers them. Numbers of high school students, seemingly oblivious to the heated rhetoric that made headlines for months, have struggled diligently to promote harmony and understanding. In the elementary schools, there are indications that black children are learning to read with greater speed and comprehension than formerly. And now, as antibusing legislation is debated in Congress and talk of a possible constitutional amendment is in the air, there is a distinct uneasiness, a fear that the progress which has been achieved by the school system may be wiped out.

That system, a consolidated one, serves Charlotte and surrounding Mecklenburg County, a prosperous urban area in central North Carolina with a population of 360,000, distinguished by its fanatical devotion to a championship minor-league ice hockey team and its equally fanatical devotion to native-son evangelist Billy Graham. Moderately consevative, the city finally approved liquor by the drink in a referendum just a year ago; but the matter is ensnarled in the courts, and there are no bars amidst the sprawl of new apartment complexes, Holiday Inns, shopping malls, and interstate highways. What there is, however, is an assortment of 82,500 students, 3600 teachers, and 104 schools, not to mention some 530 buses, and the charred remains of the offices of Julius Chambers, the black civil rights attorney whose handling of the desegregation suit resulted in an arsonist's midnight attack in February 1971.

Charlotte supports the forty-third largest school system in the United States, and is the first of such size to implement extensive cross-busing. And its name is permanently inscribed on the 1971 decision in which the Supreme Court unanimously upheld busing as a means of desegregating dual school systems throughout the South: *James E. Swann v. Charlotte-Mecklenburg Board of Education,* or as lawyers abbreviate it, *Swann v. Mecklenburg.*

Despite the gradual subsidence of hysteria, it is still unusual to discuss the case in Charlotte without arousing an emotional response. I talked to one distressed woman who lived next door to an elementary school but must rise before dawn to be sure that her children catch the 7:40 a.m. bus which carries them to another school nine miles away. One teacher told me of her deep professional satisfaction when she showed vacation slides to her desegregated class and then realized that six of her black second-graders had not previously heard of the Grand Canyon. And there was the strange combination of sadness and *déjà vu* on the part of parents who had circulated protest petitions in 1970 and now hear news reports of similar efforts in Detroit and Richmond.

SHORTHAND

The results of two and a half years of busing in Mecklenburg County are most difficult to assess. To begin with, busing, the very term, is actually a shorthand symbol for the redistribution of a city's student population, leaving no school segregated and, in certain localities, each school with an enrolment approximating the white-to-black ratio in the population at large—about seven to three in Charlotte. Furthermore, not all students are assigned beyond their own neighborhoods, not all parents who express dissenting opinions are bigots, and not all blacks are necessarily in favor of busing. An incidental irony is the fact that the school bus, pictured in the mind's eye as it bounces down a narrow road lined by cornfields, has until recently been a source of pride for Americans, especially in North Carolina, which during the 1950's labeled itself as "the school-busingest state in the Union."

School administrators from cities now facing total desegregation for the first time fly to Charlotte and seek to use it as a primer. The best concise answer to these questions that can be given at the school system's headquarters is that busing is working slightly better than its opponents feared, not quite as well as its backers hoped, and considering the furor of the last three years, probably as smoothly as could be expected.

The Education Center two blocks from downtown Charlotte was among the targets of picketers who took to the streets almost as soon as U.S. District Court Judge James McMillan's original desegregation order was announced in April 1969. Just on the other side of the skyline of high-rise bank buildings lies the black community, the city's teeming northwestern quarter. Essentially, after lengthy hearings, McMillan ruled that discriminatory laws enforced by local government had concentrated most of the black population in a single section, that a dual system had been maintained because integration had not been actively sought (42 percent of the schools were, for all intents and purposes, segregated), and that busing could be used to correct the educational inequities.

The decision set off a sociological earthquake. Sign-carrying crowds gathered at the U.S. post office and courthouse, on the lawn

of McMillan's home, and in front of the Charlotte *Observer*, a newspaper which had staunchly supported busing until the economic effect
of a drop in circulation caused a tempering of its position. Groups of
all sizes, from the Queen City Jaycees to the Classroom Teachers Association, came out against busing, as did the vocal school board
chairman, William Poe, whose intransigence was primarily responsible
for the system's inability to comply with the court order or to draw
up a workable desegregation plan of its own. Ultimately a plan was
blueprinted by a court-appointed educational expert.

Ministers denounced busing from the pulpit. The Charlotte *News*
condemned McMillan—a successful local lawyer, a pillar of the community for twenty-two years before he rose to the federal bench in
1968—on its editorial pages. Poe launched a blistering face-to-face
attack against school superintendent William Self, who found himself
caught between a judge's mandate to desegregate and the school
board's unwillingness to do so. At one of the dozens of antibusing rallies
held in school auditoriums, an ex-soldier said, "I served in Korea, I
served in Vietnam, and I'll serve in Charlotte if I need to."

"THE IMPORTANT THING"

Staging those rallies, dispatching envoys to Washington to plead
Charlotte's case before selected congressmen, and accumulating eighty
thousand signatures on antibusing petitions was the task of a new organization, the Concerned Parents Association (CPA). Not all its supporters were racist; many of the stoutest of liberal consciences were put
to the test by busing. Some CPA supporters didn't care for the inconvenience of busing; some were afraid that their children would be
exposed to the crime and drugs of the ghetto; some resented judicial
interference with a school system which as early as 1966 was able to
boast that every student was taught, at one time or another, by an
instructor of another race. Nevertheless, the CPA's rabid emotionalism
had the sound and feel of racism, and its rhetoric was an exacerbating
and divisive force, offering its backers the ill-founded hope that the
Supreme Court would reverse *Swann v. Mecklenburg* and bring to an
end the busing that began in September 1970. "Though we were busing," says Self, "the city was not committed to the program. Many felt
it would be over with as soon as the Supreme Court ruled."

The CPA's influence began to diminish even before news of the
Court's landmark decision, validating busing so long as the distances to
be traveled are reasonable, flashed onto teletype machines at Charlotte's radio stations one afternoon in April 1971. After their planned
boycott fell short of predictions, even CPA spokesmen began to send
their children to school during the second week of that first semester

of busing. Throughout Charlotte over the next several months, obstinacy mellowed into resignation. A woman who had been involved in the planning of private classes to circumvent busing chose instead to allow the public schools a trial. "It hasn't upset my child like I expected," she said. "And though I'm surprised to hear myself saying this, I think in years to come, we'll see that it's something that had to be done." A beleaguered CPA fund praiser was told by another mother, "I wouldn't care if they bused my children to South Carolina, I'm so tired of it all." EDUCATION IS THE IMPORTANT THING lapel buttons popped up across the city.

The CPA, a single-issue political phenomenon, shrank and split into factions, finally dropping from sight. Later, although three of the CPA's antibusing candidates were elected to the school board, one of them, William Booe, went so far as to write a letter to the editor, pleading for less emotionalism on the subject of school bus safety.

Minor breakdowns and delays, chiefly in the older vehicles hurriedly pressed into use to double the school system's transportation capacity, are not at all uncommon; but the 47,000 students who ride buses each morning and afternoon are accustomed to rattles and squeaks. The steering and braking mechanisms are kept in good repair, and serious accidents are exceptionally rare.

The buses operate under a now stabilized plan in which every white school district has a corresponding satellite district in a black community. Basically, of the 25 percent of the students who are bused solely for desegregation, black children in grades one through four are taken to white neighborhoods, and white fifth- and sixth-graders are carried to predominantly black areas. With six elementary schools feeding two junior high schools, which in turn supply a single senior high school, a pupil can tell from the day he enters the system where he will attend classes in any given year.

It is sheer fiction to depict the school bus as a gloomy yellow dungeon on wheels. The average one-way trip takes only thirty-five minutes. Some drivers throw picnics for their passengers, and mothers often realize that eight-year-olds would rather ride home boisterously aboard the bus than meet the family station wagon in front of the school.

Elementary school teachers report that slow learners are becoming increasingly competitive and inquisitive and that white-black barriers are virtually nonexistent. It is in the high schools, where the races tend to segregate themselves purposely in classroom and cafeteria, that major obstacles are yet to be overcome. For instance, as achievement tests show, students in all-black schools can fall four semesters behind those who attend desegregated classes; and once they reach adolescence, many are unable to catch up. Educationally thwarted, some develop discipline problems. Tension multiplies when a black feels that he is slighted in extracurricular activities because he must get on a bus immediately after the dismissal bell rings; when a white resents attending a high school other than the one in his neighborhood to which he developed an allegiance; when the charged atmosphere leads an oversensitive student to interpret a teacher's careless words as racist comment.

Such human variables also enabled three black girls, participating in a panel discussion of busing, to conclude that it had brought the races closer and fostered brotherhood, while a fourth shouted, "Like hell it has."

"WORTH ANYTHING"

Disturbances, large and small, have flared at most of Charlotte's junior and senior high schools. A riot which swept across one campus a year ago especially underscored the point that racial progress is not without setbacks.

Located in the city's plush southeastern section, Myers Park High School has long been the flagship of Charlotte's educational system, known for its legions of National Merit Scholars and All-State quarterbacks. During the spring of 1971, when violence struck several other schools, Myers Park's student body had spontaneously trooped to its football stadium for a singing, clapping, swaying demonstration of interracial unity. But one day last fall, fighting broke out on the Myers Park campus. Before it was quelled by police, twenty-two persons had been injured and sixty-eight windows smashed.

To a heartening extent, though, students have striven to make the revolution work. From the night a high school boy took the floor at an early CPA meeting and, speaking through a barrage of catcalls, said, "We'd be willing to try busing . . ." the young have quickly and repeatedly assumed the initiative. A press conference was called by a senior high school's student government to refute rumors that blacks continually harassed and intimidated whites. At a junior high, eighth-graders regularly intervene if a racial scuffle seems imminent. A series of seminars and discussions for student leaders did much to make the second year of desegregation more harmonious than the first; the third should be even quieter. Still, a principal whose school has had no violence says, "I'll be glad when we get back to worrying about the curriculum rather than how we're going to keep everyone in the classroom."

Just before commencement march last June, a woman's advice to a line of graduates was, "Don't cry." That prompted a girl, later writing an essay on her experiences with busing, to ask, "Cry? About what? I felt very unsentimental in comparison to those who had described to me their own feelings of loneliness and sadness at leaving so much behind at graduations past."

Widespread change has taken place in Charlotte's educational system, from the obvious addition of better playground equipment at schools that were once all black to the subtle new mood of solemnity articulated by a graduating senior. The worst seems to be past. Some four thousand parents are actively involved as teacher's aides. As classes grow more accustomed to busing and desegregation and move upward, they gain stability.

Nonetheless, Charlotte's progress proves little about busing in cities substantially larger, cities where the school system is not so good, cities afflicted with more severe racial tensions. A simplistic interpretation of busing in Charlotte was propounded when an Associated Press reporter quoted a member of the Community Relations Committee: "'If it can work here,'" read the widely printed article, "'it can work anywhere in the nation.'"

What the man, a liberal, actually said was, "If it can work anywhere, it can work in Charlotte. Some cities are going to have a terrible time with it; and because busing has so many disadvantages to begin with, I just can't see it becoming the uniform policy on desegregation across the country."

It would also be incorrect to think that total desegregation is fully and unanimously accepted in Charlotte. No, the discontented are still there, encouraged by President Nixon's antibusing speech in March, listening to congressional proposals in September.

On the third floor of a building in downtown Charlotte is the office of Julius Chambers, the civil rights attorney who prosecuted *Swann v. Mecklenburg*. A short and bespectacled man, undaunted by a firebomb which destroyed his office, he too watches the antibusing agitation in the high places of government. Leaning back in his swivel-based leather chair, he ponders a question about the future of busing. "What you are asking," he says, "is whether the schools in the South are going to have desegregation. I'm not any kind of prophet. But if they are to be desegregated, meaningfully, there will have to be transportation. Buses."

It is late on a Friday afternoon, his staff has departed, and Chambers himself is weary. For a moment he is silent.

"There is," he says, "a growing respect, small though it may be, between black kids and white kids, an appreciation for each other as humans. If you look beyond the lawsuits, the court decisions, the protesters' debates, all of it, that's what you find—that growing respect. To me, it's worth anything."

The Buses Reach Their Destination

NEIL V. SULLIVAN

Neil V. Sullivan was Director of the Free Schools of
Prince Edward County, Virginia, and Head of Public
Education in the State of Massachusetts. His article on
busing is based on his experiences as superintendent of
the Berkeley, California, public schools. His books include *Bound for Freedom*, *Now is the Time*, and *Walk,
Run, or Retreat: The Modern School Administrator*.

On February 1, 1966, came the first bus ride to the schools in middle
Berkeley and the hills to which 238 Negro children had been assigned for the rest of their elementary years—the first day of classes,
the first mixing on the playground. How would it work; how would it
feel?

At Hillside School, the children had discussed how the new children would feel when they came to Hillside. They recognized the
fear and loneliness they themselves would feel if they had to change
schools. "They probably are going to be scared." . . . "I would be very
scared and shy." . . . "I would feel scared that someone is going to
make a joke about me." . . . "We might fight with them, we might
tease them, but they might do the same to us." . . . "I would feel
mad and quite frightened." . . . "When I came here from Houston,
Texas, I was good and scared, and these new kids will feel the same
way." . . . "New kids feel scared of everybody. They're afraid to do
anything wrong because they think everybody will laugh." . . . "You

Neil V. Sullivan, "The Buses Reach Their Destination," *Now is the Time* (Bloomington: Indiana University Press, 1970), pp. 97–110.

feel funny about everything at first. Everyone looks like strangers. You don't know anyone so you play by yourself."

The Hillside pupils had made suggestions in class, such as: "I feel if we all try to make friends with them they will not feel so shy and unwanted." . . . "We should try to get along and be good friends with them." . . . "We can show them around the school." . . . "I am going to help these kids feel comfortable here, sort of like they were still at Columbus."

And a very practical idea: "When the new kids come, I will tell them where the bathroom is."

From the Administration Building we followed the whole move carefully. Evelyn Stewart, in her "public information specialist" role, turned reporter and watched it personally during those first busing days and at intervals thereafter, looking and listening, talking with children, teachers, counselors, bus drivers, and custodians. I shall long remember her return from the first day of the busing project as she came into an administrative staff meeting to report her enthusiasm. That first day she rode the bus with the Negro group from Lincoln School in the ghetto to their new base at Emerson in the hills, and her report reflects the excitement.

The Lincoln children, kindergarteners to mid-sixth-graders, mounted the bus at 8:15 a.m. at the designated pickup point—a side-street leading into a main thoroughfare that runs from ghetto to hills. A Negro mother, employed as an aide for the first few weeks, was there with them. So was one of the neighborhood aides employed to supervise the whole bus-riding operation as it got started. A few mothers had come to see their children off. There was the big yellow bus and its driver, a lean Texan in blue jeans and jacket and big black cowboy hat. "Hi, kids!" he said, then corrected himself and said, "Good morning, girls and boys!" "Hi!" they responded, and, then, copying him, "Good morning!" Pretty soon, as they waited to mount the bus, one child got up the courage to ask him, "Are you a cowboy?" and the driver answered, "Sure enough. I used to be." Now the kids felt better.

It was a cool grey morning—what Berkeley calls cool at 65 degrees —with rain possible, although just as likely the sun would emerge about 10 o'clock and shine brightly. Some of the boys wore shiny black or yellow slickers and fireman's rainhats. Every child was well dressed, most of them in simple neat school clothes, a few—at their request—in their Sunday best because this was a big day in their lives. Almost every reporter who covered the first busing day remarked on how well the children were dressed, how neatly groomed, writing as if the white race has a monopoly on pride in good appearance.

Although the children had ridden the bus before on a "dry run"—a get-acquainted ride, including a visit to their "new" school—the experience was still new and fresh. The children clustered together, sitting close to one another, some chattering and giggling as the bus rode upward, some quiet—slowly at first through early morning traffic, more rapidly as it mounted into the hills. They saw University student apartments, with pairs of socks or shirts hanging to dry in the window, an assortment of gift shops, art galleries, coffee houses, street cafes, churches quite unlike the simple ones they attended, the cluster of modern dormitories termed the "UC Hiltons," students hurrying to the University on foot, bicycles and Hondas—all comprising a different glimpse of living from what they knew. As they drove up into the residential section, they saw big old houses painted much less recently than their own, also many fine new ones. They saw beautiful gardens. But how much they took in on this exciting first day is a question.

The older children sat in pairs or small groups. Some sat alone. One sixth-grade boy who sat apart, looking tense and serious, was asked if he was glad to be going to Emerson. "At first I wasn't, but now I am," he said. "I liked it at Lincoln with my friends. But after I talked a lot with my teachers and parents, I decided I wanted to go. Anyway, I decided I ought to go."

Soon they arrived at Emerson—all too short a ride for the little ones who love to ride buses, and for the older ones who were more aware of their burden as ghetto pioneers entering a new world. Now they had to leave the security of the bus and the friendly cowboy driver and enter the strange white school. The Emerson children were waiting for them on the playground. The principal, a grave man of few but well-chosen words, was standing at the bright red door of the newly modernized school and almost before the bus came to a stop he walked out to welcome them. He stepped into the bus. "Good morning, boys and girls," he said. "Welcome to your new school. Your teachers are ready, your classrooms are ready. Are *you* ready?"

The children answered with one loud and hearty, "Yes!"

They entered the playground gate slowly in a single file. In no time at all, however, girls and boys in red caps, who had been assigned or had volunteered as hosts and guides, came to them, said "Hi," and began mingling them with the others to go into the classrooms. Some stood apart smiling self-consciously. Once in the classrooms, it was "business as usual," no palaver—just the first day of the spring semester

when all must be briefed on such routine matters as what to do with
lunch money and the usual regulations.

On the second day, Mrs. Stewart rode the bus to Hillside School
with the children from Columbus. This was an even more dramatic
ride—a more striking glimpse of how the other half lives, for the approach to Hillside winds steeply upward on a narrow road through
some of the most beautiful homes in Berkeley. Hillside is an old grey
stone building, its arched entrance a great carved oaken door that
might be the entrance to a church. Although the surroundings are
wooded and the houses with their fine gardens merge in friendly
fashion into the school grounds, it must have seemed awesome to the
new children.

Carefully prepared by their principal the young hosts and hostes-
ses were busy making the new children feel at home. One Hillside boy
was heard saying to a new boy, "Hey, I'm your buddy, you know. You
gotta play with me."

In the days that followed we gathered many more significant
glimpses and heard of many interesting incidents at the hill schools.
White children seemed to use mainly language to get acquainted;
Negro children tended to use the sense of touch. With boys, whatever
their color, the sense of touch often meant friendly wrestling and
often, too, not so friendly fighting. Boys at certain age levels just have to
express themselves with their bodies, tumbling and rolling around
together.

Two Negro boys were seen slugging a white boy. Standing nearby
was a white sixth-grader—a quiet, intellectual boy. He moved up and
said: "That is no way to solve your problems." His quiet criticism was
so startling that the boys immediately stopped their punching and
walked away.

The girls had playground problems, too. It turned out that the
Negro girls jumped rope faster, higher, and longer than the white girls
could. When the best Negro jumper of all was excluded from the
game, a noisy argument ensued which ended in the vice-principal's
office. The vice-principal took them to task, rather in the manner of a
coach. "We play fair," he said, "or we don't play." He discussed the
problems of getting acquainted, of learning to work and play together,
and wound up philosophically with the comment, "Some people are
better in some things; some, in others. That's the way life is."

Some of the problems were more serious than playground tussles.
Many newcomers needed individual attention. A fourth-grade teacher
at Cragmont found herself using a little spontaneous therapy on Henry,
a Negro newcomer. Henry is a little boy, almost the smallest in the

class. He had a history of problems but had been regarded as sufficiently stable to be transferred. Also he had begged to go because his
older sister would be enrolled in an upper class. But in the new
classroom, Henry was aggressively hostile, easily upset, a trouble-
maker. He talked back to his teacher and pushed younger children
around on the playground. One day, his teacher reported, he came in
and she saw that the whole class, including some Negro classmates,
had turned against him.

"He was so alone," his teacher said. "I felt sorry for him. I just
went to him and wrapped my arms around him tight, then led him to
his desk. The other children looked sort of surprised but also pleased.
This helped Henry, but I don't know if it will last."

Meanwhile his sister—a beautiful girl, self-confident and a good
mixer—was a shining star in the sixth-grade. Within a few weeks her
class elected her group captain. Another Negro girl stood out at once
for her ability in creative writing and music composition. She wrote
for the school magazine and composed a song for her class.

The few children of upper middle-class Negro families who have
long lived in the hill area reacted variously according to their per-
sonalities. One, who is lively, attractive and popular in her hill school—
a "big wheel"—mixed spontaneously with the less privileged newcomers. The new Negro girls were proud of her and she became for
some a model; they too tried to be outgoing, lively and popular.
Another hill Negro student was torn and miserable when the "outside"
Negro children came into the school. She was sorry for the new girls.
"They're lonely and unhappy," she said, when asked how the girls
were getting along. "They want to go home," she said. But she herself
could not help them. She stayed apart from the newcomers, clung to
her long-time white chum.

The younger the children were, the easier the adjustment was.
But not for all. David, a second-grader, was one of several who begged
to go back to his old school. He was an appealing little fellow, who
almost never smiled. He missed his friends and his sisters and brothers
downtown. "No, I *don't* like it," he insisted. "They don't play with you.
The bus is the only part I like. I wish I could never get off!"

David's parents also asked if he could be returned to his former
school, but had to be told, despite understanding and sympathy for the
child, that he could not. Implicit in the agreement of transfer—and
necessarily so—was that it would last long enough to be given a fair
chance.

Some interesting generalizations emerged. With the exception of
young David and a few others his age, primary-grade children mixed
easily. They were interested in external differences like skin and hair

but basically they felt alike and quickly became good friends. They played happily together, shared notes on scrapes and bruises, exchanged toys, learned to accept one another. Here as one counselor expressed it are "school kid" personality problems, not white kid or black kid problems.

It was much harder for fifth- and sixth-graders. Some as a group, others separately, set themselves apart. At Whittier, some of the transfer students formed a sports team and would not let anyone else in. They would not even play with the other Negroes from the Whittier area. They apparently came to Whittier feeling different and insisted on reinforcing that feeling. The principal and teachers broke up the clique by talking it over and by relentlessly insisting that they include other players. "But the change is on the surface," said one deeply concerned teacher. "The boys have been guided into mixing with their fellows. But in their hearts, they still feel separate and apart. Perhaps, for them—at ages 11 and 12—integration is too late."

The older Negro girls, by and large, adjusted better than the boys, both socially and academically. A few fifth- and sixth-grade boys, when they could not keep pace with their white contemporaries in the classroom turned sullen and recalcitrant. Back and forth they went to the principal's office. Some got over the hurdle, some did not. This, however, is the usual boy-girl growth difference—the girls mature earlier, more quickly gain social skills. If the Negro girls were lonely and afraid, they concealed it in the classroom. But in the nurse's room, unoccupied when the part-time nurse was not there, one often found a Negro girl, excused from the classroom for "not feeling well," lying on the couch to rest a while. And soon a friend "from home" came to sit with her.

As the busing transfer progressed, a graduate student in education at San Francisco State College, and a Berkeley parent, made a study of feelings of social belonging at Emerson School. She chose Emerson because, although its school population is primarily Caucasian, its children come from diverse backgrounds—from families of University faculty, business and profesional fields and single-parent homes—and the area is primarily middle income.

Her sample totaled 107 children of whom 19, or 18 per cent, were Negro transfers from Lincoln School. The children queried were in grades 3, 4, 5, and 6. They were asked to state in order their choice of three people in the class they would like to sit by. Some were then interviewed about their choice or rejection. Interviews went like this: Q. "On the card you put some choices of those you would like to sit by in school. How did you happen to choose her (or him)?" The children's typical answers were either general statements, He's my best friend. I like him; or expressed a special relationship; We play together. She helps me. He gives me things; or revealed attributes and behavior they admired. She's pretty. The other kids like her. She's a good student. Or, in case of rejection, opposite remarks in the same categories.

The study indicated some expected, some surprising effects of integration on children's attitudes:

Emerson children were chosen at about a 2-1 advantage over Lincoln children.

Lincoln children tended to choose Emerson children and reject Lincoln children (of their own race).

Girls experienced a higher level of social belonging than boys.

Lincoln children tended to choose Emerson children on the basis of attributes and behavior, while Emerson children chose Lincoln children on the basis of relationship.

Choices tended to be built around interpersonal and play relationships. Rejections tended to center in the classroom experience.

At the end of the school year, after one semester of busing, a major study was made of the total ESEA project's first year by ESEA's coordinator and ESEA's evaluation consultant, in a 68-page report submitted to the California State Department of Education. According to the findings about the busing project gained from 420 interviews with mothers, both at the receiving and sending schools, and with teachers, "Responses pertaining to the busing program and integration of the schools reveal a strong majority approval." Eighty-one per cent of mothers of bused children, and 65 per cent of mothers of children in classes with bused children, felt it had been "good" for their children to be in contact with children from another neighborhood and another race. Only one mother from the ghetto said it had been "bad" for her child. A majority of mothers reported that their children had made new interracial friendships.

Ninety per cent of mothers of children in receiving schools, who attended classes with bused children, as well as those mothers whose children were not in classes with the newcomers, said they favored busing as a means of relieving overcrowding in other schools. Ninety-one per cent said they were for it as a means of improving learning. "The overwhelming favorable response to these questions indicates a widespread and unselfish concern for educational excellence and educational equality," the evaluator summed up.

Ninety per cent of the 420 mothers—378—had said Yes to busing. Half of them were Negro mothers, many of whom felt it was an honor for their children to be chosen to be transferred—to be regarded as sturdy enough to weather the experience. Along with their children they had taken on the busing burden when the school district asked them to be the pioneers. Among the Caucasian mothers sampled, a few truly wanted their children to have the interracial experience, but many would have chosen the "wait until" road. For the majority, I believe it was an act of faith in board and administration leadership. The board, which they had elected, had committed itself to this small first step in elementary integration. The administration had planned, discussed, and persuaded. The parents had listened, thought, argued, and gone along.

Berkeley's first busing of 238 Negro children from ghetto to the almost pure-white hills was a testing of the wind . . . an experiment . . . hopefully a showpiece of integration. Under the regulations of the federal grant financing the program, the primary aim of busing was to relieve the overcrowded classrooms of the target schools and to enhance every means of education for the resultant smaller classes in the ghetto. But in Berkeley we felt the important long run effect of busing would be on the receiving schools, not the target schools. We hoped this experiment in elementary integration would prove to our citizens that true enrichment of education comes through quality integrated schools, not through patchwork on particular schools that have been overlooked in the past.

The pilot busing project was a success as gauged by the study after six months, and another one at the end of one year of the experiment. My own judgment of its success would be positive—but. . . .

Elements of success were the rise in achievement by the Negro children bused while the achievement of their Caucasian classmates remained stable; the social impact on children of both races who, to some extent at least, stayed to play after school and visited one another's homes in hills and flats on weekends or during summer vacation; and parental acceptance to such an extent that a sizable group of Caucasian parents said they would be willing to bus their children to the Negro schools.

But there is another side to the busing story. Great loneliness accompanies the role of warriors in the cause of equality. It is not an easy role, not a light burden for young shoulders to bear. Now they see the "differences" as they ride the bus into middle Berkeley and the hills—the greener gardens, the expensive homes, the ways of living denied them in the ghetto. Now the facts of housing discrimination are engraved on their souls.

The Negro youngsters, especially the youngest among them, loved the bus ride. Robert Coles wrote in *Integrated Education*

(February-March 1966): "The very bus ride gives Negro children vision, a sense of cohesion with one another, and even a feeling of pride. It is *their* bus; it is taking them places they have never seen before, places which, to them, mean a better life in the future." Their roles in their own environment are changed. "They become leaders in both their families and their neighborhoods, sources of information about the 'white world,' children who have 'been there' and return daily with stories to tell—and examples to inspire. . . ."

Nevertheless, this type of tokenism, essential as I believed this venture to be, accentuates differences. It exposes the contrast between the living patterns of the poor and the privileged; it contributes to the black and white division; it sharpens the pain of discrimination. The bus itself is a symbol of separateness, enclosing in temporary security a tightly-knit unit of Negro children who must dismount in an alien place. Perhaps busing even encourages the children to cling together as Negroes rather than mix with the whites.

Token busing also separates siblings, taking one and leaving the others down there. We were asked, again and again; "Why can't all our children be chosen? Why take one and not the others?" And it pushes down the reputation of the Negro schools. It proclaims, in effect, that the Caucasian hill schools are superior to the ghetto schools, that it is a privilege for a Negro child to be chosen to attend them. And white children, unlike the Negroes, never get a look at the other side of Berkeley—the ghetto.

All these factors were clear to us as we planned the busing move. We waited impatiently for the day when all children would attend totally integrated schools, eliminating the racial stigma of busing. This tokenism was a demonstration to speed up that day of integration. We made clear to the Negro parents involved our ultimate hopes for this experiment—we hoped it would show to all the need for, advantages of, and relative normalcy in total integration. "We *did* try to pick the youngsters who could work in well at the hill schools," Mrs. Harriet Wood, Director of Elementary Education, explained. "We did not want to perpetuate the stereotype of inferiority. We did not want to send large groups of nonachievers. We wanted the first move toward elementary integration to be successful."

An honor to be chosen, a privilege to be a pioneer in integration—this the parents and children understood and accepted. But when one or more children in a family were left behind in the ghetto schools, the experiment was harder to take.

Consider this parent of four children, who came to me for help. Two of her children were being bused to Emerson School in the hills, two remained at Lincoln in West Berkeley. She took an adamant position that all four children must attend Emerson. I explained that it was our policy to transfer siblings when vacancies occur in the receiving schools. I found it would be possible to transfer her third child but not her fourth because the grade he would attend was already overcrowded. This she would not accept. I said perhaps we could move the two children now at Emerson back to Lincoln, although we had a strict policy against transferring back. The mother could not accept this as a solution either. She liked what was happening to her children at Emerson. At Lincoln, she said, they had been getting A's, but getting them easily because they had little competition and because teachers expected less of them. At Emerson they were challenged, they had to work harder, and although they were not getting A's, as formerly, they were truly achieving. She also wanted them to continue to gain the experience of integration. She was proud of them. But why couldn't her other two children go to Emerson?

We were getting more and more such problems. We were deeply concerned that in fact we were adding to the stereotype of superiority-inferiority, reinforcing the feelings of parents whose children the bus divided that the receiving hill school was superior and soft pedalling the increasing excellence of their own schools. It was the integration experience that was superior, not the hill school. But again, if some of your children were chosen and others were not, how would you feel?

We worked for the time when we could say "Yes" to these mothers —*Yes*, all your children may take the bus, *all* your children may go to schools where integration will not be a token but an accomplished fact. We worked for the time when there would be no ghetto schools, no separation.

But the bus kept rolling, its course increasingly smooth. For the young ones, it did not start rolling too late; for the older ones, its value was not lost. It was, as we well knew, only a fragment—an experiment to point the way.

Our ESEA coordinator, put it well in a periodic report to the people.

> The busing has allowed us the chance to show that integrated education is the only quality education. The transfer program has awakened parents to the educational problems of both Negro and white ghetto schools. Segregated schools are beneficial to neither the Caucasian nor the Negro.
>
> Kids learn from each other and their environment. For the 238 bused youngsters, and for all the children in the receiving schools, the environment has been broadened.
>
> The West and South Berkeley community is greatly limited in breadth by not only the absence of Caucasians but of upper- and mid-

dle-class Negroes, many of whom have left. The children of this community come in contact only with kinds of like backgrounds and experiences. They don't have contact with children of different aspirations—the word is "different," not necessarily "better."

Parents volunteered their children for the busing program because they were very dissatisfied with the "separate but equal" concept of schooling.

Integration will come when the Negro community no longer accepts second-class education. It will come when West and South Berkeley parents are joined by West Berkeley educators as well as educators and citizens throughout Berkeley in the demand for truly quality education, which means full, integrated, equal education for all.

They Don't Burn Buses Anymore in Pontiac

WILLIAM SERRIN

William Serrin is a reporter for the *Detroit Free Press*
and author of *The Company and the Union,* a study of
the relations between General Motors and the United
Auto Workers.

At about 7:15 every weekday morning, Mrs. Janice Zehnder, a housewife and mother of two, drives her car into the Pontiac school district
bus yard at Saginaw and Montcalm streets, just south of the gigantic
General Motors Pontiac assembly plant and foundry complex in this
grimy factory city of 85,000, thirty miles north of Detroit. Mrs. Zehnder
parks her car, walks across the lot, and climbs into school bus number
three. If the bus has dirt on the floor, she gets a broom and sweeps it
out.

Meanwhile, another seventy-five or so drivers climb into other
buses, sweep them, and rev up the engines. The early morning bustle
smacks of the commotion just before reveille on an army company
street. The drivers—blacks, whites, men, women—josh and poke each
other. It is easy to forget that on this spot last August ten buses were
dynamited and burned in protest against the city's school busing plan.

At 7:25, Mrs. Zehnder, who is white, brown-haired, and in her
early thirties, drives bus number three slowly out of the yard, turns
down Montcalm, and drives to her first stop—McConnell School at
Willard and Paddock streets—where about twenty black grade-school
children scramble aboard. She waits about five minutes for stragglers

William Serrin, "They Don't Burn Buses Anymore in Pontiac," *Saturday Review,*
June 24, 1972. Copyright © 1972 by Saturday Review, Inc. First appeared in
Saturday Review of Education, June 24, 1972. Used with permission.

to arrive, and then, with about thirty children on the bus—all but one of them black—drives to the McCarroll School on the white side of town. The ride takes another five or six minutes.

There is much exuberant banter among her passengers during the ride. Then the children pile off and race toward the school building, and Mrs. Zehnder proceeds to her other stops, picking up kids and depositing them at two other schools in Pontiac. In the afternoon, she plies her course in reverse. Across Pontiac other buses make similar trips, transporting children to school in the morning and back to their neighborhoods in the afternoon. Mrs. Zehnder, like the other drivers, feels that everything is "fine." The children are no problem, she told me one day recently when I rode with her. In fact, she says, they are a delight.

In Pontiac, the first large northern city to be ordered by a federal court to bus children to achieve school integration, busing goes much better than expected. The children seem happy. For the first time in several years, the city, which has approximately 23,000 blacks and Mexican-Americans, has not had to close a school because of racial strife. The President may oppose busing; most congressmen may oppose it; most parents in Pontiac may oppose it, including blacks. But two facts remain: First, Pontiac schools would not be integrated without a busing program, and, second, that program is working. "The majority of our kids seem to get along fine," says Pontiac School Superintendent Dana Whitmer. "We got a lot of love going on," adds Andrew Petress, director of the city's Human Relations Commission.

Bringing busing to Pontiac and subsequently integrating its school system was a tortuous process. It began in 1969 when the 1,500-member Pontiac National Association for the Advancement of Colored People filed a class-action suit against the Pontiac school system on behalf of a black Pontiac woman, Mrs. Sadie Davis, and her son Donald, charging that the Pontiac schools were segregated in violation of the *Brown v. Topeka* U.S. Supreme Court decision of 1954, which held that segregated schools were inherently unequal.

The Pontiac chapter received little support from the national NAACP; it thought the case could not be won. In February 1970, however, U.S. District Judge Damon J. Keith, a black jurist appointed by President Lyndon Johnson, ruled that the Pontiac schools were indeed segregated and observed that between 1964 and 1970 city leaders had drawn and redrawn school districts so as to keep the system segregated. Judge Keith ordered the school board to institute a busing system to achieve integration. Pontiac's enrolment is about 33 per cent black. Under the Keith plan each of the city's thirty-six predominantly white schools were to become 20 to 36 per cent black.

The Pontiac seven-member school board responded by appealing Keith's ruling to the U.S. Circuit Court of Appeals in Cincinnati, which held the case for more than a year as it waited for the U.S. Supreme Court to express its position on busing as a method to achieve school integration. In April 1971 the High Court, after considering a Charlotte, North Carolina, school case, ruled that busing was one method that courts might properly use to bring about school integration. The circuit court thereupon upheld Keith's order. The matter, however, was still far from being settled.

During the summer an antibusing organization called the National Action Group (NAG) came into being under the leadership of a handful of militantly segregationist white mothers, including Mrs. Irene McCabe—the voluble, blonde housewife who later marched 620 miles to Washington to dramatize the NAG position. An antibusing rally was held in Pontiac's Wisner Stadium. Alabama Governor George Wallace expressed his support for the local segregationists. On the night of August 30 a hole was cut in the chain-link fence surrounding the school bus yard, and ten buses were dynamited and burned. The loss cost the city about $50,000. Two weeks later the Federal Bureau of Investigation charged six alleged members of the Ku Klux Klan with conspiracy in the crime, including Robert Miles, the leader of the Michigan Klan. (Michigan, where Governor Wallace won 51 per cent of the votes in the Democratic primary in May 1972, has long been a stronghold of the Klan in the North.)

On September 7, the day school opened, five women chained themselves to a gate at the bus yard to prevent buses from leaving. They were arrested, as were four other women who sat down in front of the gate. White pickets ringed a number of schools and yelled "Nigger, Nigger" at black children and black teachers. Rocks were thrown at buses. At Alcott Elementary School, sheriff's deputies and state police had to be called in to escort black children to their classes.

Only 66 per cent of the white students attended school on opening day. There were bomb threats and a number of clashes between white and black students. On the second day of school, attendance climbed to about 72 per cent. For the rest of the week, despite sporadic outbreaks of violence between white and black students, the percentage of students attending school did not drop far below the 80 per cent. White parents started a campaign to establish freedom schools, but although nearly 1,500 children registered for these schools in the first week, the number of those who attended them soon dropped sharply. It is now estimated that about 150 to 200 students attend these private all-white schools.

By Friday of the first school week the situation was getting back to normal. Protests continued, however. On September 15 the National Action Group massed pickets outside General Motors' Fisher Body plant in Pontiac and forced GM to close it down after a majority of the 4,200 workers refused to cross the line. In October, Senator Robert Griffin, the Michigan Republican, asked for a constitutional amendment to prevent busing, stating that the Pontiac busing program was "counterproductive" and was resulting in "bitterness and polarization." The Detroit area's suburban congressmen, most of them whites with reputations for being relatively liberal, soon capitulated and joined Senator Griffin in declaring that they, too, opposed busing.

The majority of students evidently felt differently. When asked his opinion of busing, a fifth-grader replied, "It's great." Another white student commented: "We've got a lot of friends who are black. . . . I don't want to stay out. I want to see my friends."

What many of their parents oppose, of course, is not busing in and of itself but—despite their claims to the contrary—integration. To begin with, Pontiac does not have a particularly massive busing program. About 9,000 children, or 37 per cent of the city's students, are bused under the Keith integration order. The longest distance any must travel is about six miles, a trip that takes about thirty-five to forty minutes. The average distance is about two-and-one-half miles, a trip that takes fifteen to twenty minutes. Many students have less than a five-minute bus ride to school.

There is no busing for kindergarten children; they attend their neighborhood schools. In grades one to six, students are bused for three years—either from grades one through three or from grades four through six. In the years they are not bused they attend their neighborhood schools. In junior high school grades seven through nine, students are bused two of the three years. The third year they go to school in their neighborhoods. There is no busing in the city's two high schools, which were integrated several years ago. Thus, students are bused three of seven elementary years and two of three intermediate years—or five of the thirteen years they spend in the Pontiac schools.

The large-scale violence predicted by many parents and politicians has not materialized in Pontiac. L. Brooks Patterson, an attorney for NAG who is using the publicity gained from his efforts to run for Oakland County prosecutor, insists that the school board is hiding or refusing to count racial incidents. Mrs. McCabe, the NAG leader, seconds Patterson's charge. Yet there seems to be little substance to what they say. Victor Boucheart, executive secretary of the Pontiac Education Society, observes that while racial incidents in the Pontiac schools do occur, as they do in all urban schools these days, "there are, if anything, fewer incidents now with racial implications than there were before the Keith plan was instituted."

That busing and integration are going as well as they are in Pontiac is a tribute to the majority of the parents and students as well as to the Parents-Teachers Association. (Last fall the PTA efforts and other positive programs received little attention from the press, which concentrated on Mrs. McCabe and NAG and on the bombing and demonstrations.) Certainly, there has been little assistance from the city's business and labor leadership, particularly General Motors, which employs about 35,000 in the Pontiac area, and the supposedly liberal United Automobile Workers.

General Motors historically has declined to take sides on controversial issues. David Doherty, executive director of the Pontiac Urban Coalition, explains that if GM had attempted to work for busing, this would have been resented by the Pontiac working class, whose members cannot afford to escape the city as the executives have done. Yet, surely, General Motors could have made funds available and exercised influence as it has for years in other areas of Pontiac community life.

The UAW, which traditionally hails the working man's nobility and intelligence, lacked the courage to confront its membership on the busing issue. "The UAW hasn't done anything," Superintendent Whitmer says. Would working-class whites have been less violently opposed to busing had the UAW attempted to inform its members about school integration? One suspects so but will never know, since UAW's leaders failed to take any action.

It is too early to say whether integration will increase achievement in Pontiac classrooms. Tests will be taken at the end of the school year and the results compared with those of tests taken when school began last fall. To ensure that the finding are valid, Pontiac officials plan to extend this testing program over a three-year period.

William Waterman, one of the attorneys who argued the Pontiac case in federal court, believes the tests will show that both black and white students are making more progress in their studies. In reply to blacks who oppose busing—as does Roy Innis, director of the Congress on Racial Equality, and as did the National Black Political Convention whose members recently adopted an anti-busing resolution in Gary, Indiana—Waterman says that isolation always has been destructive to blacks. He believes that most blacks approve of integration and notes that black leaders who oppose busing are for the most part not elected officials who know that their constituents favor it. Waterman points out that many white workers in Pontiac are themselves trapped in squalid working-class ghettos and adds, "Until all people, black people and poor white people, get together, neither will have a real voice."

In March, nine Pontiac students went to Washington to testify before the House judiciary subcommittee conducting hearings on a proposed constitutional amendment to ban busing as a means of integrating schools. The gist of their testimony was that integration was working in Pontiac and that they did not wish to return to the segregated system. Chris Reynolds, a fifteen-year-old white student, said, "Maybe someday we can be not only a United States but a united people." Maria Alfaro, an eighteen-year-old Mexican-American, stated, "Kids always thought that we of Mexican background sneaked around with knives ready to stab them. But since integration we have made many new friends of all races." Marty Brown, a black, added, "There is a new kind of learning this year. We're learning from one another, and also what the entire Pontiac community is all about."

How Busing Works in Britain

ANGUS DEMING

Angus Deming works in the London bureau of *Newsweek*.

It is a mild and sunny day in England (how often is it otherwise!), and in the borough of Ealing, a sprawling area of factories, shops, and low- to middle-income homes on the western outskirts of London, a familiar morning routine is taking place. On a dozen street corners, particularly in the densely populated Southall district of Ealing, neatly dressed children stand in little clusters, patiently awaiting the arrival of the school bus. There is a somewhat exotic air about this otherwise prosaic scene: Almost without exception the mothers, who stand serenely watching over their offspring, are dressed in silken jodhpurs and saris of a variety of bright pastel shades, and some wear ruby-red caste marks in the center of the forehead. They are Indians, Bengalis, and Pakistanis (save for the scattering of West Indians in their midst), and theirs are among the 10,000-odd immigrant children in Britain who are transported each day to schools outside their own neighborhoods in order to achieve a better racial balance in the classroom.

The British version of busing—or "dispersal," as it is officially termed—has been attempted in one way or another ever since 1963, primarily in those areas of London and the industrial Midlands in which immigrants from India and Pakistan have settled in large numbers over the past decade. But unlike its American counterpart, to which it bears superficial resemblances, busing in Britain could hardly qualify as a national political issue. Indeed, although certainly not without its critics, dispersal has been carried out in such typically low-key British fashion that many Britons quite probably are unaware that busing is no longer a uniquely American phenomenon.

Such controversy over busing as does make its rare way into print is most apt to be focused on the borough of Ealing, where busing was pioneered in Britain and where dispersal is still practiced on as large a scale as anywhere in this country. Every day some 2,200 children, most of them primary school pupils from Southall in the five-to-eleven-years-of-age bracket, are dispersed to schools all over the borough—entailing for some of them a bus ride of as much as six miles in each direction.

In Southall the jumping-off point for many dispersed children is a gloomy mass of red-brick Victoriana known as the Featherstone Infants School. At least a dozen bus loads of Asian and West Indian youngsters (in Britain they are all conveniently lumped together under the heading of "colored" children) leave from there at 8 a.m. each day, though by 7:30 a.m.—in fair weather or in foul—the school's courtyard is already overflowing with boys and girls waiting to clamber into buses chartered by the Borough of Ealing Education Authority.

The coach I boarded was, like the others parked along the sidewalk, a far cry from your friendly, neighborhood American school bus. No top-heavy crate in familiar yellow paint this, but a classic example of the stately British tour bus, complete with red-plush, tilt-back seats. My bus was designated "Route No. 1," the longest itinerary taken by any of the dispersed children in Ealing: a forty-five minute ride, much of it through heavy commercial traffic, to the Acton Wells School some six miles distant.

I was prepared for a tedious journey with a bunch of boisterous, screeching kids. Instead, I found myself riding with forty very appealing, brown-skinned, black-haired boys and girls whose behavior was beyond reproach. "Now, no talking please, and sit back in your seats in case we have to stop suddenly," clucked the kindly, gray-haired Englishwoman who had come along in the mother-hen role of school bus "escort."

That was just as we were getting under way, and it proved to be the only time she felt called upon to raise her voice. Glancing about at my fellow passengers, I noticed two little girls engrossed in something called *The Humpty Dumpty Comic Book*. Several other children whispered quietly among themselves. Many simply gazed, somewhat sleepily, out the bus's picture windows. Not a pigtail was pulled; not a punch was traded; not once was the pop of bubble gum heard.

Indian and Pakistani children, I was later told, are inclined to be serious and placid, but these youngsters seemed to be little paragons.

I found myself seated beside a studious little Punjabi girl with large, brown eyes, a radiant smile, and a bouquet of red roses, which she clutched in her lap. She told me that her name was Anita Sharma, that she was eleven years old, that her father was a schoolteacher in London, and that she was one of five children. Her younger sister, Parvin, aged five, sat beside the bus escort just across the aisle, and she, too, clutched a bouquet of roses. The flowers, Anita explained, were for her teacher at Acton Wells and had been picked that morning from her own garden.

"Did you vote Labor or Conservative in the 1970 general elections?" Anita suddenly asked me. Somewhat startled by her question, I explained that I was American and therefore could not vote in British elections. So she came right back with another one: "Then who would you rather have for your next President—Mr. Nixon or Mr. McGovern?" After that she wanted to know: "Is it true that Indians are still being persecuted in California? I mean *red* Indians, of course."

When it came to the subject of busing, Anita was surprisingly philosophical. "It *is* an inconvenience," she admitted in her impeccable English, "but the drivers of these buses are very nice; they are very good and very careful." She added: "Of course, they should really build more schools in Southall. Then they wouldn't have to put us on buses every morning. But that would mean knocking down lots of houses and parks to make room for the school buildings, and, if they did that, then nobody would come to live here anymore."

The fact that so many of those who *have* come to live in Southall are immigrants from a totally alien culture explains why busing was undertaken here in the first place. Indians and Pakistanis began congregating in Southall as far back as the mid-1950s, partly because of the natural tendency of an out-group plunged into a strange environment to flock together, partly because of the area's proximity to the industrial complex in which they found jobs, often of the most menial kinds, such as sweeping factory floors. By 1963 Southall had become such a high-density enclave of Indians and Pakistanis—the majority of them Sikhs from the predominantly rural Punjab—that the neighborhood's primary schools were becoming inundated with Asian immigrant children, a large percentage of whom spoke little, if any, English. "Native" English children in Southall were becoming increasingly a minority, vastly outnumbered by the offspring of former colonial subjects. To authorities and parents alike, the major preoccupation was, not that such an ironic twist had been given to the decline of Empire, but that teachers in Southall found themselves spending more and more time just teaching basic English. Everyone was being penalized: the white-skinned English pupils whose education was being retarded by an influx of Punjabi-speaking immigrant kids, the immigrant Asian children who were rapidly becoming ghettoized. Authorities in Southall thus began busing their surplus immigrant children to outlying schools. By doing so, they not only relieved some of the pressure on their own overburdened schools but also, they contended, helped the immigrant children themselves by placing them in an integrated (i.e., racially balanced) school environment within which they would learn English more rapidly and be more apt to learn to adjust to the strange new country to which they had come to live.

The basis of the operation was a somewhat arbitrary quota system: Not more than 30 percent of any one school's enrolment—the figure soon had to be raised to a more realistic 40 per cent—should be immigrant children. (As defined by the Department of Education, these are children born abroad of foreign parents or children whose foreign-born parents have lived in Britain less than ten years.) Whenever a school's quota was exceeded, "surplus" immigrant children were to be dispersed to schools in other areas.

In 1965 the Department of Education, though by no means urging that it become standard policy, specifically suggested dispersal as one means of coping with the problems of educating increasingly large numbers of immigrant children. Some of the sixty-odd school districts having large numbers of immigrant pupils embarked upon busing, but the majority did not, either because they considered the scheme impractical or because they just didn't cotton to the idea. Today there is a sort of hit-or-miss dispersal in about one-quarter of these school districts, but in only eleven of them is daily busing practiced as a matter of established policy.

A few communities are likely to phase out busing, partly because their immigrant populations have begun to decline. But Southall can afford no such luxury. Out of some 65,000 persons residing here, roughly 17,000 are Indians and another 3,000 are Pakistanis (there are also 3,000 West Indians). Indian and Pakistani children constitute well over 20 per cent of the total school population in the borough of Ealing, and in Southall more than 60 per cent. And the numbers keep increasing. Southall already has its own Indian and Pakistani movie-houses, signs printed in Punjabi as well as English, and slews of food stores redolent of curry. Small wonder that Anita Sharma, seeing two bearded and turbaned Sikhs walk by, remarked: "Southall gets to look more like India every day."

Although education authorities regard busing as an imperfect solution, they feel it is achieving positive results. "There's no doubt that, if we didn't disperse, we'd have some schools that would be well over ninety per cent colored," says Michael Elliott, chairman of the Borough of Ealing School Committee. "It would become impossible to teach them English. It would also amount to segregation, and we would be opposed to that."

In theory, at least, dispersal has always been carried out for purely educational reasons. "We are merely seeking an intelligent educational balance. It is not based on color; we feel very strongly about that," says Mrs. F. J. Bews, the comely headmistress of Acton Wells, 119 of whose 453 boys and girls come by dispersal bus each day. This is confirmed by the Department of Education, which states: "To approach this matter on racial grounds would not only be contrary to educational tradition but would, under the Race Relations Act of 1968, be against the law."

Members of the immigrant community in Ealing do not really question the high-mindedness of such declarations. But some of them, including members of the Ealing Community Relations Council, maintain that busing as practiced in Britain is inherently discriminatory. They note, for example, that British busing—unlike the American version—is a one-way proposition: Only immigrant kids get bused. Busing of native-born English children into immigrant areas has never been attempted and, because of the furor it would cause among English parents, doubtless never will. Unavoidably, therefore, the children who are dispersed are all "colored"—a fact that could play upon latent prejudices. "If we continue dispersal, we are making the color of a child's skin the most important part of it," says a member of the Ealing Community Relations Council. "Children see these children as different because they come by a special bus."

Apart from these implications of color prejudice, many immigrant parents object to dispersal because of the logistics of busing. They dislike having their children wait outdoors for the school bus in bad weather; they regret the fact that satisfactory parent-teacher relationships are extremely difficult to establish when a child attends a remote school; and they share their children's regret that busing makes it virtually impossible to maintain classroom friendships after school hours.

Weighing all these factors, the Ealing Community Relations Council recently declared that the disadvantages of busing infant or elementary school children "so clearly outweigh the advantages" that the practice should cease at the earliest opportunity. Instead, said the council, noting that "many people will be surprised to see [the council] apparently in the same camp as President Nixon," there should be a progressive and speedy return to neighborhood schooling of all children in the borough. That, however, does not seem likely for the foreseeable future. "Our position now is that, even if we wanted to stop busing, we could not," says School Committee Chairman Elliott. "If we stopped dispersing, we would have to build at least six new schools in the borough right away, and we just don't have that kind of money."

"Stifling"
Pasadena's Integration

TOM WICKER

Tom Wicker is an associate editor and regular column-
ist for *The New York Times*. His books include *Kennedy Without Tears, JFK and LBJ: The Influence of
Personality Upon Politics*, and, most recently, a political novel, *Facing the Lions*.

A new school board with an antibusing majority is about to take
office in Pasadena, California, where integration of the schools was
achieved in 1970 through heavily increased busing. The new board
is committed to abolishing "forced busing," primarily because of its
belief that busing has been the main reason for a decrease in white
enrolment from 49 to 43.6 per cent in the lower grades and from 58.2
to 50.1 per cent in high and junior high schools.

That decline certainly has taken place since 1970 but has it been
because of busing and integration? Pasadena school administrators can
show that, in 1948, Pasadena schools were just over 90 per cent white—
but that this percentage has been steadily declining, as the racial,
ethnic and economic character of the Los Angeles suburban community
suffered familiar contemporary processes of change. In 1958, the white
percentage was down to 82.7; by 1965, it had dropped to 65.5; and the
decline was so steady that when integration began in the fall of 1970,
its speeding up—according to this view—was only marginal.

Now, school administrators insist, the rate of loss is back to the
pre-1970 level, and in 1972–3 the downward trend of recent years
actually was reversed in grades one to three; hence, they say, whatever "white flight" may have resulted from busing appears to have

been stanched. Nor do they concede that integration and busing caused any more than a temporary increase in "white flight."

Equally or more important, they argue, was the beginning of construction of a freeway and interchange complex that wiped out about 11 per cent of all family dwellings in Pasadena; the long decline in aerospace industry employment in Southern California; and the fact that for these and other reasons white families have not for years been moving into Pasadena at anything like the rate needed to replace the white pupils normally finishing public school.

But if the question of "white flight" in Pasadena is arguable, the antibusing slate insists that its margin in the election—about 58 per cent—left no room for dispute. A. L. Lowe, the present school board chairman, who was defeated in the spring election, is not quite willing to concede even that. He suggested that Pasadena, a strongly Republican community, had been less influenced by its own experience than by the antibusing stand of President Nixon, by the switch to an antibusing position of the Department of Justice (which originally brought the suit that resulted in the Pasadena busing program) and by the outspoken antibusing views of Gov. Ronald Reagan, Representatives Carlos Moorhead and John Rousselot, and State Senator H. L. Richardson, all influential in Pasadena.

Mr. Lowe also pointed out that many Pasadena voters were older people whose children had long since completed school, who thus had no personal experience with integration, and who responded favorably to appeals for "neighborhood schools" as against "forced busing." Yet, he said, in the two and a half years of integration through busing, there had been no riots, no school closed for violence, a decrease in racial confrontations, a favorable change in the schools' insurance from a $50,000-deductible to a $25,000-deductible policy and operating experience in integration to the point where "the waves ought to be smoothing out."

While there is no particular evidence of black educational gains, integration has resulted in some striking innovations—for instance, an upgraded "alternative school," a night high school, and special reading centers—that might not otherwise have been instituted and which school administrators believe will have a profound ultimate effect on education in Pasadena.

Mr. Lowe does not, in fact, believe that the new school board can roll back the busing-integration program completely; that would require the approval of Federal District Judge Manuel Real, who ordered integration in 1970, and who pointed out that public sentiment could not relieve Pasadena of its constitutional obligations.

What Mr. Lowe fears most is a significant failure of integration in the four years in which the antibusing forces will have a school board majority. "It's hard enough to make an integrated school system work when you're working at it," he said. "When your leadership is against it, I worry that it may not be possible at all."

Thus, he suggested, in its efforts to hold down busing, the new board might adopt policies that would undo some of the educational innovations of the last few years, inhibit the administrators' freedom of innovation, slack off on "staff development" efforts to accustom teachers and administrators to black and Spanish-speaking students, and fail to reassure white families who might otherwise move to Pasadena about the realities of integrated education.

"They probably can't roll back integration," Mr. Lowe said. "But they can stifle its success."

IV

Busing and
Black Political Strategy

The Nationalist vs. the Integrationist

CHARLES V. HAMILTON

Charles V. Hamilton is Ford Foundation Professor of Urban Politics at Columbia University. He is author of *The Black Preacher in America* and co-author (with Stokely Carmichael) of *Black Power: The Politics of Liberation in America.*

In the nineteen-fifties, when there was growing talk about integration and officials at all levels were beginning to feel the impact of a rapidly developing civil-rights movement, black people led by Dr. Martin Luther King Jr. boycotted the buses of Montgomery, Alabama. The protest, which was ultimately won in the Federal courts, was aimed at ending segregated seating on the city buses.

Today the bus is still a major vehicle in the racial struggle, only now it is used in some places to transport children from one community to another in order to end segregated schools.

But while there was virtually unanimous agreement among blacks on the first action, there is not nearly such unanimity today over the current use of the bus. In May of this year a National Urban League analysis of three national surveys of school busing found that only 52 per cent of blacks favor busing, although the proportion of blacks who say they oppose busing has declined from 41 per cent in 1970 to 34 per cent in 1972.

This is no minor debate; it relates to the broader issue of integra-

Charles V. Hamilton, "The Nationalist vs. the Integrationist," *The New York Times Magazine,* October 1, 1972. © 1972 by the New York Times Company. Reprinted by permission.

tion and what has happened in the civil-rights movement in the last decade, and it is reflected in the black attitudes toward the present Presidential campaign. In the late fifties and early sixties, "integration" clearly meant ending overt forms of racial segregation; it meant outlawing segregated travel facilities, segregated places of public accommodation, segregated schools, segregated residential areas and so forth. The signs were there—on the doors to waiting rooms and rest rooms, over drinking fountains, in employment ads in the newspapers. The fight for integration was substantially a *legal* fight to end *de jure* segregation. It was mainly a fight, or so it seemed, to "desegregate" facilities, and it was easy for blacks and many whites to identify themselves as integrationists.

Then in the mid-sixties, precisely when many gains were being won—such as the Civil Rights Act of 1964, the Voting Rights Act of 1965—a noticeable change in attitude began to develop on the part of a perceptible number of blacks. They began to be less immediately concerned with what had been the primary goals of the earlier struggle and to focus on goals that reflected a rise of black nationalist sentiment. That did not mean that they wanted to return to the days of *de jure* segregation (they continued to believe in desegregation), although, to be sure, the new attitude was interpreted as having that consequence by many who persisted in the traditional integrationist goals.

The new attitude is a result of a number of things: disappointment with the pace of the earlier struggle; rapid politicization stemming from the violence of several summers in the late sixties; the killings and trials of those considered more militant, like the Black Panthers and Angela Davis; the growing concern with Africa and Vietnam, especially among the young blacks.

So, for example, the Congress of Racial Equality, once an avowedly pacifist-integrationist organization, now is strongly nationalist. Roy Innis, the national director, discussing the 1954 Supreme Court decision ordering school desegregation, objects that "the liberals converted this into *integration.*" Integration, Innis feels, "is not in the cards" for a majority of blacks, and even if it occurred, blacks would be in a perpetual minority. The primary goal, then, should be for blacks to try to control as many of the political, economic, educational and social institutions as possible in their communities. By doing so, they would get "a slice of the guaranteed institutional capital."

Thus it is now possible to talk about at least two major strands in black political thinking: integrationist and nationalist. This distinction might be an oversimplification, of course, but it is nonetheless helpful to understanding the new tensions that exist among blacks.

The integrationists insist that the earlier struggles to overcome *de jure* segregation must be continued beyond merely declaring segregation unconstitutional. There is very heavy reliance on an interpretation of the Constitution that argues that officials must take affirmative action to insure that there will be integration of the races. This means busing of school children if necessary; it means deliberately placing blacks in public housing projects in all-white neighborhoods if necessary. In other words, the integrationist position is that there cannot be exclusive reliance on *voluntary* action of private citizens if a meaningful amount of racial integration (in schools, in housing, on jobs) is to occur in this country.

The nationalists, on the other hand, are much more inclined to form all-black organizations and to push for goals that emphasize, in their view, the consolidation of black control over institutional policies. This spans a wide range of concerns, including busing, child adoption, scatter-site housing and community control of schools and the police.

In terms of mass support, it is certain that there are more "card-carrying" integrationists than nationalists at the present time. The National Association for the Advancement of Colored People, which much be considered in the integrationist camp, has a membership of about 390,000, is well organized and is one of the oldest such groups in the country (founded in 1909). Most nationalist organizations (CORE, Congress of African Peoples, Republic of New Africa) have neither nationwide networks nor elaborate membership lists; however, it is known that their dues-paying membership does not come anywhere near that of the N.A.A.C.P. Many nationalist groups, though, rely less on regular dues-paying members and more on widespread sympathy and sporadic support geared around periodic causes and, to be sure, crises. And they are able to mobilize considerable support from time to time on given issues.

It is instructive to note how the two attitudes divide on specific questions. Some integrationists, such as Vernon E. Jordan Jr., executive director of the National Urban League, see the busing controversy today as a "phony issue." That is, they point out that there were no loud protests from many circles when children were bused long distances in order to *maintain* segregated schools. The current antibusing stance of many whites is seen as a guise for basically racist attitudes. "It's not the Distance, 'It's the Niggers'" (a quote from a Southern white matron) is the title of a recently issued study of school busing released in May by the N.A.A.C.P. Legal Defense & Educational Fund Inc. The study takes strong exception to President Nixon's call for a moratorium on further execution of court-ordered school busing. It stated: "These proposals, which would curtail only one kind of busing —busing to desegregate schools—and not any other kind of pupil transportation, barely camouflage their racist motivation. They signal the reversal of the momentum of equal justice which during the sixties ended a century of Congressional silence on the legal rights of the nation's racial minorities."

The nationalists, on the other hand, feel that busing will not solve educational problems for the mass of black children. Some nationalists welcomed a recent controversial article on busing by Prof. David J. Armor reporting findings that showed no significant improvement in academic achievement for black students who were bused. The nationalists prefer to concentrate on establishing alternative semi-private schools in black communities that would experiment with new curricula and teaching techniques; as one spokesman put it, "schools that convey to our children that peculiarly black culture and spirit combined with solid academic standards." They also prefer to push for effective community-controlled public schools. Bryant Rollins, executive editor of New York's *Amsterdam News*, wrote recently, "Dr. Armor's study is important to black parents in that it arms those of us who feel that the present solution to urban educational problems is not through busing and other methods of integration, but through a massive two-pronged attack to bring quality education to the inner city. . . . One of the major blocks in the development of alternative all-black schools and the struggle for quality education in inner-city public schools has been the way in which blacks in leadership positions and ordinary middle-class blacks as well, have assumed that they had to move out in order for their children to learn well. This has had the effect of fracturing and dividing our energies."

The two attitudes have also been focused by the issue of child adoption. Last May the National Association of Black Social Workers, in its fourth annual convention in Nashville, Tennessee, condemned the placement of black children with white families for either foster care or adoption. The group called such placements "a growing threat to the preservation of the black family." The convention was substantially dominated by a sense of black consciousness and black nationalism and the need to develop black institutions. To counter interracial adoptions, the association suggested the alternatives of single and grandparent adoptions and special recruitment programs among blacks for adoptive and foster families. One resolution stated that "all black professionals upon completion of professional schools, should attend a finishing school in black awareness."

Bayard Rustin of the A. Philip Randolph Institute takes exception to this position. "It is not," he said, "interracial adoptions which threaten the stability of the black family but rather the absurdities of our welfare system and a black unemployment rate in excess of 10 per cent." While recognizing the existence of racial prejudice and discrimination, Rustin believes that "poverty, and all the evils attached to it, is not due solely or even largely to racism, but to an economic system already weighted to those with wealth and power." As an integrationist (as the category is used here), he is opposed to all-black organizations. "Separatist organizations are further weakened by their need to adopt unrealistic and sometimes irresponsible public positions in order to justify their existence. This often takes the form of unsound criticism of their own profession, as, I believe, is the case in the adoption resolution."

Another issue of profound disagreement between integrationists and nationalists concerns the merger of school districts. The N.A.A.C.P. Legal Defense & Educational Fund brought suit in Richmond, Va., calling for the merger of the predominantly black school district of that city with two surrounding predominantly white suburban school districts. To some in the nationalist camp, this was a major mistake. A black economist, David H. Swinton of the Black Economic Research Center in New York, sees such a merger, if it were to occur (the case was won by the N.A.A.C.P. Fund in the Federal District Court, reversed by the Court of Appeals, and is being appealed to the Supreme Court), as jeopardizing the eventual control by blacks of the city school system. Swinton says, "This includes the power to make the major decisions about curriculum, personnel and general educational policy. Perhaps of almost equal importance is control over the economic power represented by the budget of a large school district. This includes the ability to hire and to fill top salary positions, as well as the ability to make purchases and to let construction contracts. The potential importance of these things for Black development is extremely great." Swinton concludes: "The movement to gain control over a number of significant American cities and the strategy of demanding community control are much sounder strategies."

The integrationists are not persuaded by these arguments. They believe that, in the words of one prominent integrationist, the "real way blacks gain power ultimately is to be where the decisions are made, and this is not done by isolating oneself." Bayard Rustin has stated it this way:

> Those who support community control because they believe it will give minorities a measure of self-government, a "piece of the action," see only half of the picture. For inherent in the concept is the surrender of the suburbs to white domination. Blacks, in other words, will have the ghetto, with its drug addiction, soaring crime rate, high unemployment, and deplorable housing. Whites will keep the suburbs,

where job opportunities are expanding, the air is unpolluted, housing is decent, and schools provide superior education. Separatism, no matter what form it takes or how slickly it is packaged, has always worked to the detriment of the black man.

The nationalists' response to Rustin frequently follows the argument made by Swinton:

> The mistake in logic on which much of the integrationist thrust is based is an all too common one. Integration advocates confused the symptom with the cause. They commit what is closely akin to the *post hoc, ergo propter hoc* fallacy in logic. Segregation has accompanied, preceded and has been generally correlated with the undesirable economic situation of blacks. It is therefore an easy but fallacious step to conclude that segregation caused all of the undesirable manifestations that it accompanies.
>
> Segregation, however, is clearly only a symptom of the lack of effective power in the black community. It is not itself the cause of the myriad problems confronting the black community in the area of education and elsewhere. To attack the symptom may do nothing at all to eradicate the disease. . . . The true cause of the black problem is the lack of basic economic, political and social power, as is indicated by the black people's inability to take the decisions and allocate the resources that are required to deal with the black situation. This lack of power results from white dominance of the instruments and processes of power.

It is important to note that this is not a new debate in the history of black Americans. In the early nineteenth century, there was intense disagreement over the issue of colonization.

The Marcus Garvey movement, which reached its zenith in the early nineteen-twenties, saw thousands of blacks rally to the banner of "Back to Africa" and the creation of a black empire on that continent. Even some blacks who vehemently disagreed with Garvey about his African plans nonetheless felt that the development of separate black organizations and institutions in this country was the wisest course to pursue. This issue was perhaps the major one dividing Dr. W. E. B. Du Bois and the organization he helped to found, the N.A.A.C.P. In the nineteen-thirties, Du Bois began to advocate a particular kind of black economic nationalism. While he denied that it was either nationalism or a segregated economy he was proposing, he did say:

> The only thing that we not only can, but must, do is voluntarily and insistently to organize our economic and social power, no matter how much segregation it involves. Learn to associate with ourselves and to

train ourselves for effective association. Organize our strength as consumers; learn to cooperate and use machines and power as producers; train ourselves in methods of democratic control within our own group. Run and support our own institutions.

But the civil rights-integration movement of the forties, fifties and sixties maintained that it *was* possible to make substantial gains without leaving the country and without forming separate organizations. Whatever else it was (and is), that movement was very much a moral one. It relied heavily on moral arguments to make its case, and this meant that it painted a picture of those opposed to racial integration as bad people, basically immoral and unethical. The integrationists, on the other hand, were on the side of justice, goodness and God. They emphasized "brotherhood," "one society" and "color-blindness."

Moralizing the race issue had other consequences. It meant that blacks were viewed as unfortunate victims, persons to be pitied and helped. They were considered "culturally deprived" and almost perpetually dependent on the good will of others. The background of slavery undoubtedly contributed to this mentality. Whites were to take care of blacks, unlike other groups that came to this country who were expected to take care of their own. (In 1655, the following announcement greeted Jews arriving in New Amsterdam: "These people may travel and trade to and in New Netherland and live and remain there, provided the poor among them shall not become a burden to the Company or the community but be supported by their own Nation.")

While blacks have started a number of all-black, self-help organizations throughout their history, the civil rights-integration movement has been the most prominent organizational thrust for civil and political equality. And this movement has been, from the beginning, heavily populated with whites—as leaders and as rank-and-file participants. They could feel morally superior to the segregationists. They could free themselves of whatever guilt feelings they might have, and they could expect gratitude from blacks in return.

This is why some black nationalists call the integration movement basically a pleading-beggar movement. Blacks pleaded with whites to take them into their schools, their neighborhoods, restaurants, churches, etc. And this begging approach could only create a paternalistic relationship between black and white. If the integrationists responded that they were only seeking their constitutional rights, the nationalists' retort would be that in the final analysis constitutional rights could only come from political power, not from benevolent handouts.

The traditionally understood integration movement was, in a profound sense, demeaning to many black nationalists. Not so much in the goals it sought (freedom from racial segregation and discrimination), but in some of the methods it used. Many nationalists felt it was fundamentally demeaning to have whites in leadership positions in black civil-rights organizations. (Leadership of other racial or ethnic groups always reflects the primary composition of the groups.) When the integrationists responded that color was irrelevant, that commitment and skill were the only requirements, the nationalists would label this view unrealistic and point to the many other organizations set up along ethnic lines.

It was demeaning—if only because it reflected a reasonably accurate picture of things—to conclude that frequently whites had to intercede for blacks. I recall in the fall of 1970, a black colleague and I were invited to a book party at Columbia University in a university-owned apartment-hotel near the campus. When we entered the lobby, the doorman (an elderly white man) questioned us closely and would not let us enter the elevator unless we showed very precise identification and gave clear indication where we were going. This was not required of others (all white) entering the building at the same time. We protested on the spot, drawing a crowd. A white faculty wife, going to the same party, came along and offered to help. "Come," she said, "there'll be no problem. You can go in with me." But we had to explain to her that although she wanted sincerely to help, that was exactly the condition under which we had to refuse to enter the premises.

I related the incident to a black integrationist friend of mine several days later, and after firmly disagreeing with our refusal to accept the offer of assistance, his final comment was, "We Negroes are 11 per cent of the population. We simply cannot fight this battle alone. We need help. We need friends. We need allies. Any other strategy is suicide."

If the nationalists were able to work their will and have their way, their programs would range all the way from starting an entirely new, sovereign nation, the Republic of New Africa, carved out of five Southern states, to flying the black, red and green liberation flag over schools in black communities as was done recently in Newark, N. J. In general, nationalist groups would like to insure that such institutions as schools, police and health facilities in black communities are controlled by blacks; that is, no final decisions affecting their operation would be taken by any but black people acting in official capacity. This means that they would staff these facilities, whenever possible, with blacks—teachers, policemen, social workers, etc. They are immediately aware, of course, that this puts them in direct conflict with existing public-service unions. They would also require black control over the allocation of tax funds for the various agencies. (The integrationists see this goal as the most utopian of all.)

The nationalists would base electoral representation on the proportion of blacks in the population. A statement issued at the black political convention held in Gary, Indiana, in March 1972, read:

> We want the establishment of Black Congressional representation in proportion to our presence in the national population. We are at least 15 per cent of the population. Through constitutional amendment—or any other means necessary—we ought to have a minimum of 66 Representatives and 15 Senators; that until such time as the House and Senate represent black people fairly, our due seats are to be filled by persons elected at-large by the national black community. The same principle should obtain for state and local governments.

The nationalists would "see to it that no cable television comes into our communities unless we control it," and they would have at least two more black persons appointed to the Federal Communications Commission.

If the nationalists had their way, there would be a publicly funded, black-controlled agency like the Tennessee Valley Authority "to function as a planning, coordinating, and management structure for a rural industrial development program in the Black Belt." They would establish a National Commission/Foundation for Black Education, funded from private and public sources, to develop and encourage national and local research, planning and experimentation toward the creation of new models of black education at all levels.

The problems the integrationists have with these points relate not only to whether they are politically feasible. Integrationists simply do not believe that such matters as economic development and educational improvement should be dealt with on the basis of race. Thus, they question not only the gall but the goals of the nationalists. And in spite of occasional attempts to unite the two camps politically, it is unlikely that this will happen in any permanent sense.

At the Gary convention, for example, the 3,000 delegates held together for a time under the banner of "Unity Without Uniformity" until antibusing and anti-Israel resolutions (nationalist sponsored) were introduced and adopted. But even without these, it was clear that the N.A.A.C.P. and some other groups and prominent spokesmen could not accept the generally nationalist tone of the convention. In fact, in May, the N.A.A.C.P. withdrew its affiliation. The black nationalist, Imamu Amiri Baraka (formerly LeRoi Jones), one of the three co-chairmen of the convention (along with Mayor Richard

Hatcher of Gary and Michigan Congressman Charles Diggs), asked Roy Wilkins of the N.A.A.C.P. to reconsider. "Teddy Kennedy doesn't withdraw from the Senate when the Goldwater forces outvote him on an issue," Baraka said. "He stays in the organization to fight on other issues."

This is true, but the Senate (a closer analogy would have been one of the two major parties) is seen by both Kennedy and Goldwater as a legitimate institution which deserves to be protected and preserved. The black convention, however, simply is not viewed in the same way by the nationalists and the integrationists. The former believe in and work toward the building of viable all-black organizations and institutions. Therefore, their commitment to the preservation and growth of the convention is strong. Not so with the integrationists. They prefer interracial organizations and institutions, and this means that their commitment to the convention is at best tenuous.

In addition to having basically different orientations toward goals and tactics, the two groups have rather seriously divergent views about each other. The integrationists see the nationalists as unwilling to compete in the open market, as being insecure in competition with whites. This, they say, explains in large part the demand for black-studies programs in colleges and universities just at the time when vastly increased numbers of black students are entering predominantly white schools, the thinking being that such programs are academically easier. They see the nationalists as frustrated and disappointed with the pace of civil-rights progress, largely from a lack of historical perspective. If the nationalists had greater knowledge of history, they would know that major changes have occurred. Since much of the nationalist thrust comes from younger people, the integrationists accuse them of not knowing very much, if anything, about the struggle before Watts or the assassination of Malcolm X or the rise of the Black Panthers—all mid- to late-nineteen-sixties phenomena.

The integrationists are also prone to see many nationalists as hustlers, out to line their own pockets off the "new industry of blackness." And in the process, they accuse the nationalists of being not only hypocritical, but mostly rhetorical, not substantive, capable only of posturing, not producing. They do not understand "real power"; they engage largely in symbols—in clothing, hair styles, handshakes and speech.

Finally, the integrationists constantly point out that the nationalists naively give aid and comfort to racial bigots and conservatives. For example, Gov. George Wallace could only be pleased by an antibusing resolution passed by blacks. And when the black group, the National Economic Growth and Reconstruction Organization (NEGRO), supported the residents of Forest Hills, Queens, against a low-income housing project being built there, integrationists accused the group of being used by forces of racial bigotry. Nationalism, the integrationists point out, can create strange political bedfellows in the racial struggle, as black nationalists line up with Southern segregationists and Northern conservatives like Senator James Buckley.

The nationalists, on the other hand, are convinced that because the integrationists rely so heavily on money furnished by whites, the integrationists have no real voice of their own. They are controlled.

The nationalists see the integrationists as being overly impressed with whites and too willing to go to whatever lengths necessary to "prove" themselves to whites.

Above all, the integrationists are perceived as possessing a great deal of self-hate, which, again, is a form of adopting a characteristic of the larger society, that is, rejection of blacks.

If the nationalists are considered naive in politics, they, in turn, view the integrationists as too idealistic about human beings. The integrationists' alliance with white liberals (whom the nationalists see as insultingly paternalistic) is one that overlooks the fact that all people operate on the basis of self-interest, not altruism. The nationalists want the integrationists to realize that the white liberal is no better, in the end, than the white conservative—the end constituting the lack of willingness to relinquish power to black people.

Finally, the nationalists accuse the integrationists of not being flexible enough in the racial struggle, of not being willing to examine new strategies and tactics. David Swinton says, "The whole integration fight has been proceeding so long and has so involved those who are participants in that struggle, that it is now moving on its own momentum. Inertia keeps the fight going despite the fact that the social, moral, economic and political gains its advocates had hoped for have not materialized and in fact logically cannot. . . . The legal apparatus assembled to fight for integration should not continue to press cases out of habit." Thus, while the nationalists are charged with a lack of historical perspective, they accuse the integrationists of being too much committed to a particular historical approach.

These differences can show up in everyday life as well as in theoretical discussions. In one desegregated elementary school in a New York suburb not too long ago the white teacher was having a discussion with her fifth-grade class. The topic was how the children were going to spend their upcoming winter vacation. A substantial portion of the white children were from middle-class families whose parents were taking them to Florida to escape the dreary New York February weather. Most of the black children were from lower-class families who lived in a nearby public-housing project, and some were bused from another part of town.

The discussion from the white students was spirited and full of exciting accounts of flight plans, hotel reservations, Florida beaches and play areas. The black students sat silently. When a visiting black parent, who had observed the session, spoke to the teacher afterwards, the teacher was quite elated over the lively discussion and enthusiasm of the students. The parent, however, complained that that session was precisely the kind of insensitive education to which she felt the black students should not be exposed. The teacher was puzzled and hurt; she saw or heard nothing wrong or offensive in the discussion at all. The parent explained that the black children were totally excluded because their parents could not afford to take them on expensive vacations. Their sense of inferiority was reinforced, and they were made to feel that watching television and running the halls of the housing project during the week while their parents worked could not match the glamour and thrills of a week's vacation in the Florida sun. The teacher explained that she was unaware of the race of those students who did and did not participate. This episode, to the parent, was an example not of the admirable trait of color-blindness but of the insensitivity of the educational system to the needs of the black children, and it was further evidence of the dubious benefits of integration on both racial and class bases.

Strong exception to this view was taken by a black integrationist parent who also observed the class. Rather, she thought this was exactly the kind of educational experience to which the black children should be exposed. It broadened their vision; it introduced them to other worlds. "We Negroes must stop being so sensitive. Our children need those wider contacts. The parents can't give it to them, and that is just why school integration is important."

Thus, one parent saw the class as stifling, parochial and harmful. The other saw it as enlightening, stimulating and helpful.

This is not an insignificant debate. While it is not one that consumes all the time of masses of people—most of whom are simply trying to eke out a living and provide for their children as best they can—it is still not limited to black élite spokesmen. And neither is the debate academic. The courts, the Congress, the executive, state legislatures, city halls and city councils are going to be dealing with these issues, one way or another, for some time to come. Their decisions (or nondecisions) will affect masses of blacks directly.

Politicians will continue to look to various segments of the black community for signals, and they will be getting back conflicting answers. I doubt if this will change very much on some issues which are deeply embedded in ideological conflict.

One of the consequences of the schism is that it has permitted both major Presidential candidates to avoid forcefully addressing themselves to some issues in the present campaign. Instead, both black integrationists and nationalists have lined up in Demorcratic and Republican camps. Some nationalist-leaning blacks are supporting President Nixon because they feel that blacks for too long have been taken for granted by the Demorcatic party. Others, however, believe that the black-capitalism self-help emphasis of the Republicans is only a palliative not calculated to benefit the long-run interests of masses of black Americans. The fact remains that the present Presidential campaign is conspicuously lacking in any meaningful discussion of issues and goals of critical concern to blacks. Both national parties apparently recognize the national mood not entirely sympathetic to the goals of either integrationists or nationalists. And the ideological divisions among black spokesmen has permitted both President Nixon and Senator McGovern the luxury of avoiding treading on explosive ground.

The two groups broadly described here simply have little, if any common ground to share over the basic issue, say, of dispersal of the black community—in housing or school attendance. Nationalists firmly believe that blacks can begin to consolidate their political power only if they remain geographically consolidated. Integrationists believe in "breaking up the ghetto." (Indeed, the debate extends to the different uses of terms: The nationalists see a "black community" that should be strengthened and controlled by blacks; the integrationists see a "black ghetto" that should be broken up and integrated into the mainstream.)

Some doubt that a *rapprochement* can ever be worked out between the two groups; I believe, however, that if both groups are as politically sophisticated as each claims to be, they should be able to unite around ideologically neutral issues. While the principles involved in this debate certainly are important, only the politically immature would permit dogmatic adherence to them to impede broader political progress and blind them to other areas of cooperation. It is very clear, for instance, that one need not be a nationalist or an integrationist to know that the black community must be cleansed of the plague of narcotics. There ought to be consensus and cooperation on this issue, because it is certain that there will be neither effective community control nor successful integration as long as drugs remain a pervasive problem in black communities.

The same is true with tackling the problem of finding more jobs for able-bodied people. Both groups are coming to see public welfare in its present form as little more than the mechanism for perpetuating a dependent populace. Increased employment in the public and private sectors should be a goal permitting cooperation. Substantially improved health care is another area. There should be no ideological hang-ups over this issue.

Whether one is a nationalist or an integrationist, it is difficult to perceive *any* effective political leverage as long as black voter-registration and turn-out rates remain abysmally low. The political interests of both groups, it would seem, would be served by cooperating and dealing with this problem.

There are many issues that black voters of whatever orientation should be vitally concerned about and on which they should be requiring candidates Nixon and McGovern to commit themselves definitively one way or another: full employment, drugs, health care, adequate housing.

It is quite true that solutions to these kinds of problems are not as clear-cut as solutions to desegregating the Montgomery buses or Woolworth's or the ballot boxes in the South. But in the same sense that united action was necessary and possible to achieve those goals, it is no less clear that such action is necessary and possible to pursue certain current problems. Ideological debates are interesting and, at times, vitally important. But it is also important to keep in mind what Dr. Bu Bois once admonished those critics who disagreed with a particular position the N.A.A.C.P. took during World War I. He calmly reminded them, "We face a condition, not a theory." The politically mature ought to know when to concentrate on the one and when to subordinate the other. In the final analysis, this may well be the important challenge inherited from earlier years of struggle, with all the strengths and weaknesses and victories and defeats associated with that period.

A Proposal for Community School Districts

CONGRESS OF RACIAL EQUALITY

The Congress of Racial Equality (CORE) started on the University of Chicago campus in 1942 as a small group with Christian pacifist roots. Beginning with the Freedom Rides in 1961, it was a major force in the civil rights movement in the South. Under the direction of Roy Innis, CORE has in recent years espoused black nationalism and black separatism.

SCHOOL SEGREGATION: ITS TRUE NATURE

School segregation is a system designed and structured to serve the needs of Whites at the expense of Black pupils. When normal standards of educational excellence are applied to Black schools under segregation, it becomes clear that they are inferior to White schools. This is a fact with which no one can argue. Unfortunately, it has caused those who did not in the past and do not now understand the true nature of segregation to arrive at the faulty conclusion that all-Black schools are inherently inferior under any set of circumstances. A simple extension of logic prompts the following questions:

If racial exclusivity means inferior schools, then why are the schools—White *and* Black—not equally inferior? If the racial composition of a school *in and by itself* causes that school to be inferior, where then are our inferior all-White schools?

Let us take the "isolation equals inferior schools" theory to its

---

Congress of Racial Equality, *A True Alternative to Segregation: A Proposal for Community School Districts* (New York: Congress of Racial Equality, 1970).

farthest logical extension: President John Kennedy and many of his socio-economic class attended schools that were not just isolated from Blacks, but from Whites belonging to different socio-economic classes as well. Needless to say, one would not even consider looking for the kind of inferiority in Mr. Kennedy's schools that so often characterizes Black schools.

The "inherently inferior" theory is not only spurious on its face but insidiously racist in its implication that Black children alone among the different races and groups of the world must mix in order to be equal. Blacks who subscribe to this theory are suffering from self-hatred, the legacy of generations of brainwashing. They have been told —and they believe—that it is exposure to Whites *in and by itself* that makes Blacks equal citizens.

Years of heavy propaganda from liberal well-wishers on one side, and ugly declarations from racists on the other have further confused the issue. This confusion must be cleared up now if we are to proceed in an orderly fashion toward the achievement of true equality in education.

Whether or not a given school is inferior or superior has nothing, *as such*, to do with whether or not it has an admixture of racial and/or ethnic groups, but it has everything to do with who *controls* that school and in whose best interest it is *controlled*.

Many social scientists who have issued papers and written books on education have missed this very salient point. They have shown too much concern with spatial relationships, and not enough or none at all with the relationship between those who govern a school and those who are served by that school.

No, the problem is not *simply* that Blacks and Whites attend different schools. A look at segregated school systems, whether *de jure* or *de facto,* will show that they generally have, aside from attendance of White and Black pupils at different schools, three common characteristics which make segregation the obnoxious system that it is.

The first of these is that Whites set Blacks apart, by law or in fact, without their choice or consent. This constitutes the arbitrary imposition of authority from without. The act of Whites telling Blacks what schools they can or cannot attend stigmatizes Blacks and is a slap at their dignity.

The second characteristic of a segregated system is that the local school board, usually all White or predominantly White, exercises control over both White and Black schools and favors the White schools. The school board enjoys a more intimate relationship with the White community and White parents than it does with the Black community and Black parents. It is more sensitive to their problems, their needs and aspirations than it is to those of Blacks. This deprives Black educators and pupils of much-needed support from the policy makers and managers of the schools and literally guarantees the failure of the Black school to achieve excellence in education. A positive relationship between parents and those who govern the school is one of the most important factors affecting the quality of schools. Under segregation, Black parents have not enjoyed that kind of relationship.

Finally, the local school board systematically deprives Black schools of resources. The money allotted by law to each and every school district when received by the local board is directed as the local board sees fit. Traditionally, part of the money intended for Black schools has been directed by the local board to White schools. (This is true of Southern schools as well as Northern schools.)

In short, it is the local school board, the dispenser *and* regulator of money, rewards, good will, and other benefits, which makes Black schools inferior. Under segregation, Blacks have been locked into a system over which they exercise no control, for which they have no responsibility and for which they are powerless to effect meaningful change.

When segregation is placed in its proper context and defined in terms of who manages and controls the schools, it becomes apparent that the chief characteristic of a segregated school system—the imposition of oppressive outside authority—makes school systems in the North no different from those in the South.

The surest measure of how much Blacks can trust any school system to educate their children is how much actual—not illusionary —control they have over that system. Therefore, whatever is proposed to replace segregation must be measured strictly in terms of how much control is held by the Black community itself. This is the surest possible guide to determining the potential success of any proposed new system.

SCHOOL INTEGRATION: IS IT A GOOD ASSUMPTION?

Having learned from bitter experience that White schools are favored by White school boards and having become tired of the stigma attached to being told where their children could go to school, it was natural that Black people considered sending their children to White schools. Since 1954 at least, the assumption has been that the segregated and unequal treatment of Black children could be rectified by integrating them into White schools. What is basically wrong with this assumption?

1. There is a failure to recognize Black people as a valid special interest group with needs that are unique to Black people.

2. There are a number of agreed upon components of a good education. It has not been established that integration guarantees these components.

3. Equal education implies more than just equal physical space in the same classroom, the same teacher, or the same principal. It implies equal right in the curriculum; equal access to all available resources; and equal access to school policy makers and managers. The question is: Does integration guarantee Black parents these additional rights?

4. An integrated setting is as potentially damaging psychologically as a segregated setting. The assumption that integration cures all the evils of segregation does not take into consideration what the National Advisory Commission on Civil Disorders affirmed—that is, the essentially racist character of American society. Since there is no indication that racism will disappear overnight, Blacks must approach all institutional settings with extreme caution.

While integration is mandated and there is unwillingness on the part of Whites to integrate schools, Black people lose much more than they gain in such a merger. One such community was studied by the National Education Association. The following is an excerpt from their report:

The desegregation of East Texas schools is proceeding at a faster pace than in most southern states. School officials of most districts studied can report that they are in compliance either with federal desegregation guidelines or with court orders. But, as the study made abundantly clear, it is only a paper compliance. As desegregation continues, the grievances of the black community become more widespread and more severe. There is every evidence of racial discrimination in the continuing displacement and demotion of black educators; there is every evidence of racial discrimination in the increasing employment of white teachers in preference to blacks; there is every evidence of racial discrimination in the frequent exclusion of black students from participation and leadership positions in the student organizations of desegregated schools; and there is every evidence of racial discrimination in the treatment that black students commonly receive from white classmates and, in some instances, from their white teachers and principals as well.

These grievances have long remained unresolved; they continue to be unrecognized by school officials. And finally, now that the Supreme Court has ordered the immediate elimination of dualism in all southern districts the prospect is that the situation will become worse—in East

Texas and throughout the South. The frequency of teacher displacement and student mistreatment that accompanied desegregation "with all deliberate speed" is likely to accelerate as the rate of desegregation accelerates. The laws, including desegregation laws, have never worked well for black people. Unless present trends are halted, the new Supreme Court ruling will serve them no better than did the *Brown* decisions of 1954–55.

The fact is that the court can offer Black children, teachers and administrators very little protection from the crippling abuses which arise daily in an *integrated* setting where Whites don't favor the union. Some of the stories of injustices and psychological abuse emerging from integrated settings in the South are difficult to fight with litigation, but that does not make them any less damaging to the psyches of Black children, parents, teachers, and administrators:

Item: White teachers have been known to absolutely refuse to look at Black children when addressing them in the classroom.

Item: The principal of an all-Black school became the assistant principal of an elementary school under integration in one Southern town.

Item: The principal of a Black high school was replaced by a younger White man with less experience and fewer formal credentials. The principal became an assistant principal under the new White principal.

Item: Examinations are geared to favor the White child. In fights, Black children are always assumed to be in the wrong.

The sad fact of the matter is that in most cases where integration has been tried, the same White board of education that once ran the dual school system—one White, one Black—is the same board that runs the integrated system. The superintendent of education under the old system becomes the superintendent of education in the new system. The policy makers and managers are therefore the same. Since their negative attitudes towards Blacks and favoritism towards Whites remain the same, Black parents can hardly expect that any attempt will be made to change the curriculum to reflect the needs of Black pupils, or that they will have any say in the running of the school. In other words, even where integration has come about, the schools remain White-controlled.

It must not be assumed that things will get better with time. The dynamics of *forced* school integration are very different from those of *forced* desegregation of hotels, restaurants, buses, and other public facilities and services. These are what might be called transient settings of Blacks and Whites sharing or functioning in the same approximate space. Integrated schools, on the other hand, constitute an ongoing situation that is seen as far more threatening. This is underscored by the fact that the relatively mild and short-lived resistance to the desegregation of public facilities and services was nothing compared to the massive resistance that has been mounted and that will be continually mounted against integration of the schools. Moreover, when integration does occur in the schools, the few strengths Blacks did have are rapidly eroded so that with time they operate less and less from a position of strength.

Blacks who have gone along with integration have done so in search of dignity, but have found humiliation at the end of the rainbow. They integrate for equality but find they are *together but still unequal.* They have less control and less influence, if that is possible, than ever before. In short, the integration that Blacks are likely to get in most instances, North or South, has proven to be token equality, mere show and pure sham.

What about those areas where White resistance is not so high as to frustrate the integration effort? Even then we should keep in mind that effective integration is more than mere physical proximity of White and Black students. We should seriously consider whether the dispersal of Black pupils would help or hinder the chances of meeting their unique needs.

Integration, as it is designed, placed the Black child in the position of implied inferiority. Not only is he asked to give up much of his culture and identity, but with the dispersal of Blacks he loses many of the communal ties which have traditionally been the cornerstone of the Black community. Moreover, there can never be true integration between groups until there is a real parity relationship existing between them.

It is an established fact that children learn best in a supportive environment—one in which they can develop an appreciation and acceptance of self. Self-appreciation must come before one can truly appreciate others.

White schools at this time do not constitute the kind of environment which can foster the healthy development of Black children. White school boards make it difficult for even Black schools to respond to the special needs of Black children. In this respect, however, many Black teachers and administrators have tried, within the narrow limits allowed them, to try to satisfy these needs.

With the guarantee of equal resources and with the freedom to proceed as is expedient, Black schools would be a superior learning environment and could graduate students who can succeed in an interracial world.

What about the stigma attached to going to an all-Black school? That stigma was half destroyed when Blacks succeeded in smashing the laws which restricted their freedom to choose. Inasmuch as the stigma arises in part from the established inferiority of Black schools, the remaining stigma would be destroyed completely once the Black community has a board of education which could be called theirs and which would guarantee a truly equal, truly democratic education for its children.

Furthermore, Black people today have a very healthy attitude towards themselves as a people. They are not ashamed of being Black and see nothing wrong in being together and doing things together. They see strength in unity, not guaranteed failure. More than ever, Blacks place a premium on working together for progress. They are beginning to feel that it is through their strength as a group that they will win human dignity and power. If reality is taken into account when Blacks chart their course, it will become abundantly clear that in some situations school integration may not be the most effective means to equality.

From a financial, legal, economic, political, social, psychological, and most important, educational standpoint, the integrated school emerges wanting. This set of parameters must be consistently used when examining integration, segregation, and any proposed alternative to the two.

THE NEED FOR A NEW ALTERNATIVE

Desegregation is now the law of the land. Because the road is rocky and treacherous, Blacks need to chart a careful course if they are to land on their feet. The next section will offer a desegregation approach applicable primarily to urban areas, North and South. In these areas we generally find natural definable communities made up of persons with common interests and special problems.

Within Mobile County, Alabama, for example, there is a natural community comprising the Davis Avenue, Toulminville, Bullshead area. This community alone has more students than do many existing school districts throughout the state. The citizens and students in this community happen to be Black Americans. The schools attended by the youth from this community have been badly run by the Mobile County School Board. For years, the talent and energies of the best citizens of the community have been expended in fighting the school board— but without significant results. This community has many special needs different from those of the general population of Mobile County. A healthy pride and sense of purpose is evident and growing in this community. The educational hopes of the residents, however, are continually frustrated by a school board which has shown no sensitivity to their problems. The residents of this community have lost irretrievably all faith in the school board's capability of being responsive to their needs.

The tragedy is that the human input needed to solve the major educational problems which have plagued this community are within the reach of this community. The talent and energy displayed over years of struggle for relief prove that. The material input needed to solve this area's school problems lies in the public money the law presently allows if the money were to arrive directly from the source to a truly local school board. The rising aspirations, the dashed hopes, and the displaced energy will result in a steadily rising level of hostilities which will inevitably spill over into the surrounding communities.

We contend that it is possible to bring dignity and true equality of opportunity to this community without denying the human and constitutional rights of any other community. Only good sense and meaningful alteration of a faulty structure can avert this. It is in the spirit of attempting to avert chaos and establishing harmony that this proposal is presented.

THE SOLUTION: NATURAL COMMUNITY
SCHOOL DISTRICTS

The people of the above-mentioned community are seeking to exercise their basic human and constitutional right to form an institution that is accountable to them. They are seeking to be delegated by the State of Alabama to exercise its exclusive competence to determine its own educational needs and set its own educational policy, as do other peoples in America, by becoming a duly constituted state school district under the state law.

This move is not without considerable precedent in American history. One such precedent occurred early in the history of this country and culminated in a document which begins with the words, "We hold these truths to be self-evident," and includes the statement, "That whenever any form of government becomes destructive of these ends"—these ends being the securing of certain inalienable rights and "governments being instituted deriving their just powers from the consent of the governed. . . . It is the Right of the People to alter or abolish it, and to institute new government, laying its foundations on such principles and organizing its powers in such form as to them shall seem most likely to effect their safety and happiness."

The Plan

The plan is to desegregate public schools by creating state school districts which correspond to natural community lines, where the parties affected are in agreement.

The School Board

Within each school district so formed the residents would elect a school board. Each school board would be a legal entity *enjoying all the rights, privileges, and obligations as provided for by the State Education Law*. Each school board would run a unitary school system within its district.

The community school board would, pursuant to state law and as every other school district in the United States does, seek out persons with educational expertise—a superintendent who meets state qualifications as chief executive officer of the board of education, and a staff of professionals to administer and execute the policy established by the board. The board would seek the best man possible to fill the position of superintendent by selecting from a special screening committee and would solicit advice on candidates from the leading universities and professional associations as well as other organizations and individuals. Once employed, the superintendent would submit names to fill the other top-level administrative positions to the screening committee of the board and the board would choose from among the resultant list of candidates.

For the position of superintendent, the board would seek a man of unquestioned executive ability who indicates an openness to new solutions to the desperate educational problems of the community's children, and a willingness to all newly available educational innovations such as the reading program developed by the Institute for Behavioral Science for the Washington, D. C., public schools, programed instruction with audio-visual teaching machines, and use of media techniques. Most important of all, the board would seek a superintendent who is community oriented.

The community school district would hope to attract the best minds as consultants to the staff to help design the program. This would be a truly pioneering effort in the field of education.

The Teaching Staff

The community school district would welcome all teachers presently in their schools, who are excited by the prospect of being a part of this pioneering effort. Every attempt will be made to recruit to the teaching staff the best teachers regardless of race, creed or national origin. The community school district will offer in-service training programs, for up-grading, if necessary, so that all teachers in the district will have the security of having skills and training that are relevant to the unique needs of the children of the community.

The community school board would adopt fair practices with respect to teachers employed in that it is in the interest of the district to satisfy the most essential ingredient of a school system—the class-room teacher.

The community school board would seek to allow for maximum participation in the school program by encouraging strong parent associations and establishing people from the community as teacher aides and teacher apprentices so that every child will have in-depth contact with a caring adult, and the teacher will be freed to teach.

Financing

The community school district will receive public funds directly from the presently existing sources of education money—the state, the federal government and the local government unit.

State. The community school district would receive state moneys according to the existing provisions in the state law prescribing state money to school districts.

Federal. Federal moneys would come to the school districts according to the existing provisions described in the Federal Elementary and Secondary Education Act.

Local. A legal and formal agreement will be made whereby the local educational dollar will be directed to each school district on a per student basis.

IS THIS PLAN LEGAL?

It is of extreme importance that the Supreme Court's ruling on school desegregation be clearly understood. Confusion on this point has abounded, aided and abetted by those who have fallen into the trap of viewing desegregation as synonymous with integration. Integration is only one possible way—not necessarily the best or most pragmatic way—of desegregating and creating a unitary school system. The plan herein described is another way of desegregating and creating a unitary school system in a school district. It would destroy segregation, and it clearly provides for equal protection under the law. Moreover, unlike integration, this plan makes it easier to *guarantee* equal protection under the law.

A careful and unprejudiced reading of the decisions of the Supreme Court on school desegregation shows that this plan does not violate the letter or the spirit of the law.

The Supreme Court has ruled that each school board must run a unitary school system in a school district. That is, if there are White and Black children in a school district, the school board may not set them apart.

Each district proposed in this plan would be run as a unitary system. Moreover, the process of redistricting proposed here can only be done with the consent of the persons affected and with the legal agreement of the state. This is equivalent to the parties to an action arriving at a settlement out of court, without violating any law.

CONCLUSION

Schools are the transmitters of values, the molders of self-image, the instrument for providing youngsters with the technical and psychological equipment necessary to function properly in this highly competitive society. The schools in most Black communities have failed dismally on all three counts. They have not and will not, under the present school system, perform their proper function.

Integration as the means of addressing the educational problems of Black people, even if attainable, is of questionable worth. Where integration has occurred, the results suggest that it causes more problems than it solves.

Black people have tried everything there is to try under the present school structure. The escalating school crisis and the unprecedented hostility between Blacks and Whites are vivid reminders that patience is wearing thin all around. Blacks are now searching for a real solution, one which can provide dignity and true equality. We submit this plan as that solution.

It's Not the Distance, "It's the Niggers"

NAACP LEGAL DEFENSE AND EDUCATIONAL FUND

Over the past two decades, lawyers from the NAACP Legal Defense and Educational Fund have led the battle in the courts to desegregate the public schools. The Legal Defense and Educational Fund is a separate organization from the 450,000 member NAACP (National Association for the Advancement of Colored People).

CHAPTER I: INTRODUCTION

American children arrive at school via every conceivable mode of transportation, including horses, snowmobiles, boats and airplanes. Assuring their arrival on time and safely every day is big business. A vast transportation system coordinates the efforts of citizens of all racial and economic groups: trustees, administrators, patrons and children of public, private and parochial schools, Indian families on reservations, professionals who design the often-computerized travel routes, manufacturers, the suppliers and mechanics who keep the vehicles running, the safety experts, the 275,000 drivers.[1]

The school bus has now become the business of judges and politicians. Because judges have declared that the bus is one among

---

[1] N. Mills, *Busing: Who's Being Taken For A Ride,* 7 (ERIC-IRCD Urban Disadvantaged Series No. 27, April 1972).

Division of Legal Information and Community Service, NAACP Legal Defense and Educational Fund, *It's Not the Distance, "It's the Niggers"* (New York: NAACP Legal Defense and Educational Fund, Inc., 1972).

many tools necessary to eliminate racially and illegally segregated schools, politicians are clamoring for the curtailment of the power of the judiciary. A serious constitutional crisis has been precipitated. The Legal Defense Fund is deeply concerned about this attack, for it undermines the confidence in the judiciary which is vital to the effective functioning of our constitutional system. Having represented black plaintiffs for over 30 years in most of the nation's school desegregation cases, LDF lawyers know, perhaps better than any other group of private citizens, that Federal judges are extremely reluctant to impose harsh and unreasonable remedies even for clearly unconstitutional actions.

The proposed moratorium on busing threatens gains which have been made in the long and painful struggle to fulfill the constitutional rights of children to equal educational opportunities. The reopening of school cases would create pandemonium across the land and undercut the work of those courageous school officials who have provided professional leadership during the transition to unitary school systems. These proposals, which would curtail only one kind of busing—busing to desegregate schools—and not any other kind of pupil transportation, barely camouflage their racist motivation. They signal the reversal of the momentum of equal justice which during the 60's ended a century of Congressional silence on the legal rights of the nation's racial minorities.

The politicizing of the busing issue during an election year is not a mark of leadership. It has polarized our people. It has diverted attention from the urgent need to eradicate racism. "Instead of cursing the disease (segregation)," as Father Hesburgh has aptly stated, "we curse the medicine, we curse the doctors." [2] Emotions have been aroused. Wild, unsubstantiated charges about judges and about busing have been made. They must be answered. It is not the school bus which is in trouble. What is at stake is our sanity as a people, the independence and integrity of our courts, the fulfillment of our commitment to equal justice.

Our findings demonstrate that the current sentiments about busing and courts used to justify opposition to further school desegregation are popularized myths.

1. Federal courts have not exceeded Supreme Court rulings and have not ordered "massive" or "reckless" busing in order to implement desegregation plans.

---

[2] Testimony of Theodore M. Hesburgh, Chairman, U.S. Commission on Civil Rights, before Subcommittee No. 5 of the House Committee on the Judiciary, 16 (March 1, 1972).

2. Increases in busing in some cities have occurred, but these increases are not always enormous and sometimes they are due to factors other than desegregation.
3. Busing is not harmful to children. In fact, school authorities utilize busing to protect your children.
4. Transportation for various school purposes is used to improve the educational program, not to undermine it.
5. The cost of school busing is minor. It does not deplete resources for better schools.

Ever since Massachusetts enacted the nation's first pupil transportation law in 1869, American children have been transported to school under arrangements which have been regulated and subsidized by state authorities. The early horse-drawn vehicles and the ubiquitous yellow school bus have been symbols of communities that care for their children. The two major concerns which have motivated the steady increase in pupil transportation in the last century have been America's unwillingness to limit a child's educational opportunities to those available within walking distance from his home and a concern for his physical safety.

That the school bus is an established institution in American education which has received tremendous public support is evident from the following statistics:

1. 43.5% of the total public school enrolment or 18,975,939 pupils are transported to school daily, according to HEW statistics.[3]
2. There has been a steady increase in pupil transportation, with annual increases in the last decade of from .5% to 2.5%. The decades with the largest percentage gains were: 11.4% from 1939–40 to 1949–50, 9.9% from 1949–50 to 1959–60.[4]
3. American taxpayers have been willing to invest significant funds in busing. The National Highway Traffic Safety Administration reports that the total cost including capital outlay for pupil transportation for 1971–72 is $1.7 billion.[5]
4. 256,000 buses are now traveling 2.2 billion miles.[6]

---

[3] HEW Memorandum, from Constantine Menges to Christopher Cross, 1 (March 30, 1972).

[4] *Supra*, note 1, at 9.

[5] U.S. Department of Transportation, *Report on School Busing*, 1 (March 24, 1972).

[6] *Supra*, note 1, at 7.

Busing has been motivated not only by a commitment to further educational, social and humanitarian objectives, but by school administrators' concern for more efficient utilization of facilities. The major increases in busing have accompanied the moves to provide greater educational opportunities by consolidating rural schools. Urban school districts are increasingly busing children threatened by traffic hazards, a service which must usually be provided from local funds because the miles involved do not meet state requirements for reimbursement. Most states provide for the transporation of handicapped children.

The bus has made it possible for urban school districts to relieve overcrowded conditions, to use space wherever it is available in the community, to prevent double sessions and to reduce class size. The ERIC study reports the St. Louis experience where "busing was used as an alternative to having double-sessions, which would have set one set of children free in the morning and another set in the afternoon. For those transported, the benefits of the program were obvious, but they were not the only beneficiaries. As a report to the Superintendent of St. Louis Schools emphasized, 'reduction of class size, through bus transportation and other expendiences . . . made it possible for *nontransported as well as transported children* residing in the districts of these seriously overcrowded schools to suffer minimal education loss.'" [7]

Busing has made it possible for school districts to avoid expensive new school construction and not just because current available facilities can be used more efficiently. A school official in Lynchburg stated candidly that the only alternative to busing in his district would be the building of new schools in the ghetto—a capital outlay requiring bond issues which he felt the taxpayers probably would not approve.[8]

The desire of local school authorities to use the school bus as a vehicle for enriching the educational program, particularly of disadvantaged children, can be seen in their use of ESEA Title I funds for this purpose. In 1967–68, $18 million of Title I money was used nationally for transportation. Sixty percent of the Title I districts in California and 75% in Massachusetts had transportation components.[9]

Now that the school bus is the center of public controversy, it is most unfortunate that there is no longer any public or private agency which annually collects and reports statistics on pupil transportation in

---

[7] *Id.* at 12–13.

[8] Interview with Harlan C. McNeil, Supervisor, Department of Transportation, Lynchburg Public Schools, April 6, 1972.

[9] U.S. Office of Education, *Elementary and Secondary Education Act of 1965 as Amended, Title I, Assistance for Educationally Deprived Children, Expenditures for Pupil Transportation Services, Fiscal Year 1968.*

the U.S. The most current national figures available are for the 1969–70 school year. These were reported by the National Association of State Directors of Pupil Transportation Services, an informal group which has no budget, office or staff. The U.S. Office of Education collects some limited information on pupil transportation as part of its larger biennial survey of educational statistics, but this information is out of date at the time it is published.

There never has been a national source of data on pupil transportation by race. Nor are any statistics available nationally on the numbers of students bused or the number of miles school buses travel to further various educational objectives, i.e., more efficient use of facilities, vocational education, summer school, field trips and special educational programs.

The current discussion suffers from a lack of uniform, objective, factual information. In order to collect some information from school districts in which desegregation orders have been implemented in this school year, Legal Defense Fund staff members interviewed local school officials in fifteen districts which implemented busing plans this year. Four state departments of education were visited to gather state-wide information on pupil transportation. In addition, national data and information were collected from the Office of Education and the Office for Civil Rights in HEW, from the Department of Transportation, the National Safety Council, the National Education Association, the National Association of State Directors of Pupil Transportation Services, and the U.S. Commission on Civil Rights. Besides court records, school budgets and monthly transportation reports were examined.

We trust that our findings from this survey, done between March 27 and April 17, 1972, will help put busing into its proper perspective and thus contribute to a rational discussion of its role in fulfilling the constitutional rights of black and brown children to equal educational opportunities. The quotes which begin the following chapters are from President Nixon's Message to Congress on March 17, 1972, the proposed Student Transportation Moratorium Act of 1972, and the proposed Equal Educational Opportunities Act of 1972, which were submitted by the White House to Congress.

CHAPTER II

Many lower court decisions have gone far beyond . . . what the Supreme Court said is necessary. . . .

Reckless extension of busing requirements. . . .

Some of the Federal courts have lately tended toward extreme remedies. . . .

The President's first reference above is somewhat difficult to identify, since the Supreme Court said in *Swann* and *Davis* (Mobile) that an adequate desegregation plan would have to achieve "the greatest possible degree of actual desegregation consistent with the practicalities of the situation," and that in measuring the performance of proposed plans against this goal, there was a *presumption* against schools all or virtually all of one race. It is apparent from a study of district court orders in school desegregation cases issued after *Swann* that most lower court judges have made a conscientious effort to apply these principles to the systems before them by being willing to consider desegregation plans requiring proportionately similar amounts of busing as were approved for Charlotte. (Chief Justice Burger's opinion denying a stay in the *Winston-Salem* case last summer urged caution in making such comparisons, but the Court eventually declined to review Winston-Salem on the merits, without any dissent.)

The immediate impact of *Swann* was that district judges insisted upon the incorporation into plans of techniques such as non-contiguous zoning and pairing, which many had refused to require prior to the Supreme Court's ruling. However, many courts rejected unusually long bus rides by applying the *Swann* standards. In Jacksonville, Fla., the court declined to order busing to the North Beach schools in the system, finding that the trip would take one-and-one-half hours each way. And in Nashville, Tenn., the court accepted an *HEW-drawn plan* which the government's experts said was deliberately designed not to desegregate some schools in outlying Davidson County areas because of the length of the bus rides.

It is undoubtedly the concern about metropolitan remedies to school segregation which the President refers to in his comment on "extreme remedies." U.S. District Court Judge Merhige ordered the consolidation of the Richmond, Va., city schools with the school districts of the surrounding counties of Henrico and Chesterfield. The Court found that to accomplish the consolidation, 78,000 of the 104,000 students in the new system would have to be transported, about 10,000 more than those in the three jurisdictions who are now bused. The Court further found that no additional buses would be necessary and that busing times and distances would not exceed those already required of the students in those countries for many years.[10]

---

[10] *Bradley v. The School Board of the City of Richmond, Va.*, 338 F. Supp. 67 (1972) (E.D. Va.).

In defense of district judges, one must point out that some comprehensive school integration plans have been initiated by local school boards and have not been compelled by district courts under a mandate from *Swann*. The Winston-Salem-Forsyth County case was on appeal at the time of the *Swann* decision. The Fourth Circuit Court of Appeals remanded the case to the district judge who ordered the school board to prepare a plan which he subsequently approved and which is currently in effect. The board subsequently objected to its own plan and has sought to amend it.

The Columbus-Muscogee County, Ga., school board developed on its own initiative a comprehensive and complicated racial balance plan under which much of the busing is done by the children of military personnel in the area. The court approved it and the black plaintiffs were pleased to support a plan which had been locally initiated.

Federal District Judge James B. McMillan entered a finding in the *Swann* case in October 1971 that the "feeder plan" which the Charlotte-Mecklenburg school board had adopted would require the transportation of 46,667 students, while the "Finger plan," which the school board rejected after it had been approved by the U.S. Supreme Court, called for transporting 39,080.[11]

CHAPTER III

Some (court orders) have required that pupils be bused long distances, at great inconvenience. . . .

Our investigations do not support the conclusion that large numbers of children are being bused long distances to implement desegregation plans. There are individual instances of long rides, but we suspect that these are far fewer than when schools were segregated. Speaking in Congress on February 28, 1970, Senator Walter Mondale mentioned counties in Georgia and Mississippi which bused black children 75 miles and 90 miles respectively to all-black schools.[12]

Judicial notice has been taken of the length of bus rides prior to desegregation. Judge McMillan observed that an analysis of principals' reports filed in *Swann v. Charlotte-Mecklenburg* had revealed that:

The average one way bus trip is one hour and fourteen minutes; 80%

---

[11] *Swann v. Charlotte-Mecklenburg*, 334 F. Supp. 623 (1971) (W.D. N.C.).
[12] *Congressional Record*, February 28, 1970, S2652–2653.

of the buses require more than one hour for a one way trip; 75% of the buses make two or more trips each day. . . .[13]

The Honorable Stephen Horn, vice-chairman of the United States Commission on Civil Rights, testified recently before Congress:

> . . . before the Charlotte-Mecklenburg decision, pupils averaged over an hour on the bus. When the desegregation plan was carried out, however, bus trips were cut to a maximum of 35 minutes. Similarly, the Richmond decision would call for average bus rides of about 30 minutes, which is less than the current average in an adjacent district involved in the decision. Where pupils are bused for the first time, trips are rarely long. The average travel time reported seems to be 20–30 minutes. Trips of an hour or more would be out of the ordinary. A trip of a half hour or so would not bring the pupil home much later than if he walked from a neighborhood school.[14]

In recent testimony before a Congressional committee, Elliot Richardson, Secretary of the Department of Health, Education and Welfare, referred to an 80-minute, oneway bus trip in Winston-Salem, N.C. Prior to the recent court order, there were at least five bus trips which were 80 minutes or over, one of which was 120 minutes long. Three out of the five schools involved were overwhelmingly white and had hardly felt the impact of integration.[15] It is difficult to evaluate how much children are inconvenienced by these long trips because the mileage reports do not show how long each child is actually riding. The mileage begins when the bus leaves the driver's home and ends when he parks his bus. Children riding varying periods of time have boarded and left the bus in the meantime.

A long bus ride or an inconveniently early departure time from home does not necessarily reflect a long distance. Sometimes children must leave home early or travel circuitous routes because local authorities refuse to provide enough buses. When it was clear that the court-ordered integration plan for metropolitan Nashville-Davidson County, Tenn. would increase the number of bused students from

---

[13] *Swann v. Charlotte-Mecklenburg Board of Education* (W.D. N. Car. Civ. A. No. 1974), unreported supplementary Findings of Fact, March 21, 1970. (See Petitioner's Appendix to Petition for Writ of Certiorari, U.S. Sup. Ct. Oct. Term 1969, No. 1713, p. 142a.)

[14] Testimony of Stephen Horn, Vice Chairman, U.S. Commission on Civil Rights, before the Committee on Education and Labor, House of Representatives, 5 (April 11, 1972).

[15] Winston-Salem-Forsyth County Public Schools, *Principal's Monthly Bus Report,* March 1971.

34,000 to 49,000, Superintendent Elbert Brooks sought funds from the Metropolitan Council for the purchase of buses. The Council refused to appropriate these funds, so the district had to rely on its existing fleet supplemented only by 18 new buses which had been bought prior to the desegregation order.[16] According to school officials interviewed by a Tennessee reporter, the shortage of buses has resulted in inconvenience and hardships for students:

> . . . with buses having to run more than one route, many children must stand in the dark to catch buses near their homes in the morning, while others who go to school later get home after dark. . . . Some children ride up to 14 miles in the morning and afternoon, spending up to an hour on the vehicles twice a day.[17]

We are indeed concerned about the inconveniences which children experience, especially when black pupils are expected to carry a disproportionately heavy share of the busing. In Pinellas County, Fla., 6.4% of the white students are bused because of the desegregation order in comparison to 75.2% of the black children.[18] (Sixteen percent of the student population is black.) An official in Hillsborough County, Fla., reports that of the elementary pupils transported because of the court order, 8,576 are black and 5,404 are white.[19] Seventy-five percent of the bused students in Jackson, Miss., are black.[20] Furthermore, black children are often bused at an earlier age. When schools are paired or clustered, it is not unusual for the plan to require black pupils to leave their neighborhoods for the early elementary grades. The formerly all-black schools receive the older elementary children, or may become sixth-grade centers or junior highs for both races— an arrangement which requires black children to travel in the earliest years.

It is the *lack* of transportation which is often the hardship. Local and Federal officials who refuse to provide transportation to pupils who must travel long distances to school and archaic state laws which

---

[16] *Hearings Before the Select Committee on Equal Educational Opportunity of the U.S. Senate,* 92nd Cong., 1st. Sess., Part 18—Pupil Transportation Costs, 9017 (October 6, 1971).

[17] *Memphis Commercial Appeal,* January 30, 1972.

[18] Speech by C. A. Hunsinger, member, Pinellas County Board of Education, *A Chronology of Pinellas County School Desegregation,* March 1972.

[19] Memorandum from W. P. Patterson, Director of Transportation, Hillsborough County Board of Education to Wayne Hull, Assistant Superintendent for Business, October 15, 1971.

[20] Interview with D. C. Windham, Transportation Supervisor, Jackson Public Schools, April 10, 1972.

discriminate against cities in their transportation reimbursements are responsible for inconveniences to children. Hattiesburg, Miss. and Texarkana, Ark. have plans which require junior high pupils to travel long distances at their own expense. Some states do not provide reimbursement for busing within cities. (See the discussion of *Sparrow v. Gill* in Chapter IV below.)

The lack of transportation in Norfolk, Va. is a real hardship to students who must pay $63 a year to ride city buses to school because the district does not operate its own transportation system. Several hundred students from poor families in Norfolk are not in school this year because they do not have transportation.[21]

Most of the school districts mentioned in this report have sought Federal funds for transportation from the Emergency School Assistance Program (ESAP). Federal officials rejected the request from Greenville, Miss. for funds to purchase buses to transport 2,000 students who had been reassigned to elementary schools out of their neighborhoods.[22]

In 1970–71, Duval County, Fla. received a grant from ESAP of which over $100,000 was used for pupil transportation. The district applied for another grant for 1971–72 and requested several hundred thousand dollars for transportation. The total application was approved but not the use of the funds for busing. Accordingly, the school board put over $900,000 of the grant in escrow and filed suit in Federal court to compel Secretary Richardson to authorize the use of this money for transportation.[23]

CHAPTER IV

Massive Busing

We find no conclusive evidence that the aggregate amount of busing has increased nationally or regionally as a result of court-ordered integration. In the absence of data on pupil transportation by race which would reveal how many white and black children are being bused to what kinds of schools, it is impossible to state accurately the number or race of pupils who are being bused to racially segregated or integrated schools. The cry of "massive busing" for "forced integration" is completely irresponsible.

---

[21] Interview with Mrs. Vivian Mason, member Norfolk City Board of Education, January 24, 1972.

[22] Remarks of Superintendent W. B. Thompson, Greenville Municipal Separate School District, Board of Education Meeting, August 1971.

[23] Interview with Superintendent Cecil Hardesty and Joseph J. Smith, Director of Finance, Duval County Board of Education, January 17, 1972 and April 4, 1972.

We agree with Donald E. Morrison in his testimony on behalf of the National Education Association before the House Committee on the Judiciary: "There is no statistical proof that desegregation has substantially increased pupil busing, either nationally or regionally." [24]

HEW has estimated a 3% increase in busing as a result of integration.[25] This figure represents the increase in the Southeastern states in overall pupil transportation between 1967–70 from 52.5% to 55.5%. Our investigation leads us to the conclusion that this is no more than normal growth. The Southeast has been subsidizing the transportation of more than 50% of its pupils since 1957, a larger proportion than any other region. Between 1965 (when HEW's Title VI civil rights enforcement program began) and 1970, there was a 4% increase in the numbers of pupils transported in the South. Yet at the same time the percentage of pupils increased at a more rapid rate in other parts of the nation where there were few court orders and limited enforcement activity.[26]

Nationally	4.9%
North Atlantic	4.9%
Great Lakes	5.2%

The Department of Transportation [27] estimates that the annual increase is attributable to the following causes:

Population growth	95%
Centralization	about 3%
Safety	less than 1%
Desegregation	less than 1%
Other	less than 1%

Urban school districts which have only bused minimally or not at all in the past experience a major upsurge when a comprehensive plan to eliminate the dual school system is implemented. Often, however, this does not bring the district up to the state average. All of the schools in Raleigh, N.C., were effectively desegregated in 1971–72 under a plan which contributed to the increase of bused students from

---

[24] Statement of Donald E. Morrison, President, National Education Association before Subcommittee No. 5 of the House Committee on Judiciary, 8 (March 2, 1972).

[25] Supra, note 3, at 3.

[26] Id. at 2.

[27] Supra, note 5.

1,342 to 10,126, at least 5,000 of which were *Sparrow* students. Although the district is now transporting 46.5% of its students, this is less than the North Carolina state average of 64.9%.[28]

In Norfolk, Va., where the desegregation order required most elementary students to travel outside their neighborhoods for the first time in 1971–72, approximately 39% of the district's enrolment is bused. Yet 63% of all public school students in Virginia are bused.[29]

An increase in busing may result from factors which have nothing to do with integration:

1. There has been an increased use of busing to protect children from traffic hazards. In 1971–72, 66,115 students in Florida are bused at local expense because they do not meet the 2-mile state reimbursement requirement. This is a dramatic increase from 1968–69 when only 40,792 in this category were bused. Officials report that the main reason is safety, a concern about busy streets and hazardous walking conditions. The vast majority of these are elementary pupils.[30]

2. Busing is increasing through commitments to transport younger children. School officials in Roanoke, Va. took advantage of their new school buses to provide rides in hazardous areas for kindergarten children who ordinarily walk to school.[31] Beginning in 1973–74, Florida law will mandate state-supported kindergartens. All districts will be required to provide transportation.[32] Orange County, Fla. expects to bus 4,000 kindergarten pupils that first year.[33]

3. At the time of desegregation, some school districts use their newly acquired buses to further other objectives. Lynchburg, Virginia, is transporting students for the first time this year. The school system's 37 new buses not only get students to school, they are also used to provide field trips and to facilitate string music, choir practice and R.O.T.C. in high school.

4. The decision of a three-judge Federal Court in North Carolina

---

[28] Figures supplied by local and state officials.

[29] Interview with Dr. John McLaulin, Assistant Superintendent for Research and Planning, Norfolk Public Schools, January 28, 1972. *Annual Report of the Superintendent of Public Instruction of the Commonwealth of Virginia*, 110 (December 1971).

[30] Florida Department of Education, *Mid Year Transportation Report*, 5 (May 1969); interviews with Department of Education officials, April 4 and 17, 1972; interviews with school officials in Pinellas County and Hillsborough County, April 5, 1972.

[31] Interview with Richard Via, Director, Building and Grounds, Roanoke Public Schools, April 6, 1972.

[32] Interview with Wayne Hull, Assistant Superintendent for Business, Hillsborough County Board of Education, January 27, 1972.

[33] Interview with Clifton Jones, Assistant Coordinator for Pupil Transportation, Orange County Board of Education, April 7, 1972.

in *Sparrow v. Gill* [34] has increased busing and complicates the effort to determine the impact of integration on busing. Prior to the 1970–71 school year, North Carolina law generally provided that county children who lived more than a mile and a half from school would be provided school bus transportation paid for by the state. City children, however, living a mile and a half from school were not provided school bus transportation at state expense. City children were defined as those children who lived within the 1957 boundaries of a city. Therefore, those children who lived in areas of a city which had been annexed after 1957 and lived more than one and a half miles from school did receive bus transportation at state expense. Additionally, the law was interpreted to mean that if a school was located outside of the 1957 limits, then children living within the 1957 limits more than a mile and a half from the school were eligible for transportation. Thus, prior to the 1970–71 school year there was at least some school bus transportation provided for city children. Moreover, local boards of education were free to provide bus transportation at local expense if they chose to do so. Greensboro, for instance, has for many years provided transportation for children living more than a mile and a half from school and has paid for it out of local funds.

A lawsuit was filed by white children and their parents in Winston-Salem challenging the inequity which existed where city children living more than a mile and a half from school did not receive bus transportation but county children living more than a mile and a half from school did. A three-judge Federal Court decided that classifying city children differently from county children in determining who was to receive bus transportation at public expense was constitutional. However, the Court determined that it was unconstitutional to treat children who lived in the areas of a city prior to 1957 differently from children who lived in areas of a city annexed after 1957.

The result of the *Sparrow* decision was that the State Board of Education required local school boards to offer transportation to all city children or to none. If local districts decided to offer transportation to all city children living more than a mile and a half from school, then the state would provide the money for the increased transportation. This new policy went into effect for the 1970–71 school year. Almost all cities chose to increase their transportation to include city children. Raleigh was the notable exception. It began to transport *Sparrow* pupils in 1971–72.

The comparison of transportation data before and after desegregation is complicated by the effects of the *Sparrow* decision because de-

---

[34] *Sparrow v. Gill,* 304 F. Supp. 86 (M.D. N.C. 1969).

segregation was beginning to occur in North Carolina cities at the same time that state financed transportation was being offered for the first time for city students. All of the cities were surveyed by the State Department of Public Instruction prior to the 1970–71 school year to determine how many additional children would be riding school buses to be paid for by the state. The survey revealed that an additional 54,000 students, requiring 549 buses, would become eligible throughout the state as a result of *Sparrow*. Included in this figure were 1,900 students (21 buses) in Asheville, 3,108 pupils (34 buses) in Winston-Salem-Forsyth County, 6,122 pupils (68 buses) in Charlotte-Mecklenburg, 2,281 students (25 buses) in Greensboro and 3,801 students (42 buses) in Raleigh.[35]

Therefore, to calculate the extent of increased transportation occasioned by desegregation requirements, it is necessary to subtract the number of children bused in the year prior to desegregation from the number of children bused after desegregation and then subtract the number of additional city children who would have received transportation under the new state policy. The resulting figure should also be discounted further by such factors as normally expected growth, increases for special education, and pre-school education, etc.

· Whether integration brings an overall increase in busing is difficult to assess. One might expect the implementation of a busing plan to result in an increase in both the number of students bused and the mileage. Actually:

1. Arlington, Va., buses 1,000 fewer pupils.[36]
2. Pinellas County, Fla., buses about the same number of students but the buses travel 3,200 more miles daily.[37]
3. Duval County, Fla., has increased the number of pupils bused but there has been a substantial decrease (11 miles or 20%) in the average number of miles per day per bus.[38]
4. Busing to desegregate in Alabama, according to the United States Commission on Civil Rights, has resulted in 1 million fewer passenger miles than the previous year under segregation.[39]

---

[35] North Carolina Department of Public Instruction, Division of Transportation, *Status of School Transportation Within Municipal Corporate Limits* (September 3, 1969).

[36] Interview with Rene Couleman, Supervisor of Transportation, Arlington County Public Schools, March 29, 1972.

[37] Figures supplied by Florida Department of Education, Transportation Section.

[38] *Id.*

[39] *Supra,* note 14, at 6.

5. From 1965–66 to 1970–71, the number of pupils transported in Mississippi has decreased from 312,085 to 292,472.[40]

CHAPTER V

Rather than require the spending of scarce resources on ever-longer bus rides . . . , we should . . . [put] those resources directly into education. . . .

Implementation of desegregation plans will in many cases require local educational agencies to expend large amounts of funds for transportation equipment, which may be utilized only temporarily, . . . thus diverting those funds from improvements in educational facilities and instruction which otherwise would be provided.

The cost argument against pupil transportation rests on the assumption that busing costs are so great that they seriously deplete funds for the regular educational program. But the facts do not support this assumption. The latest national figures available show that 3.7% of all educational expenditures in the United States were spent on pupil transportation of all kinds. This percentage has declined slightly since the 1953–54 school year, as Table 2 on busing costs 1953–54 through 1967–68 shows. Table 5 on pupil transportation costs for individual school districts reveals that even with increased costs, pupil transportation remains a small percentage of all educational expenditures.

The broad allegations of the cost burden must also be reviewed against the fact that each state reimburses local school districts for both capital and operating costs. There are wide variations among states in their patterns of reimbursement, and there is no national average of state reimbursement of pupil transportation costs. In Florida in the 1970–71 school year, $11.2 million of the total transportation expenses of more than $23 million for all school districts were reimbursed by the state.[41]

In North Carolina, the state pays a vast majority of all pupil transportation costs incurred by local school jurisdictions. For example, the state pays the cost of operating all school buses which transport students eligible for state reimbursement. It pays for replac-

---

[40] *Reports of Advisory Study Groups, Public Elementary and Secondary Education and Junior Colleges To The Legislative Education Study Committee, Vol. 1* (December 1961); Mississippi State Department of Education, Division of Administration and Finance, *Statistical Reports* 1961–62 through 1970–71; R. Barber, *Mississippi School Busing,* April 1972.

[41] Figures supplied by Florida Department of Education, Transportation Section and Finance Department.

ing all school buses. If a local district chooses to contract with a private company, the state pays the company even if its charges are higher than the average level of state reimbursement. The main financial burden for local school districts is limited to (1) the initial purchase of the bus, (2) maintenance and upkeep of facilities, (3) some administrative costs, and (4) the cost of busing pupils who are not eligible for state reimbursement.[42]

Cities which have never subsidized busing before desegregation claim a terrible financial burden when ordered to desegregate, yet sometimes the wild projections of costs have been completely misleading. In the spring of 1971 shortly after the court ordered desegregation in Pinellas County, Florida, a local school official was quoted as saying that the order would require the busing of an additional 11,000 students. In fact, about 1,700 additional students were transported to comply with the court order. In Pinellas County, Florida, approximately 2,000 white children left the school system and the district ceased transporting 1,413 students who were ineligible for busing because they lived within walking distance of their school. Even if these 3,413 were transported in addition to the 1,700 who were bused for desegregation purposes, still less than half of the projected 11,000 students would have had to be transported.[43]

The Raleigh, N.C., school district projected that in order to comply with its desegregation order, it would have to spend $980,956 from local funds for the 1971–72 school year. Of this amount, $828,000 was for 138 new buses and $26,500 was for drivers' salaries.[44] The $26,500 represents a local supplement in excess of state reimbursement for drivers' salaries. In fact, the total local expenditures required to meet the court order were $643,054, and of that sum, about $444,993 represented the cost of buses which were not delivered in the 1971–72 school year.[45]

The major cost of desegregation is the initial capital outlay for new buses. This cost can be handled by school authorities in several ways. If the money is spent all in one year, it represents assets that are carried over a number of years. However, if the district borrows money for new buses, the actual cost is carried over the duration of the loan and does not constitute a one-time expense.

---

[42] Interview with officials of Transportation Division, North Carolina Department of Public Instruction, March 27, 1972.

[43] *Supra,* note 37. Interviews with Pinellas County school officials, April 15, 1972.

[44] Raleigh City Board of Education, *Estimated Raleigh Public School Budget—1971–72; Cost Estimates To Increase Raleigh City Schools' Bus Fleet to One Hundred Fifty Nine Buses.*

[45] Figures supplied by Raleigh Public School officials.

School officials in some districts have publicly claimed enormous expenditures for new buses. While this may sometimes be true, it may also be that some of the buses were already budgeted, that some buses are needed for non-desegregation purposes, or that some buses paid for in one year are not delivered until the following year.

In some instances, the number of students bused may vary depending on the management practices in various school districts. A Hillsborough County, Fla. school official commented to an LDF staff member that his school district transported 10,000 more children with 100 fewer buses than the Charlotte-Mecklenburg, N.C. district did.[46]

The Norfolk, Virginia, public schools had not subsidized bus transportation prior to desegregation. When the school district was ordered to desegregate its schools, the school board and the city council refused to purchase buses to get children to their assigned schools. The 15,000 children who ride a bus to get to school must pay $63 per student per year, a financial burden which families have had to bear. Yet, if Norfolk operated its own bus fleet, it would cost less than half that much, or $26.17 (the Virginia cost per pupil for cities),[47] to transport students. Furthermore, if Norfolk were to operate its own buses, it would be eligible for 47% of its operating costs from the state.[48]

The U.S. Court of Appeals for the Fourth Circuit on March 7, 1972, ordered the Norfolk school board to provide free transporation as a part of its desegregation plan on the grounds that without transportation to the assigned school, the whole desegregation plan is a "futile gesture" and a "cruel hoax." The Court recognized that the cost of transportation would be a burden, but held that $3 million capital outlay for buses and maintenance could be amortized over the normal life of the equipment and that the $600,000 increase in annual operating costs was reasonable in a district with a total school budget of $35 million.[49]

The decision of this Administration to prohibit the use of ESAP funds for any transportation costs created severe problems in a number of school districts. Dr. Elbert Brooks testified before Congress that at a meeting with southern school superintendents in Atlanta in July 1971, he and other superintendents were led to believe by HEW

---

[46] Interview with W. P. Patterson, Director of Transportation, Hillsborough County Board of Education, April 5, 1972.

[47] Annual Report of the Superintendent of Public Instruction of the Commonwealth of Virginia, 125 (December 1971).

[48] Brewer v. School Board of the City of Norfolk, 456 F.2d 943 (1972) (4th Cir.).

[49] Id. at 8–9.

officials that their requests for help to pay busing costs would be honored by HEW. But in August, after President Nixon's announcement, HEW refused to fund any of the requests.[50] Dr. Brooks, as well as other southern school superintendents, felt betrayed.

In other cases, it was not only the President, but also local municipal authorities who prohibited the use of public funds to buy school buses to meet the requirements of the court's order. The Nashville Metropolitan Council refused to approve new buses for desegregation, and as a result schools are operating on staggered hours, some extracurricular activities have been curtailed and students and parents have been inconvenienced. Despite all these problems, Dr. Brooks reported that "the regular program should not be hurt." [51]

In some instance, school districts may spend extra money for transportation in order to provide conveniences for students. North Carolina only reimburses local districts for "mixed" buses, i.e., buses which carry elementary, junior and senior high school students at the same time. Winston-Salem-Forsyth County, however, has had a practice for several years of taking elementary students home in the afternoon before junior and senior high schools are let out for the day. Thus, the local board must pay for the costs of transporting these elementary students from local funds.[52]

Some districts pay busing costs out of local funds because they undertake supplementary costs which are not state reimbursed. For example, in 1971–72 Winston-Salem-Forsyth County decided to hire adult bus drivers for the first time. They pay each adult driver $80 a month more than state reimbursement. The district projected in September that it would cost them about $150,000 this year for this driver-salary supplement.[53]

Inflation has caused increases in busing costs. In North Carolina, for example, state reimbursement for bus driver salaries has gone up considerably in the past few years after bus drivers came under the minimum wage laws. Salaries for mechanics have shown a sharp upward trend recently in North Carolina, as have the costs of parts and gas.[54]

Two North Carolina school systems—Greensboro and Asheville—desegregated their schools at no additional expense to local districts. In Greensboro, the additional busing of 6,000 students in 1971–72 was

---

[50] *Supra,* note 16, at 9016–9017.

[51] *Id.* at 9022.

[52] Interview with Morris Hastings, Transportation Director, Winston-Salem-Forsyth Board of Education, March 30, 1972.

[53] *Id.*

[54] *Supra,* note 42.

accomplished by the city's existing fleet, by county buses already utilized by the city to transport some city children, and by the borrowing of 86 buses owned by the county and maintained by the state. In Asheville, no local money was spent to bus over 2,000 children to accomplish desegregation because all transportation is done by private bus companies which are reimbursed by the state.[55]

CHAPTER VI

Curb busing while expanding educational opportunity.

School officials see busing and expanding educational opportunities as complementary and not contradictory objectives. Their views are directly contrary to those of the President who sees busing as a "symbol of social engineering on the basis of abstractions." [56] School districts throughout the country use their transportation systems to promote a variety of educational and social goals including school consolidation, improved vocational education programs, broadened horizons for their children through field trips, and expanded summer programs and pre-school education. No one, to our knowledge, has ever held out these objectives as "social engineering."

As Donald E. Morrison of NEA has testified:

> School systems have not hesitated to bus children to vocational education programs and special education programs concentrated in particular geographical areas. School children are regularly bused on field trips serving some educational purpose. In some school districts, such as Cleveland's Shaker Heights, children have been bused home for lunch to give teachers duty-free time.[57]

Educators have supported school busing to promote educational opportunity. The Council of Chief State School Officers in November 1971, stated:

> Although transportation of students as a method of achieving desegregation has become a highly controversial issue throughout the nation, the members of the Council of Chief State School Officers believe it is a viable means of achieving equal educational opportunity and should be supported.[58]

---

[55] Interview with R. S. Walthal, Director of Transportation, Greensboro Board of Education, March 30, 1972.

[56] The President's Message to Congress, 4 (March 17, 1972).

[57] *Supra*, note 24, at 9.

[58] Council of Chief State School Officers, *Policies and Resolutions* (November 17, 1971).

Transportation is still a relatively modest percentage of all educational expenditures. (See discussion above in Chapter V.) Even if the nation were to re-allocate for compensatory education all funds currently allocated to pupil transportation, including those which subsidize affluent, middle-class children attending suburban schools which have never been involved in integration, we would have little more than is currently in the budget for Title I. This program has yet to prove its effectiveness in raising the levels of academic achievement of educationally disadvantaged children.

The effect of transportation for desegregation on the regular education program has varied from district to district. In Pinellas County, Fla. desegregation resulted in a decrease in extra-curricular activities but not an increase in the number of pupils bused.[59] But in Roanoke, Va. school authorities report that because of the new buses required for the desegregation plan, the district can now "do more in a central location than could formerly be done in separate places." Roanoke operates five educational centers for elementary school children, including an oceanography center and a Japanese garden exhibiting the culture of the Far East. Students are bused to these centers as part of their regular program. The cost of duplicating such centers in each elementary school would prohibit the use of such educational innovations.[60]

Finally, Lynchburg, Virginia, school authorities report a 3.5% increase in school attendance this year over last year. This is the first year that the city has transported students to school, and officials say the only factor to which they can attribute improved attendance is busing.

CHAPTER VII

The school bus . . . has become a symbol of helplessness, frustration and outrage—of a wrenching of children away from their families. . . .

If this sentiment represented the prevailing attitude, school systems and local taxpayers would long ago have stopped busing. Many southern school districts have bused 70–100% of their students for years prior to desegregation.[61]

Many school officials are obviously proud of their buses and

---

[59] Interview with Superintendent N. G. Mangum and Assistant Superintendent Mathew Stewart, Pinellas County Board of Education, April 5, 1972.

[60] *Supra,* note 31.

[61] *Supra,* note 12.

pleased with the advantages which busing has brought. When interviewed by our representative, a Roanoke, Virginia, official observed that busing has meant "better control, better schedules, and happier kids." [62]

Of the students who were bused prior to desegregation, 98% in Winston-Salem-Forsyth County, N.C., and over 90% in Greensboro, N.C., were white.[63] Did the citizens of those communities see the school bus as an outrage? We doubt it.

A Hillsborough County, Florida, school official, noting apparently for the first time that the complete desegregation of the school system might require a one percent increase in total expenditures, mused aloud that, "maybe it isn't so bad after all; maybe it is really worthwhile!" [64]

It is true that reports of problems with discipline and with vandalism involving buses have increased. Whether this is a concomitant to integration is a mixed picture. Some incidents have involved persons of the same race. Tensions which occurred on newly integrated buses have sometimes subsided. Some problems seem to be the result of having young, inexperienced and untrained drivers, many of whom are students themselves. Where districts have employed drivers of a different race from the majority of pupils, especially white drivers for all-black busloads, they have invited trouble.

As the bus has become politicized, it has become the symbol of racial divisiveness. Buses have been turned over and burned by irate white parents. White hostility against integration has been directed against the bus. However, some officials whom we interviewed believe that the current problems have little to do with race. They are convinced that parents lack confidence in public schools, that the bus as a symbol of the educational establishment is an easy target, and that those who commit acts of vandalism are merely reflecting the prevailing disenchantment with public education.

In view of this problem, citizens have urged the employment of monitors and the training of bus drivers. Norfolk, Virginia, sought ESAP funds for monitors and was turned down by HEW officials who referred to President Nixon's veto of the use of ESAP funds for any purposes related to transportation. As a direct consequence of the

---

[62] *Supra,* note 31.

[63] Principal's Annual Bus Report, June 29, 1970; *Simkins v. Greensboro Board of Education,* C. N. C–34–G–70, Answers to Interrogatories, September 10, 1970. Annual Pupil Transportation Report 1969–70; *Scott v. Winston-Salem-Forsyth County Board of Education,* C. N. C–174–WS–68, Answers to Interrogatories, December 19, 1969.

[64] *Supra,* note 32.

President's decision, the Norfolk school board decided to use city police on the buses for the first month of school.[65]

CHAPTER VIII

Excessive transporation of students creates serious risks to their health and safety. . . .

The risks and harms created by excessive transportation are particularly great for children enrolled in the first six grades.

One of the most emotional appeals against busing is that riding a school bus risks the health and safety of children, especially those in the first six grades of school. National safety statistics refute this contention.

Data on student accident rates from the National Safety Council reveal that it is safer to ride a bus to school than to walk. The accident rate for boys riding a school bus is .03 per 100,000 student days compared with .09 for walking. For girl students the accident rate is similar—.03 when riding a bus and .07 when walking to school.[66] These rates for the 1968–69 school year are based on the reports of more than 35,000 school jurisdiction accidents, that is all types of accidents during a school day. The National Safety Council warns that since reporting is voluntary, the figures may not be representative of the national accident picture. But the figures do show that of school accidents reported, risks to student safety on a bus were much lower than risks to students in other school activities, such as sports and classroom instruction.

The risks to health and safety are presumed by the President to be even greater for younger children, those in the first six grades. This unsupported assumption has risen to the status of a "finding" set forth in the President's legislation establishing national standards for equal educational opportunity, yet Table 1 demonstrates that accident rates on school buses for boys and girls in grades 1 through 6 are slightly *lower* than the total accident rate for all ages for both sexes.

Any discussion of safety must recognize that without adequate vehicles to transport children to school, students may be subjected to unwarranted hazards. Dr. Elbert Brooks, the Director of the Nashville Metropolitan schools, testified before the Senate Select Committee

---

[65] Interview with Dr. John McLaulin, Assistant Superintendent for Research and Planning, Norfolk Public Schools, January 28, 1972.

[66] National Safety Council, *Accident Facts*, 90–91 (1971 Edition).

TABLE 1. STUDENT ACCIDENT RATES BY SCHOOL GRADE.

Location and Type	Total	Kgn.	1–3 Gr.	4–6 Gr.	7–9 Gr.	10–12 Gr.	Days Lost per Inj.
Boys—Student Accident Rates by School Grade [a]							
Going to and from school (MV)	.19	.40	.22	.13	.20	.15	3.56
School bus	.03	.04	.02	.02	.06	.02	1.24
Public carrier (incl. bus)	.01	.02	.01	.01	.01	.02	3.57
Motor scooter	.01	0	0	*	.02	.02	2.42
Other mot. veh.-pedestrain	.09	.33	.16	.08	.04	.02	4.53
Other mot. veh.-bicycle	.02	0	.02	.02	.03	*	3.34
Other mot. veh.-other type	.03	0	.01	.01	.04	.06	3.01
Girls—Student Accident Rates by School Grade [a]							
Going to and from school (MV)	.14	.29	.13	.08	.14	.19	8.26
School bus	.03	.01	.01	.03	.04	.02	2.01
Public carrier (incl. bus)	.01	.02	0	*	.01	.02	4.31
Motor scooter	.01	.01	*	*	.01	.02	1.83
Other mot. veh.-pedestrain	.07	.23	.10	.04	.06	.04	14.14
Other mot. veh.-bicycle	*	0	.01	*	.01	0	4.50
Other mot. veh.-other type	.03	.01	.01	.01	.02	.10	1.95

Source: National Safety Council, Accident Facts, 90–91 (1971 Edition).
[a] The figures in the tables are rates which show the number of accidents per 100,000 student days.
* Less than 0.005

on Equal Educational Opportunity that because the school board had been unable to purchase the necessary number of buses some children left home and returned home in the darkness of winter days and that some buses made trips on an inter-state highway to shorten the trip. Dr. Brooks felt that such practices did create risks, but that such risks were directly due to the fact that both the Nashville City Council and the President of the United States had made it impossible for the school board to purchase enough buses to eliminate these potential hazards.[67]

School officials are not unmindful of potential risks to children who walk to the nearest school, but who must cross busy streets, walk down roads with no sidewalks, and traverse railroad tracks in order to get to their neighborhood school. In such instances, local school systems often provide transportation for these students even though they would not otherwise be eligible for busing. For example, Roanoke, Virginia, this school year purchased 20 new yellow school buses in order to comply with their desegregation order. These were the first large passenger buses to be operated by the district itself. The new vehicles permitted the school system not only to bus children to desegregated schools, but also to bus kindergarten children who last year had to walk unsafe streets to get to class.[68]

In the state of Florida during this school year, 66,115 children who are ineligible for state-reimbursed transportation because they live within walking distance of their school, are nonetheless bused to school. School officials report that this busing was done at local expense, that it was done mostly for safety reasons, and that the vast majority of these children are in the elementary grades.

The following chart [69] shows, for five Florida school districts, the number of students who were ineligible for state-reimbursed transportation but who were bused primarily for reasons of safety or

District	1968–69	1969–70	1970–71	1971–72
Duval	3,397	3,030	3,630	5,764
Hillsborough	1,879	3,211	5,408	3,565
Pinellas	2,701	3,194	2,142	729
Manatee	613	504	748	822
Orange	3,767	4,635	6,347	7,834

[67] *Supra*, note 16, at 9018–9019.

[68] *Supra*, note 31.

[69] Florida Department of Education, *Mid-Year Transportation Reports* for 1968–69, 1969–70, 1970–71. Interview with officials of Transportation Section, Florida Department of Education, April 17, 1972.

convenience. Again, the majority of these children are in the elementary grades.

Apparently, it is the judgment of local educational officials that busing elementary school students is not a risk to their health or safety. Indeed, such busing is deemed a protection of young children.

CHAPTER IX

A remedy for the historic evil of racial discrimination has often created a new evil of disrupting communities and imposing hardships on children. . . .

Who has disrupted communities, imposed hardships, and torn us apart as a people?

It is not the Federal judges who have exercised judicial restraint.

It is not black citizens who are still trying to secure equal educational opportunities for their children.

It is not the school bus.

It is the present Administration which has used the power and majesty and authority of the President's office to stir dissension, confusion, and uncertainty among us by politicizing the busing issue.

HILLSBOROUGH COUNTY, FLORIDA—A PROFILE

Florida is a state of metropolitan school districts. Every city in Florida, no matter how large, is part of the county school system in which it is located. Cities like Miami and Jacksonville are located in county school systems which also have rural areas, many municipalities, and burgeoning suburbs. In spite of the state's size and population, it has only 67 school districts.

Hillsborough County, which includes Tampa, is a sprawling metropolitan area, composed of diverse racial and ethnic groups. About 20% of its 500,000 citizens are black and nearly 20% are Spanish-speaking. Within its 10,034 square miles are some four municipalities which range in population from 5,500 to almost 40,000. There are also many unincorporated, but heavily populated areas in this county. Like many metropolitan areas in Florida, significant population growth has occurred in the county, but little of that growth has occurred in Tampa itself. The county has experienced an increase in population from 398,000 in 1960 to nearly 500,000 in 1970, while the Tampa population during that same period grew from 275,000 to 278,000 persons.

Hillsborough County also has a very large, metropolitan school system with about 103,000 students (about 20% black) attending 129 schools. During the 1969–70 school year, the dual system was still intact. Freedom of choice had produced only some token desegregation in a few formerly white schools. In 1970–71, many other formerly white schools became desegregated for the first time as a result of a Federal Court order.

In the spring of 1971, black plaintiffs filed a *Swann* motion with the U.S. District Court asking that the Hillsborough County schools be desegregated. Accordingly, the Court directed the board to devise an appropriate school desegregation plan. The plan adopted by the board and approved by the Court called for each school in the system to be about 80% white and 20% black. The plan, which had the approval of the superintendent, the school board, the Chamber of Commerce, civic groups and the press, was a combination of pairing, clustering and non-contiguous zoning. The clusters were composed of one formerly black school and a few formerly white schools, with the black schools becoming middle-grade centers and the white schools serving grades 1–5. Thus, white students now attend formerly black schools in grades 6–7 only, while black students attend formerly white schools for 10 of their 12 school years.

Some resistance to this plan existed prior to the opening of the current school year. A significant portion of the resistance was in the black community. There were threats of demonstrations by blacks at the two formerly black high schools. The Court-ordered Bi-Racial Advisory Committee, which reflected the sentiment in the black community, told the Court that the plan "essentially establishes a 'community school concept' for white students. . . . The plan's undue effort to minimize white flight serves to maximize black busing." The elimination of the two black high schools, the Advisory Committee said, ". . . deals a punitive blow to the black community and by so doing . . . is inconsistent with the short or long range harmony between the races desired and needed to implement school desegregation in the community at large." Some white citizens attempted to thwart the Court's order, but no major organizations opposed the plan or caused disruptions in the schools.

In 1969–70, 164 buses were used to transport more than 27,600 students over 15,200 miles daily. In 1970–71, 179 buses transported some 32,400 students more than 15,700 miles, an increase of about 5,000 students.

Just before the Court approved the current desegregation plan last summer, the board projected that the proposed plan would require the additional transportation of about 15,700 elementary, 7,400 junior high and 2,200 senior high school students, a total of 25,300. The projection was close; 25,200 students are bused this year for the purpose of desegregation. However, 1,800 fewer elementary students are bused than projected. Of the 14,000 elementary pupils who are bused, 8,600 are black and 5,400 are white. The total number of secondary students of both races who are bused is 11,300: 8,500 in junior and almost 2,800 in senior high schools.

Transportation statistics for the 1971–72 school year in Hillsborough County reflect the increased busing necessary to implement the desegregation plan.

1. The number of buses used increased from 179 to 339, including 29 spares.
2. There are 907 separate bus trips daily this year compared with 461 last year.
3. Students were transported to 84 schools last year and 126 this year.
4. The number of elementary students bused increased from 10,600 to 22,500; junior high school students increased from 8,800 to 16,200; and senior high school students from 7,500 to 10,400.
5. Buses traveled 6,000 more "essential miles" [70] this year.
6. Total mileage has increased from 15,750 per day to 32,300 miles per day.

Two schools in the county operate on double sessions. Two separate administrative units operate within the same facility each day. The morning session has a different principal and faculty than the afternoon session. This year double sessions necessitate an additional $18,000 in bus drivers' salaries and about 5,200 "non-essential miles." [71] Double sessions result in less efficient use of buses. Since only students in particular grade levels are picked up, buses must travel further to obtain a full load and they must travel more miles empty.

Other non-essential costs have increased this year because the state computes mileage from the time a bus begins its route at the driver's house until it stops at the garage after dropping off the last student. Also, the district has had difficulty in finding bus drivers who live close to the beginning of their routes.

During the 1970–71 school year, Hillsborough County spent

---

[70] "Essential mile" is a state department term meaning the number of miles a bus travels with one or more students.

[71] "Non-essential miles" is a state department term indicating the miles a bus travels without students, or miles a bus travels off the main bus route if that detour is 1.5 miles or less one way.

$1,206,708 for transportation, or about $37.23 per pupil bused. This cost represented approximately 1.3% of the district's total budget. Out of a total budget of almost $120 million this year, the school district is spending about $1,973,728 or 1.7% for transportation. The cost per pupil bused is $37.38.

The purchase of new buses has been a significant factor in the increase in transportation costs this year. One hundred and forty-five regular buses were bought, of which 20 had already been budgeted. One million dollars was borrowed on a four-year loan to pay for the new buses.

The Florida State Department of Education recommends that school buses be replaced every ten years, yet in 1961, 1963, 1964, 1965 and 1966, Hillsborough County purchased no new buses. As a result of this delay in bus replacement, 71 buses are now 11 or more years old, and 29 buses purchased in 1957 and 1958 are now used as spares. If buses had been replaced on a regular basis, Hillsborough County's bus fleet might have more easily accommodated the increased student transportation and 29 old buses would not have had to be utilized.

This year's total anticipated educational expenditures of over $119 million are a considerable increase over 1970–71 when somewhat more than $89 million was spent. What is most interesting to note, however, is the substantial increase in the allocation for capital improvements and debt service:

	1970–71	1971–72 (est.)
Capital Improvements	$12,034,617	$32,847,393
Debt Service	2,838,883	7,741,681

The investment in new buses represents a small percentage indeed of the total capital outlay for Hillsborough County.

Despite the substantial increase in busing in Hillsborough County and the reassignment of students to new schools, the citizens of the metropolitan area, black and white alike, have accommodated to the change brought by conversion to a unitary, non-racial school system. School officials have taken steps to ease the transition. Specialists have been employed with ESAP funds to work in each secondary school in the county. Bi-racial student advisory committees have been established at each secondary school, and together with the specialists, have helped to moderate interracial antagonisms. Facilities at the formerly black schools have been improved. Air conditioning was installed and needed supplies were increased, thus reducing parent complaints. While many black students have resented losing their

identity with their old high schools, they have increasingly participated in extra-curricular activities and sports at their new schools.
Buses have been provided to transport students home after regular
school hours.

In the first week after school opened in the Fall of 1971, many
white parents did not send their children to school, and others drove
their children to school and picked them up in the afternoon because
of fear of disruptions at formerly black schools. But the disruptions
failed to materialize, and after several weeks white children began riding buses to school. Approximately 2,000 white students left the public
schools this year. The fact that there was no greater amount of
"white flight" was due to the fact that the private schools in the
county resisted expanding their enrolment for students who sought
to avoid desegregation. Superintendent Raymond Shelton has noted a
trend of white students returning to public schools.[72]

Hillsborough County is an example of what can be accomplished
when a metropolitan-wide desegregation plan becomes the vehicle
for securing the constitutional rights of black children. Most encouraging, however, is that the plan is not only working but that at least one
school official believes that, "maybe it isn't so bad after all; maybe it is
really worthwhile!" [73]

NORTH CAROLINA—A PROFILE

North Carolina has several large, urban school districts and is unique
because it is the only state in the South that has completely desegregated its city school systems. In the past four years, pupil transportation
has increased by 10% in the state, from 55% of North Carolina's enrolment to 65%. Yet only a small portion of that increase can be
attributed to desegregation of the urban areas.

In 1968–69 no school districts, including those mentioned in this
report, had desegregated school systems. During that year over 9,200
school buses transported nearly 611,000 students (almost 55% of all
students in the state) at an annual cost of over $14.2 million, which
included the cost of purchasing bus replacements. Over 352,000 miles
were traveled in that year at a cost of $23.40 per pupil.

In 1969–70 most North Carolina school systems were still segregated, including all of the large, urban school districts. In that year,
over 9,400 vehicles transported nearly 630,000 students (over 57% of

---

[72] Testimony of Chairman Theodore Hesburgh, U.S. Commission on Civil
Rights before Subcommittee No. 5 of the House Committee on Judiciary, 6–15
(March 1, 1972).

[73] *Supra,* note 32.

all the students in the state) at a cost of over $19.1 million, which included the cost of bus replacements. Over 357,500 miles were traveled at a cost of $30.39 per pupil. During this year about 15,000 special education students became eligible, for the first time, for state reimbursed transportation costs.

In 1970–71 Charlotte-Mecklenburg became the first urban district in the state to approach the elimination of the dual school system. There were other isolated cases where urban districts made beginning steps as, for example, Winston-Salem-Forsyth. Other urban districts remained almost totally segregated, such as Raleigh and Greensboro.

During 1970–71 nearly 10,000 vehicles were used to transport over 683,400 students (62% of all students in the state) at a cost of over $21.3 million, including bus replacement. 375,370 miles were traveled that year with a per pupil cost of $31.21. Significantly, this was the year when *Sparrow v. Gill* became effective.

By 1971–72 nearly all school districts in the state had made major steps in achieving unitary school systems. During this year 10,400 vehicles have transported about 717,000 students (nearly 65% of all pupils in the state).

As the above figures indicate, there has been a constant increase during each school year (before and after desegregation) in the number of vehicles, the cost of operations, the number of miles traveled annually, the number of pupils transported and the percent of pupils transported. Some items increased at a faster rate than others.

The *Sparrow* decision resulted in approximately 54,000 additional students (requiring 589 additional buses) becoming eligible for transportation. In the school year prior to 1968–69, about 5,000 additional students became eligible for transportation each year due to normal student population growth. A state transportation official believes that approximately the same pattern has existed for each school year since 1968–69.

Based upon our interviews with state officials and upon our examination of their files and documents, we conclude that of the approximately 106,200 students now transported who were not transported in 1968–69 that:

Sparrow	resulted in 54,000
Special education	accounted for 15,000
Growth (6,000 students per year × 3 years)	resulted in 18,000
Urban desegregation	caused 19,000
TOTAL	106,000

Therefore, approximately 19,000 of the 717,000 students transported in 1971–72 in North Carolina represents a net increase in pupil transportation because of urban, court-ordered desegregation. Other desegregation steps have decreased transportation in the state.

TABLE 2. BUSING COSTS, 1953–54 THROUGH 1967–68.

	Total No. Trans. U.S.	% of Enroll.	Av. Cost Per Pupil	Trans. as % of total Educ. Expend.
1953–54	8,411,719	32.8%	$36.55	4.5%
1955–56	9,695,819	35%	$36.51	4.3%
1957–58	10,861,689	36.5%	$38.34	4.1%
1959–60	12,225,142	37.6%	$39.78	3.9%
1961–62	13,222,667	38.1%	$43.59	3.9%
1963–64	14,475,778	38.7%	$46.53	3.9%
1965–66	15,536,567	39.7%	$50.68	3.7%
1967–68	17,130,873	42.0%	$57.27	3.7%

Source: U.S. Office of Education, National Center for Educational Statistics.

TABLE 3. PUPIL TRANSPORTATION BY REGION.

Region	1953–54	1955–56	1957–58	1959–60	1961–62	1963–64	1965–66	1967–68
Northeast								
No. Trans.	1,396,518	1,786,231	2,386,339	2,759,515	3,093,701	3,533,950	NA	4,487,990
% of Total	25.2%	30.1%	34.4%	36.9%	38.5%	40.6%		47%
North Central								
No. Trans.	2,140,803	2,157,035	2,807,469	3,138,674	3,441,681	3,914,131		4,863,556
% of Total	29.5%	31.3%	33.4%	34.8%	35.9%	37.7%		42.7%
South								
No. Trans.	3,895,400	4,205,068	3,730,215	3,990,808	4,254,184	4,459,630		4,855,105
% of Total	43.2%	43.6%	50.6%	50.6%	51.2%	50.7%		52.5%
West								
No. Trans.	978,998	1,247,485	1,932,666	2,296,145	2,427,901	2,568,067		2,924,222
% of Total	25.5%	29%	27.6%	28.8%	27.8%	27%		27.5%

Source: U.S. Office of Education, National Center for Educational Statistics.

TABLE 4. INCREASE IN PUPIL TRANSPORTATION IN SCHOOL DISTRICTS DUE TO DESEGREGATION COURT ORDERS.

District	Total Enroll. Prior Court Order	Total Bused in Dist. Prior Court Order	% of Enroll. Bused in District	Total Enroll. After Court Order	Total Bused After Court Order	% of Enroll. Bused After Court Order	% Public Enroll. Transported Statewide
Arlington	24,390 [b]	9,532	39.0%	23,133 [c]	8,588	37.0%	63.0%
Asheville	8,381 [a]	None	None	8,241 [b]	2,170	26.3%	62.2%
Charlotte	84,518 [a]	29,737	35.1%	82,507 [b]	39,080	47.3%	62.2%
Duval	122,493 [b]	38,750	31.6%	118,217 [c]	44,706	37.8%	NA
Greensboro	31,901 [b]	10,781	33.8%	30,105 [c]	16,689	55.4%	65.0%
Hillsborough	105,347 [b]	32,406	30.8%	102,728 [c]	52,795	51.4%	NA
Jackson	30,937 [b]	2,127	7.0%	29,031 [c]	7,300	25.0%	58.7%
Lynchburg	11,590 [b]	None	None	11,700 [c]	4,478	38.0%	63.0%
Manatee	16,923 [a]	6,628	39.2%	17,386 [b]	8,287	47.7%	NA
Nashville	94,170 [b]	34,000	36.0%	87,000 [c]	49,000	56.0%	49.0%
Norfolk	59,429 [a]	7,500	12.6%	50,791 [c]	15,000	29.5%	63.0%
Orange	85,270 [b]	32,964	38.7%	86,705 [c]	35,713	41.2%	NA
Pinellas	85,117 [a]	36,588	43.0%	86,880 [c]	36,888	42.5%	NA
Raleigh	23,469 [b]	1,342	5.7%	22,236 [c]	10,126	45.5%	65.0%
Richmond	47,988 [b]	13,916 [d]	29.0%	44,989 [c]	17,563	39.0%	63.0%
Roanoke	19,284 [b]	2,150	11.1%	18,294 [c]	4,665	25.5%	63.0%
Winston-Salem	50,462 [a]	18,444	36.5%	50,070 [c]	32,220	64.3%	65.0%

[a] 1969–70 school year.
[b] 1970–71 school year.
[c] 1971–72 school year.
[d] Of the total of 13,916, 8,500 rode Virginia Transit Co. buses and 5,416 rode school district-owned buses.

354

TABLE 5. COST OF STUDENT TRANSPORTATION IN INDIVIDUAL SCHOOL DISTRICTS WHERE DESEGREGATION OCCURRED (OPERATING EXPENSES [a]).

District	Av. Cost Per Pupil Prior to Deseg.	Total Operating Cost for Trans. Prior to Deseg.	% Trans. Cost of Total Operating School Budget Prior to Deseg.	Av. Cost Per Pupil After Deseg.	Total Operating Costs for Trans. After Deseg.	% Trans. Cost of Total Operating School Budget After Deseg.
Arlington	$61.15	$ 709,300	2.8%	NA	NA	NA
Greensboro	NA	NA	NA	NA [b]	NA [b]	NA
Jackson	79.50	169,103	.6%	$56.17	$ 410,110	1.8%
Lynchburg	None	None	None	32.90	147,350	1.3%
Nashville	39.71	1,574,790	2.3%	49.00	2,704,228	3.8%
Norfolk	None	None	None	None	None	None
Orange	30.02	989,614	1.8%	30.58	1,092,175	1.9%
Raleigh	75.01	100,669 [c]	.7%	24.69	250,061	1.7%
Richmond	32.31	175,000	.4%	28.46	500,000	1.1%
Roanoke	55.58	137,393	.8%	30.65 [e]	207,699	1.1%
Winston-Salem	20.26	373,838	1.8%	30.67	988,454 [d]	4%
Asheville [f]	None	None	None	56.95	123,598	NA
Charlotte	15.97	475,000	.8%	27.32	1,067,691	1.6%
Duval [f]	31.90	1,236,157	1.3%	48.91	2,186,590	2.2%
Hillsborough	37.23	1,206,708	1.35%	37.38	1,973,728	1.7%
Manatee	51.70	342,696	2.3%	46.39	384,468	2.5%
Pinellas	29.40	1,075,850	1.4%	55.38	2,042,970 [g]	2.4%

[a] Some figures may include spare parts or minor capital outlays.

[b] No city school district money was spent. State expenditures are not available.

[c] This includes lunchroom and administrative salaries; thus transportation above is considerably less.

[d] About $269,300 is paid from local funds for supplements for bus drivers' salaries and for transporting elementary students who are not eligible for state reimbursement.

[e] For elementary students on school owned buses. $35.00 per student per year is spent for 900 elementary students on public buses contracted for by the district. This cost is based upon the number of routes. $63.00 per student per year is spent for 1,000 secondary students who cannot afford the student fare. The cost is based upon 35¢ per day per student times 180 school days.

[f] Asheville and Duval Counties own no buses but contract with a private carrier for all transportation.

[g] Includes leasing of 18 private buses.

355

TABLE 6. 1971–72 BUSES PURCHASED AND TOTAL SCHOOL BUDGETS.

District	Number of Regular Buses Purchased	Total Cost of Buses	Total School Budget (All Monies)
Arlington	8	$ 56,000 (Est.)	NA
Asheville	None [b]	None [b]	NA
Charlotte	NA	$ 68,231 [a]	$ 67,252,036
Duval	None [b]	None [b]	$101,909,630
Greensboro	None	None	$ 23,971,934
Hillsborough	145 [c]	$1,160,000 [c]	$119,099,553
Jackson	69	$ 500,000 (Est.)	$ 23,084,121
Lynchburg	37	$ 272,387	$ 12,543,342
Manatee	19	NA	$ 15,298,905
Nashville	18 [d]	$ 315,000	$ 71,567,152
Norfolk	None	None	
Orange	None	None	$ 64,000,000
Pinellas	90	$ 794,237 [e]	$ 85,094,490
Raleigh	89	$ 534,993 [f]	$ 18,063,007
Richmond	115	$ 874,000	$ 60,000,000 (Est.)
Roanoke	16	$ 120,672	$ 18,157,764
Winston-Salem	59 (Est.)	$ 343,456 [g]	$ 37,103,968

[a] About half of this amount was for "major replacements" and the other half represents purchase of new "buses, trucks, and garage equipment."

[b] Asheville and Duval County contract all pupil transportation so there is no capital outlay.

[c] 20 buses were already budgeted; $1 million was borrowed on a four year loan to purchase 125 buses.

[d] Already budgeted for replacement.

[e] Includes $341,300 which was for 40 buses already budgeted.

[f] Five buses already budgeted and delivered in 1971–72; 10 other buses purchased and delivered in 1971–72; 74 buses purchased but will not be delivered in 1971–72.

[g] Includes about 12 replacement buses purchased by the State.